TAKING SIDES

Clashing Views in

Adolescence

McGraw-Hill **Contemporary Learning Series**

A Division of The McGraw-Hill Companies

TAKING SIDES

Clashing Views in

Adolescence

Selected, Edited, and with Introductions by

Maureen T.B. Drysdale
St. Jerome's University at the University of Waterloo

and

B.J. Rye
St. Jerome's University at the University of Waterloo

Contemporary Learning Series

A Division of The McGraw-Hill Companies

MD: To Mallory, Adam, & Megan
BJR: To Sarah, Barbara, & Donald

Photo acknowledgment
Ryan McVay/Getty Images

Cover image concept
Adam Drysdale

Cover acknowledgment
Maggie Lytle

Manufactured in the United States of America

First Edition

123456789DOCDOC9876

0-07-351508-6
978-0-07-351508-3
1933-0499

Printed on Recycled Paper

Preface

Adolescence is a critical developmental period in everyone's life. In order for us to become adults, we have to "survive" adolescence. For some, this stage of life is characterized by "storm-and-stress," while others glide through the transition unscathed. Most of us have some fond memories of pleasant and exciting experiences coupled with recollections of embarrassing and awkward experiences. Some events that occur during adolescence are universal—such as puberty, physical growth, and psychological maturation—whereas other phenomenon are a function of environmental forces—such as cultural context, family structure, school organization, and peer group practices.

How do these different forces and contexts influence the development of adolescents in Western society today? The purpose of this book is to examine some of the issues that may have an impact on adolescents in a didactic, dialectic fashion. To this end, *Taking Sides: Clashing Views in Adolescence* has been developed to foster critical and incisive thinking about issues that may have a significant impact on adolescent development in the twenty-first century. We have included interdisciplinary writings (e.g., from psychology, sociology, medicine, law, and religious studies domains) representing issues relevant to the period of adolescence in developed "Western" societies (e.g., Australia, Canada, and the United States). *Taking Sides: Clashing Views in Adolescence* presents yes/no perspectives in response to 18 questions. Consequently, 36 lively readings written by opponents who sit on different sides of the various topics under consideration are included. Each issue involves:

- A *question* that attempts to capture the essence of the debate.
- An *introduction* whereby information is presented that can be used by the reader as a background to the issue. Also available is some information about the essay authors of the debate as this may help to explain the perspective from which the writer comes.
- Two *essays* where one supports the "yes" side of the controversy while the other speaks to the "no" side of the question.
- A *postscript* presents additional information, which may help to elucidate the issue further, raise additional and thought-provoking questions, and synthesize the two authors' perspectives.

It is important to note that no issue is truly binary. There are always "gray" areas that fall in between the "yes" and the "no" perspectives. The *recommended readings* section provides additional references for the interested individual; some readers will wish to delve into particular topics in greater detail. This section was included to give some additional direction for that purpose. At the end of the book, the *Contributors to this Volume* provides additional information about each essay author. A person's training, career track, and life situation colors her/his perspective on any issue; no one is completely objective. Also, the *On the Internet* presents some useful Web site addresses (URLs) that are relevant to the issues discussed in each part.

As you read the different perspectives, you may find that you disagree with one side or both viewpoints. Regardless, it is important to read each selection carefully and critically and respect the opinions of others. This format of the textbook necessarily challenges the reader to face her or his own bias, beliefs, and values about the controversial topics presented. Two of the most important tools that a student can develop in her or his scholarly pursuits is (1) to be able to keep an open mind such that you may consider dissenting views while respecting the opinions of those who disagree with your perspective, and (2) to become a critical thinker and evaluate arguments from many different angles and viewpoints. We encourage you to challenge your own perspective so that you can develop these crucial skills.

A word to the instructor   An *Instructor's Manual*, with issue synopses, suggestions for classroom discussion, and test questions (multiple choice and essay) is available from McGraw-Hill/Contemporary Learning Series. A general guidebook, *Using Taking Sides in the Classroom*, which discusses methods and techniques for integrating the pro/con approach into any classroom setting, is also available. An online version of *Using Taking Sides in the Classroom* and a correspondence service for *Taking Sides* adopters can be found at http://www.mhcls.com/usingts.

Taking Sides: Clashing Views in Adolescence is one of the many titles in the Taking Sides series. If you are interested in seeing the table of contents for any of the other titles, please visit the Taking Sides Web site at http://www.mhcls.com/takingsides.

Acknowledgments   First, and foremost, we would like to thank our families for their patience with us during this *Taking Sides* project. Thanks to Fraser Drysdale, Mallory Drysdale, Adam Drysdale, and Megan Drysdale as well as to Sarah Forgrave, Barbara Campbell, and Donald Campbell. Your unconditional support during this *Taking Sides* undertaking was greatly appreciated.

A special thank you goes to St. Jerome's University for providing financial support for this project through the Academic Dean's Research Fund. Without this financial support, we could have never undertaken this project.

For expert assistance with researching the issues, editing, and further fine-tuning, we wish to express our heart-felt thanks to Mary-Jean Costello who was instrumental to this process. Additional thanks to Rachel Brown, Megan Drysdale, Fraser Drysdale, Glenn Meaney, Nadia Palarchio, Mallory Drysdale, and Artella Oh for their contributions to this book. Also, thank you to Adam Drysdale and Sarah Forgrave for their work on the conception of the cover.

Thanks to McGraw-Hill/Contemporary Learning Series staff for their work on this project: Marcy Mealia, Tim McLeary, and Jill Peter.

In short, thank you to the rich network of colleagues, family, and friends who helped us at various stages of this project. Your support was and is greatly appreciated!

Contents In Brief

Contents

Yvon Lapierre, a professor emeritus at the department of psychiatry at the University of Ottawa, reviewed relevant literature addressing the concern that increased suicidality was associated with the use of antidepressants including SSRIs. He concludes that the evidence currently available does not support the hypothesis that antidepressants cause increased suicidality in patients with depression. Tamar Wohlfarth, a clinical assessor, and colleagues in the Netherlands assessed antidepressant use in pediatric patients and reported an increased risk for events related to suicidality among those taking antidepressants. They caution the use of all SSRIs and NSRIs in the pediatric population.

Engels, Scholte, van Lieshout, de Kemp, and Overbeek, researchers in the Netherlands, suggest that substance use, while potentially problematic, may serve beneficial, developmental functions for adolescents. Particularly, adolescents who drink alcohol appeared to be more self-confident and sociable than those who abstained based on peer evaluations. Researcher Sandra Brown, a psychiatrist from the University of California–San Diego, argues that early onset of alcohol and drug use put youth at greater risk for neurological damage, alcohol-related injuries (e.g., from drinking and driving), and future substance dependence.

of parents support the commencement of sexual health education in elementary school or middle school. Further, parents supported the inclusion of a broad range of sexual health topics at some point in the curriculum, including birth control and safe sex practices. Robert Rector and colleagues from The Heritage Foundation, a conservative think tank in Washington, D.C., report strong parental support for abstinence programs in schools. Further, Rector, et al. report that parents strongly oppose "comprehensive sex-ed" curricula that teaches teens that sex is okay as long as contraception is used.

Aida Orgocka, a gender and development expert at the University of Illinois, presents a qualitative study of Illinois mothers' and daughters' perceptions of the sexual health school curriculum from a Muslim perspective. The participants tended to find the sex education curriculum at odds with Muslim values such that many of the girls opted to forgo the school-based sexual health classes. John Santelli, a professor of clinical population, family health and clinical pediatrics at the Mailman School of Public Health in Columbia University, and colleagues review current U.S. policies encouraging abstinence-only sexual health education and discuss the potential negative impact and ethical considerations arising from these policies on adolescent sexual practices.

Rebecca Collins and colleagues from the RAND Corporation present evidence from a longitudinal survey that adolescents who viewed more sexual content at baseline were more likely to initiate intercourse and progress to more advanced sexual activities during the subsequent year. Collins and colleagues in an earlier study suggested that entertainment television can also serve as a healthy sex educator and can work in conjunction with parents to improve adolescent sexual knowledge.

Mary Crawford, a psychology professor at the University of Connecticut, and her graduate student Danielle Popp present evidence suggesting the double standard that males are socially rewarded and females socially derogated for sexual activity exists among adolescents as it does among adults. Researchers Michael Marks and Chris Fraley oppose the above claim and suggest that there is little evidence that the traditional double standard exists among adolescents or even among adults.

PART 3   RELATIONSHIPS   235

speculative or supported only by correlational research, they make a compelling case for the benefits of teenage romances.

Psychologists Lauren Donchi and Susan Moore suggest that adolescent boys who rate their online friendships as very important are more likely to have lower self-esteem and to be lonely. Those with more face-to-face friendships have more self-esteem and are less lonely. Elisheva Gross and colleagues, researchers of adolescent psychology, conclude that adolescents mainly engage in online communication with close others, and such communication is just as effective as face-to-face communication and is mainly devoted to ordinary yet intimate topics (e.g., friends, gossip, etc.).

PART 4   ANTISOCIAL BEHAVIORS   307

Daniel Mears, an associate professor for the College of Criminology and Criminal Justice at Florida State University reports that for serious offenses, there is widespread support for sanctioning youths as adults. He points to a conservative group, fearful of crime, worrying about social order and public safety. Laurence Steinberg, Distinguished University Professor at Temple University, and Elizabeth Scott, law professor at the University of Virginia, argue that adolescents often lack the capabilities to make mature judgments, control impulses, and resist coercion from peers and therefore should not be held to the same standards of criminal conduct as adults.

Kathryne Speaker, assistant professor of education at The College of New Jersey, and George Petersen, associate professor of education at California Polytechnic State University, argue that the number of incidents of violence and the severity of these acts have dramatically increased. Dewey Cornell, professor in the Curry School of Education at the University of Virginia and director of the Virginia Youth Violence Project, provides evidence that violence in schools is not increasing.

Issue 17.   Are Girls Bigger Bullies Than Boys?   346

YES: Melanie J. Zimmer-Gembeck, Tasha C. Geiger, and Nicki R. Crick, from "Relational and Physical Aggression, Prosocial Behavior, and Peer Relations: Gender Moderation and Bidirectional Association," *Journal of Early Adolescence* (November 2005)   *348*

NO: Christina Salmivalli and Ari Kaukiainen, from "'Female Aggression' Revisited: Variable- and Person-Centered Approaches to Studying Gender Differences in Different Types of Aggression," *Aggressive Behavior* (vol. 30, 2004)   *356*

Melanie Zimmer-Gembeck, an assistant professor of psychology at Griffith University in Australia, and her colleagues report gender differences in levels of relational aggression, which is a type of bullying. In early adolescence, girls are more relationally aggressive than boys. The authors argue that girls may use relational aggression to gain and keep friends. Christina Salmivalli, professor of applied psychology, and psychologist Ari Kaukiainen, both from University of Turku, argue that boys use all types of aggression more than girls in early adolescence. This included direct aggression, verbal aggression, and indirect and relational aggression.

Issue 18.   Is the Use of "Club Drugs" a Problem Among Adolescents?   363

YES: Eric Sigel, from "Club Drugs: Nothing to Rave About," *Contemporary Pediatrics* (October 2002)   *365*

NO: Jacob Sullum, from "Sex, Drugs, and Techo Music," *Reason* (January 2002)   *376*

Eric Sigel, assistant professor of pediatrics and adolescent medicine, argues that club drugs such as Ecstasy, GHB, Rohypnol, and Special K are dangerous. Their use, especially at rave parties, allows participants to overlook social barriers and helps individuals to relate better to others. Sigel cautions that some drugs that are taken at rave parties, especially GHB, have led to date rape. Jacob Sullum, a senior editor at *Reason* magazine, contends that the effects of drugs such as Ecstasy, particularly with regard to sexual behavior, are exaggerated. He refers to the history of marijuana and how it too was deemed a drug that would make people engage in behaviors in which they would not typically engage. Sullum maintains that the public's reaction to club drugs in unjustified.

Introduction

Adolescence is a period of development marked by a transition spanning the second decade of life. Developmentally, adolescence begins at approximately age 10 and lasts into the early twenties, although from eighteen or nineteen onwards, the period is referred to as "emerging adulthood" (Arnett, 2004). Adolescence is a period of time when individuals leave the security of childhood to meet the demands of the adult world. They pull away from the structure of family in search of independence. This involves finding an identity, making a commitment, and carving out a responsible place in society. Although the transition is very individual (i.e., occurring in different ways and at different rates), it involves dealing with three sets of developmental challenges or tasks. The challenges involve the biological, psychological, and social changes occurring during this crucial period of development. The biological changes are the most visible, with puberty and hormones driving the changes in body appearance. Adolescents must learn to cope and accept these changes. The psychological changes involve advances in cognitions and enhanced emotional development, leading to stronger decision making, mature judgment, better planning, and advanced perspective taking. The task here is to cope with these new characteristics and to use them to adapt to the transition and find a place in the world. The third challenge is to find a responsible role in society and commit to a revised sense of self. The social changes (i.e., relationships, newfound independence) taking place during this time permit the adolescent to explore different roles. Taken together, the challenges and changes result in children becoming adults.

History of Adolescence

Historically, the period between childhood and adulthood has been recognized as distinct; however, it was not researched or given a specific name until the twentieth century. In ancient Greek times, Plato, Socrates, and Aristotle had specific views of adolescence. Plato, for example, recognizing the advances in thinking and judgment during the second decade of life, believed that formal education should only start at this time. Socrates, also aware of the advances in cognitions, argued that the stronger thinking skills allowed youth to become better at arguing. In addition he recognized the down side to this developmental advancement, arguing that youth were inclined to contradict their parents and tyrannize their teachers. Aristotle argued that the most important aspect of this period of development was the ability to choose. He believed that human beings became capable of making rational choices and good decisions during the second decade. Aristotle also recognized that, although youth exhibited gains in thinking, they were still immature and different from adults. His strong opinion and knowledge about youth is clearly stated in the following passage:

> "The young are in character prone to desire and ready to carry any desire they may have formed into action. Of bodily desires it is the sexual to which they are most disposed to give way, and in regard to sexual desire they exercise no self-restraint. They are changeful, too, and fickle in their desires, which are as transitory as they are vehement; for their wishes are keen without being permanent, like a sick man's fits of hunger and thirst. They are passionate, irascible, and apt to be carried away by their impulses. They are the slaves, too, of their passion, as their ambition prevents their ever brooking a slight and renders them indignant at the mere idea of enduring an injury. They are charitable rather than the reverse, as they have never yet been witnesses of many villainies; and they are trustful, as they have not yet been often deceived. They are sanguine, too, for the young are heated by nature as drunken men by wine, not to say that they have not yet experienced frequent failures. Their lives are lived principally in hope. They have high aspirations; for they have never yet been humiliated by the experience of life, but are unacquainted with the limiting force of circumstances. Youth is the age when people are most devoted to their friends, as they are then extremely fond of social intercourse. If the young commit a fault, it is always on the side of excess and exaggeration, for they carry everything too far, whether it be their love or hatred or anything else" (Aristotle 4th Century B.C.).

The early philosophical views such as those mentioned above were unchallenged for many centuries. However, by the late nineteenth century/early twentieth century, this changed, and the age of adolescence was recognized. It was argued that children and youth were not miniature adults and, therefore, should not be treated in the same way as adults, especially with respect to labor and family responsibility. As a result, child labor laws were implemented, followed by mandatory schooling until age 16. Basically, children were being protected and not permitted to work; however, they could not be left unsupervised, aimlessly wandering about, getting into trouble. The solution: "Keep them in school until they can work." With these changes in the early 1900s, the concept of adolescence became more defined. Adolescents were not children and were not yet adults, resulting in the recognition that they were unique in their development and, as such, deserved special attention.

At this time (i.e., circa 1900), G. Stanley Hall began studying adolescence in terms of their behaviors, their emotions, and their relationships. Known as the father of adolescent research, he concluded that children went through turmoil and upheaval during their second decade of life and as such were in a state of constant *storm-and-stress*, a term he coined from the German "sturm und drang." Hall identified three key aspects of adolescent storm-and-stress: risky behaviors, mood disruptions, and conflict with parents. Hall argued that the physical changes occurring during this period of the lifespan (e.g., growth spurts, sexual maturation, and hormonal changes) resulted in psychological turbulence. He further argued that the turmoil was both universal and biologically based. In other words, it was inevitable regardless of other factors. To disseminate these arguments, Hall published *Adolescence* (1904), the first text on adolescent development, making the study of adolescence both scientific and scholarly. Since the time of Hall's book, research on adolescence has attracted attention from many disciplines such as psychology, sociology, anthropology, and medicine.

Soon after Hall's view of adolescence, Margaret Mead published *Coming of Age in Samoa* (1928), which challenged Hall's view of universal adolescent storm-and-stress. After conducting observational research in Samoa (a distinctly different culture than Western society), Mead explained how Samoan adolescents experienced a gradual and smooth transition to adulthood because of the meaningful connections made between their roles during adolescence and the roles they would perform as adults. She argued that the transition through adolescence was not simply biological, but rather sociocultural, and the turmoil identified by Hall was environmentally and culturally specific and certainly not universal. Some cultures, she stated, provided a smooth, gradual transition that allowed adolescents to experience minimal, if any, storm-and-stress.

For many years, Mead was alone in arguing against Hall's view. Most social scientists based their research on what Richard Lerner (a current and eminent developmental researcher) called Hall's deficit model of adolescence where developmental deficits caused turmoil resulting in problem behaviors such as alcohol use, drugs, school failure, teen pregnancy, crime, and depression. Essentially, Hall's deficit model and view of storm-and-stress as universal was not disputed or challenged until the 1960s when it was realized that not all adolescents had a turbulent time during the transition from childhood to adulthood. Research in the 1960s began providing evidence to support Mead's perspective, arguing that many adolescents had good relationships and strong core values with few, if any, problem behaviors. Researchers, in supporting Mead, were not necessarily disputing Hall. They recognized that, while some adolescents did in fact experience an intense period of storm-and-stress, many had a smooth and uneventful transition. This led to the more recent view of a *modified storm-and-stress* period of development. From this perspective, conflict with parents, mood disruptions, and risky behaviors are on a continuum dependent on many psychological, sociological, cultural, and environmental factors.

Theories of Adolescent Development

During the twentieth century, many theories have been proposed to explain human development. A simple overview of a few of the key theories is provided with a particular emphasis on the period of adolescence.

Psychoanalytic theory states that development is unconscious and dependent on early experiences with parents. It is predicated on the premise that personality is comprised of three mostly unconscious psychological constructs: the Id, where raw desires, urges, and drives are housed (e.g., sexual desires, hunger, thirst); the Ego, which "manages" the desires and tries to appease or satisfy the wants of the Id, while working within the constraints of the real world (e.g., satisfying unacceptable sexual desires with fantasies or substituted behaviors); and the Superego, which is the social conscience of the personality (e.g., where parental and societal values reside). Within the framework of psychoanalytic theory, these three hypothesized constructs must work in harmony in order for the person to be well-adjusted and to function effectively within society. The development of these structures arises out of different psychosexual stages, which are a series of sexual obstacles the child must overcome in order to proceed to the next stage of development. Sigmund Freud (1938) and daughter Anna Freud (1958) argued that the balance previously achieved between the Id, the Ego, and the Superego is destroyed during adolescence because of the new pressures on the ego. As a result, the sexual drives brought on by puberty and hormonal changes affect an adolescent's sense of reality and subsequent behavior. From a psychoanalytic point of view, a positive sense of self, prosocial behavior, and overall healthy development can occur only if psychosexual development was not restricted in earlier years. Essentially, the sexual reawakening during adolescence (i.e., the genital stage) leads to healthy adult sexuality and overall well-being if children are not restricted during any of the previous psychosexual stages (i.e., oral, anal, phallic, and latency).

From a *cognitive perspective*, human development is a bidirectional process, explained in terms of an individual's action on the environment and the action of the environment on the individual. As a child matures, he or she becomes more active in his or her environment and more advanced cognitively. Jean Piaget, a pioneer of cognitive developmental theory, proposed that children proceed through a sequence of distinct developmental stages: the sensorimotor stage (birth to age 2), the preoperational stage (ages 2 to 5), the concrete operational stage (age 6 to early adolescence), and the formal operational stage (early adolescence to adulthood). Piaget argued that, between the ages of 11 and 15, adolescents enter the formal operational stage. Abstract and hypothetical thinking emerges during this stage, and as a result, children attain the ability to see that reality (e.g., how others treat them) and their thoughts about reality (e.g., how others "should" treat them) are different. They gain the ability to generate and recognize hypotheses about reality. The ability to think abstractly also allows adolescents to project themselves into the future, distinguish present reality from possibility, and think about what might be. Piaget also argued that adolescents, once in the formal operational stage, gain competence in formal reasoning, which is marked by a transition from inductive reasoning (e.g., "Jane had unprotected sex and did not get pregnant; therefore, if I have unprotected sex, I will not get pregnant.") to deductive reasoning (e.g., "There are risks involved when having unprotected sex, and because Jane did not get pregnant, does not mean that I will not get pregnant."). This transition means that adolescents are not only able to systemize their ideas and critically deal with their own thinking to construct theories but they are also able to test their theories logically and to scientifically discover truth. They can devise many interpretations of an observed outcome (e.g., pregnancy may be the result of unprotected sex, failed contraception, or in vitro fertilization), and they can anticipate many possibilities prior to an actual event (e.g., unprotected sex may lead to pregnancy, an STI, or HIV/AIDS).

Currently, there is debate as to whether Piaget was correct in saying that adolescents gain the competencies cited above by age 15. Neuroscientists argue that the adolescent brain may not be fully developed until late adolescence or early adulthood. Neuroimaging indicates that the prefrontal cortex (the home of the executive functions) is the last part of the human brain to develop, not reaching full maturity until the early twenties or later. This would mean that, until the brain has reached maturity, adolescents would not be competent in planning, setting priorities, organizing thoughts, suppressing impulses, weighing out consequences, and formal reasoning. Without these competencies in place, adolescents may have a difficult time with decision making. Neuroscientists therefore tend to attribute bad decisions to an underdeveloped brain (see Issue 15 for more on this argument).

Social cognitive theory (Bandura, 2005) is another approach to understanding adolescent development and behavior. From this perspective, adolescent development is understood in terms of how adolescents reason about themselves, others, and the social world around them. Theorists such as David Elkind (1967; 1978) describe adolescent reasoning and thinking in terms of the advances in metacognition. With the ability to "think about their own thinking" (metacognition), adolescents spend most of their time focused on themselves. They daydream more and, as they become preoccupied with their own thoughts, they come to believe that others are or should be as preoccupied with them as they are with themselves. As a result, they think everyone notices them. A typical example is the adolescent who cannot possibly go to school because of a facial blemish. To the distraught adolescent, everyone will notice and criticize them. David Elkind uses the term adolescent egocentrism to describe these changes in behavior and thought.

Moving toward a more social perspective is Erik Erikson's (1959) *psychosocial theory* of ego development, which encompasses the entire life span. He describes development from birth to old age as occurring in eight stages with each stage characterized by a crisis between two opposing forces (e.g., trust versus mistrust) that must be resolved successfully. According to Erikson, the resolution of a crisis is dependent on the successful resolution of all previous crises. For example, the adolescent crisis of *identity formation* versus *role confusion* can only be resolved if adolescents were successful in resolving the previous four crises of childhood (i.e., having a sense of trust vs. mistrust, autonomy vs. shame and doubt, initiative vs. guilt, and industry vs. inferiority). In addition, the resolution of the adolescent identity crisis will affect the resolution of future crises. Resolving the identity crisis means showing commitment toward a role–personal, sexual, occupational, and ideological (i.e., a concept about human life that involves a set of beliefs and values). Once complete, the established identity is a distinctive combination of personality characteristics and social style by which the adolescent defines himself/herself and by which he or she is recognized by others.

The last theory presented here is Urie Bronfenbrenner's *ecological systems theory* (1979), which examines the role of five different environments on an individual's development and well-being. Imagine the adolescent at the center of a large circle with each system radiating outward. The first system immediately surrounding the adolescent is the microsystem. This is the setting in which a person lives and includes one's family, peers, school, and neighbourhood. The second system, called the mesosystem, consists of the relationships between the different microsystems. An example is the relationship between an adolescent's family and school. According to Bronfenbrenner, the relationship between these two microsystems has a different effect on the individual than each microsystem separately. The third system is the exosystem, which comprises the linkages between different settings that indirectly involves the adolescent. An example is the relation between the home and a parent's workplace. Outside the exosystem is the macrosystem. This is essentially the cultural and social influence on an individual, such as belief systems, material resources, customs, and lifestyles, which are embedded in each of the previous inner systems. Finally, there is the chronosystem, which involves environmental events and transitions over time. For example, adolescents who were directly involved in a major trauma such as 9/11 or hurricane Katrina will have different life experiences affecting their development than adolescents who were not directly involved.

The theories presented above provide only an introduction to understanding human behavior and, in particular, adolescent behavior. Other theories exist and contribute to the interdisciplinary approach currently used to enhance our understanding of adolescence. For a more comprehensive discussion of these theories, refer to the suggested readings list at the end of this introduction.

Adolescence in the Twentieth Century

Adolescence in and of itself is a period of human development marked by many changes, transitions, and both positive and negative behaviours. Since the study of adolescence first began in the early twentieth century, researchers have examined how particular events and issues affected adolescent attitudes and behaviors. In this third section of the introduction, we provide an overview of how events shaped the way adolescents behaved and how they dealt with particular issues. For example, in the 1920s, when the period of adolescence was officially recognized, North American youth responded with a sense of newfound freedom. They were essentially given permission to stay young and have fun while they could. The decade became known as the Roaring Twenties, with increased autonomy and freedom. An interesting effect was that many adults responded to the behaviors of the young by adopting a similar appealing lifestyle with more music, dancing, and partying. This was short-lived, however, with the Great Depression of the 1930s followed by World War II in the 1940s. Irresponsibility and the age of adolescence were put on hold during these difficult times. Many young people were forced to seek employment or to serve their country in the war. The exposure to poverty, family struggles, war, violence, and death resulted in a drive for stability and security following the war. The 1950s were a time when adults focused on ensuring this security and stability for their families. During this time, adolescents were considered to be the "silent generation" because life seemed perfect. They had only their futures upon which to focus. In North American society, getting a college degree, finding a good job, getting married, and raising a family were the goals for the adolescents of the fifties.

In the 1960s, there was once again disruption to stability and security with the Vietnam War and the assassinations of North American politicians and leaders. Many adolescents reacted with anger and frustration. They did not trust politicians or decision makers because they were seen as disrupting their perceived ideal world and sense of security. They held political protests to voice their views of idealism. They challenged authority and promoted peace, love, and freedom with drug use, loosening of sexual behavior, and cohabitation. This peace movement of the sixties is remembered with phrases such as "make love not war" and "reject authority." For most, there was no focus on working hard and establishing a stable career. Attending university was as much about fun and freedom from parents as it was about studying.

The sexual revolution of the 1960s lasted into the 1970s, with adolescents becoming more focused on their own needs and goals but not without further struggles. Adolescent girls and young women, aware of the opportunity differential and stereotyped careers for men and women, began the long and difficult fight for equality. The previous argument that women would have babies and be unreliable was no longer valid. Thanks to the contraceptive pill, which was introduced in the sixties, women gained control over their reproduction and the freedom to choose if and when they would have a family. Gender inequality was no longer an issue of biology. The success of the Women's Movement in the seventies and eighties resulted in many more young women attending college and university—eventually bridging the gender gap in many professions such as medicine, law, and engineering. With more women attending to their careers, and postponing childbearing or deciding to be childless, two-income families became more popular. Small families, large homes, travel, and material possessions such as the "best" home computers became the goals. This way of life has had a profound effect on children born since 1980. For example, a carryover effect from the sixties and seventies is the notion that if you want something badly enough, you can get it. Parents have become so involved in their childrens' lives, providing material possession upon material possession, that kids have come to expect it. Large screen televisions, personal computers, electronic devices, cell phones, and disposable income are common expectations among many of today's youth. The adolescents of the twenty-first century, known as the Millennials, are unique and different from adolescents of the past.

Adolescence in the Twenty-First Century

Today's adolescents have unique experiences and issues not encountered by previous generations. There are many factors contributing to this. For instance, the advances in technology have been influential in shaping the lives of adolescents today. Many carry a cell phone, an MP3 player, and have their own personal computer, enabling them to communicate with anyone—regardless of where they are. These devices also give them instant access to music, computer games, and information. Essentially, we have technologically savvy adolescents who spend much of their time alone with inanimate objects.

A second factor contributing to the uniqueness of today's adolescents is their perceived sense of entitlement. Parents have protected and given so much to their children that, once they leave home for university or work, they come to expect the same. Parents, having had to fight for rights in the sixties and seventies, have taught their children "if you want something, it's your right to have it." As university educators, we have seen firsthand the effect this has had. For example, Millennial students are often more demanding and persistent in their demands compared to previous cohorts of the eighties and nineties. A typical example is demanding an exam be rescheduled because of personal travel plans. Millennials are also more likely to have their parents involved in their post-secondary education, making calls to professors and administrators requesting information or favors for their adolescent.

A third unique factor contributing to the novel experiences of the youth of the Millennial age involves sexual freedom. That is, youth of today experience a more open sexual discourse because of significant social events including the Sexual Revolution and Women's Movement of the 1960s and 1970s, the Gay Rights Movement of the 1970s and 1980s, as well as the HIV/AIDS crisis of the 1980s and onward. Different forms of media have also played a large role in opening up knowledge and discussion about sexuality; for example, the Internet has made many sexually oriented Web sites accessible to youth despite efforts to provide filters. Some of these Web sites are informational, while others would be characterized as obscene or pornographic. Television, films, as well as magazines and books tend to involve more overt sexuality, as regulations regarding these media have been relaxed over recent decades. These changes have had an impact on social programs including more explicit and precise sexual health education in the school system—although this has involved considerable controversy. All of this cumulates in a more sexually savvy adolescent than perhaps was the case in previous generations.

The Millennial cohort is probably more aware of pregnancy and STI prevention as well as issues surrounding sexual violence—more so than previous generations. According to a recent report published by the Centers for Disease Control and Prevention (Abma, Martinez, Mosher, & Dawson, 2004), the teenage pregnancy rate has dropped from 1990 to 2000. From 1982 and 1995 to 2002, teen intercourse has decreased (i.e., there has been an increased rate of adolescent "virginity"). Among sexually active teen girls, there has been increased condom use and decreased "no protection" during intercourse, as well. All of these changes might be positive side-effects of the increased openness and more positive attitudes toward the sexuality of adolescents.

Not only has sexual behaviors of adolescents changed across the generations, but gender roles have also changed significantly. This involves the roles of girls and boys in relation to "feminine" and "masculine" traits. Gender rigidity has declined, and greater tolerance for gender variation has increased, although early adolescence is known as a time when youth are less understanding of violations of gender rules. Regardless, this has made the youth of the twentieth century more accepting of lesbian, gay, bisexual, and transgender people

(Ponton & Judice, 2004). In sum, sexual behaviors, attitudes, and roles have changed dramatically for the Millennial generation and, while always an important aspect of adolescent development, these topics have become more central in adolescent research.

The introduction thus far has provided an overview of adolescence from when the term was first coined to the present. Through the twentieth century, adolescents were faced with many hurdles and issues that affected their development and overall transition from childhood to adulthood. The goal of this book is to present issues facing adolescents in the first decade of the twenty-first century. We address controversies such as adolescent use of antidepressants, alcohol consumption, and youth justice. We debate adolescent consent for abortions, condom availability, and comprehensive sex education. We also cover divorce and family disruption, body image, cyber-friendships, sex on television, sexual behavior, sexual orientation, and dating. Finally, we examine behaviors such as club drug usage, bullying, school violence, and criminal behavior.

These issues will shape the behaviors of tomorrow's adolescents and guide future research. As is evident from the issues listed above, this book presents adolescence as an interdisciplinary topic. We have selected issues that can be used in a variety of disciplines and courses.

References and Suggested Readings

Abma J.C., Martinez, G.M., Mosher, W.D., & Dawson, B.S. (2004). Teenagers in the United States: Sexual activity, contraceptive use, and childbearing, 2002. National Center for Health Statistics. *Vital Health Stat* 23(24).

Arnett, J. (2004). *Adolescence and emerging adulthood*, 2nd edition. New Jersey: Prentice Hall.

Bandura, A. (2005). The evolution of social cognitive theory. In Ken G. Smith & Michael A. Hitt (Eds.). *Great minds in management. The process of theory development* (pp. 9–35). New York: Oxford University Press.

Bronfenbrenner, U. (1979). *The ecology of human development.* Cambridge, MA: Harvard University Press.

Elkind, D. (1967). Egocentrism in adolescence. *Child Development*, 38, 1025–1034.

Elkind, D. (1978). Understanding the young adolescent. *Adolescence*, 13, 127–134.

Erikson, E. (1959). Identity and the life cycle. *Psychological Issues*, 1, 1–171.

Freud, A. (1958). Adolescence. *Psychoanalytic Study of the Child*, 13, 255–278.

Freud, S. (1938). *An outline of psychoanalysis.* London: Hogarth Press.

Hall, G. S. (1904). *Adolescence.* New York: Appleton.

Lerner, R. Brown, J., & Kier, C. (2005). *Adolescence: Development, diversity, context, and application.* Toronto: Prentice Hall.

Mead, M. (1928). *Coming of age in Samoa.* New York: Morrow.

Ponton, L.E., & Judice, S. (2004). Typical adolescent sexual development. *Child & Adolescent Psychiatric Clinics of North America*, 13(3), 497–511.

Santrock, J. (2005). *Adolescence*, 10th edition. New York: McGraw-Hill.

Steinberg, L. (2004). *Adolescence.* New York: McGraw-Hill.

On the Internet . . .

Antidepressants Facts

This Web Site provides basic information on anti-depressants and its side effects. It also features research articles, studies, personal experiences, and doctors' suggestions about anti-depressants.

http://www.antidepressantsfacts.com/

National Institute on Alcohol Abuse and Alcoholism

National Institute on Alcohol Abuse and Alcoholism is a part of the National Institutes of Health. They provide information on alcohol and its related health issues. Pamphlets, brochures, and posters regarding alcohol abuse are also available.

http://www.niaaa.nih.gov/

Planned Parenthood Federation of America, Inc.

This Web Site provides abortion facts, side effects, research, and health information. It is operated by Planned Parenthood, an organization which provides reproductive health care and sexual health information to women, men, and teens.

http://www.plannedparenthood.org/pp2/portal/medicalinfo/abortion/

Canadian Federation for Sexual Health

Canadian Federation for Sexual Health is a pro-choice, charitable organization which promotes reproductive health and rights in Canada and all over the world. This Web Site keeps up-to-date information on legal issues regarding abortion in Canada.

http://www.cfsh.ca

National Abortion Federation

National Abortion Federation (NAF) is a pro-choice organization that supports abortion. This Web Site provides abortion facts and information on how to obtain an abortion.

http://www.prochoice.org/

National Right to Life

National Right to Life is a pro-life organization opposing abortion, euthanasia, and infanticide. This Web Site provides information on pro-life legislation and is updated with current research findings regarding abortion.

http://www.nrlc.org/

National Organization for Women Foundation

This Web Site, operated by the National Organization for Women Foundation, promotes positive body image. It provides different ways and tips women can do to learn to accept the body they are in. Facts on body image, eating disorders, addiction, and cosmetic surgery are also available.

http://loveyourbody.nowfoundation.org/moreideas.html

PART 1

Adolescent Health

*A*dolescent physical and psychological health has important implications for future well-being. An adolescent who is both mentally and
physically fit has a better chance to develop into a strong, productive,
and happy adult. There are a multitude of adolescent health-related
issues that could have an influence on the healthy development of a
teen. In the following part, four issues that relate to different aspects of
adolescent health are examined.

- Should Adolescents Be Taking Antidepressants?

- Should Adolescents Be Allowed to Drink Alcohol?

- Should Parental Consent Be Required for Adolescents Seeking Abortions?

- Do Boys Worry about an Ideal Body Image as Much as Girls Do?

ISSUE 1

Should Adolescents Be Taking Antidepressants?

YES: Yvon D. Lapierre, from "Suicidality with Selective Serotonin Reuptake Inhibitors: Valid Claim?" *Journal of Psychiatry & Neuroscience* (vol. 28, no. 5, 2003)

NO: Tamar D. Wohlfarth, et al., from "Antidepressants Use in Children and Adolescents and the Risk of Suicide," *European Neuropsychopharmacology* (vol. 16, 2006)

ISSUE SUMMARY

YES: Yvon Lapierre, a professor emeritus at the department of psychiatry at the University of Ottawa, reviewed relevant literature addressing the concern that increased suicidality was associated with the use of antidepressants including SSRIs. He concludes that the evidence currently available does not support the hypothesis that antidepressants cause increased suicidality in patients with depression.

NO: Tamar Wohlfarth, a clinical assessor, and colleagues in the Netherlands assessed antidepressant use in pediatric patients and reported an increased risk for events related to suicidality among those taking antidepressants. They caution the use of all SSRIs and NSRIs in the pediatric population.

Researchers have estimated that 2 percent of children and 4–8 percent of adolescents suffer from depression, and that the lifetime prevalence for major depressive disorder (MDD) by adolescence ranges between 15 and 20 percent (American Academy of Child and Adolescent Psychiatry, AACAP, 1998). Depressive disorders are generally chronic among adolescents with an average episode in a clinical setting lasting 8 months. Unfortunately, children and adolescents with clinical depression often go untreated, and untreated depression is a major risk factor for substance abuse, school failure, impaired relationships, and personality disorders. Depression is also the strongest predictor of suicidal ideation, attempts, and completions; suicide completions are now the third leading cause of death in 10 to 19 year olds (Anderson, 2002).

Furthermore, depression during adolescence is a major risk for depression, suicide, and long-term psychosocial impairment in adulthood.

Given the serious nature of the disorder, along with the fact that the peak onset of depression is in adolescence, early recognition and effective treatment are crucial. Effective treatments for children and adolescents with depressive disorders most often include psychotherapy and antidepressant medications. Studies have indicated that a combination of both treatments is most effective, although studies have also found antidepressants alone to convey almost as much benefit as the combined treatment.

Antidepressants introduced since 1990, especially selective serotonin reuptake inhibitors (SSRIs), have become a preferred treatment option for children and adolescents with depression. Compared to their predecessors (the tricyclic antidepressants, TCAs), SSRIs such as fluoxetine (Prozac), sertraline (Zoloft), paroxetine (Paxil), and citalopram (Celexa) are better tolerated, have a lower frequency of cardiac events and sudden death, have fewer anticholinergic effects (dry mouth, somnolence, and constipation), and have superior efficacy (Hamrin & Scahill, 2005). SSRIs work by blocking the reuptake of serotonin (5HT), a neurotransmitter in the central nervous system involved in a range of physiological and behavioural functions including sleep, wakefulness, appetite, emotional response, and thought process. Although the etiology of depression is unknown, serotonin is believed to play an important role: Depression may be associated with reduced serotoninergic function. Therefore, antidepressants such as SSRIs appear to be effective in treating the disorder. However, the safety of prescribing antidepressants to children and adolescents has been the subject of increasing concern.

The controversy about the safety and efficacy of antidepressants, particularly SSRIs and newer antidepressants such as selective norepinephrine reuptake inhibitors (SNRIs), began in June 2003. At that time, the U.S. Food and Drug Administration (FDA) conducted an investigation of antidepressants. The meta-analysis of 24 SSRI trials resulted in the FDA issuing a black-box warning describing an increased risk of worsening of depression and suicidality for all current and future antidepressants used in those under the age of 18. The FDA investigation resulted in only fluoxetine receiving approval for major depression in children and adolescents. Of note, however, is that of the data reviewed by the FDA, no completed suicides were reported in any of the randomized controlled trials (RCTs) of adolescents taking any of the above medications.

The controversial black-box warning has since led to an active debate regarding the appropriate treatment of depression in younger patients. Just how safe are antidepressant, and do they increase the risk of suicidal behaviour? Ecological studies provide mixed evidence on the risks and benefits of SSRIs; some show that increases in SSRI use are associated with reductions in suicide rates, while others show the opposite to be true.

In the selections that follow, Yvon Lapierre argues that the available research does not support the hypothesis that the risks of taking antidepressants outweigh the benefits. On the other hand, Tamar Wohlfarth and colleagues are firm in their argument against the use of antidepressants among adolescents due to the increased risk of suicidality and other related behaviours.

YES

Yvon D. Lapierre

Suicidality with Selective Serotonin Reuptake Inhibitors: Valid Claim?

Introduction

A plethora of new antidepressants followed the introduction of the selective serotonin reuptake inhibitors (SSRIs) with the associated claims of their relative innocuity compared with the previous generation of tricyclics antidepressants (TCAs) and monoamine oxidase inhibitors. These claims seem to have reached their high point, and SSRIs as well as other antidepressants are now undergoing a second phase of critical review. . . .

One considerably controversial issue has been the risk of suicide in relation to SSRI antidepressants. The issue arose from a series of case reports of patients who developed intense suicidal preoccupations and intense thoughts of self-harm while taking antidepressants. The initial reports implicated fluoxetine,[1] and this was followed by reports suggesting a similar phenomenon with other SSRIs, thus leading to the speculation of a class effect.[2] . . .

[A first concern] is whether there is a temporal cause–effect relation between the administration of a specific drug and the development of suicidal ideation and of suicide. The order of such a cause and effect relation may then be examined and attributed, if applicable, as either a primary drug effect, a paradoxical drug effect, an expected side effect of the drug or, finally, an action that may be secondary to a side effect of the compound. A second issue to be addressed is whether this effect is drug specific or class specific. The question of validity of any imputed causality must be critically re-evaluated throughout this process. Once these issues are clarified, strategies that would improve the outcome of treatment for patients with depression may arise.

This paper will address the problem by first looking at issues of efficacy and suicide data and then discussing the case for the alleged link between suicide and SSRI and other antidepressant therapies.

Efficacy Issues

The efficacy of a widely used intervention may be evaluated by assessing its impact on the population at large through epidemiological approaches and then on the experiences obtained from clinical trials and clinical practice.

From *Journal of Psychiatry & Neuroscience*, vol. 28, no. 5, September 2003, pp. 340–347. Copyright © 2003 by CMA Management. Reprinted by permission. References omitted.

Epidemiological observations suggest that there has been a gradual increase in the incidence of depression in post-World War II generations. There are indications that this illness will become an ever-increasing burden of disability in Western societies. Given that depression is the predominant risk factor for suicide, one would expect that with the increased numbers of depressed individuals, there would be an increase in suicide rates. Furthermore, if there is validity to the claim that SSRIs play a causative role in suicide, there would be an even greater increase in suicide rates since the advent of these drugs. Although this may not have materialized as such, these speculations are not necessarily dismissed as being completely invalid.

Epidemiological studies on the issue of antidepressant treatment and suicide have been conducted in a number of countries. In Italy, there was found to be a possible relation between increased SSRI use from 1988 to 1996 and suicide rate. There was a slight increase in suicide rates for men but a more pronounced decrease for women; however, these changes were not significant.[3] In Sweden, from 1976 to 1996, increased utilization of antidepressants paralleled a decrease in suicide rates.[4] . . .

In the National Institute of Mental Health Collaborative Depression Study, Leon et al assessed the possibility of an increased suicidal risk associated with the SSRI fluoxetine. In the 185 patients in follow-up, there was a trend for a decrease in the number of suicide attempts compared with patients receiving other treatments. Although this cohort was at higher risk because of a history of repeated suicide attempts, treatment with fluoxetine resulted in a nonsignificant reduction of attempts in these patients.

The findings of these epidemiological studies do not provide any indication that the use of antidepressants, and more specifically SSRIs, contribute to an increased risk of suicide in population bases or in depressed populations.

The main sources of information on psychopharmacological agents are the data from clinical trials. Then, post-marketing studies are intended to provide the alerts on safety and potentially new indications for the drug. Both of these sources have limitations and biases, however, inevitably adding fuel to the present debate.

Given that RCTs are designed to primarily identify clinical efficacy and acute or short-term safety of antidepressants, there are limitations on the gathering of exhaustive data on unwanted side effects. The selection of patients for an RCT generally excludes those who are considered to be at risk for suicide. This is usually determined clinically, and the judgment is based on clinical indicators that have, in past experience, been associated with increased risk. Up to 80% of depressed patients may experience thoughts of suicide, and there is a greater than 15% risk of suicide with depression, making the elucidation of suicidal thoughts and intent increasingly relevant to a valid assessment of risk.

This rationale is based on the premise that suicidal ideation is the precursor to and is likely to lead to suicidal acting out. Suicidal acts in the recent past, as well as a number of other associated factors, contribute to the evaluation of risk and the decision of inclusion or exclusion. This inevitably leads to a skewed population, where those appearing to be most clearly at risk and those more severely depressed are often excluded.

The experimental design most often used is a single-blind placebo-washout phase followed by a double-blind randomized phase with a placebo control, a standard active treatment control and an experimental treatment arm. Because of the pressures against the use of placebo in RCTs, as well as cost considerations, there is a trend toward having unbalanced groups, with fewer subjects in the placebo and control arms. This results in reduced statistical power and the need for more patients in the studies. . . .

[Another methodological problem] occurs in post-marketing surveillance studies. The source of data varies from one jurisdiction to the next, as do the methods and obligations to report adverse events. Clinicians are known to adopt different prescribing patterns for patients presenting more severe states of depression and for those considered to be at greater risk for suicide. The former group are more likely to receive a TCA, whereas the latter are more likely to receive a "safer-in-overdose" SSRI. Thus, a significant bias in patient selection arises in the evaluation of suicidal risk under one form of treatment or another. . . .

[Finally,] meta-analyses of RCTs have yielded conflicting results. The short duration of RCTs, which are the basis of these meta-analyses, may not provide valid long-term data, but they do contribute to an understanding of acute therapeutic effects. There is an inherent deficiency in meta-analyses because of the intrinsic limitations of post hoc analyses. Nevertheless, a few of these reports suggested that fluoxetine was associated with a greater incidence of suicidal thoughts. This was followed by other reports suggesting that sertraline, fluvoxamine, paroxetine and citalopram produced similar effects. This led to the speculation of a class effect of SSRIs. On the other hand, there are meta-analytic and other types of studies that just as strongly suggest that emergent suicidal ideation was lessened by these same SSRIs. In the Verkes et al study,[5] the findings are more convincing because of the high-risk population involved. Others have suggested that, not only do SSRIs reduce suicidal ideation, but the symptom is increased in patients taking norepinephrine reuptake inhibitors.[6]

A meta-analytic study of treatment with fluoxetine, tricyclic antidepressants and placebo in large samples of patients with mood disorders ($n = 5655$) and nonmood disorders ($n = 4959$) did not identify statistically significant differences in emergent suicidal thoughts between groups, and there were no suicides in the nonmood disorder group.[7] These data do not support a suicidogenic effect of SSRIs or TCAs. . . .

Suicide

The risk of a depressed patient committing suicide with prescribed antidepressants has been a long-standing concern of clinicians treating depressed patients. This was particularly significant with the older generation tricyclics and was one reason to advocate the use of the newer agents (because of their reported lower lethal potential in overdose). On the other hand, it is surprisingly rare for patients to use prescribed antidepressants for suicidal purposes. Data on the agents used for suicide from a number of countries suggest that only about 5% of overdoses are with antidepressants. . . .

An important finding in these reports is that patients tend to use previously prescribed undiscarded antidepressants as their drug of choice. This points to the important role of therapeutic failure in a number of patients who commit suicide.

The advent of the SSRIs brought a renewed impetus in physician and public education on depressive disorders to not only raise professional and public awareness of depression but also publicize the profile of the new antidepressants in their treatment. This, in addition to other factors, has led to many of these educational activities being sponsored by the pharmaceutical industry, with the inevitable ensuing risk of bias. These efforts have certainly contributed to a heightened awareness of depression by professionals and to less reluctance in using antidepressants because of improved safety profiles with equivalent efficacy.

Although antidepressants have been pivotal in the treatment of depression for more than 4 decades, a number of unanswered questions remain. The therapeutic superiority of antidepressants has been taken for granted despite the inconsistent robustness in many controlled studies, where their superiority over placebo is not always clearly demonstrated. Recent data on the latest generation of antidepressants, the SSRIs and serotonin–norepinephrine reuptake inhibitors suggest that only 48% of placebo-controlled studies show a consistent statistically significant superiority of the antidepressant over placebo. This figure may be inferior to the generally accepted greater success rate and emphasizes the need for individualized therapeutic strategies. This becomes critical for poor responders, where the limitations of available treatments become obvious. Depression is the main risk factor for suicide, the final and fatal outcome of non-response to treatment. If, as is suggested by some, the risk of suicide is increased by antidepressants, which are considered to be the cornerstone and most widely accepted treatment for depression, the use of such agents would obviously necessitate a critical re-evaluation.

Suicidality and suicidal actions induced de novo by SSRIs was suggested by a few clinical papers. . . . Because of the paradoxical nature of these observations, a number of retrospective analyses of large cohorts were then conducted. The analyses of the US Food and Drug Administration database . . . looked at suicidality and suicide rates in a cohort of 23 201 patients participating in clinical trials of antidepressants. Overall suicide rates for patients were 627/100 000 compared with a general population rate of 11/100 000. There were no significant differences between rates for placebo, comparator drugs and new-generation investigational drugs. The mortality rates ranged from 0.19% for placebo to 0.14% for the investigational drugs and 0.11% for the active comparators. There were no significant differences in patient exposure years between these 3 groups, although the numerical values were higher for the antidepressant groups. The attempted suicide rate ranged from 0.66% for the investigational drugs to 1.37% for the comparators to 1.39% for placebo (no significant differences). Patient exposure years also did not differ significantly. These findings do not provide information on the duration of exposure to treatment but include the data on all patients who participated in the trials and are thus quite representative of short-term studies. Patient exposure years, which cumulates the duration of treatment and the number of patients treated, did not show differences either. These data do not support the suggestion that SSRIs add to suicide risk.

A similar study was done in the Netherlands[8] . . . on data submitted to the Medicines Evaluation Board of the Netherlands for 12 246 patients treated in short-term (< 8 wk) clinical trials. Attempts at suicide occurred in 0.4% of patients in both placebo and active drug groups. Completed suicide occurred in 0.1% of patients in both placebo and active treatment groups. In longer-term studies (> 8 wk) involving 1949 patients, attempted suicide occurred in 0.7% of patients in both groups, and completed suicides occurred in 0.2% (2 patients) of the active drug group (no significant difference). These results also do not support a suicidogenic effect of these antidepressants. . . .

Discussion

SSRI antidepressants as a class are among the most frequently prescribed drugs in the Western world. Their applications have broadened from their initial indication in depression to a number of other psychiatric conditions such as obsessive–compulsive disorder, generalized anxiety disorder and, more recently, late luteal phase disorder. This provides a wide spectrum of conditions under which the SSRIs are administered and allows for a much broader clinical experience for the appraisal of the drugs in question. There have not been any reports of suicide in patients taking SSRIs for these other conditions.

Suicide is a leading public health problem in all societies. It is estimated that known suicides account for 1 million deaths worldwide annually. Given that depression is a significant factor in nearly 50% of these cases, the treatment of depression merits critical appraisal, especially if this treatment contributes further to suicidal behaviour, as has been suggested. This partly explains the reaction to the initial reports of increased suicidality during treatment with fluoxetine and then with the other SSRIs. These reports have led to a healthy second look at the available data and to the pursuit of additional studies and observations.

Clinical studies and meta-analyses indicate that an overwhelming number of patients experience a decrease in suicidal ideation while taking SSRIs. The fact that these meta-analyses were based on data collected primarily to demonstrate efficacy does not diminish their validity. Although the method of evaluation has been criticized (i.e., a single item on the HAM-D) and the evidence of decreased suicidality admittedly not highly nuanced, the data still reflect the observed clinical reality. A decrease in suicidality must be considered to reflect an improvement in the depressed condition.

Despite the availability of less toxic antidepressant drugs, the increasing use of antidepressants has not consistently been associated with a significant decline in suicide rates. As the SSRIs gain popularity, the use of the older TCAs as instruments of suicide by overdose has decreased. However, other more violent means are resorted to, thus indirectly reducing the positive safety impact of the SSRIs. It would be simplistic to make conclusions on single causality in suicidal behaviour without recognizing the complexities of the behaviour and circumstances that lead to the outcome.

Although evidence from large studies points to a reduction in suicidal ideation, the few reports of the appearance of intense suicidal thoughts in a few patients must not pass unnoticed. There were sporadic reports of suicidality with zimelidine, the first SSRI. This did not hold up to statistical testing and, because the drug was discontinued shortly after being launched, there was no follow-up. There were no major concerns at this time because most patients experienced an improvement in suicidal thoughts. A sporadic paradoxical effect to a psychotropic agent is a well-known phenomenon. It is well documented with antipsychotic agents such as the phenothiazines, where excitement and even worsening of the psychotic disorder have been observed. These are rare events but must be kept in mind so they will be recognized when they do occur. It is also essential to recognize that the emergence of suicidal thoughts may simply be attributable to underlying psychopathology.

Studies of fluoxetine have reported that this drug, in addition to causing some increase in agitation in some patients, may also cause akathisia. High levels of anxiety and agitation are known to accompany increased suicidal behaviour. In such a situation, the behaviour would be secondary to a side effect of the drug, rather than to its primary action. . . .

Despite anecdotal reports implicating most of the SSRIs, a drug-specific or class effect is not substantiated. Unfortunately, SSRIs have not been compared critically with other classes of antidepressants. On the other hand, the common pharmacological action of serotonin reuptake inhibition does not explain all of the actions of these drugs. A comparison of fluoxetine with its activating properties and citalopram with its more sedating profile illustrates the different effects SSRIs can have. Fluoxetine is known to occasionally cause some agitation. This may be experienced independently from akathisia which may, albeit rarely, also result from fluoxetine. The combination of the 2 (i.e., akathisia and agitation) has been associated with increased suicidal tendencies in depressed patients, but it is unlikely that this would support a class effect or phenomenon. It is more likely a consequence of a rare side effect of the drug.

A pharmacological explanation for a rare event is difficult to establish because it is, by definition, unpredictable. However, it is not beyond the realm of possibility and merits further exploration, although it is unlikely to attract interest simply because of the rarity of the event and the unpredictability of a host of variables.

Conclusion

Any conclusions based on these few reports of sporadic cases of increased suicidality with SSRIs must be limited and highly tentative. The most these cases can suggest is an individual paradoxical effect, and these can be compared with the large number of patients who experience a diminution of suicidality and an improvement in depression. Another significant factor is that as the use of these antidepressants has broadened, the initial reports have not been followed by an increasing number of cases. Results of clinical studies are inconclusive, with some supporting a link and others refuting one. However, the awareness of the possibility of increased suicidality with SSRI treatment must be taken in the context of the risk of suicide in treating depression with any other antidepressant. Suicide is an inherent risk in the context of depression, but this should not deter from adequate treatment.

A review of this issue serves as a reminder of the basic principles of good therapeutics that recommend that the complete profile of the drug be taken into account when selecting a pharmacotherapeutic agent. Once the primary (desired) and secondary (unwanted or not) effects have been fully considered, the total profile of the drug can be tailored to the clinical profile of an individual patient.

The newer SSRI antidepressants were never considered to be superior in efficacy to the TCAs, but their entry into the therapeutics of depression has reduced the risk of iatrogenic intoxication and, most likely, the overall risk of suicidal outcome in adequately treated patients. There is, at this time, insufficient evidence to claim that they lead to suicide.

References

King RA, Riddle M, Chappell PB, Hardin MT, Anderson GM, Lombroso P. Emergence of self-destructive phenomena in children and adolescents during fluoxetine treatment. *J Am Acad Child Adolesc Psychiatry* 1991;30:171–6.

Lane RM. SSRI-induced extrapyramidal side effects and akathisia: implications for treatment. *J Psychopharmacol* 1998; 12:192–214.

Barbui C, Campomori A, D'Avanzo B, Negri E, Garattini S. Antidepressant drug use in Italy since the introduction of SSRI's: national trends, regional differences and impact on suicide rates. *Soc Psychiatry Psychiatr Epidemiol* 1999;34(3):152–6.

Isacsson G. Suicide prevention-a medical breakthrough? *Acta Psychiatr Scand* 2000;102(2):113–7.

Verkes RJ, Van der Mast RC, Hengveld MW, Jolien P, Zwinderman AH, Van Kempen GMJ. Reduction by paroxetine of suicidal behaviour in patients with repeated suicide attempts but not major depression. *Am J Psychiatry* 1998;155: 543–7.

Filteau MJ, Lapierre YD, Bakish D, Blanchard A. Reduction in suicidal ideation with SSRI's: a review of 459 depressed patients. *J Psychiatry Neurosci* 1993;18:114–9.

Tollefson GD, Fawcett J, Winokur G, Beasley CM Jr, Potvin JH, Faries DE, et al. Evaluation of suicidality during pharmacologic treatment of mood and non-mood disorders. *Ann Clin Psychiatry* 1993;5:209–24.

Storosum JG, Van Zwieten BJ, Van den Brink W, Gersons BPR, Broekmans AW. Suicide risk in placebo-controlled studies of major depression. *Am J Psychiatry* 2001;158:1271–5.

Antidepressants Use in Children and Adolescents and the Risk of Suicide

1. Introduction

An increasing number of children and adolescents are treated with antidepressants. However, evidence to support such treatment in this age group is lacking. In fact, most pharmacological treatments of paediatric patients in most fields of medicine lack supportive empirical evidence. Regulatory authorities in Europe and the US have undertaken various measures, including guidelines (EMEA, 1999) and legislation (FDA, 1997) in order to try and correct for this situation. These efforts have led to the initiation of numerous randomised clinical studies in paediatric patients, including studies of antidepressants medications.

As the results of these studies have become available, an apparent signal with respect to suicide-related events has begun to emerge, first with respect to paroxetine and later with respect to other antidepressants. These findings have instigated renewed attention to the question whether SSRIs have the potential to induce suicidality. . . . The review of the results of clinical trials in children by Whittington et al. (2004) concluded that the risk involved in the treatment with SSRIs of children with depression outweighs the benefit except for fluoxetine.

Examining a partly overlapping data set, regulatory authorities have concluded that all antidepressants that were examined are associated with a signal of suicidality, and hence recommended issuing a warning against the use of all antidepressants in children and adolescents (EMEA, 2004a; FDA, 2004). The purpose of this paper is to describe the evidence these recommendations were based on. . . .

2. Methods

Altogether 22 short-term randomised double-blind placebo-controlled clinical trials are examined. These studies were conducted and submitted to the registration authorities for the purpose of obtaining a registration for the treatment of depression and anxiety disorders in children and adolescents. . . .

The studies involved eight different pharmaceutical products and included over 4000 paediatric patients. Pharmacodynamically, these products were selective serotonin and/or noradrenerge reuptake inhibitors: SSRIs and NSRIs.

The studies were conducted between 1984 and 2002. Most studies, however, were of recent date. Most trials (15) included patients with major depressive disorders (MDD), four trials were of patients with obsessive—compulsive disorder (OCD), two with generalised anxiety disorder (GAD), and one with social anxiety disorder (SAD).

Diagnoses were made by psychiatrists and were based on DSM-III or DSM-IV criteria, depending on the time period in which the trial was performed. The design of the trials varied with respect to instruments used to measure efficacy. However, most depression trials used the revised version of the Children Depression Rating Scale (CDRS-R) and all OCD studies used the Child Yale-Brown Obsessive Compulsive Scale (CY—BOCS). The mean severity scores at baseline indicated that most patients included in the studies suffered from moderate to severe disorders. Trials varied with respect to the age range of patients, with some including only children, some only adolescents and some both age groups. The duration of the trials varied between 6 and 12 weeks.

The study reports were searched for descriptions of adverse events that could indicate suicide or events related to suicidality. The following strings were searched for: 'suic-', 'self-', 'harm', 'injury', 'injurious', 'intentional', 'non-accidental', 'hostility', 'emotional' and 'lability'. Event descriptions that included the string 'suic-' were defined as adverse events related to suicidality. Events that included any of the other terms but not the term 'suic-' were classified as 'self-harm', 'hostility' or 'emotional lability', unless clearly indicated that these were accidental. Case reports that were identified were counted so that each patient could be counted only once in each category. . . .

2.1. Data Analysis

No tests of significance were performed on event rates in the individual studies, as the studies were not powered in order to detect differences between treatment groups in the rates of these rare events. Instead, for each study, the existence of a signal for suicidality was defined as any rate observed in the treatment group that was higher than that seen in placebo. In addition, where possible, point estimates for the relative risk (RR) were calculated (i.e. if the rate in the placebo group was not zero).

A random effect meta-analysis was conducted over all the studies. The ORs and RDs (with 95% confidence intervals) were calculated based on a random effect model. . . .

3. Results

. . . No completed suicides were reported in any of the studies. . . .

[Events] (including self-harm, hostility and emotional lability), which are thought to have the same underlying mechanism as suicide-related events, occurred more frequently in the treatment groups compared to the placebo groups. . . .

Signals appeared in studies of longer duration (i.e. 10–12 weeks) as well as in studies of shorter duration (i.e. 6–8 weeks) and in studies that included only adolescents as well as in studies that included both children and adolescents. Therefore, it was concluded that there is no association between the appearance of the suicidality signal and the duration of the studies or with the age range of the patients included. Furthermore, an examination of the cases with suicide-related events in studies that included both children and adolescents indicated that an equal number of children and adolescents were involved in these behaviours.

A meta-analysis for the MDD studies showed an overall significant odds ratio (OR) of 1.67 (95% CI: 1.05–2.65, $\chi^2_{(13)}$ heterogeneity $= 8.93$, $p = 0.78$) and a significant risk difference (RD) of 1.4% (95% CI: 0.36%–2.46%, $\chi^2_{(14)}$ heterogeneity $= 11.25$, $p = 0.66$).

Results for the anxiety disorders studies showed an overall non-significant OR . . . and a non-significant RD. . . .

Meta-analysis of the MDD trials indicated that efficacy results are heterogeneous across trials and hence an overall measure of efficacy could not be meaningfully interpreted. Furthermore, examination of the design of the trials indicated that there were significant differences between the trials in the methods used to select patients into the trials that are likely to lead to differences in the included patient populations. Thus, heterogeneity between the trials with respect to design and with respect to efficacy makes it difficult to derive an overall statement about efficacy with respect to MDD. Because efficacy could be detected in some trials that used more stringent inclusion procedure (e.g. placebo run-in), it may be that some of these compounds are efficacious in a subgroup of children and adolescents who suffer from more severe and more persistent depression.

The trials of the various anxiety disorders were positive in some but not all products. The meta-analysis for the anxiety trials indicated no significant heterogeneity across trials . . . and an overall effect size of 0.39 (95% CI: 0.27–0.51), indicating a small to medium overall effect.

4. Discussion

The review of all trials that were submitted to the European registration authorities has shown that no completed suicide was reported in any of these trials. However, a signal pertaining to suicidality and related behaviours was detected in all products that were examined.

The combined OR for events related to suicidality in all the depression studies (1.67) has reached statistical significance while the OR in the anxiety disorders studies was weaker (1.33) and did not reach statistical significance. However, the existence of a risk for suicidality in patients treated for anxiety cannot be ruled out. Failure to reach statistical significance may be because the studies were not powered to detect differences in this rare event.

The conclusion from the clinical trials data, therefore, is that in children and adolescents, there is an association between the use of all the antidepressants that were examined and suicide-related events.

No relationship to patients' age, gender or duration of the study was detected, although the numbers are too small to allow any definitive conclusions with regard to these factors.

The evidence concerning efficacy seems to suggest that the MDD trials were heterogeneous with respect to both efficacy and methodology, specifically the methods used to recruit patients. Trials that used long and extensive diagnostic procedure and placebo run-in had better efficacy results than trials that did not. These results may indicate that these compounds may be efficacious in a select group of patients who suffer from more severe and more persistent depression. Efficacy results were stronger and more homogeneous in the anxiety trials, indicating that antidepressants may be effective in treating anxiety disorders in children and adolescents. . . .

The FDA has reached similar conclusions to the ones arrived at in this review (FDA, 2004). Two sets of analyses, using different case ascertainment strategies to define suicide-related events, were run by the FDA. The first used cases of suicide-related behaviours that were identified by the sponsors of the studies. The second analysis relied on events that were classified as suicide-related by a group of suicide experts, under the coordination of researchers at Columbia University. Despite this and other differences in the methods, the two analyses arrived at similar results and reached similar conclusions and recommendations. The analyses presented in this paper are similar to the first FDA analysis in the way cases were identified, but differ in that the number of patients rather than the number of person years at risk were used for the denominators. In addition to other technical differences, the analysis in this paper is based on a slightly different set of studies, corresponding to antidepressants that are registered in Europe. In spite of all these differences, similar conclusions were arrived at, namely that all antidepressants are associated with suicide-related events. . . .

Another source of information that may be relevant to the issue at hand is the General Practice Research Database (GPRD), a computerised database of longitudinal clinical records from 777 GP practices covering about 5% of the UK population. Analyses of the GPRD data set (Martinez et al., 2005) have suggested that suicidality in paediatric patients is associated with the use of SSRIs. However, it is known that patients who are at higher risk for suicidality are more commonly prescribed SSRIs as opposed to TCAs. Hence, the observed association might be due to this selection process rather than to a relatively high risk associated with SSRIs compared to TCAs.

Yet another source of evidence outside RCTs are ecological studies investigating co-occurring time trends in the prescription of SSRIs and suicide rates. Several studies have demonstrated that increases in the use of SSRIs are associated with reductions in suicide rates in the total population, among adults (Isacsson, 2000) as well as among male adolescents (Olfson et al., 2003). These findings provide indirect evidence suggesting that, on the group level, SSRIs may be beneficial in their effect on suicidality. However, these findings should be interpreted with caution, as reduction in suicide rates may be due to other trends in risk factors.

In summary, there are grounds for concerns regarding the use of antidepressants in the paediatric population due to the increased risk of suicidality and related behaviours. Although the signal that is detected is weak, the fact that it is consistently found in a large number of studies indicates that this might not be a chance finding. The fact that a signal was detected in studies of all products that were examined suggests that the process responsible for this phenomenon (although the nature of this process is, as of as now, unclear) may be operating in all instances of antidepressants use in paediatrics and not only in those products for which data happened to be available. Hence, the evidence indicates that a warning concerning the use of antidepressants in the paediatric population is called for. While the evidence for efficacy is inconsistent, especially with respect to the treatment of MDD, this does not necessarily indicate that those antidepressants are ineffective in all cases of depression in children or adolescents. Negative results may be due to failures in the design of the studies (e.g. not stringent enough inclusion criteria).

Altogether these results call for caution in the use of all the examined SSRIs and NSRIs in the treatment of paediatric patients. The need for caution also applied to other types of antidepressants (e.g. tricyclic antidepressants). As long as no contradictory information is available, it is safer to assume that the same risks apply to these medications as well. . . .

References

European Agency for the Evaluation of Medicinal products (EMEA), 1999. Committee for Proprietary Medicinal Products: Guidelines for studies in children (CPMP/ICH/2711/99, Topic E11 Note for Guidance on Clinical Investigation of Medicinal Products in the Paediatric Population. http://www.emea.eu.int/pdfs/human/ich/.

European Agency for the Evaluation of Medicinal products (EMEA), 2004a. Press release on Paroxetin. London, 22 April 2004a. Doc. Ref. EMEA/D/11206/04/Final. http://www.emea.eu.int/pdfs/human/press/pr/1120604en.pdf.

Food and Drug Administration (FDA), 1997. Modernization Act, enacted Nov. 21, 1997. http://www.fda.gov/cdrh/modact97.pdf.

Food and Drug Administration (FDA), 2004. http://www.fda.gov/cder/drug/antidepressants/default.htm.

Isacsson, G., 2000. Suicide prevention: a medical breakthrough? Acta Psychiatr. Scand. 102, 113–117.

Martinez, C., Rietbrock, S., Wise, L., Ashby, D., Chick, J., Moseley, J., Evans, S., Gunnell, D., 2005. Antidepressant treatment and the risk of fatal and non-fatal self harm in first episode depression: nested case-control study. BMJ 330, 373–374.

Olfson, M., Shaffer, D., Marcus S.C., Greenberg, T., 2003. Relationship between antidepressant medication treatment and suicide in adolescents. Arch. Gen. Psychiatry 60, 978–982.

Whittington, C.J., Kendall, T., Fonagy, P., Cottrell, D., Cotgrove A., Boddington, E., 2004. Selective serotonin reuptake inhibitors in childhood depression: systematic review of published versus unpublished data. Lancet 363, 1341–1345.

POSTSCRIPT

Should Adolescents Be Taking Antidepressants?

Major depression is a serious illness in children and adolescents and, therefore, it is important to identify safe and effective medications for the treatment of this disorder in our youth. Recent warnings of the potential serious negative effects of antidepressants, especially SSRIs, raise questions about the risk-benefit ratio of these drugs. Arguments against their use focus on the increased risk of suicidal behaviours, while those in favour argue that untreated adolescents are at greater risk for suicide.

The two selections for this issue are excellent examples of these opposing views. Wohlfarth and colleagues, for example, argue that empirical evidence outlining the benefits of treating adolescent depression with antidepressants is lacking. Although no completed suicides were reported in their meta-analysis of 24 RCTs, self-harming behaviours (related to suicidality) occurred more frequently in all treatment groups (i.e., all antidepressant products) compared to placebo groups. They concluded that, for children and adolescents, there is a significant association between the use of all antidepressants and suicide-related events. Wohlfarth et al.'s conclusions are consistent with results from previous meta-analytical studies such as Whittington et al. (2004) and Jureidini et al. (2004). Further, their results also support the warnings made by the FDA in 2003.

On the other hand, Lapierre argues that the warnings are based on mixed findings from studies with methodological problems and limitations, specifically issues of efficacy and suicide data. For example, the epidemiological and meta-analytic studies examining the safety of antidepressants are often biased with respect to patient selection and suicide risk evaluations. He argues there is often pressure against using a placebo. This can often result in very small sample sizes for the placebo cells, causing an imbalance in groups and, thus, reducing statistical power. Lapierre concludes that the data from the studies do not support the argument that SSRIs add to suicide risk. In fact, many studies report a decrease in suicide ideation while taking SSRIs—this decrease must be considered an improvement in the depressed condition. Lapierre's conclusions are similar to those reported by Emslie et al (2002) and Hamrin and Scahill (2005).

There are obvious opposing views on this issue but perhaps with future publications of methodologically sound clinical trials, the costs and benefits of antidepressants will become clearer. In the meantime, these selections raise awareness of adolescent depression and, given that suicide is a risk in the context of depression, they also strengthen the argument that safe and effective treatment is essential.

References/Further Readings

American Academy of Child and Adolescent Psychiatry. (1998). Practice parameters for the assessment and treatment of children and adolescents with depressive disorders. *Journal of the American Academy of Child and Adolescent Psychiatry*, 37(suppl.), 63S–83S.

Anderson, R. (2002). Deaths: Leading causes for 2000. *National Vital Statistics Report*, 50, 1–85.

Emslie, G., Heiligenstein, J., Wagner, K. D., Hoog, S., Ernest, D., Brown, E., Nilsson, M., & Jacobson, J. (2002). Fluoxetine for acute treatment of depression in children and adolescence: A placebo-controlled, randomized clinical trial. *Journal of the American Academy of Child and Adolescent Psychiatry*, 41, 1205–1215.

Hamrin, V., & Scahill, L. (2005). Selective serotonin reuptake inhibitors for children and adolescents with major depression: Current controversies and recommendations. *Issues in Mental Health Nursing*, 26, 433–450.

Jureidini, J., Doecke, C., Mansfield, P., Haby, M., Menkes, D., & Tonkin, A. (2004). Efficacy and safety of antidepressants for children and adolescents. *British Medical Journal*, 328, 879–883.

Seroczynski, A., Jacquez, F., & Cole, D. (2003). Depression and suicide during adolescence. In G. R. Adama & M. D. Berzonsky (Eds.), *Blackwell Handbook of Adolescence* (pp. 550–572). Oxford: Blackwell Publishing.

Whittington, C., Kendall, T., Fonagy, P., Cottrell, D., Cotgrove, A., & Boddington, E. (2004). Selective serotonin reuptake inhibitors in childhood depression: Systematic review of published versus unpublished data. *The Lancet*, 363, 1341–1345.

U.S. Food and Drug Administration (2004). PDA News. FDA launches a multi-pronged strategy to strengthen safeguards for children treated with antidepressant medication. Retrieved Thursday, June 22, 2006 from http://www.fda.gov/bbs/topics/news/2004/NEW01124.html.

ISSUE 2

Should Adolescents Be Allowed to Drink Alcohol?

YES: Rutger C.M.E. Engels et al., from "Peer Group Reputation and Smoking and Alcohol Consumption in Early Adolescence," *Addictive Behaviors* (vol. 31, 2006)

NO: Sandra A. Brown, from "Providing Substance Abuse Prevention and Treatment Services to Adolescents," Testimony Before the U.S. Senate, Subcommittee on Substance Abuse and Mental Health Services (June 15, 2004)

ISSUE SUMMARY

YES: Engels and colleagues, researchers in the Netherlands, suggest that substance use, while potentially problematic, may serve beneficial developmental functions for adolescents. Particularly, adolescents who drink alcohol appeared to be more self-confident and sociable than those who abstained based on peer evaluations.

NO: Researcher Sandra Brown, a psychiatrist from the University of California–San Diego, argues that early onset of alcohol and drug use put youth at greater risk for neurological damage, alcohol-related injuries (e.g., from drinking and driving), and future substance dependence.

Alcohol use prevention may not seem like it should be a controversial issue. After all, alcohol use is strictly regulated and illegal for adolescents. Substance abuse can create a host of social, health, and legal problems; therefore, adolescent prohibition is easily justified. Organizations such as MADD (Mothers Against Drunk Driving) and AA (Alcoholics Anonymous) attest to the potential harm of alcohol use; this harm is more detrimental for adolescents than adults. So, what makes alcohol use among adolescents a controversial issue?

The majority of youth will try alcohol at some point during their adolescence. Among youth, the prevalence of current alcohol use in 2003 increased with age, from 3 percent at age 12 to about 70 percent of persons 21 or 22 years old; however, among adults, the prevalence of alcohol use decreased with increasing age, from 62 percent among 26- to 29-year-olds to

34 percent among people aged 65 or older (Substance Abuse and Mental Health Services Administration, 1999; 2003). Further, the highest prevalence of both binge and heavy drinking in 2003 was for young adults aged 18 to 25 (42 and 15 percent, respectively), with the peak rate of both measures occurring at age 21. Of concern, however, is that about 80 percent of adult respondents receiving alcohol treatment reported that they first became intoxicated before the age of 18, although not all youth who experiment with alcohol will become dependent as adults (Substance Abuse and Mental Health Services Administration, 1999; 2003). This finding suggests that youth drinking patterns may have a significant impact on future alcohol dependence.

Most countries have regulations governing the use and sale of alcohol, called alcohol control measures. One common control measure is an "age of majority." This age differs from place-to-place; for example, in Wisconsin, the age of majority for drinking alcohol is 21 years, while in Quebec, it is 18 years of age. In some European countries (e.g., France), 14-year-olds can drink wine but not hard liquor. These laws have been demonstrated as effective at reducing youth alcohol consumption.

However, there are drinking norms to which adolescents must conform or risk being labeled as less social, less mature, or even deviant. Adolescents who abstain from drinking may suffer social sanctions (e.g., stigma) from their peers. Particularly, males may have their masculinity called into question if they do not drink alcohol. This could perhaps explain the gender difference in alcohol consumption. Thus, there are many reasons (e.g., social pressure) for adolescents to consume alcohol despite the many deterrents (e.g., laws prohibiting consumption and restricted access to alcohol).

In the following selections, Engels et al. suggest that there may be some significant social benefits for adolescents who drink alcohol. They suggest that *not* drinking in youth can be indicative of some significant developmental social problems (e.g., issues with developing intimate relationships with peers). In contrast, Brown's paper—where she reviews some of the negative consequences of alcohol use by youth such as neurological deficits caused by early alcohol consumption—is disturbing and alarming and seems to suggest that groups such as parents, schools, health care professionals, and government should ban or eradicate alcohol consumption by youth. As you read the two selections, consider how these two viewpoints could be reconciled.

YES    Rutger C.M.E. Engels et al.

Peer Group Reputation and Smoking and Alcohol Consumption in Early Adolescence

1. Introduction

National surveys in Western societies, such as the United States, Great Britain, and the Netherlands have shown that experimentation with risk behaviors, such as cigarette smoking, marijuana use and alcohol consumption is rather normal among adolescents. The widespread uptake of alcohol in adolescence focuses attention on the developmental tasks to be realized in the teenage years. The transition from adolescence to adulthood is characterized by intensified contacts with peers and an entrance into new social contexts and activities. The relevance for adolescents to achieve intimacy goals, such as closeness and trust, shifts from parents towards peers. It is essential for young people to establish contact with new friends or to strengthen existing affiliations. In this way they can reflect their own ideas and opinions. From 14, 15 years on, youngsters spend more time with friends outside the parental home in comparison with children and early adolescents. Going out to pubs, discos and parties is considered to be important for the development and maintenance of friendships as well as romantic relationships. Since some leisure time activities take place in settings, such as bars, discos and parties, in which certain risk behaviors (e.g., smoking, drinking) and the development of peer relations come together, some risk behaviors can be assumed to facilitate peer group integration. We will discuss three lines of research that reflect this reasoning.

First, research has shown that compared to drinkers, abstainers are less sociable, spend less time with their friends and are less likely to have a chumship, and have less adequate social skills. With prospective and concurrent analyses, Maggs and Hurrelmann (1998) found small but consistent support for the positive effects of substance use (including smoking) on peer relations. In addition, findings from a few longitudinal studies suggested that abstaining late adolescents and young adults are less likely to develop a steady intimate relationship than drinkers.

Second, when youngsters are asked what motives they endorse for their drinking or smoking behavior, they often mention the social aspects of substance use. It seems to make parties more fun, it makes one more relaxed, makes it easier to approach others, or to share feelings and experiences. The literature on drinking motives, for instance, illustrates that people who endorse enhancement (i.e., drinking to feel relaxed and at ease) and social motives (i.e., drinking to celebrate, to have a good time with friends), are more likely to report high drinking levels in social contexts. Research on alcohol expectancies has shown that the expected reinforcing social elements of drinking are related to, and predictive of, frequency and quantity of adolescent alcohol use. Apparently in the eyes of the beholder (i.e., youngsters themselves), substance use is interconnected with sociability and associated with social interactions.

Third, research on social images, stereotypes and self-other identification, and substance use strongly relies on the assumption that people value smoking or drinking peers positively. For example, people may have self-consistency and self-enhancement motives for using cigarettes; not only those who perceive their self-image to be similar to a smoking stereotype (peer smoker) are more likely to initiate smoking, but also those who value the characteristics of a typical smoking peer (stereotype) higher than their own image are more likely to start smoking. In sum, people who link substance use to desired social characteristics that are represented in peers are more likely to be engaged in substance use.

These three lines of research [support] the assumption that substance use has social benefits, or that young people at least perceive that this is the case. However, the overwhelming majority of studies used self-report data on social performance in relations. A limitation of self-reports is that there might be discrepancies in how people think they act in social encounters, and how others perceive them interacting. It is therefore essential to gather data among an individual's peers. If the social or psychological functions of substance use are primarily in the eyes of the beholder, and peer group members do *not* associate social skills or performance with substance using peers, this might be essential and valuable information for challenging prevailing distorted cognitions of substance using early adolescents on the social consequences of their behavior. Further, it might be possible that, though substance use is related to social benefits, it is also associated with negative behaviors, such as aggression, inattentiveness, and poor school performance. Therefore, it is relevant to get a more comprehensive picture by gathering information on traits and behaviors of substance using and non-using early adolescents from their immediate peer group members.

In the present study, we examined the association between peer group reputation and substance use. As is the case in sociometric research, members of a specific group (i.e., pupils in a school class) are asked to nominate class members who have specific characteristics that are related to social behavior, such as sociability, aggression, achievement motivation, withdrawal, emotional stability, and self-confidence. When the findings confirm that drinkers and smokers possess certain positive *social* characteristics, and not negative characteristics, such as aggression, emotional instability or loss of control, as perceived by their own peers, we have gained more insight into the etiology of adolescents' uptake of substance use. . . .

2. Method

2.1. Participants

Participants were 3361 adolescents (1430 girls, 1931 boys) attending 17 first ($n = 361$, mean age 12.5 years), 42 second ($n = 1032$, 13.4 years), 44 third ($n = 983$, 14.5 years), and 45 fourth and fifth ($n = 985$, 15.6 years) grade secondary school classes in the Arnhem-Nijmegen region in The Netherlands. The age of the students ranged from 12 years to 18 years. . . .

2.2. Measures

2.2.1. Substance Use

The average number of cigarettes smoked per day over the past month was measured using a 9-point scale (0, 1, 2, 3, 4, 5, 6–10, 11–20, >20). The average number of glasses of alcohol (i.e., beer, wine, mixed drinks) consumed over the past month was measured using a 10-point scale (0, 1–2, 3–4, 5–6, 7–10, 11–15, 16–20, 21–30, 31–50, >50).

2.2.2. Peer Group Reputation

Peer group reputation was based on 20 "Guess who" peer nomination items. The 20 items concerned attributes of an individual's peer group functioning. Per item, the students had to nominate three to five classmates. To correct for unequal numbers of nominating students per class, all of the nominations received from all nominating classmates on a particular item were summed and transformed per class into probability scores (p-scores) for each subject. . . .

The 20 items comprise . . . five . . . peer group reputation factors: *Aggression–Inattentiveness* (e.g., being perceived as quarrelsome, lazy, absent-minded, irritable), *Achievement–Withdrawal* (e.g., being perceived as persistent, hard working, shy, reserved, withdrawn), *Self-confidence* (e.g., being perceived as sensible, secure, steady, sincere), *Sociability* (e.g., being perceived as enthusiastic and considerate), and *Emotionality–Nervousness* (e.g., being perceived as emotional, anxious, nervous, uncreative). . . .

3. Results

3.1. Descriptives

Of all adolescents, 67% had never smoked. The adolescents who smoked had smoked on average 4 cigarettes a day during the past month, with 25% of them reporting having smoked on average more than 10 cigarettes a day. No differences existed between boys and girls in smoking. With respect to drinking, 38% of all adolescents reported that they had not consumed any alcohol during the past month. Adolescents who drank, had consumed on average between 6 and 10 glasses. Gender differences indicated that boys had consumed significantly more than girls. . . .

3.2. Variable-Centered Approach

First, we calculated . . . correlations between peer group reputation scores and substance use. It appeared that all five peer group reputation measures were . . . associated with smoking and alcohol use. Respondents who were evaluated by their class members as being high on aggression–inattentiveness, self-confidence and sociability were more likely to smoke and drink. In contrast, respondents who were evaluated as being high on achievement–withdrawal and emotionality–nervousness were less likely to smoke and drink. . . . In addition, boys were more likely to report higher levels of alcohol use and lower levels of smoking as compared to girls. Age was associated with increased substance use.

3.3. Person-Centered Approach

. . . [Cluster] analyses were computed and four clusters were obtained. [Cluster analysis identifies similar groups of people based on the peer reputation variables. A cluster might be thought of as a profile of traits or characteristics.] Adolescents in cluster 1 ($n = 961$) were characterized by high scores on self-confidence and sociability and low to moderate scores on achievement–withdrawal and emotionality–nervousness. Cluster 2 adolescents ($n = 432$) were characterized by high scores on aggression–inattentiveness and emotionality–nervousness, and low scores on self-confidence, achievement–withdrawal and sociability. Adolescents in cluster 3 ($n = 1169$) had high scores on emotionality–nervousness and achievement–withdrawal. Finally, adolescents in cluster 4 ($n = 772$) were characterized by moderate scores on all five peer group reputation scores. . . .

In a second step, we calculated the scores on smoking and drinking for the four clusters. . . . [The] four groups [CLUSTERS] of adolescents [here compared] on smoking and drinking. . . . [The groups (clusters) were significantly different in terms of their alcohol use and cigarette smoking.] Highest scores on alcohol and cigarette use were found for cluster 1, with respondents high on self-confidence and sociability. Lowest likelihood of engagement in substance use was found for cluster 3, with respondents characterized by emotionality–nervousness and achievement–withdrawal. Hardly any differences were found between smoking and drinking across the different clusters. Apparently, students do not attribute different traits or behaviors to either substance. . . .

4. Discussion

Variable- and person-centered approaches employed in the present study demonstrate that students draw distinctions between substance using and nonusing classmates. According to the variable-centered approach, drinkers and smokers appear to be more self-confident, sociable and aggressive, and less nervous, emotional, oriented on achievement and withdrawn. The person-centered approach provides a more precise picture, demonstrating that particularly pupils who are self-confident and sociable, but are low on nervousness and achievement–withdrawal according to their class mates, are engaged most strongly in smoking and drinking. It is important to mention that students who combine high aggressiveness–inattentiveness and emotionality–nervousness, are also likely to engage in more smoking and drinking when compared to those who score moderately low on all peer group reputation measures or those who combine particularly high scores on achievement–withdrawal and emotionality–nervousness.

These findings are in line with research showing that adolescents who drink report that they are more sociable, have more friends and spend more time with their friends. Apparently, these self-perceptions are in line with the opinions of others in the direct social environment of adolescents. On the other hand, it is quite clear that those who drink or smoke score lower on achievement and school performance, and score higher on aggression and inattentiveness. The groups identified with the person-centered approach show that two categories of early adolescents drink and smoke more than others: those who are sociable and self-confident, and those who are aggressive and emotionally insecure. In particular concerning alcohol use, it would be interesting [to know] whether especially the latter category is associated with the negative consequences of binge drinking and alcohol misuse in adolescence. Drinking in adolescence, especially riskful drinking patterns, such as binge drinking or problem drinking, is not only a predictor of alcohol misuse and problem drinking in adulthood, but drinking in adolescence is also related to car accidents, suicide, delinquency, aggression, and sexual assaults. It would be interesting to know whether in particular early starting, aggressive and emotional drinkers experience negative consequences of drinking later on.

A limitation of the current study is that we could not carry out a longitudinal investigation. We could not test the long term association of engagement in substance use by adolescents and peer reputation. This affects the generalizability of our results. For instance, it might be possible that our findings are limited to early adolescence, and that if we would interview all respondents in late adolescence, the reputation of substance users among their peers is different. Thus, some of the differences in social and emotional development could disappear if our sample were reinterviewed later on. It is also crucial to understand that we do not make causal inferences from our data. We do not imply that smoking leads to self-confidence and social acceptance. It is possible that those who start to drink and smoke in early adolescence have a high social status in the group, and therefore positive social and personal attributions are made by others. Or that sociable and self-confident adolescents are more likely to spend time with friends at parties where they consume alcohol. Longitudinal research should reveal whether substance use leads to specific peer reputation scores, the other way around, or both. Since the main result of this study could be viewed as encouraging smoking and drinking, it should be stressed that the main goal was to explore the social reputation of drinkers and smokers in the eyes of their peers.

It is questionable to what extent our findings can be generalized to other countries and cultures. The legal age for entering public drinking places in the Netherlands is 16 years. At this age, youngsters are allowed to order soft

alcoholic beverages, such as beer and wine. The legal age to purchase cigarettes is also 16 years of age. Since in some western countries the legal age for
pub-going, alcohol use and cigarette smoking is substantially higher, attention
must be paid to the significance of age groups and comparability of findings
across countries.

Nevertheless, our findings illustrate that early adolescents who engage in
smoking and drinking are not only perceived as self-confident and sociable,
but also with less interest in school and academic performance, emotionality
and nervousness, and aggression. Further, some subgroups of higher engagement are distinguished. Although part of these patterns is already reported in
the literature using self-reports, this is, to our knowledge, the first study
employing reports by peers (i.e., classmates) on adolescents' social and personal
development.

Reference

Maggs, J. L., & Hurrelmann, K. (1998). Do substance use and delinquency have
differential associations with adolescents peer relations? *International Journal
of Behavioural Development, 22,* 367–388.

Sandra A. Brown

 **NO**

Providing Substance Abuse Prevention and Treatment Services to Adolescents

Introduction

Recent research supported by the National Institutes of Health and other agencies is leading to a common understanding about the critical role of age of onset of addictive disorders in their course, consequences and progression. Researchers are finding that these disorders often begin during adolescence and sometimes even during childhood; therefore early intervention may prevent many of the social, behavioral, health, and economic consequences caused by alcohol and drug abuse as well as provide an opportunity to treat problems before they become full blown and damage in the lives of our youth.

Early Onset

NIAAA [National Institute on Alcohol Abuse and Alcoholism] and NIDA [National Institute on Drug Abuse] supported researchers are finding that alcohol and other drug addictions commonly start earlier than previously understood, and the earlier youth start the greater the lifetime risk for dependence. New findings regarding early patterns of abuse and dependence dramatically underscore the importance of reducing underage drinking and drug use. The age of most prevalent tobacco dependence onset is 15 and for alcohol dependence age 18 is the most common period of first diagnosis of dependence. It is now clear that most cases of alcohol dependence begin before age 25. After that age, new cases drop off precipitously. The epidemiological research message is obvious: youth is a critical window of opportunity for preventing alcohol, tobacco and other drug disorders. Previous studies have suggested that this is so, but the new research findings, corroborated by independent sources, have confirmed these findings.

Ongoing research may reveal a cause-and-effect relationship between early use and subsequent dependence, or it may reveal that common biological and environmental factors drive the risk for both use and dependence, as well as other addictive and psychiatric disorders. In either case, these new data

APA Congressional Testimony, June 15, 2004. Note: The complete text of this article contains many references to specific studies described. The interested individual should refer to the original publication for these extensive citations. These references have been omitted here in the interest of brevity.

are a powerful indicator of the need for more effective preventive interventions for youth.

Given the new epidemiologic findings, the fact that alcohol use is so widespread among children and adolescents is troubling. Alcohol is the primary substance of abuse among American children and adolescents.

- 47 percent of 8th graders, 67 percent of 10th graders, and 78 percent of 12th graders have used alcohol.
- 11 percent of 6th graders have reported binge drinking (5 or more drinks per occasion for males; 4 for females) in the past 2 weeks.
- 30 percent of high-school seniors have reported binge drinking at least once a month.
- 44 percent of college students have reported binge drinking in the past 2 weeks.
- 23 percent have reported that they binge drink frequently.
- Youth who drink alcohol before age 14 are 4 times more likely to become alcohol dependent in their lifetime than those who wait until age 21 or older.

Neurodevelopmental Studies

A series of recent studies indicate that exposure to drugs of abuse during adolescence may produce more adverse effects than exposure during adulthood in part because of the important changes occurring in the brain during adolescent development. Advances in science have now brought us to a point where researchers can use new animal models, modern brain imaging technology and other neurobehavioral assessment tools to probe the effects of alcohol, tobacco and other drugs on the developing brain and determine immediate as well as its long-term behavioral consequences.

Emerging findings from neuroimaging studies demonstrate that brain structures change during adolescence to become more specialized and efficient in their functioning. Our developmentally focused research indicates important neurocognitive disadvantages among adolescents with alcohol and drug use disorders as compared to teens without substance involvement. For example, even after three weeks of abstinence, alcohol dependent youth display a 10% decrement in delayed memory functions. Neuropsychological testing of these youth followed up to eight years demonstrates that continued heavy drinking during adolescence is associated with diminished memory of verbal and nonverbal material, and poorer performance on tests requiring attention skills. Alcohol and drug withdrawal over the teen years appears to uniquely contribute to deterioration in functioning in visuospatial tasks. Recent brain imaging studies of alcohol and drug using youth compared to youth without such experience have also shown reduced hippocampal volumes, white matter microstructure irregularities, and brain response abnormalities while performing cognitive tasks among those with early alcohol/drug exposure. Additionally, youth who have extensive experience with alcohol have increased brain response when viewing alcohol advertisements compared to other beverage advertisements.

Animal studies are consistent with the findings that alcohol or drug exposure during adolescence has more adverse consequences than delayed (adult) exposure. In these investigations, adolescent alcohol exposure is associated with more frontal lobe damage and poorer spatial memory. Further research is needed to understand how age of drinking or drug use onset and duration of abstinence at the time of assessment affect cognitive and behavioral findings. Longitudinal studies are needed to clarify neuromaturational changes associated with early alcohol and drug exposure and patterns of resiliency. Although the magnitude of effects observed in adolescents' neurocognition is modest, the implications are major given the prevalence of alcohol involvement, and the important educational, occupational, and social transitions that occur during adolescence.

These new directions in adolescent research will help to inform us on important aspects of cognition, decision-making, motivation, emotional regulation, and risk perception during adolescence, and will help us determine how these factors play a role in the use and consequences of alcohol and drugs. Armed with new knowledge about how adolescents make decisions, control their impulses and desires, and what motivates their behavior, researchers and agencies will be poised to design better preventions and interventions to reduce alcohol, tobacco and other drug experimentation, abuse and dependence, as well as other risky behaviors. Adolescents have in common unique neurobiological and neurocognitive developmental factors that affect risk and resiliency vis-à-vis substance use. Few studies have addressed these developmentally specific neurobiological and neurocognitive mechanisms and consequences of heavy drinking/use in this group despite the importance of these for long-term development.

Vulnerability

While early initiation of substance involvement is a powerful predictor of subsequent dependence, not everyone who uses at a young age later develops abuse or dependence. Even among youth with two alcoholic parents, only about one-half become alcohol dependent. The outcome is determined largely by the interplay of environmental and genetic/biological factors.

Environmental factors have the biggest influence on whether a child first uses alcohol, tobacco or other substances. However, genetic factors have an influence on whether a child continues to use. Understanding how these factors result in initiation and continuation of use or make resolution of drinking/drug use more difficult is essential to disrupting the developmental process of addictive behavior. Thus, a focus on genetic/biological aspect of use may clarify how variations in genes result in differences in how our bodies absorb, distribute, and eliminate substances and variability in tolerance.

Binge Drinking

Binge drinking, episodes of heavy drinking (5 or more drinks for males; 4 or more drinks for females), is a problem for people in any age group, whether or not the drinker is addicted to alcohol. An alarming number of children and adolescents binge drink and that it is increasing. Drinking too much, too fast in this manner carries additional risks especially for youth. They include car crashes, injury, death, property damage, encounters with the justice system, and family, school, and workplace problems. Each drink increases the fatal crash risk more for youth than adults. At a blood alcohol level of 0.08% in every age and gender group there is at least a 11-fold increase in single vehicle fatal crash risk. Among males 16–20 at a blood alcohol level of 0.08% there is a 52-fold increase in single vehicle crash risk compared to sober drivers the same age.

Epidemiology studies have shown beyond doubt that genes play a role in risk of alcohol, tobacco and other drug dependence. Research toward discovering which genes are involved, what biochemical pathways they influence in brain cells, and how these pathways translate into specific behaviors is the next step to this line of investigation. Such findings provide information about genetic/molecular events in the brain that influence use, and provide potential targets for pharmacological intervention. For example, new findings about a naturally occurring marijuana-like substance in the brain also provide potential new molecular targets for pharmacological intervention.

Prevention of Abuse and Dependence

Prevention of alcohol and substance use problems among youth need to be understood as a continuum of services and consequently research needs to span this continuum. This continuum ranges from **universal** prevention (those appropriate for all children and adolescents who might use alcohol, tobacco or other drugs) to **selective** preventative measures for subgroups with risk factors for abuse or dependence, to **indicated** preventative measures for those individually at high risk for the disorder. Preventive interventions for alcohol, tobacco, and other drug use disorders and related problems can be improved through early detection and diagnosis, and through testing of new behavioral strategies at the individual, family, and community levels. Of particular interest are longitudinal data on children entering the age of risk, adolescents and young adults in high-risk environments (college and the military), youth who resolve use/problems without formal treatment, and women of childbearing age. New interventions to prevent early-onset of use can be gleaned through studies that identify developmental and environmental features as well as biological factors that stimulate or suppress addictive behavior.

It is important to evaluate prevention programs on an ongoing basis as well as disseminate research findings to communities, educators, parents, and health care providers who are the first line of defense against alcohol, drugs and other risky behaviors. Both NIAAA and NIDA offer free educational materials designed to help students learn about the impact of alcohol and drugs on the brain and body. Parents, educators, and community leaders can use these materials to help guide their thinking, planning, selection, and delivery of drug abuse prevention programs at the community level. NIAAA and NIDA also have websites that offer science-based information specifically designed for teens. *The Leadership to Keep Children Alcohol-Free* has recruited 33 Governors' spouses to spearhead a national prevention campaign which influences both public policy and local practices. *The Task Force on College Drinking* has brought together university presidents and researchers, and is making headway in efforts to reduce the seemingly intractable problem of drinking by college students.

Clearly, alcohol and substance use disorders are the result of a complex combination of genetic and environmental interactions that influence how people respond to the substance and their initial propensity for using alcohol and drugs. Longitudinal studies of these genetic and environmental factors are crucial for understanding (1) early initiation of drinking and drug use, (2) transition to harmful use, abuse, and dependence, and (3) remission and abatement of alcohol and drug related problems in untreated populations. This is particularly critical for youth as some resolve problematic use without treatment and research in this area can teach us how to facilitate changes in alcohol and drug involvement in ways that are most developmentally appropriate and acceptable to youth. Developmentally specific research in these areas has potential to help identify mechanisms of vulnerability and protection which can be used in prevention.

Improving Effectiveness of Treatment

Findings from the National Household Survey on Drug Abuse indicate that about 10 percent of 12- to 17- year-olds (about 2.3 million) are heavy users of alcohol or drugs, yet only 187,000 (8%) received services. Although estimates of the cost-effectiveness of early intervention are speculative, research suggests that early treatment has the potential to be cost-effective, especially in comparison with incarceration or treatment for a long-term abuse problem. For instance, cost benefit research on drug and alcohol treatment generally (Office of National Drug Control Policy, 2001) suggest that the range of savings is between $2.50 and $9.60 for every dollar spent on treatment. Unfortunately, only one person in seven who would qualify for treatment was admitted to treatment in 1999 (National Institute on Drug Abuse Community Epidemiology Work Group, 1999). The proportion of youth who are admitted to treatment is even smaller.

Much progress has been made in developing behavioral/psychosocial interventions for alcohol and other substance use disorders, but much remains to be investigated. Controlled research trials provide evidence that several psychosocial treatment approaches may be effective in reducing alcohol and other drug use while also improving associated behavioral, familial, and psychosocial outcomes. These outcomes are enhanced when a combination of modalities are offered in a comprehensive, integrated treatment plan that addresses alcohol and drug abuse and a broad range of biopsychosocial problems, skills deficits, and comorbid psychiatric problems. For example, having families involved in the treatment program increases the likelihood of success in youth. Brief Strategic Family Therapy (BSFT) and Cognitive Behavioral Interventions are examples of promising youth specific treatment already in the field. The evaluation and dissemination of more evidence-based interventions in a variety of community venues, including schools, healthcare settings, and prisons, should be a high priority. Developing, evaluating, and improving efficacy and cost-effectiveness of treatments is a central goal in alcohol, tobacco and drug research. Adolescent focused treatment research lags behind adult treatment research. Studies are needed to develop and test new behavioral therapies; conduct clinical trials in existing treatment settings, examine cost-effectiveness of behavioral and pharmaceutical therapies; clarify mechanisms of action that make effective treatments successful; and conduct trials of dissemination strategies, to test how effective they are at introducing behavioral and pharmacological treatments into real-world clinical practice.

Alcohol, tobacco and other drugs affect genders and subpopulations differently, and some groups suffer more adverse effects of alcohol, tobacco and drugs than other groups. For treatment of these youth problems to be optimally effective, research to study the role of gender, ethnicity, socioeconomic status, and other variables in determining the effects of various substance abuse interventions is sorely needed. For example, we need to support studies on specific facilitators and barriers to alcohol and drug treatment in minority and rural populations.

Clearly multifaceted longitudinal research is sorely needed to fully understand the development and resolution of alcohol and drug use disorders in the context of child and adolescent development. Through such focused process research (e.g., changes in brain structure and recovery of functioning, decision making process, social and family dynamics) can improved prevention and intervention policies emerge.

POSTSCRIPT

Should Adolescents Be Allowed to Drink Alcohol?

The two selections presented here do not necessarily contradict each other because the phenomena and issues surrounding adolescent drinking are complex. Brown's paper clearly speaks to potential negative effects of adolescent alcohol use, while Engels et al. found some social benefits of drinking for many teens. However, Engels et al. also found that users of alcohol and cigarettes were perceived by their peers as highly aggressive, nervous, insecure, and lacking in sociability. Engels et al. speculated that this group *might* be at-risk for longer-term, more negative outcomes of substance use (e.g., adult alcohol problems). This may be a group at whom specific prevention and intervention efforts need to be aimed.

A key question still remains: Can we differentiate adolescents who will "benefit" from alcohol use from those who may suffer long-term harm so as to intervene with the latter group? Brown calls this approach selective prevention. Or, should we simply be more conservative and maintain the ban on adolescent alcohol use (which is as high as 21 years in some U.S. states)? Alternatively, would it be more advantageous to allow youth to drink alcohol legally and therefore, less covertly, in order to avoid the potential problems associated with youth prohibition (i.e., drinking in unsafe, unsupervised environments)? Then, we can intervene with those who are actually experiencing the negative consequences of alcohol use. Brown calls this approach indicative intervention.

Some harm-reduction programs have been developed to educate youth on alcohol use. Such programs are not necessarily aimed at eradicating adolescent drinking but are designed to foster safer alcohol-related attitudes, reduce how often and how much youth drink, and reduce unsupervised drinking, which is correlated with alcohol-related injuries. For example, McBride et al. (2004) demonstrate the sustained effects of a harm-reduction program: The intervention group continued to demonstrate more positive effects relative to a control group 17 months after completion of the intervention. Like McBride et al., others have argued that promoting complete abstinence in adolescent drinking through intervention is likely to be ineffective and unsuccessful.

Alcohol education can be effective when presented within a harm-reduction framework. This would be consistent with Brown's universal prevention while also perhaps maintaining some of the potential benefits of adolescent drinking as identified by such researchers as Engels et al. However, Engels et al. and Brown would agree that it is critical that selective prevention and indicative intervention programs exist for those youth who demonstrate problems or who are at increased risk for alcohol abuse-related problems.

Regardless of what approach we take, programs aimed at reducing alcohol consumption should be part of a broader societal response. Youth attitudes about alcohol likely reflect the modeling of adult attitudes and behavior.

References/Further Readings

Alcohol & Public Policy Group (2003). Alcohol: No ordinary commodity. *Addiction,* 98, 1343–1350.

Babor, T.F., Caetano, R., Casswell, S., Edwards, G., Giebrecht, N., Graham, K., Grube, J., Gruenewald, P., Hill, L., Holder, H., Homel, R., Osterberg, E., Rehm, J., Room, R., & Rossow, I. (2003). *Alcohol: No Ordinary Commodity—Research and Public Policy.* Oxford & London: Oxford University Press.

Hill, L., Hamilton, G., Roche, A., Anderson, P., & McBride, N. (2004). Commentaries on McBride et al. *Addiction,* 99, 292–298.

McBride, N., Farringdon, F., Midford, R., Meuleners, L., & Phillips, M. (2004). Harm minimization in school drug education: Final results from the School Health and Alcohol Harm Reduction Project (SHAHRP). *Addiction,* 99, 278–291.

Substance Abuse and Mental Health Services Administration, Office of Applied Studies (2003). National Survey on Drug Use and Health: Results. Rockville, MD: Department of Health and Human Services. Retrieved on June 23, 2006 from: http://oas.samhsa.gov/NHSDA/2k3NSDUH/2k3results.htm#ch3.

Substance Abuse and Mental Health Services Administration (1999). Treatment of Adolescents with Substance Abuse Disorders, Treatment Improvement Protocol (TIP), Series 32. Rockville, MD: Department of Health and Human Service.

ISSUE 3

Should Parental Consent Be Required for Adolescents Seeking Abortions?

YES: Teresa Stanton Collett, from Testimony Before the Sub-committee on the Constitution, Committee on the Judiciary, U.S. House of Representatives (September 6, 2001)

NO: Nancy E. Adler, Emily J. Ozer, and Jeanne Tschann, from "Abortion Among Adolescents," *American Psychologist* (March 23, 2003)

ISSUE SUMMARY

YES: Teresa Stanton Collett, law professor at the University of St. Thomas School of Law in Minnesota, testifies in front of the U.S. House of Representatives in support of the federal Child Custody Protection Act. She advocates parental involvement in a minor's pregnancy, regardless of the girl's intention to carry or terminate the pregnancy.

NO: Nancy Adler, a professor of medical psychology at the University of California-San Francisco, and colleagues argue that the empirical data do not support the assumptions that adolescents are at a higher risk of psychological harm from abortion and are unable to make an adequately informed decision. In fact, studies suggest a relatively low risk associated with abortion, and adolescents seeking abortion appear to make an informed choice.

In 1973 the United States Supreme Court decision *Roe v. Wade* guaranteed a woman's right to access abortion without restriction during the first trimester. The decision did not mention, however, the age of the woman seeking the abortion. A number of individual states, therefore, have statutes that require a girl under the age of 18 to either receive one or both parents' or legal guardians' consent in order to obtain an abortion, or to notify one or both parents. In Canada, abortion was illegal until 1969, when Parliament amended the Criminal Code to allow abortion to be legal under certain circumstances. Then, in 1988, the Supreme Court of Canada struck down the amended law involving the "certain conditions" as unconstitutional (called the Morgentaler decision). Currently, Canada has no laws surrounding abortion, and it is treated like any other medical procedure. Canada has no age restrictions, and nothing similar to the U.S. parental notification/consent laws is required when adolescents seek abortion.

A U.S. Supreme Court decision, *Belotti v. Baird*, upheld the rights of states to place these restrictions on girls—provided there is an option for a "judicial bypass." This means that a girl can appear before a judge and either demonstrate that she is mature enough to make the decision to have an abortion or explain why notifying her parents would be detrimental to her. As the *Belotti* decision says, "[if] the court decides the minor is not mature enough to give informed consent, she must be given the opportunity to show that the abortion is in her best interest. If she makes this showing, the court must grant her bypass petition." As of June 2006, 34 states required parental involvement with an adolescent's decision to have an abortion (Guttmacher Institute, 2006). All of these states allow for judicial bypass.

Any discussions around abortion rights are rooted in the fundamental support or opposition to abortion itself. It can be challenging, therefore, to separate out the question of abortion from the question of whether or not minors can make an informed decision. Even adults who consider themselves to be pro-choice may support an adult woman's right to choose whether to carry or terminate a pregnancy, while feeling differently about girls under the age of 18 being able to make this decision for themselves. Others are clear on their belief that abortion is wrong regardless of the circumstance or age of the girl or woman involved. And still others believe that any girl or woman, regardless of age, is able and has the right to make this personal decision for herself. Specific to the debate around parental notification is the issue of someone other than a parent facilitating an abortion for a girl under the age of 18.

Because the Canadian legal situation is quite different from that of the United States, parental notification is not an issue. When considering abortion and receiving sexual health counseling, teen girls are encouraged by counselors to communicate with their parents *if* the girl has raised the issue of parental discussion. When having a therapeutic abortion, a teen typically has a support person accompany her to the appointment, and this is sometimes a parent. Sexual health counselors and abortion counselors, when discussing abortion with a young person, are legally bound to report to authorities (e.g., Child and Family Services and/or police) in exceptional circumstances outlined by the Criminal Code of Canada. These circumstances include: (1) when the client is under the legal age to consent to sexual activity (i.e., the girl is under 14 years of age and her sexual partner is not her peer—this means that he is at least 2 years older than the girl, (2) when there is reported child abuse or neglect or a violation of an authority relationship (e.g., a teacher having an affair with a 15-year-old student), or (3) when the client expresses intent to harm herself or others. Thus, there is no mandatory parental notification in Canada, but there is reporting to authorities in the circumstances outlined above.

Theresa Stanton Collett demonstrates what she feels is widespread support for parental involvement laws, focusing in particular on the Child Custody Protection Act. Nancy Adler et al. discuss key issues raised by, and often used to justify, parental involvement laws. These authors do not believe these reasons are sufficient to warrant laws enforcing parental notification and/or consent.

YES

Teresa Stanton Collett

Prepared Testimony of Teresa Stanton Collett

UNITED STATES HOUSE OF REPRESENTATIVES
Committee on the Judiciary
Subcommittee on the Constitution
Congressman Steve Chabot, Subcommittee Chair
September 6, 2001

. . . I am honored to have been invited to testify on H.R. 476, the "Child Custody Protection Act" . . . My testimony represents my professional knowledge and opinion as a law professor who writes on the topic of family law, and specifically on the topic of parental involvement laws. It also represents my experience in assisting the legislative sponsors of the Texas Parental Notification Act during the legislative debates prior to passage of the act, and as a member of the Texas Supreme Court Subadvisory Committee charged with proposing court rules implementing the judicial bypass created by the Texas act. . . .

It is my opinion that the Child Custody Protection Act will significantly advance the legitimate health and safety interests of young girls experiencing an unplanned pregnancy. It will also safeguard the ability of states to protect their minor citizens through the adoption of effective parental involvement statutes. . . .

Parental Rights to Control Medical Care of Minors

[In 2001], in a case involving the competing claims of parents and grandparents to decisionmaking authority over a child, the United States Supreme Court described parents' right to control the care of their children as "perhaps the oldest of the fundamental liberty interests recognized by this Court." In addressing the right of parents to direct the medical care of their children, the Court has stated:

> Our jurisprudence historically has reflected Western civilization concepts of the family as a unit with broad parental authority over minor children. Our cases have consistently followed that course; our constitutional system long

From U.N. Convention on the Rights of the Child by Teresa Stanton Collett, 2001.

ago rejected any notion that a child is "the mere creature of the State" and, on the contrary, asserted that parents generally "have the right, coupled with the high duty, to recognize and prepare [their children] for additional obligations." *Surely, this includes a "high duty" to recognize symptoms of illness and to seek and follow medical advice. The law's concept of the family rests on a presumption that parents possess what a child lacks in maturity, experience, and capacity for judgment required for making life's difficult decisions.*

It is this need to insure the availability of parental guidance and support that underlies the laws requiring a parent be notified or give consent prior to the performance of an abortion on his or her minor daughter. The national consensus in favor of this position is illustrated by the fact that there are parental involvement laws on the books in forty-three of the fifty states. Of the statutes in these forty-three states, eight have been determined to have state or federal constitutional infirmities. Therefore the laws of thirty-five states are in effect today. Nine of these states have laws that empower abortion providers to decide whether to involve parents or allow notice to or consent from people other than parents or legal guardians. These laws are substantially ineffectual in assuring parental involvement in a minor's decision to obtain an abortion. However, parents in the remaining twenty-six states are effectively guaranteed the right to parental notification or consent in most cases.

Widespread Public Support

There is widespread agreement that as a general rule, parents should be involved in their minor daughter's decision to terminate an unplanned pregnancy. This agreement even extends to young people, ages 18 to 24. To my knowledge, no organizations or individuals, whether abortion rights activists or pro-life advocates, dispute this point. On an issue as contentious and divisive as abortion, it is both remarkable and instructive that there is such firm and long-standing support for laws requiring parental involvement.

Various reasons underlie this broad and consistent support. As Justices O'Connor, Kennedy, and Souter observed in *Planned Parenthood v. Casey,* parental consent and notification laws related to abortions "are based on the quite reasonable assumption that minors will benefit from consultation with their parents and that children will often not realize that their parents have their best interests at heart." This reasoning led the Court to conclude that the Pennsylvania parental consent law was constitutional. Two of the benefits achieved by parental involvement laws include improved medical cane for young girls seeking abortions and increased protection against sexual exploitation by adult men.

Improved Medical Care of Minors Seeking Abortions

Medical care for minors seeking abortions is improved by parental involvement in three ways. First, parental involvement laws allow parents to assist their daughter in the selection of a healthcare provider. As with all medical procedures, one of the most important guarantees of patient safety is the professional competence of those who perform the medical procedure or administer the medical treatment. In *Bellotti v. Baird*, the United States Supreme Court acknowledged the superior ability of parents to evaluate and select appropriate abortion providers.

For example, the National Abortion Federation recommends that patients seeking an abortion confirm that the abortion will be performed by a licensed physician in good standing with the state Board of Medical Examiners, and that he or she have admitting privileges at a local hospital not more than twenty minutes away from the location where the abortion is to occur. A well-informed parent seeking to guide her child is more likely to inquire regarding these matters than a panicky teen who just wants to no longer be pregnant.

Parental involvement laws also insure that parents have the opportunity to provide additional medical history and information to abortion providers prior to performance of the abortion.

> The medical, emotional, and psychological consequences of an abortion are serious and can be lasting; this is particularly so when the patient is immature. An adequate medical and psychological case history is important to the physician. Parents can provide medical and psychological data, refer the physician to other sources of medical history, such as family physicians, and authorize family physicians to give relevant data.

Abortion providers, in turn, will have the opportunity to disclose the medical risks of the various procedures to an adult who can advise the girl in giving her informed consent to the procedure ultimately selected. Parental notification or consent laws insure that the abortion providers inform a mature adult of the risks and benefits of the proposed treatment, after having received a more complete and thus more accurate medical history of the patient.

The third way in which parental involvement improves medical treatment of pregnant minors is by insuring that parents have adequate knowledge to recognize and respond to any post-abortion complication that may develop. In a recent ruling by a Florida intermediate appellate court upholding that state's parental involvement law, the court observed:

> The State proved that appropriate aftercare is critical in avoiding or responding to postabortion complications. Abortion is ordinarily an invasive surgical procedure attended by many of the risks accompanying surgical procedures generally. If post-abortion nausea, tenderness, swelling, bleeding, or cramping persists or suddenly worsens, a minor (like an adult) may need medical attention. A guardian unaware that her ward or a parent unaware that his minor daughter has undergone an abortion will be at a serious disadvantage in caring for her if complications develop. An adult who has been kept in the dark cannot, moreover, assist the minor in following the abortion provider's instructions for post-surgical care. Failure to follow such instructions can increase the risk of complications. As the plaintiffs' medical experts conceded, the risks are significant in the best of circumstances. While abortion is less risky than some surgical procedures, abortion complications can result in serious injury, infertility, and even death.

Abortion proponents often claim that abortion is one of the safest surgical procedures performed today. However, the actual rate of many complications is simply unknown. At least one American court has held that a perforated uterus is a "normal risk" associated with abortion. Untreated, a perforated uterus may result in an infection, complicated by fever, endometritis, and parametritis. The risk of death from postabortion sepsis [infection] is highest for young women, those who are unmarried, and those who undergo procedures that do not directly evacuate the contents of the uterus. . . . A delay in treatment allows the infection to progress to bacteretnia, pelvic abscess, septic pelvic thrombophlebitis, disseminated intravascular coagulophy, septic shock, renal failure, and death."

Without the knowledge that their daughter has had an abortion, parents are incapable of insuring that the minor obtain routine post-operative care or of providing an adequate medical history to physicians called upon to treat any complications the girl might experience.

Increased Protection From Sexual Assault

In addition to improving the medical care received by young girls dealing with an unplanned pregnancy, parental involvement laws are intended to afford increased protection against sexual exploitation of minors by adult men. National studies reveal that "[a]lmost two thirds of adolescent mothers have partners older than 20 years of age." In a study of over 46,000 pregnancies by school-age girls in California, researchers found that "71%, or over 33,000, were fathered by adult post-high-school men whose mean age was 22.6 years, an average of 5 years older than the mothers. . . . Even among junior high school mothers aged 15 or younger, most births are fathered by adult men 6–7 years their senior. *Men aged 25 or older father more births among California school-age girls than do boys under age 18.*" Other studies have found that most teenage pregnancies are the result of predatory practices by men who are substantially older.

Abortion providers have resisted any reporting obligation to insure that men who unlawfully impregnant minors are identified and prosecuted. Just [recently] a lawsuit was filed in Arizona alleging that Planned Parenthood failed to report the sexual molestation of a twelve-year-old leading to her continued molestation and impregnation. If true, this conduct is consistent with the position of many abortion providers who argue that encouraging medical care through insuring confidentiality is more important than insuring legal intervention to stop the sexual abuse. While seemingly well intentioned, this reasoning fails since the ultimate result of this approach is to merely address a symptom of the sexual abuse (the pregnancy) while leaving the cause unaffected. The minor, no longer pregnant, then returns to the abusive relationship, with no continuing contact with an adult (other than the abuser) knowing of her plight. The clinic won't tell, the police and parents don't know, and the girl, still under the abuser's influence, is too confused or afraid to tell. . . .

States adopting parental involvement laws have come to the reasonable conclusion that secret abortions do not advance the best interests of most minor girls. This is particularly reasonable in light of the fact that most teen pregnancies are the result of sexual relations with adult men, and many of these relationships involve criminal conduct. Parental involvement laws insure that parents have the opportunity to protect their daughters from those who would victimize their daughters again and again and again. The Child Custody Protection Act would insure that men cannot deprive these minors of this protection by merely crossing state lines.

Effectiveness of Judicial Bypass

In those few cases where it is not in the girl's best interest to disclose her pregnancy to her parents, state laws generally provide the pregnant minor the option of seeking a court determination that either involvement of the girl's parent is not in her best interest, or that she is sufficiently mature to make decisions regarding the continuation of her pregnancy. This is a requirement for parental consent laws under existing United States Supreme Court cases, and courts have been quick to overturn laws omitting adequate bypass.

Opponents of the Child Custody Protection Act have argued that its passage would endanger teens since parents may be abusive and many teens would seek illegal abortions. This is a phantom fear. Parental involvement laws are on the books in over two-thirds of the states, some for over twenty-years, and there is no case where it has been established that these laws led to parental abuse or to self-inflicted injury. Similarly, there is no evidence that these laws have led to an increase in illegal abortions.

It [is] often asserted that parental involvement laws do not increase the number of parents notified of their daughters' intentions to obtain abortions, since minors will commonly seek judicial bypass of the parental involvement requirement. Assessing the accuracy of this claim is difficult since parental notification or consent laws rarely impose reporting requirements regarding the use of judicial bypass. The Idaho parental consent law enacted in 2000 is one of the few exceptions to this general rule. Based upon the reporting required under that law, no abortions obtained by minors were pursuant to a judicial bypass. From September 1, 2000 through April 3, 2001, thirty-three minors have been reported as obtaining an abortion in Idaho. Thirty-one of these abortions were performed after obtaining parental consent. One minor was legally emancipated and did not need parental consent, and one report did not indicate the nature of the consent obtained prior to performance of the abortion.

Obtaining comparable information in states having parental involvement laws with no mandatory reporting requirement is difficult. State agencies will not accumulate such information absent a legislative mandate. Nonetheless, it is safe to say that the use of judicial bypass to avoid parental involvement varies significantly among the states. While commonly used in Massachusetts, judicial bypass is seldom used in many states. In 1999, 1,015 girls got abortions in Alabama with a parent's approval and 12 with a judge's approval, according to state health department records. Indiana also has few bypass proceedings according to an informal study. In Pennsylvania, approximately 13,700 minors obtained abortions from 1994 through 1999. Of these only about seven percent or 1,000 girls bypassed parental involvement via court order. Texas implemented its Parental Notification Act in 2000. During the state legislative hearings, the Texas Family Planning Council submitted a study indicating that a parent accompanied 69% of minors seeking abortions in Texas. After passage of the Texas Parental Notification Act, 96% of all minors seeking an abortion in Texas involved a parent.

Conclusion

By passage of the Child Custody Protection Act [see Addendum from the Editors], Congress will protect the ability of the citizens in each state to determine the proper level of parental involvement in the lives of young girls facing an unplanned pregnancy.

Experience in states having parental involvement laws has shown that, when notified, parents and their daughters unite in a desire to resolve issues surrounding an unplanned pregnancy. If the minor chooses to terminate the pregnancy, parents can assist their daughters in selecting competent abortion providers, and abortion providers may receive more comprehensive medical histories of their parents. In these cases, the minors will more likely be encouraged to obtain post-operative check-ups, and parents will be prepared to respond to any complications that arise.

If the minor chooses to continue her pregnancy, involvement of her parents serves many of the same goals. Parents can provide or help obtain the necessary resources for early and comprehensive prenatal care. They can assist their daughters in evaluating the options of single parenthood, adoption, or early marriage. Perhaps most importantly, they can provide the love and support that is found in the many healthy families of the United States.

Regardless of whether the girl chooses to continue or terminate her pregnancy, parental involvement laws have proven desirable because they afford greater protection for the many girls who are pregnant due to sexual assault. By insuring that parents know of the pregnancy, it becomes much more likely that they will intervene to insure the protection of their daughters from future assaults.

In balancing the minor's right to privacy and her need for parental involvement, the majority of states have determined that parents should know before abortions are performed on minors. This is a reasonable conclusion and well within the states' police powers. However, the political authority of each state stops at its geographic boundaries. States need the assistance of the federal government to insure that the protection they wish to afford their children is not easily circumvented by strangers taking minors across state lines.

The Child Custody Protection Act has the unique virtue of building upon two of the few points of agreement in the national debate over abortion: the desirability of parental involvement in a minor's decisions about an unplanned pregnancy, and the need to protect the physical health and safety of the pregnant girl. I urge members of this committee to vote for its passage.

Addendum from the Editors

The Child Custody Protection Act would have made it a federal crime for any person other than a parent/guardian to transport a minor across state lines to obtain an abortion. While the U.S. House of Representatives passed the act in 2002, the Senate did not pass it. On April 27, 2005, the House of Representatives passed a companion bill, the Child Interstate Abortion Notification Act. Like the Child Custody Protection Act, the Child Interstate Abortion Notification Act amends the federal criminal code to prohibit transporting a minor across a state line to obtain an abortion to avoid parental involvement laws in a minor's home state. The Child Interstate Abortion Notification Act also requires an abortion provider who performs an abortion on a minor who is a resident of a state other than that in which the abortion is performed to provide at least 24 hours actual notice (in person) to a parent of the minor before performing the abortion (or if actual notice is not possible after a reasonable effort, 24 hours constructive notice by certified mail). Transporting a minor with intent to evade parental involvement laws or performing an abortion without complying with the Child Interstate Abortion Notification Act's requirements may result in a criminal fine or imprisonment up to 1 year, or both. Civil law suits are also available to any parent who suffers harm from a violation of the Act. As of May 2006, this legislation has not been addressed in the Senate. In essence, the Child Interstate Abortion Notification Act would create two federal crimes: (1) making it illegal for anyone but a parent/guardian to transport a minor out-of-state for the purpose of abortion and (2) making it illegal for a physician to perform an out-of-state abortion without parental involvement.

Nancy E. Adler, Emily J. Ozer, and
Jeanne Tschann

 **NO**

Abortion Among Adolescents

Issues of abortion for adolescents are embedded in the status and meaning of abortion in the country in which they are living. For adolescents in much of the world, particularly in developing countries, the major problem is access to safe, legal abortion. One quarter of women in the world live in countries in which abortion is either completely prohibited or permitted only to save the woman's life. These restrictions are not limited to adolescents but apply to women of all ages. . . . In the United States, safe, legal abortion is available, but access is more limited for adolescents than for adults. The most common restriction is the requirement in some states for parental involvement or consent.

Worldwide, there has been a move toward liberalizing abortion laws. In the second half of the 20th century, most industrialized nations and many developing countries reformed and eased their abortion laws. As legal abortion becomes more widely available, issues of adolescents' access become more salient. Most of the available research on adolescent abortion is from the United States but may be useful for other countries that are contemplating potential consent requirements. Below, we review the current status of abortion laws pertaining to adolescents worldwide, examine questions raised by parental involvement laws in the United States and by the relevant psychological research, and discuss the issues facing adolescents seeking abortions in the United States and internationally.

Parental Involvement Laws

Out of 158 countries in which legal abortion is available, 55 countries permit abortion only when necessary to save the life of the woman. Parental authorization for abortion is required in 28 countries, including 5 countries in which abortions may only be performed to save the woman's life. Cuba, Denmark, Italy, Norway, Turkey, and most Eastern European countries require written parental consent for adolescents to have an abortion, and in Turkey, married women must have the consent of their husbands. In several Western countries, including Denmark, Italy, and Norway, a court or hospital committee may bypass this parental consent restriction. As of 2001, France no longer requires parental consent for adolescents but does require an adult of the minor's choice to be involved in the abortion process.

From *American Psychologist,* vol. 58, no. 3, March 2003, pp. 211–217. Copyright © 2003 by American Psychological Association. Reprinted by permission. Note: The complete text of this article contains many references to specific studies described. The interested individual should refer to the original publication for these extensive citations. These references have been omitted here in the interest of brevity.

Thirty-two states [34 as of June 2006] in the United States currently restrict adolescents' access to abortion. Parental notification laws require that one or both parents be notified prior to the adolescent having her abortion; parental consent laws require explicit permission from one or both parents. Fifteen states enforce parental notification laws; 17 enforce parental consent laws. Several states permit another adult family member such as a grandparent to give consent instead of a parent. As of 2001, all but 4 states with parental consent or notification laws allow for an alternative judicial bypass of parental involvement. This is granted by a judge if (a) the minor is deemed capable of giving informed consent or (b) the abortion is in the best interests of the adolescent and parental involvement would likely cause harm or abuse of the minor.

Issues Raised by Parental Involvement Laws

The stated purposes of most parental involvement laws in the United States are to protect adolescents from making a harmful decision and to promote family functioning by assuring that parents become involved in their daughters' decision making and/or care. Parents of legal minors are responsible for their children's well-being, including the authorization of medical treatment. However, adolescents are allowed to make some decisions regarding reproductive health independently; for example, all 50 U.S. states and the District of Columbia allow minors to consent to testing and treatment for sexually transmitted diseases. Such testing and treatment are considered to be *sensitive services*. Laws regarding sensitive services recognize that such services are inextricably bound to issues of adolescents' sexuality and that minors may be hesitant to seek them if they have to inform their parents. A recent survey confirmed that parental notification can have adverse effects on service utilization and on health. [One study] found that almost 60% of current female patients under the age of 18 said that their utilization of services would change if parental notification were required. Anticipated adverse effects included delay and discontinuation of services, including sexual health care and STD testing. Most states do not require parental involvement for prenatal care or delivery if adolescents decide to continue their pregnancies. Thirty-four states and the District of Columbia explicitly permit a minor mother to place her child for adoption without her own parents' permission or knowledge. Eleven states make no distinction between minor and adult parents.

Parental involvement laws differentiate abortion from other sensitive services on the premise that this is a high-risk decision. . . . Below, we examine the three key rationales for restrictive laws regarding adolescents: (a) that abortion poses a significant risk, (b) that adolescents are incapable of making an adequately informed decision, and (c) that adolescents benefit from parental involvement that results from notification or consent. . . .

Risk of Harm From Abortion

Abortion itself carries relatively few medical risks, especially compared with the risks of childbearing. Although overall pregnancy-related mortality rates in the United States are 9.2 per 100,000 live births, the mortality rate is 0.3

per 100,000 legal abortions. In other countries where abortion is safe and legal, rates are comparably low compared with pregnancy-related deaths.

Well-designed studies of psychological responses following abortion have consistently shown that risk of psychological harm is also low. Some women experience psychological dysfunction following an abortion, but postabortion rates of distress and dysfunction are lower than preabortion rates. Moreover, the percentage of women who experience clinically relevant distress is small and appears to be no greater than in general samples of women of reproductive age. A recent study . . . showed not only that rates of disorders such as depression and posttraumatic stress disorder (PTSD) were not elevated in a large sample of 442 abortion patients followed for two years but also that the incidence of PTSD was actually lower in patients postabortion than are rates in the general population.

Although overall risks of psychological harm from abortion are low, one might still worry that adolescents are at heightened risk. The empirical data, however, do not support this. The best study of adolescent abortion followed 360 adolescents over two years after they had been interviewed when seeking a pregnancy test (Zabin, Hirsch, & Emerson, 1989). Some adolescents had a negative test, some were pregnant and carried to term, and some were pregnant and aborted their pregnancy. The adolescents who underwent an abortion showed significant drops in anxiety and significant increases in self-esteem and internal locus of control from baseline to two years later. In addition, the abortion patients appeared to be functioning as well as—or even better than—adolescents who had had a negative pregnancy test or who had carried to term. Two years after baseline, the abortion group showed lower trait anxiety than the other two groups, had higher self-esteem than the negative pregnancy group, and had a stronger internal locus of control than the childbearing group. They were also more likely than those in the other groups to be in school or to have graduated from high school, more likely to be at grade level if they were in school, and less likely to have a subsequent pregnancy, as well as having higher economic well-being.

Recent studies have examined directly whether legal minors are at greater risk of negative psychological responses following abortion than are older patients. Quinton, Major, and Richards (2001) compared responses of 38 abortion patients under age 18 versus 402 adult patients. On . . . a standardized measure of depression, there were no differences either one month or two years postabortion. One month postabortion, the minors reported somewhat less satisfaction and benefit in relation to their abortion than did the adults, but over time, minors' ratings became more positive, and two years later there were no differences by age. Thus, the minors increasingly reported having benefited from the abortion, whereas the adults reported such benefits at both time periods. Even at the one-month assessment, the mean levels for adolescents were in the positive range. Similar results were obtained [in another] one-month-[study comparing] postabortion functioning of 23 patients under 18 years of age with that of 40 patients ages 18–21 years. There were no significant age differences on standardized measures of depression, self-esteem, anxiety, or positive states of mind or on emotional responses to abortion.

[Minors] reported less comfort than adult patients with their decision one month postabortion, but the absolute values signified that most minors were comfortable with their decision. In this sample, there was no difference by age in patients' feelings about whether abortion was the right decision. Notably, results suggested that adolescents were not harmed by the abortion experience; in fact, there were significant decreases in scores on the Beck Depression Inventory and on negative emotions, and there was a significant increase in positive emotions from preabortion levels to one month postabortion.

In sum, the available data show that mean postabortion scores on psychological measures are well within normal bounds for minors as well as for adults. The data do not suggest that legal minors are at heightened risk of serious adverse psychological responses compared with adult abortion patients or with peers who have not undergone abortion.

Informed Consent

A second rationale for restrictive laws is that adolescents are not capable of making an adequately informed choice. Although adolescents are often viewed as irrational and less capable of informed action than adults, the empirical data suggest a more complex view. Studies examining the extent to which adolescents believe themselves to be invulnerable to bad outcomes have concluded that adolescents are no more biased in their perceptions than are adults. Other research has found that adolescents are consistent in their reasoning and decision making, behaving in ways that conform to rational models of decision making. [One study] found that young adolescents age 14 did not differ significantly from adults in their responses to hypothetical treatment choices; they were no different in their understanding of treatment options or the reasonableness of their decision as evaluated by health professionals. Koocher and DeMaso (1990), in discussing children's competence in relation to medical procedures in general, noted that "children are often more capable of expressing preferences and participating in making major life decisions than is generally recognized in medical settings or under the law" (p. 68).

Competence is domain specific; performance in one sector does not necessarily generalize to performance in other sectors, and there is no single measure of competence. This limits the extent to which research in areas other than health can be applied to evaluating adolescents' capacity to give informed consent for abortion. For example, one area where there is substantial discussion of competency regards the competency of adolescents to stand trial as adults. Research on adjudicative competence cannot be readily applied to competency to consent for abortion, however. For one thing, the competencies needed to make decisions regarding one's legal defense in a trial are markedly different from those needed to decide about pregnancy. Components of adjudicative competence include such things as the ability to work collaboratively with an attorney, to testify at trial, and to understand the sequence of pretrial and trial events. These place different demands than does the abortion decision. In addition, adolescents involved in these two domains are different in important ways. As discussed below, adolescents who are seeking abortion may have more psychological and social resources and be more capable of making an informed choice than are their peers. The reverse is likely to be true for adolescents facing prosecution for criminal activities, who have higher than average rates of mental disorders.

Studies examining the quality of adolescents' reasoning regarding hypothetical or real decisions about abortion provide further caution about applying findings on adolescent reasoning in general to understanding adolescents' abilities to consent to abortion. In a study of 90 female adolescents in their first trimester of pregnancy who had decided to have an abortion, [there were] differences in global moral reasoning between younger (12–14 years) and older (17–19 years) adolescents but [no] differences in reasoning about abortion. [College] students anticipated a different process of seeking advice and consultation in deciding about an abortion than they would for other types of decisions. Among other differences, the students reported that they were relatively more likely to consult with their significant other for an abortion decision than for a medical, a career or educational, or an interpersonal decision. They also showed different patterns with respect to consulting family members, friends, and professionals for abortion than for other decisions.

Ambuel and Rappaport (1992) . . . examined the decision making of 75 patients seeking a pregnancy test, comparing legal adults ages 18–21 years with two groups of younger adolescents: ages 14–15 years and ages 16–17 years. Some were considering abortion, and some planned to carry to term. Patients' interviews with a pregnancy counselor were evaluated on four indicators of competence; (a) volition, or the voluntary and independent nature of the decision; (b) global quality of reasoning; (c) awareness of consequences of the decision; and (d) the types of considerations expressed regarding the decision. Neither younger nor older adolescents considering abortion differed from legal adults on any of the components of competency. Among patients not considering abortion, there was no difference in competency between those ages 16–17 and those ages 18–21, but the youngest adolescents who planned to carry to term were significantly lower in volition, awareness of consequences, and global quality of the decision. An earlier study of 26 adults and 16 adolescents seeking a pregnancy test also found little difference in the decision-making processes of adolescents ages 13–17 and adults ages 18–25.

The findings by Ambuel and Rappaport (1992) are consistent with the view that adolescents seeking abortion are relatively more capable than their peers of making an informed choice. The youngest adolescents who planned to carry to term showed lower quality decision making than legal adults, whereas same-aged adolescents considering abortion did not differ from adults in their decision processes. Similarly, among teens studied by Zabin et al. (1989), those who subsequently had an abortion differed in key ways from those who subsequently carried to term. At baseline, adolescents who subsequently chose abortion had higher educational achievement, had more-educated mothers, and were from families in better economic circumstances; all of these factors are likely to be associated with greater competence. . . .

In sum, this research suggests that under current conditions, adolescent abortion patients may represent a subgroup that is more competent than pregnant adolescents who are not considering abortion. The actual experience in judging adolescents' competence and justification for abortion supports this view. Where it has been studied, it appears that virtually all adolescents' requests for judicial bypass are granted by judges assessing their competence and reasons for requesting bypass of parental consent.

Consequences of Parental Involvement in the Abortion Decision

Although parental involvement laws aim to promote family communication and functioning, there is little empirical data about whether they actually do so. Forcing communication between parents and children around the abortion decision may not have the desired positive effects. Health care providers and investigators have voiced concern about possible physical or emotional harm to adolescents who are forced to involve their parents in their abortion decision. Many, if not most, adolescents voluntarily tell their parents. Studies have reported widely varying numbers ranging from 35% to 91% of adolescents who inform their parents even when parental consent is not mandated; younger adolescents are more likely to inform their parents than are older adolescents. Adolescents who do not tell parents about their pregnancy cite fear of disappointing their parents, fear of anger, concern that their parents would punish them, and worries that a parent might become physically violent.

Young women who do not tell their parents about their pregnancy appear to have different family circumstances than those who do. Those who do not involve their parents perceive their family communication to be less open, feel less free to talk about feelings in general, and are less comfortable talking to their parents about sex than are young women who tell their parents about their pregnancy. Zabin and Sedivy (1992) found no differences in satisfaction with the decision to terminate or to continue to term between adolescents who consulted with a parent who supported their decision and adolescents who did not consult with a parent. However, adolescents who consulted with a parent who did not support their decision were less happy than were either those who never consulted their parents or those who consulted their parents and received support. Zabin and Sedivy concluded that "the small number who did not communicate made a responsible decision" (Zabin & Sedivy, 1992, p. 323).

One problem with mandatory parental notification is that young women with serious concerns about the consequences of notifying their parents may pursue other avenues to obtain abortions. As a result, some adolescents subject themselves to risk of injury and death by seeking an illegal abortion. For example, Becky Bell, a teenager in Indiana, died from the complications of an illegal abortion. She underwent this procedure because under Indiana law she would have had to obtain consent from one of her parents for a legal abortion, and she did not want to disappoint them. Parental consent requirements may also cause adolescents to seek legal abortions in another state. In some states, within-state abortions among minors decreased by as much as 50% after passage of parental consent laws, while out-of-state abortions obtained by minors in states not requiring parental consent increased in the same period.

Research by Henshaw and Kost (1992) provides indirect-evidence about the potential harm in forcing adolescents to notify parents of their pregnancy.

In that study, adolescents whose parents found out about their pregnancy without the adolescent telling them reported more adverse consequences due to parental knowledge compared with adolescents who voluntarily told their parents about the pregnancy. These adverse consequences included parents making them have an abortion, physical violence, and being forced to leave home.

Current Debate in the United States

Debate in the United States about adolescent abortion is occurring largely in the courts in the context of legal challenges to parental consent legislation. The American Psychological Association has filed several amicus briefs arguing against restrictions on adolescents' access to abortion. This is an area where legal and scientific arguments and conventions are not well aligned. [Research] cannot prove "no difference"; not finding a difference between adolescent and adult competence (or psychological response) is not equivalent to proving that there are no differences. This dilemma derives from the difficulty of proving the null hypothesis. In the current situation, where several studies have not found a difference in psychological functioning or in competency, one can at least say that the scientific evidence does not provide justification for the assumptions on which restrictive legislation is built. Though one cannot say there is no difference, one can say with some confidence that the available data are consistent with the view that there are no meaningful differences between adolescents and adults.

One challenge to this view is that the null findings could result from inadequate statistical power in studies with small numbers of participants. However, although it would be helpful to have large-scale studies of representative samples, this may not be necessary to draw some conclusions. A key issue is the clinical significance, not simply the statistical significance, of a difference between groups. Studies with large samples can result in statistically significant differences even when the effect size is quite small. For example, with large numbers of participants, a half-point difference on the Beck Depression Inventory between adolescents and adults could be statistically significant. However, such a small difference would have few implications for mental health because the vast majority of both adolescents and adults score well below the cutoff for moderate or severe depression. Only where there are large enough effects to have public health implications should one demand policy intervention. If adolescents are markedly less competent than adults or if adolescents show substantially worse psychological outcomes after abortion than do adults, this should show up as a medium or large effect, which would not require a large sample to show a difference between groups.

U.S. and International Issues

Adolescents throughout the world are having abortions, but their experiences vary dramatically depending on where they live. A major determinant is the legal status of abortion for all women; a secondary one is the restrictions placed on adolescents. Even within the United States, there are marked differences by state and region. An urban teen in New York or California, where parental consent is not required and public and private providers are available, will have a much easier time than adolescents who live in states such as North Dakota or Mississippi, which require consent of both parents, or who live in a rural area where there are no providers. There are some countries, notably the Scandinavian countries, where abortions may be easier to obtain than in the United States and may carry less stigma, in part because adolescent sexual activity is itself less stigmatized. Yet, in many parts of the world, teens seeking to terminate their pregnancies face far greater risks and obstacles than do their counterparts in the United States.

Unfortunately, there are few comparative data on adolescents from other countries. Among industrialized counties with similar or less restrictive abortion laws, the small number of psychologically oriented studies have focused largely on adolescents' attitudes toward abortion or on the psychological effects of abortion (Quinton et al., 2001). With few exceptions, research on adolescents and abortion in developing countries has mainly been concerned with basic issues of access and safety. It seems likely that psychological responses would be more negative in countries and states where adolescents experience greater risk, in terms of both physical safety and social stigma, in terminating an unwanted pregnancy.

The legal and social status of abortion within countries is often closely tied to predominant religious teachings. Agostino and Wahlberg (1991) studied adolescents in Italy and Sweden. The majority of Italian adolescents in that study indicated that abortion is only justified on medical grounds, whereas most Swedish adolescents in the study believed that nonmedical reasons also provide sufficient grounds for abortion. The authors attributed this difference in attitudes to greater Catholic influence in Italy and its prohibition of abortion. Yet countries with the same predominant religion may vary with respect to abortion laws. In Islamic law, for example, the killing of a soul is strictly prohibited, and the fetus is generally considered to develop a soul at the time of quickening, when the mother can detect fetal movements. However, although some Islamic countries permit abortion prior to quickening, others prohibit abortions completely. Thus, adolescents in other countries are likely to be affected both by secular laws and by their own religious beliefs about abortion, similar to the U.S. political and religious debate over when life begins.

It is important to note critical differences in the social roles of adolescent women across the industrialized and developing world. Although adolescent urban elites in many developing countries occupy social roles similar to those of many U.S. adolescents with respect to pursuing higher education and career experience prior to marriage, large numbers of adolescents from rural or less elite backgrounds marry and begin families as adolescents. In these countries, adolescent pregnancy does not necessarily imply single parenthood, as is more often the case in the United States. In India, for example, roughly 30% of rural female adolescents are married by age 15, and 40% of all women ages 15–19 are married, despite laws prohibiting marriage before age 18 for females. Early marriage is often accompanied by strong pressures to quickly prove fertility because a young woman's security in the home of her husband's family may be largely determined by her ability to bear children—particularly a son. Adolescent women in such cultural and familial settings may experience little real power in decisions regarding abortion; those in rural settings must further contend with limited access to reproductive health services.

In sum, the overriding issue regarding abortion for adolescents in the international context is that abortion is frequently completely prohibited. Other issues are the age at which young women marry and are considered adults, the power that women have to determine their own fertility, the availability of safe abortion, and the stigma associated with abortion due to societal norms and religious beliefs. If the international trend toward liberalization of abortion laws continues in both industrialized and developing nations, the issues that currently are of concern in the United States may become more central in those countries. Within the United States, the focus of debate on adolescent abortions has been on the need for parental involvement and/or consent. Although it seems obvious that it is better to have parents involved in their minor daughter's decision making and care, there is little evidence that adolescents benefit from having this mandated. Moreover, there is reason to be concerned about the potential adverse effects of legislating parental involvement. Parental consent legislation has also been predicated on the assumption that it is needed because adolescents are at high risk for adverse responses to abortion and are not capable of making an adequately informed choice. Research to date provides no backing for these assumptions.

It is tempting to end this article by calling for research on adolescents' decision making about abortion and their psychological responses in the United States and internationally, and such research would certainly be useful. In the United States, for example, it would be informative to compare adolescents' experience with and responses to abortion in states with different parental consent laws. This could assess whether hypothesized benefits of parental notification or consent (e.g., involvement of parents in their daughter's care, better medical and psychosocial outcomes, increased communication within the family, and strengthened relationships between parents and children) occur more often in states with consent laws. Similarly, the relative prevalence of potential hazards (e.g., increased rates of abuse, increased conflict between parents and children, increased stress for adolescents who have to go through a court hearing, more midtrimester abortions, and more adolescents going out of state or seeking illegal abortions) should be examined. Some of these effects have been studied, but there is too little information to allow for a comprehensive analysis of costs versus benefits. At this time, there is no evidence that parental consent is either needed or beneficial. Further debate and policy discussion would benefit from studies that directly test the consequences of requiring parental notification or consent for abortion.

At the same time, the research suggested above is not the most critical need. In all countries, abortion generally represents the failure to prevent an unwanted pregnancy. In some countries, this is due to lack of access to effective contraception; in others, it may be due to high rates of rape, incest, or other coerced intercourse. In still other countries, abortion rates may be affected by a preference for male children. While all women, including adolescents, who need to terminate an unwanted pregnancy should have access to safe, legal abortion, it is also necessary to focus on the conditions that lead to the need for abortion.

References

Agostino, M. B., & Wahlberg, V. (1991). Adolescents' attitudes to abortion in samples from Italy and Sweden. *Social Science and Medicine, 33,* 77–83.

Ambuel, B., & Rappaport, J. (1992). Developmental trends in adolescents' psychological and legal competence to consent to abortion. *Law and Human Behavior, 16,* 129–154.

Henshaw, S. K., & Kost, K. (1992). Parental involvement in minors' abortion decisions. *Family Planning Perspectives, 24,* 196–213.

Koocher, G. P., & DeMaso, D. R. (1990). Children's competence to consent to medical procedures. *Pediatrician, 17,* 68–73.

Quinton, W., Major, B., & Richards, C. (2001). Adolescents and adjustment to abortion: Are minors at greater risk? *Psychology, Public Policy, and Law, 7,* 491–514.

Zabin, L. S., Hirsch, M. B., & Emerson, M. R. (1989). When urban adolescents choose abortion: Effects on education, psychological status and subsequent pregnancy. *Family Planning Perspectives, 21,* 248–255.

Zabin, L. S., & Sedivy, V. (1992). Abortion among adolescents: Research findings and the current debate. *Journal of School Health, 62,* 319–324.

POSTSCRIPT

Should Parental Consent Be Required for Adolescents Seeking Abortions?

The abortion debate, like many other controversies, is often viewed in extremes. One is pro-choice or one is anti-choice. There is no gray area in between. At the same time, however, introducing a minor into the discussion often alters the discussion—particularly the younger the girl is who is seeking the abortion. In some cases, the younger a girl is, the more protection adults may feel she needs. In other cases, the younger she is, the more likely some abortion opponents might be to make an exception, citing a preference for the "necessary evil" of abortion over letting a 14-year-old girl become a parent.

An important factor to keep in mind is the fact that not everyone has sexual intercourse by choice. While many abortion opponents will make an exception for pregnancies that are caused by rape or incest, others maintain that a pregnancy is a pregnancy and that no potential life should be punished even if it were conceived in a violent manner. If a state law requires that a parent be notified, and the parent who is notified is the one who caused the pregnancy, then parental notification may have stopped an abortion only to put a girl's safety or life in jeopardy. On the other hand, in cases of incest, parental notification could help to bring rape or incest—which are all too frequently hidden or kept private—out into the open so that it will not happen again, and the perpetrator, if known, can be arrested and the abuse stopped.

Legislating personal decisions is, as always, a slippery slope. How far do we go? How do laws legislating one behavior or type of procedure affect others? For example, parental consent is currently not required in order for a minor to obtain birth control. Controversy remains around one particular type of birth control, Emergency Contraception, formerly known as the "morning-after" pill. A form of emergency contraception, Plan B (levonorgestrel), is dispensed by a pharmacist without a prescription in Canada. Emergency Contraception is not an abortion; it prevents pregnancy from happening. In fact, if a woman is pregnant without knowing it, has unprotected intercourse, and then takes Emergency Contraception, her pregnancy should not be affected by the Emergency Contraception. At the same time, however, since one of the ways in which Emergency Contraception works is by preventing a fertilized egg from implanting, those who believe that life begins at conception argue that Emergency Contraception is the same thing as abortion. Therefore, the door that is open to parental notification and consent laws remains open to support for parental notification or consent before Emergency Contraception can be dispensed. This in turn could lead to legislation requiring parental notification or consent for birth control pills and condoms. How would such notification be enacted and enforced within a pharmacy as condoms and emergency contraception pills (in Canada) are relatively easily accessible?

In an ideal world, people would not have sex before they are old enough and established enough in their lives to be able to manage the potential consequences of being in a sexual relationship. In an ideal world, abortion would not be necessary because no pregnancy would be unplanned or come as the result of rape or incest. However, we do not live in an ideal world. People, regardless of age, have unprotected sex or use contraception incorrectly. People, regardless of age, are raped and sexually abused. Women, regardless of age, have pregnancies that may need to be terminated for medical reasons. In some households, the revelation of an unplanned pregnancy can result in violence against the pregnant teen and/or her partner.

Is there a solution between these two extremes that could enable parents to show their care and support of their adolescents while at the same time letting them make their own decisions? Where do feelings about abortion, in general, come into play in one's thoughts and opinions on this particular matter?

It is important to note that studies do indicate that many adolescents seek the advice of parents or trusted adults when considering abortion. In fact, as many as 9 out of 10 girls seeking an abortion consult with a parent. This figure was higher for younger girls, girls who live with their parents, and girls who have good communication with their parents. In summary, it appears that regardless of the legislation, the majority of adolescent girls consult with a parent regarding their abortion decision. This perhaps is indicative of an adequate level of maturity and competence in making important life decisions regarding abortion.

References/Further Reading

Alford, S. (January 2003). *Adolescents and abortions: The facts.* Washington, D.C.: Advocates for Youth. Available online at: http://www. advocatesforyouth .org/publications/factsheet/fsabortion.htm.

Benson, M.J. (2004). After the adolescent pregnancy: Parents, teens, and families. *Child & Adolescent Social Work Journal,* 21(5), 435–455.

Center for Reproductive Rights (January 2006). The Teen Endangerment Act: Harming young women who seek abortions. Available online at: http://www.reproductiverights.org/pub_fac_ccpa.html.

Collett, T. S. (2006). Transporting minors for immoral purposes: The case for the Child Custody Protection Act & the Child Interstate Abortion Notification Act. *Health Matrix,* 16, 107–150.

Earll, C.G. (2000). Frequently asked questions: Parental involvement in minor abortions. *Citizen Link: Focus on Social Issues.* Colorado Springs, CO: Focus on the Family. Available online at: http://www.family.org/ cforum/fosi/bioethics/faqs/a0027733.cfm.

Finken, L. (2005). The role of consultants in adolescents' decision making: A focus on abortion decisions. In J.E. Jacobs & P.A. Klaczynski (Eds.), pp. 255–278. *The development of judgment and decision making in children and adolescents.* Mahwah, NJ: Lawrence Erlbaum.

Guttmacher Institute (June 2006). State policies in brief: Parental involvement in minors' abortions. New York: Guttmacher Institute. Available online at: http://www.guttmacher.org/statecenter/spibs/spib_PIMA.pdf.

Jones, R. K., Purcell, A., Singh, S., & Finer, L. B. (2005). Adolescents' reports of parental knowledge of adolescents' use of sexual health services and their reactions to mandated parental notification for prescription contraception. *Journal of the American Medical Association,* 293(3), 340–348.

Hull, N.E.H., and Hoffer, P.C. (2001). *Roe v. Wade: The Abortion Rights Controversy in American History* (University Press of Kansas).

ISSUE 4

Do Boys Worry about an Ideal Body Image as Much as Girls Do?

YES: Donald R. McCreary and Doris K. Sasse, from "An Exploration of the Drive for Muscularity in Adolescent Boys and Girls," *Journal of American College Health* (May 2000)

NO: Duane A. Hargreaves and Marika Tiggemann, from "Idealized Media Images and Adolescent Body Image: 'Comparing' Boys and Girls," *Body Image* (vol. 1, 2004)

ISSUE SUMMARY

YES: Donald McCreary and Doris Sasse, researchers at Brock University, suggest that adolescent boys are just as likely to experience body image dissatisfaction likely influenced by the portrayal of the "macho" muscular body as an ideal image in many men's health magazines.

NO: Duane Hargreaves and Marika Tiggemann, researchers in the School of Psychology at Flinders University, state that adolescent girls are more vulnerable to body image pressures than boys. They argue that the glamorization of eating disorders among female celebrities and the media play a significant role.

Many young adolescents are dissatisfied with their bodies. Research maintains that 50–70 percent of adolescent girls diet, and an even higher number maintain a feeling of dissatisfaction with their body and a longing to be thin. It is also reported that body weight dissatisfaction and affiliated weight-loss strategies may be a precondition for developing an eating disorder (Tomori and Rus-Makovec, 2000). Research also indicates that adolescent boys have concerns about their bodies. Specifically, an estimated one-third of adolescent boys desire a thinner body while another third desire a larger more muscular build. McCabe and Ricciardelli (2001) report that as many as 50 percent of boys are trying to lose weight while just as many are engaged in muscle-building strategies.

These statistics indicate that physical appearance is on the minds of many adolescents. In fact, for both boys and girls, satisfaction with one's body is an important developmental issue during adolescence. It plays a significant role in predicting self-esteem, physical appearance self-concept, emotional distress, depression, eating disorders, and overall psychological adjustment. For this reason, it is important to understand the variables that affect body image and to examine whether the risk factors and rates differ for boys and girls.

The role of sociocultural pressures regarding the ideal thin body has been researched extensively among adolescent girls. Although many factors can contribute greatly to unhealthy beliefs regarding adolescents' weight and shape, one particularly significant factor is the media. The media plays a powerful role in bombarding girls with images of acceptable and unacceptable body shapes. In magazines and on television, the ideal female body is tall, thin, and perhaps even prepubescent looking. Research has indicated that as girls' progress through adolescence, they become more aware of the sociocultural ideal and as a result, increase their attempts to achieve it (McCabe & Ricciardelli, 2005). Essentially, there is a "drive for thinness" among many adolescent girls. In reality, few girls have the genetic makeup for the ideal body type portrayed in the media.

Little research however has examined the increasing number of ideal male body images in the media and the effects on male body satisfaction. As with females, there is a clear sociocultural ideal for males, specifically a V-shaped, lean, and muscular build. Where there is a drive for thinness for females, one could say there is a drive for muscularity among males. However, is the drive for muscularity for males similar to the drive for thinness for females? The drive for thinness has been associated with weight loss strategies such as excessive dieting and exercise, while the drive for muscularity has been associated with muscle-building strategies such as excessive exercise, bodybuilding, and anabolic steroid use (Ricciardelli & McCabe, 2004). Do these similarities mean that boys and girls worry equally about an ideal body image, or are girls more influenced by the sociocultural pressures regarding an ideal body type?

As previously mentioned, body image and psychosocial adjustment has been well documented for girls and women; however, the relationship is less clear for boys and men. The increase in boys and men's magazines depicting the ideal lean and muscular body has led to a need to examine the effects on male body image. As such, many researchers are including a sample of boys in their research design.

Two such studies examining body image satisfaction among boys and girls are presented below. In the first selection, McCreary and Sasse suggest that adolescent boys are just as likely to experience body image dissatisfaction. In the second selection, Hargreaves and Tiggemann report that adolescent girls are more vulnerable to body image pressures than boys.

YES

**Donald R. McCreary and
Doris K. Sasse**

An Exploration of the Drive
for Muscularity in Adolescent
Boys and Girls

To date, many empirical investigations have found that adolescent girls are significantly more dissatisfied with their bodies than adolescent boys. As a result, girls are more likely than boys to use dieting and other weight-reduction methods (eg, fasting and laxative abuse) to help achieve a more socially desirable shape. This *drive for thinness* is so pronounced that, at any given time, between one half and two thirds of adolescent girls may be on a diet.[1]

Researchers point to the many cultural factors that reinforce an unhealthy, overly thin standard of bodily attractiveness in girls and women. For example, it has been shown that TV actresses, magazine models, and beauty pageant contestants are significantly less curvaceous (in terms of both their bust-to-waist ratio and their weight) than average women in the population.[2] In addition, female-oriented magazines subject girls and women to large numbers of both implicit and explicit messages that they should be thin; diet and aerobic exercise are the two most common weight-reduction techniques promoted by these types of publications.[2] The toys that young girls play with also may reinforce unrealistic expectations of women's body shapes. In one study, researchers used anthropometric data to translate the shapes of the infamous Barbie and Ken dolls to those of adult women and men. They found that Barbie's body shape is so distorted that it has a probability of occurring in only 1 out of every 100 000 women, whereas the shape of the male doll, Ken, is much more realistic and can be found in 1 out of 50 men.[3]

But what about boys and men? Do they also strive to be thin? Are the cultural imperatives the same for boys and men as they are for girls and women? Research has shown that the drive for thinness is relatively rare in boys and men[4] and is found most often in those who need to be light for recreational or occupational purposes (eg, swimmers, wrestlers, runners). Instead, the most desirable body shape for men emphasizes muscle mass and physical bulk, what researchers refer to as the *muscular mesomorph*.[5] Research into perceptions of ideal body shapes for men reveals two consistent findings: (a) that men will often pick the muscular mesomorphic shape as their ideal, and (b) that men also believe that women look for muscularity in their ideal man.[5] The validity of the latter belief has been demonstrated empirically—

From *Journal of American College Health*, vol. 48, May 2000, pp. 297–304. Copyright © 2000 by Heldref Publications. Reprinted with permission of the Helen Dwight Reid Educational Foundation. Published by Heldref Publications, 1319 Eighteenth St., NW, Washington, DC 20036–1802. Note: The complete text of this article contains many references to specific studies described. The interested individual should refer to the original publication for these extensive citations. These references have been omitted here in the interest of brevity.

women tend to rate men with more highly developed pectoral muscles (ie, the classic inverted triangle) as more attractive than men with less well-developed chests.[6]

Western society reinforces the stereotype of the muscular mesomorph by emphasizing the link between muscularity and masculinity. Although the tale of the "95-pound weakling" is one extreme, other messages are found in male-oriented magazines. These typically describe how men can become more popular with women by becoming more muscular.[5] Even action toys present unrealistic expectations of muscularity to boys. In a recent study, researchers showed that a popular action figure marketed to boys (GI Joe) has become unrealistically muscular over the past 30 years. When the degree of muscularity found on these toys was anthropometrically mapped onto the average male frame, the findings showed how the toys presented a degree of muscularity that even the most advanced bodybuilders could never attain.[7]

Additional evidence for this *drive for muscularity* in men and boys comes from several sources. Research on body image and body satisfaction shows that young men tend to see themselves as thinner and less muscular than they really are. In fact, between 28% and 68% of all normal-weight adolescent boys are trying to gain weight (or want to).[8] [Studies] exploring the reasons behind this desire to be bigger suggest that boys and men really want to become more muscular; half of all the boys and men in these studies expressed a desire for larger pectorals, biceps, wrists, shoulders, or forearms, and flatter abdominal muscles.[8] Researchers also have shown that men are more motivated than women to participate in weight training. Furthermore, the more boys and men are involved in weight training activities, the more satisfied they are with their bodies, regardless of their overall muscle mass.[9]

Like the drive for thinness, the drive for muscularity can have detrimental physical and psychological consequences. The physical consequences resulting from a heightened drive for muscularity are different from those typically associated with the drive for thinness. Whereas those who want to be thinner tend to abuse laxatives, undergo extreme dieting regimens (eg, fasting), and often engage in self-induced vomiting, researchers suggest that boys who want to be more muscular tend to engage in binge eating but do not purge afterward.[8]

Wanting to be more muscular also has been shown to be associated with an increased likelihood of using anabolic androgenic steroids and other types of performance-enhancing supplements. Although very little is known about the risks associated with most of the nutritional supplements taken by those who want to be more muscular (eg, creatine), the adverse health consequences of anabolic steroid abuse are well documented. They include greater risk for coronary heart disease (CHD), kidney and liver damage, and reduced functioning of the immune system.[10] . . .

If the drive for muscularity is associated with boys' and men's body images, then adverse psychological reactions may also be associated with the drive. For example, those high in the drive for thinness tend to have low levels of self-esteem and high levels of depression. We expect the same pattern of relationships for those high in the drive for muscularity.

However, whether the psychological problems associated with this drive are the same for boys and men and for girls and women has become an interesting empirical and theoretical question. A recent article suggested that, whereas gender-related drives or motivations (eg, gender-role traits, attitudes, behaviors, and gender-related stressors) are internalized in the same way by both men and women, they are not equally important to both sexes.[11] As a result, the associations between these drives or motivations and psychological or physical outcome variables will be sex-differentiated. This concept is referred to as *differential salience*. [For] men, the male role was strongly associated with alcohol use and alcohol problems (factors for which men have significantly more problems than women). By contrast, the associations were not present for women.[11]

[Work] on the relationship between the male role and alcohol involvement shares several notable similarities with the present research on the drive for muscularity and its association with adverse psychological outcomes: Both men and women have internalized the notion that it is desirable for men to be big (either muscular or fat). Society is more accepting of the notion of overweight men because people may confound being overweight with being muscular. As a result, men more often want to be bigger and more muscular whereas women want to be thinner. This suggests that, for men, the drive for muscularity is more salient than it is for women. If this is the case, then men should be higher in the drive for muscularity than women are. However, we also think that the drive should be more strongly correlated with psychological problems, such as lower self-esteem and greater depression in boys or men than in girls or women. In other words, we are curious about whether gender will moderate the association between the drive for muscularity and psychological outcome measures.

In this study, we sought to begin developing the concept of a drive for muscularity. Before we could achieve this goal, however, we needed to find a way to measure the drive. To do this, we polled a group of weight-training enthusiasts about the factors that motivate them to train and how they feel when they miss a weight-training session. We also analyzed the content of various weight-training magazines for the same factors. From these sources, we developed a list of motivations. We then asked a group of women and men involved with weight training to determine the face validity of the various attitudes and behaviors on our list. Using their recommendations as a guide, we created a 15-item Drive for Muscularity Scale. . . .

We also tested [the] notion of differential salience[11] as it applies to the drive for the muscularity construct by examining the associations between the drive and psychological outcomes separately for boys and for girls. If the drive for muscularity was associated with poor self-esteem and depression for boys, but not for girls, then evidence for a differential impact of the drive would have been found.

Method

Participants

One-hundred ninety-seven high school students (101 girls and 96 boys) . . . participated in the study. They ranged in age from 16 to 24 years ($M = 18$ years). . . .

Measures

Drive for Muscularity

The DMS is a 15-item questionnaire developed for the present study that measures attitudes and behaviors that reflect the degree of people's preoccupation with increasing their muscularity. . . . Each item is scored on a 6-point scale from *never* to *always*. We averaged responses to the 15 items; higher scores indicate a greater drive for muscularity.

Behavioral Indicators

We included three indicators of a person's involvement in weight-training activities and muscle development. They were the number of times each week the respondent participated in weight training, whether the respondent was presently dieting to gain weight (yes/no), or whether the respondent was presently dieting to lose weight (yes/no).

Psychological Well-being

We included measures of both self-esteem and depression in the study. The Rosenberg Self-esteem Scale is a 10-item survey measuring global self-esteem. . . . A scale mean is calculated and higher scores are indicative of greater self-esteem. . . .

To measure depression, we used the Center for Epidemiologic Studies Depression Scale (CES-D). On the CES-D, participants indicate how frequently each of 20 statements applied to them in the past week (eg, "I felt depressed"). . . . We computed an average CES-D score [where higher] scores reflect greater levels of depression. . . .

Drive for Thinness

We included two measures of the drive for thinness in this study: the Eating Attitudes Test (EAT) and the Body Dissatisfaction (BD) subscale from the Eating Disorders Inventory (EDI). The EAT consists of 26 items that assess the maladaptive eating attitudes and behaviors associated with anorexia and bulimia nervosa. . . . We computed an average of the EAT items, with high scores representing a greater drive for thinness. . . .

The BD subscale from the EDI consists of 9 items measuring the extent to which people believe that parts of their body (eg, stomach, thighs, buttocks) are too large. . . . Higher scores reflect a greater degree of body dissatisfaction. . . .

Results

Reliability of the DMS

To determine reliability, we calculated the internal consistency of the DMS on the overall sample as well as separately for boys and for girls. . . . The alpha coefficients for the DMS—an overall alpha of .84—showed that it has good reliability. When broken out by the sex of the respondents, the alpha for boys was .84, for girls it was .78. . . .

Validity of the DMS

Face Validity
We determined face validity by examining the sex differences in each of the DMS items, as well as the scale average. If boys and men are more motivated than girls or women to be muscular, then responses to many of these questions, as well as the overall scale score, would be significantly higher for the boys than for the girls in our sample. . . .

[Significant] sex differences on 9 of the 15 items [were revealed] with the boys scoring higher than the girls on each. On the 6 items for which the sex differences were not significant, the trend was for the boys to score higher than the girls. Finally, the boys scored significantly higher than the girls on the overall scale average. . . .

Convergent Validity
We examined convergent validity of the drive for muscularity concept in several ways. The initial approach examined whether DMS scores varied as a function of whether the participants were trying to gain weight. . . . Both boys and girls who were trying to gain weight had significantly higher DMS scores (2.92) than those who were not trying to gain weight (1.99).

We also examined the DMS as a function of whether the participant was attempting to lose weight. Apart from the main effect for participants' sex . . . no other significant main effects or interactions [were found.]

The second method for examining convergent validity was to assess the correlations between the DMS and the number of times per week the participant typically engaged in weight-training activities. The frequency of weight training is positively related to DMS scores, $r = .24$, $p < .001$; those respondents with higher DMS scores tended to participate in weight training significantly more frequently than those with lower DMS scores.

The final way we examined the convergent validity of the DMS was by assessing the intercorrelations between the DMS and both self-esteem and depression. However, because we also wanted to test the concept of differential salience in the relationships between the DMS and the psychological outcome variables (ie, whether the drive for muscularity would be more salient for the boys in our sample, and therefore more likely to be associated with poor self-esteem and high levels of depression among boys but not among the girls), we examined the correlations separately for the boys and the girls. The findings confirmed the presence of differential salience: The drive for muscularity was associated with significantly poorer self-esteem ($r = -.41$, $p < .001$) and greater levels of depression ($r = .32$, $p < .001$) only in our sample of boys. For the girls, the correlations were not significant ($r = -.07$ and $r = .00$, respectively).

Discriminant Validity
To display adequate discriminant validity, the DMS should not be highly correlated with the drive for thinness, otherwise it could be argued that the drive for muscularity is merely the opposite of the drive for thinness. The findings showed that, for the sample as a whole, the DMS was uncorrelated with the EAT scale [$r = -.05$, not significant (*ns*)] and slightly negatively correlated with

the BD scale ($r = -.15$, $p < .03$). We also examined these correlations separately for the boys and the girls. For the boys, the DMS was positively correlated with the EAT scale ($r = .37$, $p < .001$) and was uncorrelated with the BD scale ($r = .09$, *ns*). For the girls, the DMS was uncorrelated with both the EAT ($r = .04$, *ns*) and the BD scales ($r = -.13$, *ns*). The small magnitude of the two significant correlations, combined with the fact that all of the remaining correlation coefficients were not significant, suggested that, as they are currently measured, the two drives are relatively independent of each other. . . .

Comment

Past research has shown that boys and men tend not to experience anorexia and bulimia nervosa to the same extent as girls and women. However, whereas boys and men may not be focused on a drive for thinness, research suggests that many wish to be bulkier and more muscular than they currently see themselves. For the present study, we created the DMS, a 15-item pencil-and-paper questionnaire that assesses people's attitudes about their muscularity and motivation to become more muscular. We then used this survey to determine (a) that boys scored higher on the DMS than girls (ie, face validity), (b) that high scores on the DMS were related to more frequent weight-training sessions per week and to dieting to increase physical bulk (ie, convergent validity), and (c) that high scores on the DMS were unrelated to the drive for thinness (ie, discriminant validity). In addition, we also determined the differential impact of the drive for muscularity. We found DMS scores were positively correlated with lower levels of self-esteem and higher levels of depression in boys, but not in girls.

With regard to the DMS, the alpha coefficients suggest that the items that make up the scale are highly intercorrelated; therefore, the scale can be considered reliable by this estimate. . . .

As we expected, the drive for muscularity appears to be stronger in boys than in girls. Furthermore, those who are high in the drive for muscularity (whether they are boys or girls) also act in a corresponding manner: they weight trained more often and they adopted a diet designed to increase bulk. Because people appear to act in a way that supports the drive for muscularity, we believe that those high in the drive (mostly, but not exclusively, men) may also be at greater risk for using anabolic-androgenic steroids. These dangerous drugs, . . . [are] associated with a number of health problems, including testicular atrophy, high blood pressure (a risk factor for CHD), fluid retention, kidney and liver problems, reduced immune function (eg, less resistance to colds), addiction, and death. Research suggests that those who use steroids have less knowledge about the side effects of the substances and engage in other forms of risk-taking behavior, including polydrug use and needle sharing.[10] . . .

Consideration of the moderating effect of a person's sex should always be considered when exploring the drive for muscularity and its effects. In some cases, such as when behavioral correlates of the drive for muscularity are being explored, a moderating effect is not expected. For example, if someone is high in the drive, he or she is likely to be trying to gain weight and engaging in a lot of weight training. This is not expected to differ between men and women. But how the drive for muscularity affects men's and women's self-concepts should be expected to differ. In the present study, we observed that boys high in the drive for muscularity had lower self-esteem and higher levels of depression; girls' self-esteem and depression levels were unrelated to their drive for muscularity. We also observed differences in the associations between the drive for muscularity and the drive for thinness.

These findings suggest that boys and men and girls and women engage in weight training for different reasons: for boys, it appears to be for an enhanced self-concept. But what other aspects of boys' and men's self-concepts are affected by the drive for muscularity? For example, why do men tend to confound being overweight with being muscular? Furthermore, research needs to address the factors that motivate girls and women to use weight-training techniques. If the girls and women are not driven to be muscular for the same reasons as men, do they weight train for all-around fitness or for some other reasons?

These findings have important implications for college health professionals. In many college environments, counselors and coaches are actively involved in identifying and reducing the prevalence of eating disorders in women (eg, through an Eating Disorders Awareness Week). However, because the rate of boys' and men's steroid use is higher than the rate of anorexia and is equal to the rate of bulimia in girls and women,[12] more emphasis needs to be given to men's body image concerns.

Discussions about the distorted way the media present women's bodies need to be balanced with a similar discussion of how the media present men's bodies. Coaches and counselors need to be alert for the signs of steroid use and should provide information about the effectiveness of other ergogenic aids as they emerge. Effective dietetic information should be made available to men, encouraging healthy eating practices and emphasizing that bulk acquired through increased caloric intake cannot be converted to muscle later. . . .

In summary, this study examined the drive for muscularity in adolescent boys and girls. It was shown that boys displayed higher levels of this drive than girls did. Regardless of a person's sex, being high in the drive for muscularity was associated with engaging in a greater amount of weight training and being on a diet to gain weight. The drive for muscularity was unrelated to the drive for thinness, and the findings suggest that it may be a body-image disorder in boys and men because of its relation to poorer levels of self-esteem and depression.

References

1. Huon GF, Brown L. Attitude correlates of weight control among secondary school boys and girls. *Journal of Adolescent Health Care.* 1986;7:178–182.
2. Wiseman CV, Gray JJ, Mosimann JE, Ahrens AH. Cultural expectations of thinness in women: An update. *Int J Eat Disord.* 1992;11:85–89.
3. Norton KI, Olds TS, Olive S, Dank S. Ken and Barbie at life size. *Sex Roles.* 1996;34:287–294.
4. Olivardia R, Pope HG, Mangweth B, Hudson JI. Eating disorders in college men. *Am J Psychiatry.* 1995;152:1279–1285.

5. Mishkind ME, Rodin J, Silberstein LR, Striegel-Moore RH. The embodiment of masculinity: Cultural, psychological, and behavioral dimensions. *American Behavioral Scientist.* 1986;29:545–562.

6. Maisey DS, Vale ELE, Cornelissen PL, Tovée MJ. Characteristics of male attractiveness for women. *Lancet.* 1999;353:1500.

7. Pope HG, Olivardia R, Gruber A, Borowiecki J. Evolving ideals of male body image as seen through action toys. *Int J Eat Disord.* 1999;26:65–72.

8. Moore DC. Body image and eating behavior in adolescent boys. *American Journal of Diseases in Children.* 1990;144:475–479.

9. Tucker LA. Effect of weight training on body attitudes: Who benefits most? *Journal of Sports Medicine.* 1987;27:70–78.

10. Korkia P, Stimson GV. Indications of prevalence, practice, and effects of anabolic steroid use in Great Britain. *Int J Sports Med.* 1997;18:557–562.

11. McCreary DR, Newcomb MD, Sadava SW. The male role, alcohol use, and alcohol problems: A structural modeling examination in adult women and men. *Journal of Counseling Psychology.* 1999;46:109–124.

12. Spitzer BL, Henderson KA, Zivian MT. Gender differences in population versus media body sizes: A comparison over four decades. *Sex Roles.* 1999;40:545–565.

**Duane A. Hargreaves and
Marika Tiggemann**

 **NO**

Idealized Media Images
and Adolescent Body Image:
"Comparing" Boys and Girls

Introduction

Body dissatisfaction, which is common among women of all ages, is especially prevalent during adolescence when body image is [a very] important component of adolescent girls' self-esteem (Levine & Smolak, 2002). Arguably the most likely cause of body dissatisfaction among adolescent girls is the current unrealistic standard of female beauty which places an inordinate emphasis on thinness, and which is unattainable for most girls (Ackard & Peterson, 2001). This ideal standard of beauty is conveyed to individuals via a number of sources including family, peers and the mass media. . . .

A small number of studies have examined the impact of media images on the body image of adolescents. Correlational studies show that adolescent girls who read more magazines and watch more television report greater body dissatisfaction (Hofchire & Greenberg, 2002). Experimental studies show that exposure to idealised media images leads to increased state body dissatisfaction for girls. To date, however, . . . few correlational studies have included boys (Botta, 2003). While a small number of experimental studies have found a negative impact of muscular-ideal magazine images on college-aged men (Leit, Pope, & Gray, 2002), no experimental studies of the media's immediate impact on the body image of adolescent boys have been conducted. Although boys' body dissatisfaction is typically less severe than for girls, they too express dissatisfaction with their body weight and appearance (Levine & Smolak, 2002; Ricciardelli & McCabe, 2001). Such dissatisfaction has been linked to a number of negative consequences including the development of dieting, excessive exercise, and low self-esteem.

Like girls, the most likely cause of body dissatisfaction among boys is an unrealistic appearance ideal. The current ideal male body is lean but highly muscular, characterised by a "well-developed chest and arms, with wide shoulders tapering down to a narrow waist" (Pope et al., 2000, p. 30). Images of this ideal have become increasingly common in the media. For example, compared to 25 years ago, men are now more often bare chested in magazines, in accord with increased sexual objectification of male bodies in mainstream advertising (Rohlinger, 2002). Repeated exposure to images of unrealistically muscular male ideals may cause men to feel insecure about their own bodies, parallel to the way in which exposure to images of unrealistically thin models promotes body dissatisfaction among girls.

The purpose of the present experiment was to examine the impact of televised images of idealised male attractiveness, in addition to female attractiveness, on adolescent body image. Effects on the underlying process, and individual differences in reaction, were also examined. Social comparison theory (Festinger, 1954) would suggest that the mechanism by which media exposure influences body image is appearance-related social comparison. Specifically, . . . viewing television, or reading magazines, prompts individuals to evaluate their own appearance by comparison to the salient and highly attractive models who pervade such media. Because this process leads most individuals to find themselves wanting, such upward social comparison produces a negative evaluation of one's own physical appearance, resulting in a state-like increase in body dissatisfaction.

In addition there are likely to be stable individual differences in comparison tendency relating to appearance (Wood, 1989). Such differences might predict who engages in "state" appearance-related social comparison to media images, and is therefore most vulnerable to the media's effect on body image. Recent evidence suggests girls are more likely to engage in appearance-related social comparison than boys (Jones, 2001). Moreover, individuals who have a trait-like tendency to engage in appearance-related social comparison or who are more strongly invested in their appearance, sometimes referred to as appearance schematics, may be particularly likely to engage in appearance comparison to media images. We propose that these stable individual difference variables (e.g., trait social comparison, appearance schematicity, and gender) interact with characteristics of the media image (e.g., salience of the model's attractiveness) to predict when media exposure will prompt appearance-related comparison and increased body dissatisfaction.

To date this perspective has been investigated only for women and girls. . . . We believe this perspective is equally applicable to an understanding of men's and boys' body image. The present study used a 2 × 2 between subjects experimental design to investigate the effects of commercial condition (thin ideal, muscular ideal, non-appearance control) and instructional set (appearance-focus, distracter) on boys' and girls' appearance-related social comparison and state body dissatisfaction. . . . It was predicted that boys (girls) would report greater body dissatisfaction and appearance comparison after viewing muscular-ideal (thin-ideal) commercials than non-appearance commercials, and that adolescents high on trait social comparison and appearance schematicity would be most strongly affected.

Method

Participants

The participants were 595 adolescent students (310 girls, 285 boys [, mean age 14.3 years)] . . . of medium socio-economic status. . . . Participants were [randomly] allocated to the thin-ideal, muscular-ideal, or non-appearance commercial condition by . . . class group ($n = 42$), and were randomly allocated to the instructional set conditions on an individual basis. This procedure resulted in a total of 153 girls in the thin-ideal commercial condition, 157 girls in the non-appearance commercial condition, 146 boys in the muscular-ideal commercial condition, and 139 boys in the non-appearance commercial condition.

Materials

State Mood and Body Dissatisfaction

A number of visual analogue scales (VAS) were used as measures of body dissatisfaction and mood. Participants were asked to indicate how they feel "right now" on a series of four mood dimensions: "Happy"; "Worried"; "Confident"; and "Angry"; and four dimensions of body satisfaction: "Fat"; "Strong"; "Dissatisfied (unhappy) with weight and shape" and "Dissatisfied (unhappy) with overall appearance." Each participant completed the VAS on two occasions: 5 min before commercial viewing and immediately after commercial viewing. . . .

Three of the four body dissatisfaction VAS were significantly intercorrelated . . . and so were combined to form a composite state body dissatisfaction variable. . . . Intercorrelations between the four mood VAS were also significant . . . and so were combined to form a composite mood variable (happy and confident were reverse coded, such that higher scores reflect greater negative affect). . . . The composite state body dissatisfaction and negative mood variables were significantly positively correlated. . . .

State Appearance Comparison

A series of self-report items . . . assessed appearance-related social comparison during commercial viewing. Participants were asked to use a Likert scale ranging from $1 = not\ at\ all$ to $7 = very\ much$ to indicate what they had thought about while viewing the commercials. The five items assessed how much they: (1) thought about the qualities of the commercials; (2) thought about the effectiveness of the commercials; (3) thought about the attractiveness of the people in the commercials; (4) compared their own appearance to the actors in the commercials; and (5) wanted to be like the actors in the commercials. Questions 2 and 3 served as a manipulation check of the instructional set which asked participants to rate the "effectiveness of the commercials" (Question 2) or the "attractiveness of actors in the commercials" (Question 3). Responses to Question 4 formed the single-item state appearance comparison variable.

Appearance Schematicity

The Appearance Schemas Inventory (ASI) (Cash & Labarge, 1996) was used to measure appearance schematicity. Using a five-point Likert scale ranging from $1 = strongly\ disagree$ to $5 = strongly\ agree$, respondents indicate their level of agreement with 14 statements (e.g., "What I look like is an important part of who I am"), . . . such that high scores reflect higher appearance schematicity. . . .

Trait Social Comparison

The Physical Appearance Comparison Scale (PACS) (Thompson et al., 1991) measures the degree to which individuals tend to compare their appearance with others. Participants indicate their agreement with five statements (e.g., "In social situations, I compare my figure to the figure of other people") using a five-point scale ranging from 1 = *never* to 5 = *always*. . . . Both trait social comparison and appearance schematicity were measured approximately 15 min after participants completed the dependent measures.

Experimental Manipulation: Videotape Stimulus

Three sets of video stimulus materials were compiled, each containing 18 television commercials. [The first set (thin-ideal commercials)] . . . contained female actors who "epitomise societal ideals of thinness and attractiveness" for women. . . . The second set . . . (muscular-ideal commercials) . . . contained images of men who epitomise societal ideals of muscularity and attractiveness. . . . The third set of commercials contained no actors who epitomised either the thin ideal for women or the muscular ideal for men. To ensure that these commercials (control condition) were of equal interest to viewers, they were matched to the first two sets on both effectiveness and product category.

[A pilot tape of 145] commercials were collected from Australian primetime television [and were tested] according to the following criteria: (1) "to what extent do the actors epitomise the current thin ideal for women?" (2) "to what extent do the actors epitomise the current muscular-attractiveness ideal for men?" and (3) "how effective is the commercial?" [The] 15 commercials that most epitomised the muscular ideal for men were chosen first [followed by the] 15 commercials that most epitomised the thin ideal for women. . . . [Finally] 15 commercials that contained women and men of "normal" appearance were matched to these commercial sets. . . . A further three non-appearance commercials were selected and included in all three commercial sets to help disguise the purpose of the study.

Experimental Manipulation: Instructional Set

Instructions for viewing the commercials were manipulated using a commercial rating task. Half the participants were asked to rate the attractiveness of the actors (appearance focus condition) in each commercial. . . . In contrast, the other half of participants (distracter condition) were asked to rate the overall effectiveness of each commercial. . . .

Results

The Effect of Television Commercials on Girls' and Boys' Body Dissatisfaction

The results [showed] significant main effects of gender, $F(1, 586) = 25.20$, $p < 0.001$, . . . commercial condition, $F(1, 586) = 5.34$, $p < 0.05$, . . . and instructional set, $F(1, 586) = 11.87$, $p < 0.05$. . . . The appearance focus instructions produced more body dissatisfaction than the distracter instructions. The main effects of gender and commercial condition were modified by a significant Gender × Commercial condition interaction, $F(1, 586) = 12.26$, $p < 0.001$. . . . As predicted, girls viewing thin-ideal commercials had significantly greater body dissatisfaction ($M = 32.7$) than those viewing the non-appearance commercials ($M = 27.7$), $F(1, 307) = 16.08$, $p < 0.001$. . . . In contrast, boys in the muscular-ideal condition did not report greater body dissatisfaction ($M = 25.1$) than boys in the non-appearance condition ($M = 26.1$), $F(1, 282) < 1$, $p > 0.05$. There were no further significant two- or three-way interactions. . . .

The Effect of Television Commercials on Girls' and Boys' State Mood

. . . [The results showed] that girls ($M = 23.5$) reported greater negative mood than boys ($M = 20.3$), $F(1, 586) = 16.46$, $p < 0.001$, . . . and that girls and boys in the ideal appearance condition reported significantly greater negative mood ($M = 23.1$) than girls and boys in the non-appearance condition ($M = 20.7$), $F(1, 586) = 9.98$, $p < 0.01$. . . . There were no further significant effects. . . .

The Effect of Television Commercials on Girls' and Boys' Appearance Comparison

[Results] revealed a main effect of gender whereby, irrespective of experimental condition, girls engaged in greater appearance comparison ($M = 2.51$, $SD = 1.70$) than boys ($M = 2.07$, $SD = 1.35$), $F(1, 583) = 14.38$, $p < .001$. . . . There was also a significant main effect of commercial condition whereby participants in the ideal appearance condition engaged in greater appearance comparison ($M = 2.72$) than participants in the non-appearance condition ($M = 1.88$), $F(1, 583) = 45.81$, $p < 0.001$. . . . But the main effects of gender and commercial condition should be interpreted in light of a significant Gender × Commercial condition interaction, $F(1, 183) = 9.20$, $p < 0.01$. . . . [Idealized] appearance commercials led to greater appearance comparison for girls than for boys, $F(1, 296) = 17.39$, $p < 0.001$, . . . but . . . girls and boys did not differ in the non-appearance condition, $F(1, 291) < 1$, $p > 0.05$. There was no significant main effect of instructional set, . . . nor significant interaction of instructional set with either gender or commercial condition. . . .

Trait Social Comparison and Appearance Schematicity as Moderating Variables

Appearance schematicity and trait social comparison were highly correlated for both girls, $r = 0.68$, . . . and boys, $r = 0.60$. . . . Thus, the two scales were averaged to form a single appearance investment variable. [Analysis] showed that girls reported greater appearance investment . . . than boys ($t(589) = 5.28$, $p < .001$). . . . [Participants] were then divided into tertiles based on their appearance investment score. Participants in the low appearance investment group (102 girls and 125 boys) scored between 1 and 2.24, participants in the medium group scored (98 girls and 101 boys) between 2.25 and 2.99, and participants in the high investment group (103 girls and 54 boys) scored between 3.00 and 5.00.
    . . . The results for body dissatisfaction show a significant main effect of gender, $F(1, 570) = 22.19$, $p < 0.001$, . . . commercial condition, $F(1, 570) = 6.33$,

$p < 0.05$, . . . and appearance investment, $F(2, 570) = 9.07$, $p < 0.001$, . . . and a significant Gender $\times$ Commercial condition interaction, $F(2, 570) = 7.65$, $p < 0.01$. . . . There were no other significant [interactions]. A second ANCOVA for mood showed a significant main effect of gender, $F(1, 570) = 10.84$, $p < 0.001$, . . . and commercial condition, $F(1, 570) = 8.09$, $p < 0.01$, . . . but not appearance investment. . . .

Lastly, . . . results [showed] a significant main effect of gender, $F(1, 567) = 6.36$, $p < 0.05$, . . . commercial condition, $F(1, 567) = 53.32$, $p < 0.001$, . . . and appearance investment, $F(2, 567) = 50.10$, $p < 0.001$, . . . and significant two-way interactions between Gender and Commercial condition, $F(2, 567) = 6.41$, $p < 0.05$, . . . and Appearance investment and Commercial condition, $F(2, 567) = 7.24$, $p < 0.001$. . . . [Participants] high on appearance investment reported greater appearance-related social comparison with the commercials than participants in the medium and low appearance investment groups. . . . [This] effect was larger in the ideal condition . . . than in the non-appearance condition. . . .

Discussion

The present study has replicated the results of previous research for adolescent girls. As predicted, exposure to thin-ideal commercials led to significantly greater body dissatisfaction and negative affect among girls than non-appearance commercials. Although the effect sizes were only small, the results are consistent with the conclusion that exposure to thin-ideal media has a small and reliable negative effect on girls.

But the main purpose of the study was to examine the effect of idealized images of male attractiveness on adolescent boys, which has been largely neglected in previous research. The results show that muscular-ideal television commercials had only a limited impact on boys' body image, and on average, exposure to muscular-ideal commercials did not lead to increased body dissatisfaction. This finding was in contrast to some previous studies that found a negative impact of muscular-ideal magazine images on college-aged men (Leit et al., 2002). It could be that males do not develop a vulnerability to muscular-ideal media images until late adolescence or early adulthood, perhaps due to developmental changes in the salience of muscularity concerns.

A second important purpose of the study was to examine the role of social comparison processes for understanding the media's impact. While exposure to thin-ideal and muscular-ideal commercials did lead to increased appearance comparison, this effect was stronger for girls. These results suggest that, in general, girls seem to process self-related appearance information more deeply and more automatically than boys. . . .

Overall the results suggest that the media's immediate impact on body image is both stronger and more normative for girls than boys. This pattern of results reflects the general pattern of gender differences in the body image literature (Levine & Smolak, 2002), suggesting that boys' body image experiences mirror those of girls but are typically less prevalent, and when present, less severe.

In summary, the present results suggest that unrealistic ideals of beauty in the media are an important source of social comparison, and a possible cause of body dissatisfaction among certain girls and boys. It remains unclear how these short-lasting effects might generalize to real world media exposure. However, as a whole, the results support the usefulness of social comparison theory, which proposes appearance comparison as an underlying process by which the media can increase body dissatisfaction, and appearance schematic-ity/trait social comparison as explanations as to why some adolescents are more vulnerable than others to the media's immediate effect. . . .

References

Ackard, D. M., & Peterson, C. B. (2001). Association between puberty and disor-dered eating, body image, and other psychological variables, *International Journal of Eating Disorders 29,* 187–194.

Botta, R. A. (2003). For your health? The relationship between magazine reading and adolescents' body image and eating disturbances. *Sex Roles, 48,* 389–399.

Cash T. F., & Labarge, A. S. (1996). Development of the appearance schemas inventory: A new cognitive body image assessment. *Cognitive Therapy and Research, 20,* 37–50.

Festinger, L. (1954). A theory of social comparison processes. *Human Relations, 7,* 117–140.

Hofshire, L. J., & Greenberg, B. S. (2002). Media's impact on adolescents' body dissatisfaction. In J. D. Brown, J. R. Steele & K. W. Walsh-Childers, (Eds.), *Sexual teens, sexual media: Investigating media's influence on adolescent sexuality.* New Jersey: Erlbaum.

Jones, D. (2001). Social comparison and body image: Attractiveness comparisons to models and peers among adolescent girls and boys. *Sex Roles, 45,* 645–664.

Leit, R. A., Pope H. G., Jr., & Gray, J. J. (2002). Cultural expectations of muscu-larity in men: The evolution of Playgirl centerfolds, *International Journal of Eating Disorders, 29,* 90–93.

Levine M. P., & Smolak, L. (2002). Body image development in adolescence. In T. F. Cash & T. Pruzinsky (Eds.), *Body image: A handbook of theory, research, and clinical practice* (pp. 74–82). New York: Guilford Press.

Pope, H. G., Phillips, K. A., & Olivardia, R. (2000). *The Adonis complex: The secret crisis of male body obsession.* New York: Free Press.

Ricciardelli, L. A., & McCabe, M. P. (2001). Children's body image concerns and eating disturbance: A review of the literature. *Clinical Psychology Review, 21,* 325–344.

Rohlinger, D. A. (2002). Eroticizing men: Cultural influences on advertising and male objectification. *Sex Roles, 46,* 61–74.

Thompson, J. K., Heinberg, L. J., & Tantleff, S. T. (1991). The physical appear-ance comparison scale (PACS). *The Behavior Therapist, 14,* 174.

Wood, J. V. (1989). Theory and research concerning social comparisons of personal attributes. *Psychological Bulletin, 106,* 231–248.

POSTSCRIPT

Do Boys Worry about an Ideal Body Image as Much as Girls Do?

Donald McCreary and Doris Sasse examined drive for muscularity and drive for thinness among a sample of adolescent boys and girls. They found the drive for muscularity to be similar to the drive for thinness in that both had detrimental physical as well as psychological consequences. Like drive for thinness in girls and women, drive for muscularity was a body image disorder in men and boys and was associated with lower levels of self-esteem and depression. As expected, the drive for muscularity was stronger in boys than girls and was unrelated to drive for thinness, indicating that adolescents do not have a drive for both simultaneously.

Hargreaves and Tiggemann examined the effects of ideal body images in commercials on adolescent girls and boys. Commercials included the thin ideal for women, and the muscular ideal for men. After viewing the commercials, body dissatisfaction increased, and appearance comparison was stronger for girls than for boys, suggesting stronger body image vulnerability for girls.

The above studies provide evidence for the consistent findings examining body image concerns for girls; however, they also provide evidence for the mixed findings with respect to body image concerns among boys. It could be the female ideal is more prevalent in society, resulting in stronger correlations between body satisfaction and psychological well-being for girls. Boys may be as anxious but are not as comfortable expressing their dissatisfaction. This could explain the findings by Hargreaves and Tiggemann as well as those reported by McCabe and Ricciardelli (2004; 2005) indicating that girls experience higher levels of body dissatisfaction than boys. McCabe and Ricciardelli further argue that age may play a part. Specifically, they found that, opposite of girls, as boys progressed through adolescence, they became less concerned with body importance and therefore were less likely to engage in either weight loss or muscle-building strategies. Perhaps developmental age should be examined in more detail when comparing boys and girls body image concerns.

As for the McCreary and Sasse findings, the relationship between drive for muscularity and body image dissatisfaction can be further explained by the Jones and Crawford (2005) model of body dissatisfaction in males. Essentially, they report that weight and muscularity concerns have distinct pathways to body dissatisfaction. The "weight-body dissatisfaction" pathway indicates that males with the highest BMIs (i.e., significantly heavier boys) are more likely to attribute body dissatisfaction to weight and dieting concerns, whereas the "muscularity-body dissatisfaction" pathway indicates that males with lower BMIs (significantly lighter boys) are more concerned about muscle-weight–gaining behaviours. Jones and Crawford conclude that BMI (both lower and higher BMI groups) plays a significant role in predicting body satisfaction for boys. If studies include BMI as a variable, perhaps stronger correlations will be found between body image satisfaction and psychological well-being for boys.

In summary, it appears the mixed findings might be explained in terms of two moderating variables: age and BMI. Younger boys and those with either significantly low or significantly high BMIs may be as vulnerable as girls when it comes to body image dissatisfaction.

References/Further Readings

Jones, D. C., & Crawford, J. K. (2005). Adolescent boys and body image: Weight and muscularity concerns as dual pathways to body dissatisfaction. *Journal of Youth and Adolescence, 34*, 629–636.

McCabe, M. P., & Ricciardelli, L. A. (2001). Body image and body change techniques among young adolescent boys. *European Eating Disorders Review, 9*, 335–347.

McCabe, M. P., & Ricciardelli, L. A. (2004). A longitudinal study of pubertal timing and extreme body change behaviors among adolescent boys and girls. *Adolescence, 39*, 145–166.

McCabe, M. P., & Ricciardelli, L. A. (2005). A prospective study of pressures from parents, peers, and the media on extreme weight change behaviors among adolescent boys and girls. *Behaviour Research and Therapy, 43*, 653–668.

McCreary, D. P., & Sasse, D. K. (2002). Gender differences in high school students' dieting behavior and their correlates. *International Journal of Men's Health, 1*, 195.

Ricciardelli, L. A., & McCabe, M. P. (2003). Sociocultural and individual influences on muscle gain and weight loss strategies among adolescent boys and girls. *Psychology in the Schools, 40*, 209–224.

Tomori, M., & Rus-Makovec, M. (2000). Eating behaviour, depression, and self-esteem in high school students. *Journal of Adolescent Health, 26*, 361–367.

On the Internet . . .

sexualityandu.ca

This Web site, administered by the Society of Obstetricians and Gynaecologists of Canada, contains resources for youth, parents, teachers, and health professionals. It provides information on contraception, sexually transmitted infections, drugs, and sexual orientation.

http://www.sexualityandu.ca

Contraception Online

This Web site is sponsored by the Baylor College of Medicine and is an online educational resource for health care providers and educators seeking latest information on reproductive health, family planning, and contraception.

http://www.contraceptiononline.org/

Oral Sex

The University Health Center at the University of Georgia has dedicated this Web site to provide facts on oral sex and its related sexually transmitted diseases.

http://www.uhs.uga.edu/sexualhealth/oral_sex.html

AVERT

AVERT is an international HIV and AIDS charity with the aim of averting HIV and AIDS worldwide. This Web site provides tools for HIV/AIDS and sex education. AVERT also provides booklets, pamphlets, and other materials on HIV/AIDS.

http://www.avert.org/educate.htm

National Campaign to Prevent Teen Pregnancy

The goal of the National Campaign to Prevent Teen Pregnancy is to reduce the rate of teen pregnancy by one-third between 2006 and 2015. This Web site provides facts and statistics on teen pregnancy and the resources needed to prevent pregnancy.

http://www.teenpregnancy.org/

Focus Adolescent Services

This Web site provides facts and raises awareness of teen sexual behaviours. It is run by Focus Adolescent Services, which is an Internet clearinghouse of information and resources on teen and family issues.

http://www.focusas.com/SexualBehavior.html

Sexual Orientation: Science, Education, and Policy

Dr. Gregory Herek is an internationally recognized authority on sexual prejudice, hate crimes, and AIDS stigma. This Web site provides factual information to promote the use of scientific knowledge for education and public policy related to sexual orientation and HIV/AIDS.

http://psychology.ucdavis.edu/rainbow/index.html

PART 2

Sex and Sexuality

A very important part of an adolescent's development is sexuality. Unfortunately, many textbooks regarding adolescents will gloss over the topics of sex and sexuality of youth because of the controversial nature of these topics. Learning about sex and sexuality is of critical importance to youth. Also, developing sexual and romantic relationships with peers is considered a critical part of youth development. Adolescence is a time when sexual identity is explored and formed. This part examines seven key issues surrounding sexuality and adolescence.

- Should Adolescents Get Comprehensive Sex Education Outside the Home?
- Should Adolescents Have Easy Access to Condoms in Schools?
- Is There Cause for Concern About an "Oral Sex Crisis" for Teens?
- Is Comprehensive Sex Education for Adolescents Too Liberal?
- Does Sex on TV Negatively Impact Adolescent Sexuality?
- Does a Traditional or "Strong" Double Standard with Respect to Sexual Behavior Exist Among Adolescents?
- Is Female Sexual Orientation More Fluid than Male Sexual Orientation During Adolescence?

ISSUE 5

Should Adolescents Get Comprehensive Sex Education outside the Home?

YES: Angela D. Weaver, et al., from "Sexual Health Education at School and at Home: Attitudes and Experiences of New Brunswick Parents," *Canadian Journal of Human Sexuality* (Spring 2002)

NO: Robert E. Rector, Melissa G. Pardue, and Shannan Martin, from "What Do Parents Want Taught in Sex Education Programs?" *Backgrounder: The Heritage Foundation* (January 28, 2004)

ISSUE SUMMARY

YES: Results from a survey conducted by Angela Weaver, an instructor at the University of New Brunswick, and colleagues indicated that the majority of parents support the commencement of sexual health education in elementary school or middle school. Further, parents supported the inclusion of a broad range of sexual health topics at some point in the curriculum, including birth control and safe sex practices.

NO: Robert Rector and colleagues from The Heritage Foundation, a conservative think tank in Washington, D.C., report strong parental support for abstinence programs in schools. Further, Rector, et al. report that parents strongly oppose "comprehensive sex–ed" curricula that teaches teens that sex is okay as long as contraception is used.

Sex education in schools is a hotly debated issue. It is not necessarily that people think sex education should not be taught in schools; in fact, a recent representative U.S. survey by the Kaiser Family Foundation (2004) found that 90 percent of the general population felt it was important for schools to include sexuality education in their curriculum, while only 7 percent thought that sex education should not be taught in schools. This study also demonstrated that there was largely agreement about what should be taught within this curriculum; for example, pregnancy and birth, sexually transmitted infections (STIs) and HIV/AIDS, contraception, and sexual relationship negotiation were endorsed as appropriate topics for school sexual education curriculum by over 90 percent of the general public.

If there is all this agreement among people, what is the problem? The controversy lies not in *should* sex education be taught, per se, nor in *what* should be taught; rather, the debate is *how* the topics should be presented and weighted within the curriculum.

More conservative organizations and special interest groups, such as The Heritage Foundation (located in Washington, D.C.) or Focus on the Family, argue strongly in favor of more conservative curricula. For example, The Heritage Foundation researchers support "authentic abstinence" programs—those that tend to devote around half or more of their curricula materials to abstinence topics including healthy relationships and marriage (i.e., typically postponing sex until one is in a heterosexual marriage). These abstinence advocates object to comprehensive sex ed programs (also described as "abstinence plus" curricula) as they focus substantially more attention on contraception and disease prevention (i.e., HIV and STIs) relative to teen sexual abstinence. They criticize the comprehensive programs as presenting too simplistic a perspective when they do discuss abstinence.

In contrast, more liberal organizations and think tanks, such as Planned Parenthood, ETR Associates, and SIECUS/SIECCAN (Sex Information and Education Councils of the United States and Canada, respectively) argue strongly in favor of more liberal sex education curriculum. They view comprehensive sex education programs as superior to abstinence-only programs because the latter type of program contains inaccurate information and are ineffective at achieving their goals. Meanwhile, comprehensive sex education programs tend to be more effective, based on empirical research.

On both the conservative and liberal sides of this debate, the authors write about what the general public and parents want taught to students in schools. For example, a commonly cited finding by conservative writers was that a Zogby International poll (2004), commissioned by the conservative Coalition for Adolescent Sexual Health, found that 73 percent of parents support abstinence education, 75 percent opposed condom-based education, and 61 percent oppose comprehensive sex education programs. In contrast, liberal writers often cite a report (discussed above; conducted by Princeton Survey Research Associates and commissioned by National Public Radio, Henry J. Kaiser Family Foundation, and Kennedy School of Government) entitled *Sex Education in America* (2004), that found that 65 to 72 percent of parents were in favor of federal funding of comprehensive sexuality education programs and that most fail to support current government policy of funding abstinence-only programs (i.e., with only 24 to 32 percent of parents endorsing the governmental abstinence-only funding). These results seem sharply in contrast to one another. The following selections by Rector, Pardue, and Martin (from The Heritage Foundation) and Weaver, Byers, Sears, Cohen, and Randall (sexology researchers from the University of New Brunswick) are illustrative of this debate.

YES

Angela D. Weaver et al.

Sexual Health Education at School and at Home: Attitudes and Experiences of New Brunswick Parents

Introduction

Adolescents rate sex education as one of their most important educational needs. However, sexual health education (SHE) is often a controversial topic, with perhaps no other subject sparking as much debate. School administrators have identified fear of parental or community opposition as major barriers to the provision of SHE. Similarly, teachers in New Brunswick have identified anticipated reactions from parents to the inclusion of specific topics as the greatest barrier to their willingness to teach SHE. Are parents in fact opposed to school-based SHE as often feared or do parents support the provision of SHE at school? The answer to this question is important because parental support is strongly associated with the success of SHE programs. Further, discussion of sexuality in the home is an important component of students' overall SHE, and school-based SHE can make it easier for parents to discuss sexuality with their child. The purpose of this study was to evaluate parents' attitudes toward and experiences with SHE at school and at home, including their ideas about the timing and content of the sexual health curriculum and their involvement in providing SHE to their children.

Attitudes Toward Sexual Health Education

Although a vocal minority can create the impression that parental objections to school-based SHE are widespread, research has consistently found that parents support SHE at school. For example, 95% of parents in one rural school district in Ontario agreed that SHE should be provided in school. The majority of parents (82%) felt that SHE should begin in the primary grades and continue through to high school. Similarly, 95% of parents of high school students in rural Nova Scotia supported school-based sexuality education and 98% of urban Ontario parents were in favour of AIDS education in the schools.

As no large-scale study has been undertaken to assess New Brunswick parents' attitudes toward SHE, it is unclear whether results of studies conducted in other provinces can be generalized to New Brunswick. It is important to

From *The Canadian Journal of Human Sexuality*, vol. 11, no. 1, Spring 2002, pp. 19–30. Copyright © 2002 by SIECCAN. Reprinted by permission. Note: The complete text of this article contains many references to specific studies described. The interested individual should refer to the original publication for these extensive citations. These references have been omitted here in the interest of brevity.

have information regarding the attitudes of New Brunswick parents as parental attitudes have the potential to affect educational policy, curriculum, and procedures in this province. Therefore, the first goal of this study was to assess parents' general attitudes toward SHE in the schools, including which topics they believe are important to their children's SHE.

Although the vast majority of parents support SHE, they do not necessarily share a common vision of the nature, content, and timing of an ideal SHE curriculum. Thus, they may agree that SHE should be provided in school, but they may disagree about how important it is to include some of the more "controversial" topics, such as masturbation or sexual orientation, or about the appropriate grade level for introducing specific topics. For example, [one study] found that the majority of parents felt that all of the sexual health topics listed in their survey should be included at some point in the SHE curriculum, although parents' views about the appropriate grade level for introducing each topic varied depending on the topic. However, . . . parents' opinions about a number of important topics, such as masturbation, correct names for genitals, and wet dreams [were not assessed]. Therefore, a second goal of this study was to investigate at what grade levels parents want various sexual health topics to be introduced using a more comprehensive list of sexual health topics.

Sexual Health Education at Home

Most parents believe that parents and schools should share responsibility for SHE. For example, . . . most parents identified parents (88%), health professionals (88%), and teachers (77%) as appropriate people to provide SHE in the school and community. Similarly, in a study of 406 students in grades 7–12 in rural Ontario, students identified family and school as their two preferred sources of sexual health information.

However, the extent to which parents are actually providing quality SHE to their children is unclear. Respondents rarely identify their parents as a primary source of sexual health information. Further, in one study, only 61% of students felt that their parents had done a good job providing them with SHE. Similarly, [another] found that 70% of the parents . . . surveyed felt that most parents do not give children the SHE they need. Although 73% of the parents surveyed felt that they had provided adequate SHE for their children, [other research] found that only 52% of parents had confidence in their own efforts to provide SHE, and only 15% had confidence in other parents.

Unfortunately, these studies did not ask parents to provide further information on the nature of the SHE they had provided. Thus, their results provide a global assessment of SHE in the home, yet tell us little about what specific subjects parents are discussing with their children or how comprehensive their discussions are. For example, there may be topics that parents feel more comfortable with and subsequently cover in more detail. Conversely, there may be topics that parents typically do not discuss with their children. Therefore, a third goal of the study was to assess what topics parents are discussing with their child at home and in what level of detail.

If parents are not providing quality SHE at home, it is important to know how they can be encouraged to provide a level of education that will promote positive sexual health outcomes for their children. There are a number of factors that may prevent parents from providing adequate SHE in the home. Many parents are concerned that they do not possess sufficient sexual health knowledge to educate their children. Further, they report that they do not know how much information is appropriate for various age levels. The final goal of the study, then, was to ask parents what could be done to support their efforts to provide SHE at home.

Method

Participants

In total, 9,533 surveys were distributed to parents of children in grades K–8 in 30 New Brunswick schools; 4,206 completed surveys were returned. Parents who received multiple copies because they had more than one child enrolled in grades K–8 in the selected schools were asked to complete only one copy and return the extra indicating that they had already completed the survey. . . .

Measure

Parents completed a survey entitled "New Brunswick Parents' Ideas About Sexual Health Education" which was divided into six parts. Part A elicited parents' general opinions, rated on 5-point Likert scales, about SHE in the schools, such as whether SHE should be provided in the schools, whether the school and parents should share responsibility for the provision of SHE, and parents' perceptions of the quality of the SHE that their children have received in school. They also indicated the grade level at which they thought SHE should begin (K–3, 4–5, 6–8, 9–12, or "There should be no sexual health education in schools"). Part B asked parents to indicate, on a 5-point scale ranging from 1 (not at all important) to 5 (extremely important), how important it is to include each of 10 topics in a sexual health curriculum. Parents were asked this question generally, and were not asked to respond with regard to a specific child. In Part C, parents indicated the grade level at which schools should begin covering each of 26 sexual health topics (K–3, 4–5, 6–8, 9–12, or "This topic should not be included"). Next, in Part D, parents were asked to evaluate the SHE they had provided to their children. Parents were provided with the same list of 10 general sexual health topics as in Part B and were asked to indicate on a scale from 1 (not at all) to 4 (in a lot of detail) how thoroughly they felt they had discussed each topic. They responded to this question with respect to their oldest child who was in grades K–8. In Part E, parents provided demographic information (gender, age, education level, and community type).

In Part F of the survey, parents were asked three open-ended questions. The first question invited parents to comment on SHE in the schools. They were then asked to indicate how the New Brunswick Department of Education or their child's school could support their efforts to provide SHE at home. Finally, they were asked whether they would be interested in attending a workshop on SHE if their child's school was to offer one and what topics they would like to see included in this type of workshop. To evaluate parents' responses to the open-ended questions, 1137 surveys (37%) were randomly selected from the 4206 completed questionnaires. In total, 547 of the 1137 questionnaires (48%) contained a response to one or more of these open-ended questions. Content analysis, commonly used in survey research to evaluate responses to open-ended questions, was used to evaluate parents' responses to these items. One of the authors reviewed all responses to each of these items and then read and reread the responses until patterns emerged. These patterns were labelled as themes. Because similar themes emerged for the first two open-ended questions, responses to these items were analyzed together.

Procedure

This study was conducted in the spring of 2000 as part of a larger project that also assessed teacher and student attitudes toward SHE. Thirty-three elementary and/or middle schools were selected geographically from around the province so that an approximately equal number of parents would have children attending rural and urban schools. Thirty of the 33 targeted schools agreed to participate.

Parents were informed about the survey by means of a notice in the school newsletter and/or a voice mail message system. Classroom teachers distributed the surveys, sealed in privacy envelopes, to students in their class, with the request that they take them home to be filled out by their parents. Surveys were returned to the school with the child, and then returned to the researchers by the school.

Results

Attitudes Toward Sexual Health Education

The vast majority of parents were in support of school-based SHE, with 94% of parents either agreeing (40%) or strongly agreeing (54%) that SHE should be provided in school. Almost all parents (95%) felt that both the school and parents have a role to play in SHE, with 33% agreeing and 62% strongly agreeing that the school and parents should share this responsibility.

Approximately equal numbers of parents reported that SHE should begin in grades K–3, 4–5, and 6–8 (33%, 32%, and 32% respectively). Thus, 65% of parents felt that SHE should begin in elementary school and 97% felt that it should begin in elementary or middle school. Only 1% of parents reported that SHE should not be provided in school. In order to determine whether parental characteristics were associated with attitudes towards SHE, parents' age, level of education, community type (rural versus urban), and age of their oldest child were correlated with these three items. . . . None of these characteristics significantly predicted parental attitudes towards SHE.

The median of parents' responses shows that parents rated each of the 10 listed topics as important to include in a sexual health curriculum. Parents rated personal safety, abstinence, puberty, sexual decision-making, and reproduction as extremely important. They rated sexually transmitted diseases, sexual coercion/assault, birth control methods and safer sex practices, and correct names for genitals as very important to the curriculum. Although parents felt that sexual pleasure/enjoyment was less important than the other nine topics, they still rated it as important overall.

Preferred Grade Level for Introducing Specific Sexual Health Topics

Parents were asked to indicate the grade level at which they thought schools should begin teaching each of 26 sexual health topics. . . . There was strong support for the inclusion of all 26 topics in the curriculum; between 73% and 99% of parents wanted each topic included at some grade level. Further, parents wanted most topics introduced by grades 6–8, and there were several topics that many parents thought should be introduced in elementary school.

The median responses of parents who felt that topics should be included in the curriculum indicated that they wanted personal safety to be introduced in grades K–3. Parents were divided with respect to correct names for genitals, body image, and sexual coercion and sexual assault. The median response suggests that parents wanted these topics introduced in grades 4–5, yet a substantial percentage of parents wanted them introduced earlier (25%–42%).

Parents' median responses for most of the other topics indicated that they felt these topics should be introduced in grades 6–8, with a minority of parents (7% to 46%) wanting them introduced earlier. These topics included: puberty, menstruation, reproduction and birth, being comfortable with the other sex, abstinence, sexually transmitted diseases/AIDS, dealing with peer pressure to be sexually active, teenage pregnancy/parenting, communicating about sex, wet dreams, birth control methods and safer sex practices, sexuality in the media, masturbation, sex as part of a loving relationship, attraction, love, and intimacy, homosexuality, sexual behaviour, teenage prostitution, building equal romantic relationships, sexual problems and concerns, and pornography. However, parents were divided with respect to several of these topics. Although approximately half of parents reported wanting puberty and menstruation to be introduced in grades 6–8, an almost equal percentage of parents wanted them introduced earlier (46% and 44%, respectively). Similarly, median responses suggest that parents want sex as part of a loving relationship as well as attraction, love, and intimacy introduced in grades 6–8, yet a similar percentage wanted these topics introduced in grades 9–12; (44% and 42%, respectively). Sexual pleasure and orgasm was the only topic with a median response indicating that parents wanted it covered in grades 9–12; yet, 41% of parents wanted even this controversial topic introduced earlier in the curriculum.

Topics that more than 10% of parents wanted excluded from the curriculum included wet dreams, sexuality in the media, masturbation, sex as part of a loving relationship, homosexuality, sexual behaviour, teenage prostitution, sexual problems and concerns, pornography, and sexual pleasure and orgasm. It is important to remember that these potentially controversial topics still had the support of the large majority of parents. For example, pornography and sexual pleasure and orgasm drew the highest percentage of parents who felt that these topics should be excluded. Yet, even for these two topics, 73% and 75% of parents, respectively, supported their inclusion in the curriculum.

Sexual Health Education at Home

Only about one-third of parents felt that the SHE they or their partner had provided to their children at home was excellent (9%) or very good (29%). An additional 38% felt that they had done a good job. Almost one-quarter of parents felt that they had done only a fair (19%) or poor (5%) job providing SHE to their children. However, when asked about the level of detail they had provided their oldest child in K–8 on 10 sexual health topics, overall parents indicated they had not discussed any of these topics in a lot of detail. According to the median responses, parents reported discussing only personal safety and correct names for genitals in some detail. In contrast, they reported discussing puberty, reproduction, sexual coercion and assault, sexually transmitted diseases, and abstinence in general terms only. Overall, they had not discussed birth control methods and safer sex practices, sexual decision-making in dating relationships, and sexual pleasure and enjoyment at all.

Because it is likely that parents provide more detailed SHE to their children as they get older, depth of coverage was examined for each of the 10 topics by the child's grade level. . . . [Analyses] revealed significant differences in the depth of coverage of all topics based on the grade level of the child. In general, parents with a child in older grades reported discussing sexual health topics in more detail than parents whose child was in younger grades. Nonetheless, according to the median responses, even parents with children in middle school had not discussed any of the topics in a lot of detail with their child.

Examination of the median responses yielded two patterns. First, there are some topics that parents appear to discuss in greater detail as the child gets older. For example, parents with a child in grades K–3 had not discussed puberty at all, whereas those with a child in 4–5 had discussed it in general terms, and those with a child in 6–8 had discussed it in some detail. For reproduction and sexual coercion and sexual assault, a more detailed discussion appears to come with middle school (some detail) as both parents of early and late elementary students had discussed this topic in general terms only. Similarly, parents with children in elementary school tended not to discuss birth control and safer sex practices, sexually transmitted diseases, abstinence, or sexual decision-making with their children at all, whereas parents with children in middle school had discussed these topics in general terms. Some detail about the correct name for genitals was given to children in grades 4–5 and middle school; early elementary school children had only been told the correct name for genitals in general terms. Second, some topics appear not to be discussed in greater depth as the child gets older—at least until the end of middle school. For example, on average, parents with children in elementary or middle school reported discussing personal safety "in some detail," and sexual pleasure and enjoyment "not at all."

Supporting Parents' Efforts to Provide SHE at Home

Three primary themes emerged from the content analysis of parents' responses to the open-ended questions representing their general comments about SHE in school and suggestions for how their efforts to provide SHE at home could be supported.

Theme #1: Evaluation of current curriculum.   Many parents made evaluative comments, positive and negative, about the current sexual health curriculum. Some parents took the opportunity to indicate strong support for SHE in school.

> Parent 1: *It is extremely important that children learn correct information early. If well-rounded information is provided, sexual education doesn't promote sexual activity. I feel it is gaps in accurate information that leads to experimentation and unwanted consequences. Some kids will experiment with or without knowledge so it is best to prepare them.*

Other parents made negative comments about the sexual health curriculum, such as suggesting that SHE should not be provided in school.

> Parent 2: *I feel sex education should not be taught in schools, because many of the topics would necessarily promote a moral agenda which may not be in keeping with that of the home. I do not believe birth control should be promoted in school, and issues such as homosexuality and relationships have no place in an academic institution. Issues such as avoiding sexual abuse and awareness of sexual coercion are issues of safety, and appropriate to a school health curriculum.*

Some parents suggested ways in which the current SHE curriculum should be expanded whereas other parents suggested ways in which it should be restricted.

> Parent 3: *There should be more updated info. {sic} And at a younger age, not outdated general videos. It should be a course once or twice a week for several weeks.*

> Parent 4: *The present program places too much emphasis on knowing all of the parts of the male and female anatomy. The amount of and level of vocabulary is excessive for middle school.*

Theme #2: Quality of teaching.   Some parents mentioned the teaching methods used for SHE and the importance of the quality of teaching. They indicated that they want their children to have a comfortable and qualified teacher and are concerned that an uncomfortable teacher would impart negative messages. Some parents provided suggestions regarding who should be involved in providing SHE (e.g., a public health nurse) and what training would be important (e.g., in-service training).

> Parent 5: *Make sure the educators are completely comfortable with the topic. When they are uncomfortable the children recognize this and it becomes a giggle session. Not every teacher can teach this, perhaps a special health education teacher is needed.*

Theme #3: Need for support for parents.   Some parents suggested ways in which they could be supported in their efforts to provide SHE to their children. Many expressed interest in attending a SHE workshop and wanted general information on a wide variety of sexual health topics. Some parents indicated that they would like to learn strategies for approaching and discussing sexual health topics with their children at home.

> Parent 6: *Respecting your body. How to help girls not succumb to pressures from boys. How to make sex something normal not hush hush or dirty.*

> Parent 7: *All of the topics, especially how to keep the communication open to our kids so we can discuss these with them.*

Some parents indicated that they would like increased communication with the schools about the SHE their children would be receiving. Parents felt that information on sexuality and suggestions on how to discuss topics with their children could help them respond to questions at home, and they suggested various ways the school could provide such information.

> Parent 8: *I think that it would be **very** beneficial for parents to know the topics that would be discussed before the children are actually exposed to it so that when they come home and start asking questions, we would be prepared for it and can respond to them openly and honestly, without being embarrassed or at a loss for words.*

Parents were asked to indicate whether they would be interested in attending a SHE workshop for parents if it was offered at their child's school. Fifty percent of parents indicated that they would be interested in attending the workshop, 20% were not interested, and 30% were not sure. Parents who indicated that they would be interested in attending a SHE workshop were asked to list the topics that would especially interest them. Of the 569 parents who indicated an interest, 362 parents (64%) commented. Nineteen percent of those parents indicated that they would like general information on *all* topics. Specific topics that parents frequently mentioned include sexually transmitted diseases and AIDS, puberty, menstruation, correct names for genitals, contraception, teen pregnancy, teen relationships, teen sexuality, dating, peer pressure, sexual decision-making, sexual coercion, sexual assault, sexual harassment, and personal safety issues. Almost one-half of parents (45%) expressed a desire to learn strategies for approaching and discussing specific sexual health topics with their children at home, including peer pressure to have sex, how to answer children's questions in a way that is appropriate for their age, and how to communicate about sexual health information in a way that makes their child feel comfortable.

Discussion

The vast majority of parents in New Brunswick support school-based SHE. Ninety-four percent agreed that SHE should be provided in school. This result is consistent with findings of 95% of parents in support of SHE in rural Ontario and 95% in rural Nova Scotia, and suggests that the fears teachers and administrators have of parental and community opposition may reflect the opinions of a small, vocal minority and not the opinions of most parents. Studies like this one can help reduce the fears administrators and teachers have about parental opposition to SHE at school. Themes that emerged from the open-ended questions suggest that some parents would like to see the current SHE curriculum begin earlier and be more comprehensive, while other parents are concerned about children receiving too much information at a young age.

Clearly, most parents want SHE to begin by middle school and many feel that at least some topics should be introduced earlier. In response to the question about the grade level in which age-appropriate SHE should begin, 65% of parents wanted age-appropriate SHE to begin by grades 4–5, and 33% by grades K–3. Thus, it appears that many parents want children equipped with knowledge and skills to keep themselves sexually healthy *before* they begin engaging in sexual relationships. Given that this survey did not provide details about what topics and what depth of coverage would be considered "age-appropriate" SHE at each of these levels, it is possible that some additional parents would support SHE in the younger grades if they knew more about the specific curriculum. Thus, it appears that there is substantial support for introducing SHE in the early elementary grades that, at a minimum, includes personal safety, correct names for genitals, body image, and sexual coercion and sexual assault. However, as there is no consensus as to when in elementary school various topics should be introduced, parents need to be kept informed of the content and rationale for the sexual health curriculum.

Further, parents rated each of 10 sexuality topics as important to the curriculum. This suggests that parents want a comprehensive SHE program that includes a full range of topics that go beyond biology, such as sexual decision-making and sexual pleasure and enjoyment. There was also support for including a broad range of sexual health topics in middle school, including some that may be considered controversial, such as masturbation, homosexuality, and sexual pleasure and orgasm. It appears that parents recognize and support their children's need for information about a broad range of sexual health issues. They also appear to support a developmental approach to SHE in which children learn the foundations of sexual health (e.g., correct names for genitals) in elementary school and, as they develop, new knowledge is introduced which builds on this base.

Parents showed support for a comprehensive SHE curriculum that starts in elementary school and thus identified a wide range of topics as important. This endorsement may reflect an awareness that parents alone are unlikely to provide comprehensive SHE at home. Almost all parents (95%) reported that the school and parents should *share* responsibility for SHE provision. However, very few parents felt that they had done an excellent job of providing SHE and few parents had discussed sexual health topics in detail with their children. While parents tended to discuss many sexual health topics with their children in greater depth as they grow up, even parents with children in middle school had not discussed any of the listed topics in a lot of detail, and some topics (e.g., sexual decision-making, sexual pleasure and enjoyment, sexual transmitted diseases) had been discussed in general terms only or not at all.

Given the variability in the implementation of SHE in schools, and our finding that parents seldom provided detailed information on SHE topics, it seems likely that many students are not receiving the kind of comprehensive and diverse education about sexuality that their parents endorse. It is probable that "safer" topics receive more coverage at home and at school, exposing students to a limited range of sexual health information. For example, parents in this survey reported that they discussed personal safety and correct names for genitals in more detail than birth control methods and safer sex practices. Even parents of students in middle school were more likely to have discussed the biological aspects of reproduction than birth control methods, safer sex, or sexual decision-making. Similarly, New Brunswick teachers reported being more willing to teach topics related to anatomy and physical development and less willing to teach about topics such as masturbation or sexual problems and concerns. These are topics that, traditionally, classroom teachers have not covered, opting instead to stick to the safe biological aspects of sexuality because they feel they have knowledge about, and are comfortable with, these topics. Parents appear to be aware of many teachers' low levels of comfort with some sexual health topics. Although not a focus of this survey, in response to the open-ended questions, a number of parents commented on the importance of teachers being both qualified to teach SHE (i.e., knowledgeable) and comfortable with discussing sexuality if children are to be fully educated about important sexual health issues.

Despite their stated desire to do so, many parents indicated that they are providing little or no SHE to their children. This is consistent with research showing that many students report that their parents have not done a good job providing SHE. It is important to look closely at the reasons why parents are not engaging in such discussions. For example, barriers, such as inadequate knowledge or personal discomfort or anxiety, may be keeping parents from having open discussions about sexual health with their children. Parents indicated two main ways that the schools could support their efforts to provide SHE in the home. First, they would like to have information from schools concerning sexuality in general. Second, they would like to be informed about the education their child will be receiving before they receive it so they will be prepared for questions that may arise at home. Taking steps to address these concerns would help provide parents with the tools they need to initiate sexual health discussions with their children. Many parents indicated an interest in attending a SHE workshop, if their child's school was to offer one. Schools might consider offering workshops for parents that cover a range of sexual health topics. Such workshops should also provide information about how to talk to a child in a way that is age-appropriate and makes the child comfortable.

The results of this study must be considered in light of its limitations. First, although there was a good response rate to the survey, with at least 46% of parents returning completed questionnaires, it may be that parents who did and did not return the survey differ in important ways. As a result, the extent to which the findings of this study can be generalized to all New Brunswick parents or to parents in other regions of Canada is not known. Second, the survey was completed primarily by mothers, so it is not clear how well these results reflect the attitudes and experiences of fathers regarding SHE at school and at home. Third, this study used only the survey method to assess parents' attitudes and experiences. Interviews or focus groups with parents might well have highlighted other salient issues. Finally, the cross-sectional nature of this study limits our understanding of parents' ideas about SHE to one point in time. Longitudinal studies that collect information from parents as their children progress from elementary to middle school may develop a more accurate picture of parents' attitudes and experiences with SHE at school and at home.

Conclusion

This study adds to a growing body of literature documenting Canadian parents' strong support for comprehensive SHE in school starting in elementary school with all topics introduced by middle school. Although most parents would like to have a role in their child's SHE, few are actively discussing sexual health topics in great detail with them. Schools have a role in supporting parental involvement in their children's SHE. Based on parents' own suggestions, there are a number of ways in which this can be accomplished, such as providing parents with sexual health information before it is disseminated to their child and providing information on how to discuss sexual health topics with their child. Involving parents in the school-based SHE their children receive could promote more discussion in the home and help encourage healthy and safe sexual development.

Robert E. Rector, Melissa G. Pardue,
and Shannan Martin

 **NO**

What Do Parents Want Taught in Sex Education Programs?

Debates about sex education have focused on two different approaches: "safe sex" courses, which encourage teens to use contraceptives, especially condoms, when having sex, and abstinence education, which encourages teens to delay sexual activity.

In recent years, advocacy groups such as SIECUS (the Sex Information and Education Council of the United States) and Advocates for Youth have promoted another apparent alternative, entitled "comprehensive sexuality education" or "abstinence plus." These curricula allegedly take a middle position, providing a strong abstinence message while also teaching about contraception. In reality, this claim is misleading. Comprehensive sexuality education curricula contain little or no meaningful abstinence material; they are simply safe-sex programs repackaged under a new, deceptive label.

Abstinence programs teach that:

- Human sexuality is primarily emotional and psychological, not physical, in nature;
- In proper circumstances, sexual activity leads to long term emotional bonding between two individuals; and
- Sexual happiness is inherently linked to intimacy, love, and commitment—qualities found primarily within marriage.

Abstinence programs strongly encourage abstinence during the teen years, and preferably until marriage. They teach that casual sex at an early age not only poses serious threats of pregnancy and infection by sexually transmitted diseases, but also can undermine an individual's capacity to build loving, intimate relationships as an adult. These programs therefore encourage teen abstinence as a preparation and pathway to healthy adult marriage.

By contrast, comprehensive sex-ed curricula focus almost exclusively on teaching about contraception and encouraging teens to use it. These curricula neither discourage nor criticize teen sexual activity as long as "protection" is used. In general, they exhibit an acceptance of casual teen sex and do not encourage teens to wait until they are older to initiate sexual activity. For example, the curricula do not encourage teens to abstain until they have finished high school. "Protected" sex at an early age and sex with many different partners

From *Backgrounder,* no. 1722, January 28, 2004. Copyright © 2004 by The Heritage Foundation. Reprinted by permission. Note: The complete text of this article contains many references to specific studies described. The interested individual should refer to the original publication for these extensive citations. These references have been omitted here in the interest of brevity.

TALKING POINTS

Although the government currently spends at least $4.50 promoting teen use of contraception for every dollar it spends to promote teen abstinence, a recent poll reveals that this contradicts the desires of parents. An overwhelming majority of the parents of teens:

- Show strong (in many cases, nearly unanimous) support for the major themes of abstinence.
- Reject "comprehensive sex-ed" curricula, which teach that teen sex is okay as long as contraception is used.
- Want sex education programs to teach teens to abstain from sex until they are married or in an adult relationship that is close to marriage.
- Believe that sex at an early age, casual sex, and sex with many partners are likely to have harmful consequences, and want their teens to be taught to avoid these behaviors.

are not treated as problems. Sexuality is treated primarily as a physical phenomenon; the main message is to use condoms to prevent the physical problems of sexually transmitted diseases and pregnancy. Comprehensive sex-ed curricula ignore the vital linkages between sexuality, love, intimacy, and commitment. There is no discussion of the idea that sex is best within marriage.

Determining Parental Attitudes Toward Sex-ed Curricula

This paper presents the results of a recent poll on basic issues concerning sex education. The poll questions seek to measure parental support for the themes and values contained in abstinence curricula as well as support for the values embodied in comprehensive sex education.

The data presented are drawn from a survey of parents conducted by Zogby International in December 2003. Zogby conducted telephone interviews with a nationally representative sample of 1,004 parents with children under age 18. Parents were asked 14 questions concerning messages and priorities in sex education; the questions used were designed by Focus on the Family. The margin of error on each question is plus or minus 3.2 percent points. The responses to the questions showed only modest variation based on region, gender of the parent, or race. The poll questions were designed to reflect the major themes of abstinence education. The descriptions of the messages contained in abstinence and comprehensive sex-ed curricula in the following text are based on a forthcoming content analysis of major sex-ed curricula conducted by The Heritage Foundation.

. . . Overall, the poll shows that parents are extremely supportive of the values and messages contained in abstinence programs. By contrast, very few parents support the basic themes of comprehensive sex-ed courses. . . .

"Sex Should Be Linked to Marriage; Delaying Sex until Marriage Is Best"

Abstinence education curricula stress a strong linkage between sex, love, and marriage. The Zogby poll shows strong parental support for this message.

> **Parents want teens to be taught that sexual activity should be linked to marriage. . . .**

Some 47 percent of parents want teens to be taught that "young people should not engage in sexual activity until they are married." Another 32 percent of parents want teens to be taught that "young people should not engage in sexual intercourse until they have, at least, finished high school and are in a relationship with someone they feel they would like to marry."

When these two categories are combined, we see that 79 percent of parents want young people taught that sex should be reserved for marriage or for an adult relationship leading to marriage. Another 12 percent of parents believe that teens should be taught to delay sexual activity until "they have, at least, finished high school." Only 7 percent of parents want teens to be taught that sexual activity in high school is okay as long as teens use contraception.

These parental values are strongly reinforced by abstinence education programs, which teach that sex should be linked to marriage and that it is best to delay sexual activity until marriage. By contrast, comprehensive sex-ed programs send the message that teen sex is okay as long as contraception is used; the underlying permissive values of these programs have virtually no support among parents.

> **Parents want teens to be taught that sex should be linked to love, intimacy, and commitment and that these qualities are most likely to occur in marriage.**

Some 91 percent of parents want teens to be taught this message about sexuality.

This is a predominant theme of all abstinence curricula. By contrast, comprehensive sex-ed programs do not discuss love, intimacy, or commitment and seldom mention marriage. Casual sex is not criticized; sex is presented largely as a physical process; and the main lesson is to avoid the physical threats of pregnancy and disease through proper use of contraception. Comprehensive sex-ed programs do not present sexuality in a way that is acceptable to most parents.

> **Parents want teens to be taught that it is best to delay sex until marriage.**

Some 68 percent of parents want schools to teach teens that "individuals who are not sexually active until marriage have the best chances of marital stability and happiness."

This theme is strongly supported by abstinence programs, all of which urge teens to delay sexual activity until marriage. It is ignored completely by comprehensive sex-ed courses, which do not criticize casual sex and seldom mention marriage.

General Support for Abstinence

The poll shows overwhelming parental support for other abstinence themes as well.

Parents want teens to be taught to abstain from sexual activity during high school years.

Some 91 percent of parents support this message. However, for most parents, this is a minimum standard; 79 percent want a higher standard taught: abstinence until you are married or near marriage.

All abstinence curricula strongly encourage abstinence at least through high school, and preferably until marriage. By contrast, comprehensive sex-ed curricula do not encourage teens to delay sex until they have finished high school; most do not even encourage young people to wait until they are older.

Parents want teens to be taught that abstinence is best.

Some 96 percent of parents support this message.

Abstinence curricula obviously support this theme. Comprehensive sex-ed programs may claim to support this message, but in reality they do not. They teach mainly that abstinence is the "safest" choice, but that teen sex with protection is safe. Their overall message is that abstinence is marginally safer than safe sex. Beyond this, they have little positive to say about abstinence.

"Sex at an Early Age, Sex with Many Partners, and Casual Sex Have Harmful Consequences"

Parents believe that sex at an early age, casual sex, and sex with many partners are likely to have harmful consequences. They want teens to be taught to avoid these behaviors.

Parents want teens to be taught that the younger the age an individual begins sexual activity, the greater the probability of harm.

Some 93 percent of parents want teens taught that "the younger the age an individual begins sexual activity, the more likely he or she is to be infected by sexually transmitted diseases, to have an abortion, and to give birth out-of-wedlock."

Abstinence programs strongly support this message; they teach teens to delay sex until they are older, preferably until they are married. Comprehensive sex-ed programs teach about the threat of unprotected sex, not about the harm caused by sex at an early age. They do not urge young people to delay sex until they are older; voluntary sex at any age is depicted as okay as long as "protection" is used.

Parents want teens taught that teen sexual activity is likely to have psychological and physical effects.

Some 79 percent of parents want teens to be taught this message.

Abstinence curricula clearly teach this message; comprehensive sex-ed curricula do not. Comprehensive sex-ed curricula focus on encouraging condom use; they do not criticize or discourage teen sex as long as "protection" is used.

Parents want schools to teach that teens who are sexually active are more likely to be depressed.

Some 67 percent of teens who have had sexual intercourse regret it and say they wish that they had waited until they were older. (The figure for teen girls is 77 percent). Sexually active teens are far more likely to be depressed and to attempt suicide than are teens who are not sexually active. Nearly two-thirds of parents support the message that sexually active teens are more likely to be depressed; a quarter of parents oppose it.

Abstinence curricula inform teens about the basic facts of regret and depression; comprehensive sex-ed curricula ignore this topic.

Parents want sex education to teach that the more sexual partners a teen has, the greater the likelihood of physical and psychological harm.

Some 90 percent of parents want this message taught to teens.

Abstinence curricula emphasize the harmful effects of casual teen sex; comprehensive sex-ed curricula do not.

Parents want teens taught that having many sexual partners at an early age may undermine one's ability to develop and sustain loving and committed relationships as an adult.

Some 85 percent of parents want teens to be taught that "having many sexual partners at an early age may undermine an individual's ability to develop love, intimacy and commitment." Another 78 percent of parents want teens to be taught that "having many different sexual partners at an early age may undermine an individual's ability to form a healthy marriage as adult."

These are major themes of abstinence programs. They teach that teen sexual relationships are inherently short-term and unstable and that repeated fractured relationships can lead to difficulties in bonding and commitment in later years. This perspective is accurate; women who begin sexual activity at an early age will have far more sexual partners and are less likely to have stable marriages as adults. Comprehensive sex-ed curricula ignore this topic completely.

"What's More Important, Abstinence or Contraception?"

Parents believe that abstinence should be given emphasis that is more than, or equal to, that given to contraception. Some 44 percent of parents believe that teaching about abstinence is more important than teaching about contraception;

another large group (41 percent) believe that abstinence and contraception should be given equal emphasis. Only 8 percent believe that teaching about contraception is more important than teaching about abstinence.

Regrettably, government spending priorities directly contradict parental priorities. Currently, the government spends at least $4.50 promoting teen contraceptive use for every $1.00 spent to promote teen abstinence.

Parents Overwhelmingly Reject Main Values and Messages of Comprehensive Sex Education

Despite the claims of advocacy groups such as SIECUS and Advocates for Youth, comprehensive sex education curricula contain weak to non-existent messages about abstinence. These programs focus almost exclusively on (1) explaining the threat of teen pregnancy and sexually transmitted diseases and (2) encouraging young people to use contraception, especially condoms, to combat these threats. Many of these curricula appear to be written from a limited health perspective. Sexuality is treated as a physical process (like nutrition), and the goal is to reduce immediate health risks.

While comprehensive sex-ed curricula do not explicitly and directly encourage teen sexual activity, they do not discourage it either. As long as " protection" is used, teen sexual activity is represented as being rewarding, normal, healthy, and nearly ubiquitous. While "unprotected" sex is strongly criticized and discouraged, "protected" teen sex is presented as being fully acceptable. There is little or no effort to encourage young people to wait until they are older before becoming sexually active. By presenting "protected" teen sex activity as commonplace, fulfilling, healthy, and unproblematic, comprehensive sex-ed courses send a strong implicit anti-abstinence message to teens.

The new poll of parental attitudes shows that less than 10 percent of parents support the main values and messages of comprehensive sex education programs. Specifically:

> **Parents oppose teaching that teen sex is okay if condoms are used.**

In comprehensive sex-ed curricula, "protected" teen sex is neither criticized nor discouraged. These courses explicitly or implicitly send the strong message that "it's okay for teens in school to engage in sexual intercourse as long as they use condoms." Only 7 percent of parents support this message; 91 percent reject it.

> **At a minimum, parents want teens to be taught to abstain from sexual activity until they have finished high school.**

Some 91 percent of parents want teens to be taught this minimum standard; most want a far higher standard. But comprehensive sex-ed curricula do not teach that teens should abstain until they have finished high school; in fact, these courses do not provide any clear standards concerning when sexual activity should begin. For the most part, they do not even encourage young people to wait until they are vaguely "older;" they are simply silent on the issue.

> **Comprehensive sex-ed courses are silent on vital issues such as casual sex, intimacy, commitment, love, and marriage.**

[Parents] overwhelmingly support the main themes of abstinence education and want these topics to be taught to their children. These themes are conspicuously absent from comprehensive sex-ed. These courses therefore fail to meet the needs and desires of most parents.

Should Abstinence Programs Teach About "Safe Sex" or Contraception?

The poll shows an apparent divergence between abstinence education and parental attitudes on only one issue: Some 75 percent of parents want teens to be taught about both abstinence and contraception. Except for describing the likely failure rates of various types of birth control, abstinence curricula do not teach about contraception.

However, the fact that abstinence programs, per se, do not include contraceptive information does not mean that teens will not be taught this material. Abstinence and sex education are seldom taught as stand-alone subjects in school; they are usually offered as a brief part of a larger course, most typically a health course. [Some 85 percent of the sex education taught in the United States is part of a larger course on a broader subject, most typically a health or biology class.]

In addition, sex education is usually taught not once, but in multiple doses at different grade levels as the student matures. When students are taught about abstinence, in most cases, they will also receive biological information about reproduction and contraception in another part of their course work. By 11th or 12th grade, some 91 percent of students have been taught about birth control in school.

There is no logical reason why contraceptive information should be presented as part of an abstinence curriculum. Not only would this reduce the limited time allocated to the abstinence message, but nearly all abstinence educators assert that it would substantially undermine the effectiveness of the abstinence message.

In general, parents tend to agree that abstinence and contraceptive instruction should not be directly mixed. [Some] 56 percent of parents believe either that contraception should not be taught at all or that, if both abstinence and contraception are taught, they should be taught separately. (Some 22 percent believe that contraception should not be taught, while 35 percent want the two subjects taught separately.)

Although most parents want teens to be taught about both abstinence and contraception, there is no strong sentiment that these topics must be combined into one curriculum. The stronger a parent's support for abstinence, the less likely he or she is to want abstinence and contraception merged into a single curriculum.

The fact that 75 percent of parents want both abstinence and contraception taught to teens should not, in any way, be interpreted to mean support for comprehensive sex-education. Comprehensive sex-ed curricula are focused almost exclusively on promoting contraceptive use and contain little or no mention of abstinence, yet only 8 percent of parents believe that schools should give greater emphasis to contraception than to abstinence.

Moreover, parents have reservations concerning the type of contraceptive education these curricula contain. While 52 percent of parents want schools to provide "basic biological and health information about contraception," only 23 percent want schools "to encourage teens to use condoms when having sex, teach teens where to obtain condoms, and have teens practice how to put on condoms." The latter aggressive type of contraceptive promotion is typical of comprehensive sex-ed curricula, though it lacks wide support among parents.

In general, parents want teens to be taught a strong abstinence message as well as being given basic biological information about contraception. The polls suggest that most parents would be satisfied if young people were given a vigorous abstinence course and were taught about the basics of contraception separately. This is probably the typical situation in most schools where authentic abstinence is taught. On the other hand, extremely few parents (7 percent to 8 percent) would be happy if abstinence education were to be replaced by comprehensive sex-ed.

Conclusion

The newly released poll shows strong (in many cases, nearly unanimous) support for the major themes of abstinence education. Abstinence programs provide young people with the strong, uplifting moral messages desired by nearly all parents.

Multiple evaluations show that abstinence programs are effective in encouraging young people to delay sexual activity. The effectiveness of these programs is quite remarkable, given that they typically provide no more than a few hours of instruction per year. In those few hours, abstinence instructors seek to counteract thousands of hours of annual exposure to sex-saturated teen media, which strongly push teens in the opposite direction.

Most parents not only want vigorous instruction in abstinence, but also want teens to be taught basic biological information about contraception. Such information is not contained in abstinence curricula themselves but is frequently provided in a separate setting such as a health class. Overall, the values and objectives of the overwhelming majority of parents can be met by providing teens with a strong abstinence program while teaching basic biological information about contraception in a separate health or biology class. This arrangement appears common in schools where abstinence is taught.

In recent years, groups such as Advocates for Youth and SIECUS have sought to eliminate funding for abstinence or to replace abstinence education with comprehensive sex-ed. This is always done under the pretext that comprehensive sex-ed contains a strong abstinence message and, thereby, renders traditional abstinence superfluous. In reality, comprehensive sex-ed curricula have weak to nonexistent abstinence content. Replacing abstinence education with these programs would mean eliminating the abstinence message in most U.S. schools; nearly all parents would object to this change.

Only a tiny minority (less than 10 percent) of parents support the values and messages taught in comprehensive sex education curricula. Since the themes of these courses (such as "It's okay for teens to have sex as long as they use condoms") contradict and undermine the basic values parents want their children to be taught, these courses would be unacceptable even if combined with other materials.

The popular culture bombards teens with messages encouraging casual sexual activity at an early age. To counteract this, parents want teens to be taught a strong abstinence message. Parents overwhelmingly support abstinence curricula that link sexuality to love, intimacy, and commitment and that urge teens to delay sexual activity until maturity and marriage.

Regrettably, this sort of clear abstinence education is not taught in most schools. As a result, the sexual messages that parents deem to be most important are not getting through to today's teens.

POSTSCRIPT

Should Adolescents Get Comprehensive Sex Education outside the Home?

Sexual health education is of critical importance for youth. Parents recognize this. Very few parents are in favor of *no* sex education being taught in the school. Over half of parents view the negative outcomes of teen sexuality such as pregnancy, STIs, and HIV as major problems facing teens today. Approximately two-thirds to three-quarters of parents think that sex education in the schools today help students avoid negative outcomes such as HIV, STIs, and unexpected pregnancies as well as help adolescents make responsible decisions about sexuality. Around half feel that sex education helps youth postpone sex. Over two-thirds of parents think that sex education in schools should be a required subject for adolescents. Very, very few parents stated that they refused to allow their children to participate in the sex education curricula in schools (based on the survey *Sex Education in America*, 2004).

How surveys such as *Sex Education in America* are interpreted by those with more liberal and more conservative perspectives on sexuality education in schools may be colored by the viewpoint of the writer. That is, how these poll results are read can be open to interpretation of the reader. How surveys are conducted can also be influenced by the wording of the questions. The items asked are often influenced by the political leanings/personal opinions of the researchers. For example, the *Sex Education in America* study found that around half of parents endorse the statement: "Abstinence from sexual intercourse is best for teens, but some teens do not abstain, so sex ed classes should provide information about condoms and other contraception." From a more liberal perspective, this endorsement may be interpreted as supporting comprehensive sex education. From a more conservative viewpoint, this statistic can be used to support the idea that abstinence needs to be advocated more strongly, the negative outcomes of early intercourse stressed, and the failure rates of various contraceptives presented. Which perspective is right, and which is wrong? Is there deliberate or malicious misrepresentation? All of us have biases and leanings; this is part of human nature. Regarding the issue of sex education and interpretation of parents' responses to questions about sex education, both those on conservative and liberal sides present what they believe to be the truth about parental attitudes. It is up to the discerning reader of these reports to take the authors' perspectives (i.e., more liberal or more conservative) on sex education into account when assessing how valid the research reported is. Can you, the reader, see the bias? Is the argument convincing, or are statements made that lack support?

Are there alternate explanations than those presented by the authors? These are questions that are critical when reading the conflicting opinions such as those presented in the selections here.

References/Further Reading

Martin, S., Rector, R., & Pardue, M.G. (2004). *Comprehensive Sex Education vs. Authentic Abstinence: A Study of Competing Curricula.* Washington, DC: The Heritage Foundation.

McKay, A., & Holowaty, P. (1998). Parents' opinions and attitudes toward sexuality education in the schools. *The Canadian Journal of Human Sexuality, 6,* 29–38.

Princeton Survey Research Associates. (2004). *Sex Education in America: General Public/Parents Survey.* Kaiser Family Foundation publication number 7017. National Public Radio/Kaiser Family Foundation/Kennedy School of Government. http://www.kff.org/newsmedia/7017.cfm.

Princeton Survey Research Associates. (2004). *Sex Education in America: Principal Survey.* Kaiser Family Foundation publication number 7016. National Public Radio/Kaiser Family Foundation/Kennedy School of Government. http://www.kff.org/newsmedia/7016.cfm.

Rector, R.E. (2004). *Facts about Abstinence Education.* WebMemo #461. Washington, DC: The Heritage Foundation. http://www.heritage.org/Research/Welfare/wm461.cfm#_ftn9.

Rector, R.E. (2005). *The War Against Abstinence.* First appeared in *The Washington Times.* Washington, DC: The Heritage Foundation. http://www.heritage.org/Press/Commentary/ed042005b.cfm.

Sex & Censorship Committee, National Coalition Against Censorship. (2005). *Abstinence-Only "Sex" Education.* New York: Planned Parenthood Federation of America. http://www.plannedparenthood.org/pp2/portal/medicalinfo/teensexualhealth/fact-abstinence-education.xml.

SIECUS. (2004). Public Support for Comprehensive Sexuality Education—Fact Sheet. *SIECUS Report—The Politics of Sexuality Education, 32*(4). http://www.siecus.org/pubs/srpt/srpt0050.html.

ISSUE 6

Should Adolescents Have Easy Access to Condoms in Schools?

YES: Susan M. Blake, et al., from "Condom Availability Programs in Massachusetts High Schools: Relationships with Condom Use and Sexual Behavior," *American Journal of Public Health* (June 2003)

NO: Alison Campbell Rate, from "Kids and Condoms," Open Doors Counselling and Education Services Inc., http://www.opendoors.com.au (February 2002)

ISSUE SUMMARY

YES: Researchers Blake and colleagues conclude that condom distribution has a positive effect on protective sexual behavior but leads to no increase in sexual behavior.

NO: Campbell Rate, executive director (Hon) of Open Doors Counselling and Educational Services in Australia, argues that condom distribution to teens is problematic for a variety of reasons and may have a negative impact on the psychological development of youth.

Adolescents and youth are groups that are targeted by public health officials as being at risk for negative consequences of unprotected sexual activity. For example, HIV and other sexually transmitted infections (STIs) are considered a major threat to the health of adolescents. Condoms are the only effective means of prevention of HIV transmission for those who are sexually active. Condoms can also help to prevent the spread of other STIs, such as chlamydia and gonorrhea, which tend to be more prevalent in younger individuals. While condoms do not provide 100 percent protection against STIs, consistent condom use is related with reduced rates of chlamydia, herpes, and gonorrhea as well as reduced likelihood of HPV symptoms (the virus that causes genital warts). Further, unexpected pregnancy can result from unprotected sex; when condoms are used properly, they are very effective at preventing pregnancy.

Proponents of condom availability programs argue that, by providing condoms in schools, barriers to condom use are reduced while access to a relatively effective means of preventing unexpected pregnancy and HIV or STI infection is improved. Some of these barriers may be financial (e.g., youth do not have the financial resources to purchase condoms) as well as embarrassment and other psychological barriers. While students may obtain condoms freely from family planning clinics, youth may not have the foresight to predict when they are going to need condoms, be able to locate the clinic, or procure transportation to the clinic, etc. Having condoms available in schools reduces these barriers. Also, having condoms available in schools may facilitate pre-sex discussions about condom use and other safer sexual behaviors, including abstinence. Finally, some studies have indicated that school condom availability programs resulted in increased condom use among sexually active students. Thus, an inexpensive condom program that results in even a small reduction of unprotected sexual behavior is justified from a cost-benefit perspective.

Opponents of condom availability programs argue that providing condoms in schools may increase the sexual behavior of students since this practice is viewed as an implicit sanctioning of teen sex. In short, there is a fear that teachers, other school officials, and other adults will be seen by students as promoting teen sexual behavior. This may also encourage young people to have sex with a greater number of partners and, consequently, incur greater risk. In addition, teachers and other school officials may not be keen on implementing condom distribution programs as they themselves may be labeled as promiscuous or "un-Christian." Distributing condoms may be against their personal value system, or they may believe that condom distribution undermines promotion of positive moral values.

Other arguments against condom distribution programs include the fact that, while students may be taking the condoms, they may be ineffective users of condoms. Several adversaries of these programs point to increased rates of pregnancy and STIs *after* the introduction of school condom distribution. For example, Jason Allardyce reported in the *Sunday Times* (London, April 11, 2004) that after the introduction of a "Healthy Respect" initiative in Lothian, Scotland, which was designed to increase teen access to contraception, early teen pregnancy rates in the region increased from 7.4 (which was the Scottish average) to 8.4 per 1000 youth. Some critics of condom distribution programs assert that youth are too immature to be allowed to make independent decisions about their sexual behavior and condom use. The critics of condom distribution initiatives often discuss abstinence promotion or abstinence-only sexuality education as the best alternative.

Susan M. Blake and colleagues describe the effects of a school condom availability program on adolescent sexual behavior in Massachusetts high schools. Results suggest students in schools with condom availability program are no more likely to have sex *but* are more likely to use condoms if they were sexually active compared to students in schools without a condom program. On the other hand, Alison Campbell Rate opposes condom distribution initiatives in the schools. She presents arguments, including method and user failure associated with condom use, on the potential negative impact of such programs on youth who are not yet sexually active, and some of the psychological implications of early sexual involvement.

YES

Susan M. Blake, et al.

Condom Availability Programs in Massachusetts High Schools: Relationships with Condom Use and Sexual Behavior

There is a continuing need for effective HIV, sexually transmitted disease (STD), and pregnancy prevention programs that discourage early onset of sexual activity and encourage protection among adolescents who are already sexually active. Despite sustained declines during the 1990s in teenage pregnancy and birth rates, as well as rates of certain STDs, approximately 1 million American teenagers continue to become pregnant each year, and three quarters of these pregnancies are unintended.[1-5] The decline in pregnancy rates has been attributed to declines in sexual activity, increased use of condoms, and longer acting hormonal contraceptive methods.[2,5,6] Yet, rates of HIV and other STDs among adolescents remain unacceptably high,[7] and it has been reported that 1 in 3 young people are infected with an STD by the age of 24 years.[8]

According to 1 study, approximately 49% of all adolescents in grades 9 through 12 reported ever having had sexual intercourse (36% within the previous 3 months), and during their most recent sexual encounter, use of condoms (58%) or other birth control methods (16%) was not universal among those who were sexually active.[9] Factors associated with condom use among sexually active youths include the following: (1) positive beliefs or attitudes about condom use (e.g., that they do not reduce sexual pleasure),[10-12] (2) perceiving peer norms as endorsing condom use,[12,13] (3) confidence in knowledge of correct condom use or negotiation techniques,[10,14] (4) believing condoms are effective and protective,[11-14] (5) discussing condom use with partners,[11,14] (6) not using alcohol or drugs in conjunction with sexual activity,[10,13-16] and (7) relationship status (i.e., use is more likely in short-term or casual relationships than in longer term or steady relationships).[17-19] Therefore, interventions designed to enhance beliefs, perceptions, and skills related to condom use could be expected to reduce the number of unprotected sexual encounters among sexually active adolescents.

The majority of school-based programs continue to focus on primary prevention to delay onset of sexual activity, particularly among younger adolescents; however, many school systems, with the support of parents and

From *American Journal of Public Health*, Vol. 93, no. 6, June 2003, pp. 955–962. Copyright © 2003 by American Public Health Association. Reprinted by permission.

community members, also provide secondary prevention programs to meet the needs of sexually active students. School health service staff in junior and senior high schools nationwide offer family planning counseling services (these services are available in 28.6% and 38.2% of such schools, respectively), pregnancy screening and testing (16.6% and 20.9%), and STD diagnosis and treatment (15.8% and 19.5%).[20] Not all teachers are comfortable discussing sensitive topics in the classroom,[21-24] but, according to one report, 33% and 58% of middle and senior high school teachers, respectively, provide instruction on condom efficacy, and 17% and 37%, respectively, demonstrate correct condom use techniques.[21]

However, the practice of making condoms available in schools is far more controversial and less likely to be openly endorsed by school administrators. One study estimated that 4.7% of all middle schools and 8.4% of high schools nationwide make condoms available.[20] In another study, 50 school districts nationwide, representing 431 schools, were identified as having condom availability programs (0.35% of all districts and 2.2% of all high schools nationwide).[25] Approximately 42% of these school districts were located in Massachusetts.

The purpose of the present study was to determine whether relationships exist between the presence or absence of condom availability programs in Massachusetts high schools and adolescent sexual practices. When condoms are available in schools and are successfully used by sexually active adolescents, they may be an effective means of preventing potentially harmful outcomes such as HIV/STDs and pregnancy.[26]

In the relatively few evaluations of the use and impact of condom availability programs that have been reported in the literature, number of condoms distributed, changes in attitudes, number of students carrying condoms, and self-reported condom use consistency have been used to measure program effectiveness.[25,27,28] Several evaluations have shown that adolescents in schools with and without programs are equally likely to become sexual active, and in 2 of 3 studies, sexually active youths were more likely to report having used condoms during their most recent sexual encounter.[29,30,31] In the present study, we expected to replicate and possibly expand on these findings by assessing levels of sexual activity and condom use in a random sample of students in high schools with and without condom availability programs after controlling for demographic differences between communities and students.

Methods

Environmental Context

The Commonwealth of Massachusetts Board of Education has adopted one of the most progressive and far-reaching state HIV/AIDS education policies in the country. The Board of Education issued a policy on HIV/AIDS prevention education in 1990, and in August 1991 the Board of Education approved a policy addendum that expanded recommendations for HIV prevention programs and directly addressed making condoms available. At the time of approval, several school districts were already considering making condoms available. The Board of Education policy recommends that all district school boards consider making condoms available in secondary schools and that this consideration involve a public dialogue between board members, the superintendent, school administrators, faculty, parents, students, and the local community. Specific venues for making condoms available were recommended for consideration; multiple channel use was encouraged.

Recognizing that making condoms available would not ensure that students would know how to use them properly, the commonwealth advised simultaneous consideration of instruction on proper condom use. Districts were advised that local decisions should include a parental information component, in recognition of the positive impact of parent reinforcement and the desire to have condom use discussed in the context of individual family values. Between 1991 and 1996, 65% of the 348 commonwealth districts held at least 1 public meeting to discuss making condoms available; 45% held discussions with the school board, as recommended by state policy. Twenty-eight percent of the districts developed explicit policies related to condom availability, and 10% of the districts with high schools approved condom availability programs in secondary schools.[32]

Research Design and Procedures

. . . Sixty-three of the state's 299 high schools with 100 or more students in grades 9 through 12 were randomly selected at a probability rate proportional to school size. The school response rate was 94%; 59 schools participated. . . . Three to 5 required classes per school were randomly selected. Passive consent procedures were used; parents were notified and given the option of refusing to allow their child's participation. Student participation was voluntary, and survey responses were anonymous. Of the 5370 students present in selected classrooms, 4166 completed the survey, yielding a 78% response rate. . . .

Results

District and School Characteristics

. . . According to a census survey of district health coordinators (response rate: 88%),[32] most districts with condom availability programs distributed condoms through school nurses (62%) or other personnel (48%), frequently gym teachers and assistant principals. Some of these districts distributed condoms through school-based health clinics (38%), but relatively few used barrier-free methods such as vending machines (10%). Parental consent to obtain condoms was not required in the majority of districts. More often than not, changes in district HIV education curricula paralleled adoption of condom availability programs.

Opportunities for public dialogue accompanied the program adoption process. Public discussions were more likely to be held in districts that made condoms available (94% vs 42% . . .) or adopted a policy (87% vs 20% . . .)

than in those that did not do so. Furthermore, public discussions were held significantly more often in districts that had adopted a condom availability policy (3.0 vs 1.7 times on average . . .) or program (18 vs 6 times on average . . .) than in nonadopting districts. In addition, condom availability districts held discussions with a greater number of constituency groups (on average, 4 vs 2 different constituent groups . . . .)[32]

Student Characteristics

Twenty-one percent of the students were enrolled in schools with condom availability programs (n = 865); the remainder (n = 3301) were not. Respondents in condom availability schools were more likely to be younger, to be from lower grade levels, and to be members of minority groups.

Differences in HIV-Related Instruction

Adolescents in condom availability schools received a greater range of HIV instruction. . . . They were more likely to have received instruction in regard to preventing HIV infection, to have heard a presentation from a person with HIV/AIDS, and to have been taught how to use a condom in school. Condom availability was not associated with adolescents having talked to their parents about AIDS.

Differences in Onset of Sexual Activity and Condom Use

Adolescents enrolled in schools with condom availability programs were no more likely to report ever having had sexual intercourse or having been sexually active in the preceding 3 months. In fact, they were slightly less likely to report having had sexual intercourse. Sexually active adolescents enrolled in condom availability schools were twice as likely to report using condoms during their most recent sexual encounter and using condoms to prevent pregnancy, but they were less likely to have used other pregnancy prevention methods. Similar differences in contraceptive use were found among adolescents who had recently been sexually active. . . .

Adolescents in schools with condom availability were more likely to use any contraceptive method and . . . more likely to use condoms during their most recent sexual encounter (68% vs 52%), whereas adolescents in schools without programs were more likely to use other contraceptive methods (21% vs 10%, . . .).

No differences were found among sexually active adolescents in regard to age at first sexual intercourse, recency of sexual intercourse, or number of recent sexual partners (past 3 months). No differences were found in the proportion of adolescents reporting or the number of times adolescents reported having been pregnant or having gotten someone pregnant. Sexually active adolescents in schools with condom availability programs were no more likely than those in schools without such programs to report that condoms were easy to obtain, and there were no differences in terms of where students would be most likely to obtain condoms if needed. . . .

Discussion

We have described a cross-sectional study designed to assess potential effects of condom availability programs in Massachusetts, a state with a history of exemplary and forward-thinking school health policies and practices.[34,35] . . .

Similar to previous research,[26,28,36–38] the data supported the potential benefits of making condoms available to sexually active students and the lack of harm in doing so for students who are not sexually active. Our study is important and relevant in that it provides a broad-based look at condom availability programs in a state with experience in implementing quality programs. In reviewing the findings, as well as the published literature, we were able to draw several conclusions and develop questions for future research.

First and foremost, sexual intercourse rates were not higher in schools where condoms were made available, which supports previous research suggesting that condom distribution in schools does not lead to initiation of sexual activity.[26,27,39–41] In fact, adolescents enrolled in condom availability schools were *less* likely to be sexually active or to report recent sexual intercourse, and no associations with age at first intercourse or numbers of sexual partners were found. Thus, the concerns of the small minority of parents who oppose providing condoms or related instruction in schools[27,39] were not substantiated in this study. Second, the presence of a condom availability program was protective; that is, sexually active adolescents in these schools were more likely to report having used condoms during their most recent sexual encounter. This finding also replicated previous research demonstrating relationships between condom availability in schools and students' use of them.[26,28]

Third, positive associations remained significant after controls for condom use instruction, suggesting that such instruction may be a necessary, but by itself insufficient, condition for condom use. These findings must not be interpreted, however, to suggest that condom use instruction is not necessary, because making condoms available to students without concurrently providing instruction may inadvertently result in improper or inconsistent condom use and might potentially increase risks for HIV/STDs and pregnancy. The preponderance of the evidence suggests that skills-based prevention programs can effectively delay onset of sexual activity, increase rates of refusal in regard to sexual activity, and reduce high-risk behaviors among sexually active adolescents.[38,42–45] The benefits of condom availability programs in regard to sexual risk taking as well as pregnancy and HIV/STD rates can be enhanced when such programs are supplemented by skills-based instruction in proper condom use.[26] Appropriately, most condom availability programs in the United States, including those in Massachusetts, are offered within a comprehensive health program framework that includes counseling and sexuality or HIV/AIDS education.[22]

The data also highlight important areas for exploration in future school health policy and program research. Several investigators have cited the need for studies designed to increase our understanding of the school health policy adoption process and its relationship to effective school health programs and practices.[46–50] The present study was conducted 4 years after adoption of a state policy that explicitly encouraged local school board consideration and public discussion of condom availability programs and instruction. Some, but certainly not all, local districts complied with state policy recommendations; 65% had discussed making condoms available, 45% held discussions with the school board (as prescribed by state policy), and 28% adopted a local policy related to condom distribution and instruction. Furthermore, 10% of the school districts statewide, and 15% of this representative sample of high schools, had adopted a condom availability program; these rates represent nearly 30 times the estimated percentage of districts nationwide with such programs (0.35%) and 7 times the estimated percentage of high schools (2.2%).[22,25]

Previous research suggests that community opinion is critical in promoting health policy initiatives.[51] In this study, districts that held public discussions about making condoms available, and those that held more public discussions with a greater number of constituency groups, were more likely to adopt a condom availability program.[32] The findings described here support the premise that state-level policies promoting public discussion have the potential to increase school districts' consideration of sensitive health issues that might otherwise go unaddressed. Furthermore, when an issue such as condom availability is opened to public dialogue, the probability of endorsement may increase (perhaps because most parents support the presence of prevention programs, including condom availability programs, in schools).[24,52–58] . . .

[In sum,] our results suggest that making condoms available, a clear indication of social and environmental support for condom use, may improve HIV prevention practices. Condom availability was not associated with greater sexual activity among adolescents but was associated with greater condom use among those who were already sexually active, a highly positive result. Finally, because we used a large, randomly selected sample of students representing an entire state and controlled for selected demographic characteristics and potential socioenvironmental influences, our findings expand on those of previous research.

References

1. Centers for Disease Control and Prevention. National and state-specific pregnancy rates among adolescents-United States, 1995–1997. *MMWR Morb Mortal Wkly Rep.* 2000;49:605–611.

2. Darroch JE, Singh S. *Why Is Teenage Pregnancy Declining? The Roles of Abstinence, Sexual Activity and Contraceptive Use.* New York, NY: Alan Guttmacher Institute; 1999.

3. *Sexually Transmitted Disease Surveillance, 1999.* Atlanta, Ga: Division of STD Prevention, Centers for Disease Control and Prevention; 2000.

4. Henshaw SK. Unintended pregnancy in the United States. *Fam Plann Perspect.* 1998;30:24–29, 46.

5. Ventura SJ, Mosher WD, Curtin SC, Abma JC, Henshaw S. Trends in pregnancies and pregnancy rates by outcome: estimates for the United States, 1976–96. *Vital Health Stat 21.* 2000;No. 56:1–47.

6. Henshaw SK. *US Teenage Pregnancy Statistics, With Comparative Statistics for Women Aged 20–24.* New York, NY: Alan Guttmacher Institute; 1999.

7. Kaplan DW, Feinstein RA, Fisher MM, et al. Condom use by adolescents. *Pediatrics*. 2001;107:1463–1469.

8. Centers for Disease Control and Prevention. Trends in sexual risk behaviors among high school students—United States, 1991–1997. *MMWR Morb Mortal Wkly Rep*. 1998;47:749–752.

9. Kann L, Kinchen SA, Williams BI, et al. Youth risk behavior surveillance—United States, 1999. *MMWR CDC Surveill Summ*. 2000;49(SS-5):1–32.

10. Basen-Engquist K, Parcel F. Attitudes, norms and self-efficacy: a model of adolescents' HIV-related sexual risk behavior. *Health Educ Q*. 1992;19:263–277.

11. Hingson RW, Strunin L, Berlin BW, Heeren T. Beliefs about AIDS, use of alcohol and drugs, and unprotected sex among Massachusetts adolescents. *Am J Public Health*. 1990;80:295–299.

12. Norris AE, Ford K. Condom beliefs in urban low income, African American and Hispanic youth. *Health Educ Q*. 1994;21:39–53.

13. Brown LK, DiClemente RJ, Park T. Predictors of condom use in sexually active adolescents. *J Adolesc Health*. 1992;13:651–657.

14. DiClemente RJ, Durbin M, Siegel D, Krasnovsky F, Lazarus N, Comacho T. Determinants of condom use among junior high school students in a minority, inner-city school district *Pediatrics*. 1992;89:197–202.

15. Ku LC, Sonenstein FL, Pleck JH. Young men's risk behaviors for HIV infection and sexually transmitted diseases, 1988 through 1991. *Am J Public Health*. 1993;83:1609–1615.

16. Lowry R, Holtzman D, Truman BI, Kann L, Collins JL, Kolbe LJ. Substance use and HIV-related sexual behaviors among US high school students: are they related? *Am J Public Health*. 1994;84:1116–1120.

17. Ford K, Norris A. Knowledge of AIDS transmission, risk behavior, and perceptions of risk among urban, low-income, African-American and Hispanic youth. *Am J Prev Med*. 1993;9:297–306.

18. Magura S, Shapiro JL, Kang SY. Condom use among criminally-involved adolescents. *AIDS Care*. 1994;6:595–603.

19. Remafedi G. Predictors of unprotected intercourse among gay and bisexual youth: knowledge, beliefs, and behavior. *Pediatrics*. 1994;94:163–168.

20. Small ML, Majer LS, Allensworth DD, Farquhar BK, Kann L. School health services. *J Sch Health*. 1995;65:319–326.

21. Collins JL, Small ML, Kann L, Pateman BC, Gold RS, Kolbe LJ. School health education. *J Sch Health*. 1995;65:302–311.

22. Blake S, Lohrmann D, Windsor R. *Dade County Public Schools HIV/AIDS Education Program Final Evaluation Report*. Washington, DC: Academy for Educational Development; 1995.

23. Forrest JD, Silverman J. What public school teachers teach about preventing pregnancy, AIDS, and sexually transmitted diseases. *Fam Plann Perspect*. 1989;21:65–72.

24. Kerr DL, Allensworth DD, Gayle JA. The ASHA national HIV education needs assessment of health and education professionals. *J Sch Health*. 1989;59:301–307.

25. Kirby DB, Brown NL. Condom availability programs in US schools. *Fam Plann Perspect*. 1996;28:196–202.

26. Wolk LI, Rosenbaum R. The benefits of school-based condom availability: cross-sectional analysis of a comprehensive high school-based program. *J Adolesc Health*. 1995;17:184–188.

27. Guttmacher S, Lieberman L, Ward D, Radosh A, Rafferty Y, Freudenberg N. Parents' attitudes and beliefs about HIV/AIDS prevention with condom availability in New York City public high schools. *J Sch Health.* 1995;65:101–106.

28. Stryker J, Samuels SE, Smith MD. Condom availability in the schools: the need for improved program evaluations. *Am J Public Health.* 1994;84:1901–1906.

29. Guttmacher S, Lieberman L, Ward D, Freudenberg N, Radosh A, DesJarlais D. Condom availability in New York City public high schools: relationships to condom use and sexual behavior. *Am J Public Health.* 1997;87:1427–1433.

30. Kirby DB, Brener N, Brown NL, Peterfreund N, Hillard P, Harrisst R. The impact of condom distribution in Seattle schools on sexual behavior and condom use. *Am J Public Health.* 1999;89:182–187.

31. Kirby DB, Waszak C, Ziegler J. Six school-based clinics: their reproductive health services and impact on sexual behavior. *Fam Plann Perspect.* 1991;23:6–16.

32. Blake S, Sawyer R, Ledsky R, Lohrmann D, Lehman T. *Commonwealth of Massachusetts Department of Education HIV/AIDS Education Program Evaluation: Technical Report and Executive Summary.* Washington, DC: Academy for Educational Development; 1998.

33. *1995 Massachusetts Youth Risk Behavior Survey Results.* Malden, Mass: Massachusetts Dept of Education; 1996. Publication 17817-58-4M-4/96-DOE.

34. Shirreffs JF. The history of health education. In: Rubinson L, Alles WF, eds. *Health Education: Foundations for the Future.* New York, NY: Macmillan Publishing Co; 1984.

35. Simons-Morton BG, Greene WH, Gottlieb NH. *Introduction to Health Education and Health Promotion.* 2nd ed. Prospect Heights, Ill: Waveland Press Inc; 1995.

36. Kirby DB, Short L, Collins J, et al. School-based programs to reduce sexual risk behaviors: a review of effectiveness. *Public Health Rep.* 1994;109:339–360.

37. Sellers DE, McGraw SA, McKinlay JB. Does the promotion and distribution of condoms increase teen sexual activity? Evidence from an HIV prevention program for Latino youth. *Am J Public Health.* 1994;84:1952–1959.

38. St. Lawrence JS, Brasfield TL, Jefferson KW, Alleyne E, O'Bannon RE 3rd, Shirley A. Cognitive-behavioral intervention to reduce African American adolescents' risk for HIV infection. *J Consult Clin Psychol.* 1995;63:221–237.

39. Kirby D, Coyle K. School-based programs to reduce sexual risk-taking behavior. *Child Youth Serv Rev.* 1997;19:415–436.

40. Schuster MA, Bell RM, Berry SH, Kanouse DE. Impact of a high school condom availability program on attitudes and behaviors. *Fam Plann Perspect.* 1998;30:67–72.

41. Zabin LS, Hirsch MB, Smith EA, Steett R, Hardy JB. Evaluation of a pregnancy prevention program for urban teenagers. *Fam Plann Perspect.* 1986;18:119–126.

42. Hovell M, Blumberg E, Sipan C, et al. Skills training for pregnancy and AIDS prevention in Anglo and Latino youth. *J Adolesc Health.* 1998;23:139–149.

43. Jemmott JB III, Jemmott LS, Fong GT. Reductions in HIV risk-associated sexual behaviors among black male adolescents: effects of an AIDS prevention intervention. *Am J Public Health.* 1992;82:372–377.

44. Kirby DB, Barth RP, Leland N, Fetro JV. Reducing the risk: impact of a new curriculum on sexual risk taking. *Fam Plann Perspect.* 1991;23:253–263.

45. Main DS, Iverson DC, McGloin J, et al. Preventing HIV infection among adolescents: evaluation of a school-based education program. *Prev Med.* 1994;23:409–417.

46. Bogden JF, Vega-Matos CA. *Fit, Healthy, and Ready to Learn: A School Health Policy Guide.* Washington, DC: National Association of State Boards of Education; 2000.

47. Gutman M, Clayton R. Progress on interventions and future directions. *Am J Health Promotion*. 1999;14:92–97.

48. McGraw SA, Sellers D, Stone E, et al. Measuring implementation of school programs and policies to promote healthy eating and physical activity among youth. *Prev Med*. 2000;31(suppl):86–97.

49. Mullen PD, Evans D, Forster J, et al. Settings as an important dimension in health education/promotion policy, programs, and research. *Health Educ Q*. 1995;22:329–345.

50. Wechsler H, Devereaux RS, Davis M, Collins J. Using the school environment to promote physical activity and healthy eating. *Prev Med*. 2000;31(suppl): S121–S137.

51. Dunt D, Day N, Pirkis J. Evaluation of a community-based health promotion program supporting public policy initiatives for a healthy diet. *Health Promotion Int*. 1999;14:317–327.

52. Colwell B, Forman M, Ballard DE, Smith DW. Opinions of rural Texas parents concerning elementary school health education. *J Sch Health*. 1995;65:9–13.

53. Gallup AM, Clark DL. The 19th Annual Gallup Poll of the Public's Attitudes Toward the Public Schools. *Phi Delta Kappan*. 1987;69:17–29.

54. Harris L. *Inside America*. New York, NY: Vintage Books; 1987.

55. Janus SS, Janus CL. *The Janus Report on Sexual Behavior*. New York, NY: John Wiley & Sons Inc; 1993.

56. Raferty Y, Radosh A. Attitudes about AIDS education and condom availability among parents of high school students in New York City: a focus group approach. *AIDS Educ Prev*. 1997;9:14–30.

57. *AIDS: Public Attitudes and Education Needs*. New York, NY: Roper Organization Inc; 1991.

58. Santelli J, Alexander M, Farmer M, et al. Bringing parents into school clinics: parent attitudes toward school clinics and contraception. *J Adolesc Health*. 1992;13:269–274.

Alison Campbell Rate

 **NO**

Kids and Condoms

"Teenagers won't be helped in their decision making about sex if we throw condoms at them and expect them to get it all together."

Looking for Solutions

The media microscope frequently focuses on adolescent sexual behaviour, and the ways in which society should understand and respond. With recent studies showing that about a third of young people are sexually active by the time they are 16 (North & Buxton, 1992; Vic Health Project, 1992), calls come regularly from health and education authorities for the installation of condom vending machines in schools in the interests of preventing teenage pregnancy and sexually transmitted diseases. Such suggestions are not new and neither are the arguments employed by the advocates.

Assuming Safety

The high incidence of teenage pregnancy and sexually transmitted disease remain largely unsolved problems. The first assumption behind the push to install condom vending machines in schools is that availability and knowledge about condoms will reduce teen pregnancy rates. By and large it won't.

In Australia, 3 out of 10 teenage girls will experience a pregnancy between the ages of 15–19 (Bennett 1985), and because only about 30% of teenagers in that age group are sexually active, this means that most sexually active teenagers can expect a pregnancy. Extensive information about and availability of contraceptives does not change this fact. A strong positive correlation has been shown between increasing use of condoms at first sexual intercourse and higher rates of teenage conceptions. Contraceptive failure is a major factor in teenage pregnancy (Pearson et al, 1995; Carnall, 1996).

While the rate of pregnancy is increasing, the trends show a decrease in live births and an increase in the number of abortions. Of the approximately 100,000 abortions performed every year in Australia, approximately 25% are performed on the 15–19 year old age group (29th Annual Report, 1998). Therefore the highest concentration of abortions is among teenagers. The people who are at highest risk of experiencing abortion and its ramifications are sexually active teenagers. This phenomenon is reflected in international adolescent health statistics.

The problem with condoms is, of course, that they fail and fail frequently. In an article about the abortion pill RU-486, Dr Edith Weisberg of the NSW Family Planning Association argued the need for the option of abortion to be available to women who experience contraceptive failure. She refers to a study of more than 2000 women electing abortion, of whom 22% said they were pregnant because of condom failure. "If we're promoting condoms for safe sex we need back-up methods for when they fail", Dr Weisberg is quoted (*Australian Doctor Weekly,* 28 October 1994). For teenagers the failure rate is even higher than for adults. One US study showed a teen failure rate of up to 36% in practice (Jones and Forrest, 1989).

An advertisement for Reality female condoms in the American journal *Family Planning Perspectives* gives comparative statistics for various contraceptive failure rates. "Typical use" failure rates for male and female condoms are given as follows, referring to the occurrence of "unintended pregnancy" while using the method.

	6 months	12 months
Reality female condom	12%	25%
Male latex condom	8%	15%

Fifteen percent of male condom users in the trial experiencing "unintended pregnancies" does not equal safe sex, but bear in mind that these figures represent many more actual failures of the method and this is where the second assumption behind the condom vending machines suggestion comes undone.

It is argued that by using condoms young sexually active teenagers will be protected from disease. Whereas the failure rate for condom use is given in terms of unintended pregnancies despite using the method, it in no way indicates the actual failure rate. This is because pregnancy does not occur with each act of intercourse. It depends on where the woman is in her cycle. If the condom fails during her infertile phase she will not become pregnant; the method will not have "failed" in that sense. But a sexually transmitted disease can be passed on at any stage. Failure rates given in terms of pregnancies do not give a true picture of failure rates in terms of exposure to STDs including HIV/AIDS. Furthermore, condoms do not provide effective protection from herpes, genital wart virus, syphilis and lice as these are passed on by skin contact.

The promotion of condoms to teenagers is particularly problematic in this regard. Teenagers don't think like adults, or reason like them. Most adults would not sit down and work all this out. Your average teenager certainly wouldn't. Yet schools, education bodies, curriculum planners, health workers, writers for television and teenage magazines, and so on, persist in selling the condom to teenagers as a safe, realistic option. The reality is more often inconsistent use, if used at all. Teenagers are not, and never have been, good contraceptive users, despite all the information in the world.

Assuming Choice

It has been argued that if a third of young people are choosing to be sexually active by the time they are 16, then it is a school's responsibility to provide easy access to condoms. This assumption of choice has to be challenged.

Dr. David Elkind, a US psychologist and professor specialising in child and adolescent studies states in his book *Parenting Your Teenager in the 1990s:* "Contrary to popular opinion, most young people engage in sexual activity for psychological rather than hormonal reasons" (Elkind, 1993).

Experienced crisis pregnancy counsellors recognise that young sexually active teenagers are often motivated to form inappropriate relationships where they have unmet needs for love, nurturing and acceptance. They are vulnerable to exploitation by a more powerful partner in return for a sense of security and affection. They may themselves be the exploiter, manipulating a weaker partner's needs into taking the relationship further and stalling the inevitable break-up. Usually these motivations are unconscious, having their roots in issues such as family dysfunction and unresolved loss. Such unresolved issues contribute to a phenomenon called pregnancy proneness—the unconscious wish to be pregnant in order to fill a psychological void.

A third of Australian young people of secondary school age "choosing" to be sexually active is not an example of democracy at work. It is not a case of free choice to be complemented by free condoms at school. It is an indication that many young adolescents—children in the eyes of the law—are using their sexuality inappropriately, are risking their health and well-being, and that of their partners, and are in need of effective intervention counselling. The presence of condom vending machines on campus will continue to divert attention away from these realities and make it harder for young people who need it to access appropriate help.

Assuming Immunity

Claims that non-sexually active students at schools would not be affected by the presence of condom vending machines into changing their sexual status must be challenged.

Adolescence is known as a stage where to appear 'normal' is an extremely strong drive. Teenagers desire to fit in, to be like their peers appear to be. A condom vending machine in a school would send a strong message that to be sexually active is an expected status for teenagers and not all teens would be immune to this message. Studies are already showing significant numbers of sexually active teenagers expressing regret at not waiting until they were older, and/or reporting feeling pressured or coerced into participating in first sexual encounters against their will (Wellings et al, 1994; Curtis et at, 1988; Dickson et al, 1998).

Would such advocates condone the installation of cigarette machines in schools for those students who by age 16 have chosen to smoke and who are too embarrassed to buy their cigarettes at the supermarket? Setting aside the legal issue, they would probably agree that such a move would send an inappropriately permissive message about tobacco use to the rest of the school population. They would not want the smokers in the teenage population to influence the other students, particularly those younger and less able to make independent decisions.

Of course not all non-sexually active teens would be influenced by the presence of a condom vending machine to the extent of changing their sexual status. Other factors come into play here upon a young person's decision making, such as the effect of parental values and expectations and the strength of personal identity formation. But teenagers battling personal problems and lacking firm role models at home upon which to hone their own developing value system would clearly be vulnerable to such an overt influence.

Reality Check

Will schools adopting this measure also place a notice alongside the condom vending machine stating that condoms have a known method failure rate and an even higher user failure rate especially for teenagers? . . . that condom failure can result in pregnancy and/or disease? . . . that condoms do not prevent the transmission of the life-long recurring disease herpes, or the genital wart virus which is linked to cancer of the cervix in women?

Will these schools in fact give as much warning about the unsafe potential of condom use as they would of cigarette, drug or alcohol use?

It seems doubtful. A large proportion of society has been hoodwinked into accepting the blanket message of safe sex with condoms without enquiring too closely into the veracity of the claims.

Safer it may be, under some circumstances and for mature adults who have their emotions, relationships and sexual reactions more under control. But for young teenagers who are not yet effective decision makers and who are busy riding the adolescent rollercoaster, safe they are not. They need a different message about sex.

Looking for Me

Helping teenagers understand that their sexuality is part of their whole identity is the key. In forming their identity through the sometimes stormy passage of adolescence they are learning to know themselves—who they are and what they believe. At the end of this journey they are, as adults, able to form an intimate relationship with someone else, not merely to be sexually intimate. It's a journey that takes time.

Sexual intimacy during adolescence cuts short this fruitful learning time, restricting what should be a period of unfettered self-discovery. Some adults who struggle now in their relationships are experiencing the effects of this foreclosure of their own journey of self-discovery as adolescents. They don't know themselves and so cannot fully give of themselves, or receive, in a relationship.

Teenagers won't be helped in their decision making about sex if we throw condoms at them and expect them to get it all together. By nature adolescents haven't got it all together yet and we shouldn't expect it of them. Giving them permission, encouragement and skills to take the time to grow freely into themselves is far more important for both their present and future happiness.

References

Bennett, DL (1985) Adolescent Health in Australia—An Overview of Needs and Approaches to Care. A health education and promotion monograph. The Australian Medical Association, Sydney.

Carnall D (1996). Condom failure is on the increase [news] BMJ 1996: 312:1059.

Curtis, HA, Lawrence, CJ, Tripp, JH (1988). Teenage sexual intercourse and pregnancy. Arch Dis Child 1988; 63: 373–379 [Summary].

Dickson, N, Paul C, Herbison, P and Silva, P (1998). First sexual intercourse: age, coercion and later regrets reported by birth cohort. BMJ 1998.

Elkind, D (1993) Parenting Your Teenager in the 90s. New Jersey: Modern Learning Press.

Jones, EF and Forrest, JD (1989) Family Planning Perspectives. 21, 3:103-9.

North, P and Buxton, M (1992). Illawarra Region Survey: Sex Education and Attitudes Year 9 High School Students Aged 14–16 Years. Illawarra Education Unit, Family Planning Association NSW, Jan. 1992.

Pearson, VAH, Owen, MR, Phillips, DR, Pereira Gray, DJ and Marshall, MN (1995). Pregnant teenagers' knowledge and use of emergency contraception. BMJ 1995; 310:1644 [full text]

29th Annual Report from Committee Appointed to Examine and Report on Abortions Notified in South Australia, 1998.

Vic Health Project, (1992). Centre for Adolescent Health Survey, Information note #3 March 1993: "Sexual Behaviour."

Wellings, K, Field, J, Johnson, AM and, Wadsworth, J (1994). Sexual behaviour in Britain. London: Penguin 1994.

POSTSCRIPT

Should Adolescents Have Easy Access to Condoms in Schools?

A recent study representative of the population of the United States (Abma, Martinez, Mosher, & Dawson, 2004; Mosher, Chandra, & Jones, 2005) reported that a little over half of teens (i.e., aged 15 to 19 years of age) have had vaginal intercourse at some point in their lives. Of those teens who have had intercourse, 25 percent of the females and 18 percent of the males used no contraceptive device for their first intercourse, while 66 percent of the females and 71 percent of the males reported using a condom during their first intercourse. Further, 94 percent of sexually active teens indicated that they have used condoms at some point in their sexual lives.

Considering a broader definition of sexuality, slightly less than two-thirds of teens have had some sort of sexual contact with another person (e.g., oral sex, anal sex, or mutual masturbation). These latter behaviors do not put couples at risk for pregnancy, but they may put sexually active teens at risk for contracting sexually transmitted infections (STIs). About one-half of STIs in the United States occur in adolescents and young adults (i.e., aged 15–24 years of age). In short, teenagers in the United States are sexually active, do use condoms at least sometimes, and may be at risk for some of the negative consequences of unprotected sexual behavior.

The proponents of condom availability programs typically present empirical studies as scientific evidence of the effectiveness of these interventions. Some research supports the success of these programs (as measured by increased condom use by sexually active students and no increase in sexual behavior) while some do not (see Kirby, Brener, Brown, Peterfreund, Hillard, & Harrist, 1999). In contrast, the opponents of condom availability programs tend to present more moral or value-oriented arguments against these types of initiatives. Blake et al.'s selection is an experiment that corresponds with and supports the proponents perspective, while Campbell Rate's paper presents a solid rhetorical discourse in opposition of the provision of condoms to adolescents.

Imagine that you are a principal of a typical high school in the United States. Knowing the statistics above and the controversy surrounding these interventions, would you want to have a condom distribution program in your school? Would there be significant opposition by parents and community leaders? Would this have an impact on the moral standards and sexual behaviors of the youth entrusted to your care? It is these types of issues that face educators today.

References/Further Readings

Abma, J.C., Martinez, G.M., Mosher, W.D., & Dawson, B.S. (2004). Teenagers in the United States: Sexual activity, contraceptive use, and childbearing, 2002. *Vital Health Statistics*, 23(24). Hyattsville, MD: National Center for Health Statistics.

Allardyce, J. (2004). Sunday Times. April 11, 2004. London.

Hartigan, J.D. (1999). The disastrous results of condom distribution programs. *CCL Family Foundation*, 25(5), 22–23.

Holmes, J. (2005). Legal 450: Legal Research and Writing: Sample brief: Curtis v. School Committee of Falmouth. Retrieved Thursday June 22, 2006 from: http://www.unix.oit.umass.edu/~leg450/Samples/samplebrief.htm.

Kirby, D. (2000). Making condoms available in schools. The evidence is not conclusive. *Western Journal of Medicine*, 172(3), 149–151.

Kirby, D., Brener, N.B., Brown, N.L., Peterfreund, N., Hillard, P., & Harrist, R. (1999). The impact of condom distribution in Seattle schools on sexual behavior and condom use. *American Journal of Public Health*, 89, 182–187.

Klein, J., Rossbach, C., Nijher, H., et al. (2001). Where do adolescents get their condoms? *Journal of Adolescent Health*, 29, 186–193.

Mosher, W., Chandra, A., & Jones, J. (2005). Sexual behavior and selected health measures: Men and women 15–44 years of age, United States, 2002. *Advance data from vital and health statistics*, no. 362. Hyattsville, MD: National Center for Health Statistics.

The Sex Information and Education Council of Canada. (2004). Sexual health education in the schools: Questions and answers. *Canadian Journal of Human Sexuality*, 13(3–4), 129–141.

Yarber, W.L., Milhausen, R.R., Crosby, R.A., & Torabi, M.R. (2005). Public opinion about condoms for HIV and STD prevention: A midwestern state telephone survey. *Perspectives on Sexual and Reproductive Health*, 37(3), 148–154.

ISSUE 7

Is There Cause for Concern About an "Oral Sex Crisis" for Teens?

YES: Sharon Jayson, from "Teens Define Sex in New Ways," http://www.USAToday.com (October 19, 2005)

NO: Alexander McKay, from "Oral Sex Among Teenagers: Research, Discourse, and Education," *Canadian Journal of Human Sexuality* (Fall/Winter 2004)

ISSUE SUMMARY

YES: Journalist Sharon Jayson argues that more than half of 15- to 19-year-olds are engaging in oral sex. She reports some experts are becoming increasingly worried that adolescents who approach this intimate behavior so casually might have difficulty forming healthy intimate relationships later on.

NO: Alexander McKay, research coordinator of the Sex Information and Education Council of Canada, argues that the discourse about oral sex is somewhat exaggerated but may be used as a vehicle for increasing discussions with teens about their motives for sexual activity, which, in turn, can help guide sex education initiatives.

Recently, there has been a surge in media attention given to the "problem" of teen oral sex. There are rumors of "rainbow" clubs—parties for teens where girls wear different colored lipstick and fellate boys. The "goal" is for boys to have many different colors of lipstick on their penis at the end of the party. Oral sex has been called the new "spin the bottle" of teenagers. A book for teens by Paul Ruditis entitled *Rainbow Party* (Simon & Schuster, 2005) brought with it a flurry of discussion on the topic of teen oral sex.

But is there any real cause for concern? When questioned about sex, Michael Learned, a television star of the 1970s, stated in an interview in the 1980s that she thought kids today are doing the same thing that she and her peer group were doing as kids—only the kids of the 1980s talked about their sexual activities more than her cohorts did. Is that the case with oral sex of the Millennial teenagers? Are they simply talking about oral sex more as opposed to "doing it" more, compared to past generations?

A variety of studies have been conducted recently in North America that have gathered some preliminary information about oral sex and adolescents. Studies such as the Canadian Youth, Sexual Health and HIV/AIDS study (Boyce, Doherty, Fortin, & MacKinnon, 2003) and Centers for Disease Control and Prevention's study on sexual behavior and selected health measures of men and women aged 15–44 years (Mosher, Chandra, & Jones, 2005), both conducted in 2002, report on oral sex activity of youth. One of the major problems, however, is comparing this data to prior studies. The Canada Youth and AIDS study (King, et al., 1988), which was conducted in the late 1980s and is the earlier counterpart to the Canadian 2003 study, did not ask teens about their oral sex behavior.

More recent studies have asked teenagers about their oral sex behaviors. Lisa Remez, in a study published in *Family Planning Perspectives* in December 2000, reviewed the formal research about oral sex and youth. An early study in the 1980s found that about 20 percent of 13–18 year olds had engaged in oral sex. Another early 1980s study of tenth to twelfth graders found that 24 percent of virgins had had oral sex. A mid-1990s study of "nonvirgin" university students found that many of them (between 57 to 70 percent) retrospectively reported having had engaged in oral sex prior to having intercourse. A study of ninth to twelfth graders indicated that about 10 percent of virgins had engaged in oral sex. One representative sample—the National Survey of Adolescent Males—in 1988 and again in 1995 suggested that receipt of fellatio had not increased significantly for boys aged 15–19 years, with 44 percent and 50 percent, respectively, having received oral sex. Studies in the 2000s tend to be consistent with these earlier studies with approximately 40 percent of older teens (15–17 years) having engaged in oral sexual activity (Prinstein, Meade, & Cohen, 2003) while 20 percent of younger teens (grade 9, around 14 years of age) have had oral sex (Halpern-Felsher, Cornell, Kropp, & Tschann, 2005). A recent representative study by the Canadian Association for Adolescent Health (February 2006) found that 19 percent of 14–17-year-old respondents reported having engaged in oral sex, while the average age for first oral sex and vaginal intercourse was 15 years (http://www.acsa-caah.ca/ang/pdf/misc/research.pdf).

While there may or may not be an increase in oral sexual activity from earlier generations of teens (McKay states that there is evidence for a modest increase), should sex educators and those who work with adolescents be concerned about teen oral sex activity? In the following selection, Alex McKay discusses the research around oral sex and youth, sex education about oral sex, and the health risks associated with oral sexual activity. McKay does not view oral sex as a problem, per se; rather he describes this as important opportunity for opening discussions with youth about sex education and increasing our acknowledgment of the role of pleasure in the sexual lives of adolescents. In contrast, Sharon Jayson, in a *USA Today* article, discusses some of the potential negative ramifications of, and some of the worries that adults may have about, teen oral sex.

YES

Sharon Jayson

Teens Define Sex in New Ways

The generational divide between baby-boomer parents and their teenage offspring is sharpening over sex.

Oral sex, that is.

More than half of 15- to 19-year-olds are doing it, according to a groundbreaking study by the Centers for Disease Control and Prevention.

The researchers did not ask about the circumstances in which oral sex occurred, but the report does provide the first federal data that offer a peek into the sex lives of American teenagers.

To adults, "oral sex is extremely intimate, and to some of these young people, apparently it isn't as much," says Sarah Brown, director of the National Campaign to Prevent Teen Pregnancy.

"What we're learning here is that adolescents are redefining what is intimate."

Among teens, oral sex is often viewed so casually that it needn't even occur within the confines of a relationship. Some teens say it can take place at parties, possibly with multiple partners. But they say the more likely scenario is oral sex within an existing relationship.

Still, some experts are increasingly worrying that a generation that approaches intimate behavior so casually might have difficulty forming healthy intimate relationships later on.

"My parents' generation sort of viewed oral sex as something almost greater than sex. Like once you've had sex, something more intimate is oral sex," says Carly Donnelly, 17, a high school senior from Cockeysville, Md.

"Now that some kids are using oral sex as something that's more casual, it's shocking to (parents)."

David Walsh, a psychologist and author of the teen-behavior book *Why Do They Act That Way?*, says the brain is wired to develop intense physical and emotional attraction during the teenage years as part of the maturing process. But he's disturbed by the casual way sex is often portrayed in the media, which he says gives teens a distorted view of true intimacy.

Sex—even oral sex—"just becomes kind of a recreational activity that is separate from a close, personal relationship," he says.

"When the physical part of the relationship races ahead of everything else, it can almost become the focus of the relationship," Walsh says, "and they're not then developing all of the really important skills like trust and communication and all those things that are the key ingredients for a healthy, long-lasting relationship."

"Intimacy has been so devalued," says Doris Fuller of Sandpoint, Idaho, who, with her two teenage children, wrote the 2004 book *Promise You Won't Freak Out,* which discusses topics such as teen oral sex.

"What will the impact be on their ultimately more lasting relationships? I don't think we know yet."

Casual Attitude Is Worrying

Child psychology professor W. Andrew Collins of the University of Minnesota says a relationship "that's only about sex is not a high-quality relationship."

In a 28-year study, Collins and his colleagues followed 180 individuals from birth. His yet-to-be-published research, presented at a conference in April, suggests that emotionally fulfilling high school relationships do help teens learn important relationship skills.

The researchers did not specifically ask about oral sex, he says. But relationships that are focused more on sex tend to be "less sustained, often not monogamous and with lower levels of satisfaction."

Terri Fisher, an associate professor of psychology at Ohio State University, says oral sex used to be considered "exotic." After the sexual revolution of the 1960s, it was viewed as a more intimate sexual act than sexual intercourse, but now, in young people's minds, it's "a more casual act."

Beyond shock, many parents aren't sure what to think when they discover their children's nonchalant approach to oral sex.

"It doesn't cross your mind because it's not something you have done," Fuller says. "Most parents weren't doing this (as teenagers) in the way these kids are."

But if parents are looking for reasons to freak out, the health risk of oral sex apparently isn't one of them. Teenagers and experts agree that oral sex is less risky than intercourse because there's no threat of pregnancy and less chance of contracting a sexually transmitted disease or HIV.

"The fact that teenagers have oral sex doesn't upset me much from a public health perspective," says J. Dennis Fortenberry, a physician who specializes in adolescent medicine at the Indiana University School of Medicine.

"From my perspective, relatively few teenagers only have oral sex. And so for the most part, oral sex, as for adults, is typically incorporated into a pattern of sexual behaviors that may vary depending upon the type of relationship and the timing of a relationship."

Data Don't Tell Whole Story

A study published in the journal *Pediatrics* in April supports the view that adolescents believe oral sex is safer than intercourse, with less risk to their physical and emotional health.

The study of ethnically diverse high school freshmen from California found that almost 20% had tried oral sex, compared with 13.5% who said they had intercourse.

More of these teens believed oral sex was more acceptable for their age group than intercourse, even if the partners are not dating.

"The problem with surveys is they don't tell you the intimacy sequence," Brown says. "The vast majority who had intercourse also had oral sex. We don't know which came first."

The federal study, based on data collected in 2002 and released last month, found that 55% of 15- to 19-year-old boys and 54% of girls reported getting or giving oral sex, compared with 49% of boys and 53% of girls the same ages who reported having had intercourse.

Though the study provides data, researchers say, it doesn't help them understand the role oral sex plays in the overall relationship; nor does it explain the fact that today's teens are changing the sequence of sexual behaviors so that oral sex has skipped ahead of intercourse.

"All of us in the field are still trying to get a handle on how much of this is going on and trying to understand it from a young person's point of view," says Stephanie Sanders, associate director of The Kinsey Institute for Research in Sex, Gender and Reproduction at Indiana University, which investigates sexual behavior and sexual health.

"Clearly, we need more information about what young people think is appropriate behavior, under what circumstances and with whom," Sanders says. "Now we know a little more about what they're doing but not what they're thinking."

The $16 million study, which took six years to develop, complete and analyze, surveyed almost 13,000 teens, men and women ages 15–44 on a variety of sexual behaviors.

Researchers say that the large sample size, an increased societal openness about sexual issues and the fact that the survey was administered via head-phones and computer instead of face to face all give them confidence that, for the first time, they have truthful data on these very personal behaviors.

"There is strong evidence that people are more willing to tell computers things, such as divulge taboo behaviors, than (they are to tell) a person," Sanders says.

More Analysis Needed

Researchers cannot conclude that the percentage of teens having oral sex is greater than in the past. There is no comparison data for girls, and numbers for boys are about the same as they were a decade ago in the National Survey of Adolescent Males: Currently, 38.8% have given oral sex vs. 38.6% in 1995; 51.5% have received it vs. 49.4% in 1995.

Further analyses of the federal data by the private, non-profit National Campaign to Prevent Teen Pregnancy and the non-partisan research group Child Trends find almost 25% of teens who say they are virgins have had oral sex. Child Trends also reviewed socioeconomic and other data and found that those who are white and from middle- and upper-income families with higher levels of education are more likely to have oral sex.

Historically, oral sex has been more common among the more highly educated, Sanders says.

Is Intimacy Imperiled?

The survey also found that almost 90% of teens who have had sexual intercourse also had oral sex. Among adults 25–44, 90% of men and 88% of women have had heterosexual oral sex.

"If we are indeed headed as a culture to have a total disconnect between intimate sexual behavior and emotional connection, we're not forming the basis for healthy adult relationships," says James Wagoner, president of Advocates for Youth, a reproductive-health organization in Washington.

Oral sex might affect teenagers' self-esteem most of all, says Paul Coleman, a Poughkeepsie, N.Y., psychologist and author of *The Complete Idiot's Guide to Intimacy.*

"Somebody is going to feel hurt or abused or manipulated," he says. "Not all encounters will turn out favorably. . . . Teenagers are not mature enough to know all the ramifications of what they're doing.

"It's pretending to say it's just sexual and nothing else. That's an arbitrary slicing up of the intimacy pie. It's not healthy."

A survey of more than 1,000 teens conducted with the National Campaign to Prevent Teen Pregnancy resulted in *The Real Truth About Teens & Sex*, a book by Sabrina Weill, a former editor in chief at *Seventeen* magazine. She says casual teen attitudes toward sex—particularly oral sex—reflect their confusion about what is normal behavior. She believes teens are facing an intimacy crisis that could haunt them in future relationships.

"When teenagers fool around before they're ready or have a very casual attitude toward sex, they proceed toward adulthood with a lack of understanding about intimacy," Weill says. "What it means to be intimate is not clearly spelled out for young people by their parents and people they trust."

Although governmental and educational campaigns urge teens to delay sex, some suggest teens have replaced sexual intercourse with oral sex.

"If you say to teenagers 'no sex before marriage,' they may interpret that in a variety of ways," says Fisher.

Talk Is Crucial

Experts say parents need to talk to their kids about sex sooner rather than later. Oral sex needs to be part of the discussion because these teens are growing up in a far more sexually open society.

Anecdotal reports for years have focused on teens "hooking up" casually. Depending on the group, teens say it can mean kissing, making out or having sex.

"Friends with benefits" is another way of referring to non-dating relationships, with a form of sex as a "benefit."

But not all teens treat sex so casually, say teens from suburban Baltimore who were interviewed by USA TODAY as part of an informal focus group.

Alex Trazkovich, 17, a high school senior from Reisterstown, Md., says parents don't hear enough about teen relationships where there is a lot of emotional involvement.

"They hear about teens going to the parties and having lots and lots of sex," he says. "It happens, but it's not something that happens all the time. It's more of an extreme behavior."

Alexander McKay  **NO**

Oral Sex Among Teenagers: Research, Discourse, and Education

T he issue of teens and oral sex has appeared on the radar screens of public and media consciousness rather abruptly. The more level-headed among us may ask whether all the talk about oral sex among teens reflects a recent major shift in adolescent behaviour (i.e., a "new teen sexual revolution") or an example of unwarranted media induced anxiety, or a combination of both. It should be stated, from the onset, that nearly all the reports in the media about an "outbreak" of oral sex among teens, and especially young teens, are based almost entirely on anecdotal accounts and speculation. Although well-conducted survey research that allows young people to anonymously report their sexual behaviour may not always be methodologically perfect, it is almost certainly a more reliable way to obtain an accurate gage of adolescent sexual behaviour than is the television camera or journalist's interview with a group of self-selected teen informants where a social desirability bias is much more likely to be present. What does the available research tell us about oral sex among teens?

Oral Sex and Teens: What the Research Says

The *Canadian Youth. Sexual Health and HIV/AIDS Study* (Boyce, Doherty, Fortin, & MacKinnon, 2003) included a sample of just over 11,000 Canadian Grade 7, 9, and 11 students. The Grade 9 and 11 students were asked about their practice of specific sexual behaviours. The survey was conducted in 2002. At that time, 32% of Grade 9 males, 28% of Grade 9 females, 53% of Grade 11 males, and 52% of Grade 11 females reported that they had engaged in oral sex at least once (Boyce et al, 2003). How does this compare to the past? A similar study involving Canadian youth conducted in 1992 found that 27% of Grade 9 males, 21% of Grade 9 females, 48% of Grade 11 males, and 47% of Grade 11 females said they had experienced oral sex at least once (Warren & King, 1992). It should be kept in mind that in these surveys, as is typically the case, teens are asked if they have "ever" engaged in a particular behaviour. This is important because it means that the figures do not differentiate between those who have had oral sex once or twice from those who are regular practitioners. In any case, if we compare the percentages between 1992 and 2002 we might cautiously conclude that there has been a modest increase in the percentages

From *The Canadian Journal of Human Sexuality*, vol. 13, no. 3–4, Fall/Winter 2004, pp. 201–202.

of teens who have ever had oral sex at least once. Very few studies have assessed oral sex among younger teens. One study of 12- to 15-year-olds indicated that 18% had experienced oral sex (Boekeloo & Howard, 2002).

The popular perception is that with respect to teen oral sex, it is more likely that there is a gender discrepancy in which females are more likely to be giving (fellatio) rather than receiving (cunnilingus) oral sex from their male partners. Unfortunately, the studies mentioned above did not distinguish between who was giving and who was receiving. However, the research that is available on this point would tend to support the idea that among teens it is more likely to be the female who is giving oral sex. For example, in a large-scale study from the United States conducted in 1995, among males aged 15 to 19, 49% reported that they had received oral sex whereas 39% said that they had given oral sex (Gates & Sonenstein, 2000).

To put these statistics on oral sex in perspective, several points should be noted. First, part of the current discussion of this issue is the belief that many young people do not consider oral sex to be the "real thing," that it's not really sex, that it's not even a particularly intimate behaviour. Attitudes towards oral sex are no doubt changing but if oral sex among teens is commonly occurring on "a lark" then we should expect that oral sex will be far more common than the "real thing" (i.e., vaginal intercourse). In other words, if we put oral sex on the traditional continuum of sexual behaviours that begins with kissing, proceeds to petting above and then below the waist, moves next to oral sex, and finally ends in intercourse, then we should expect that in the new era of oral sex as "no big deal" that the traditional continuum would have become distorted. That is, that oral sex among teens would have become significantly more common relative to other sexual behaviours. However, when we look at the findings of the *Canadian Youth, Sexual Health and HIV/AIDS Study* (Boyce et al., 2003), oral sex seems to have kept its traditional place in the continuum of behaviours. For example, when we look at the sexual behaviours of Grade 9 females we see that 67% have experienced "deep, open mouth kissing," 64% have been touched above the waist, 54% have participated in touching below the waist, 28% have had oral sex, and 19% have had intercourse (Boyce et al., 2003).

A second point that we should keep in mind is that although the media and public discourse on oral sex has disproportionately focused on youth, oral sex among adults has become, over time, a normative sexual behaviour. Data from the U.S. *National Health and Social Life Survey* indicated that, for example, among 40- to 44-year-olds, 84% of men and 73% of women had given oral sex while 86% of men and 77% of women had received it (Laumann, Gagnon, Michael, & Michaels, 1994). Perhaps even more telling is a study of married and cohabiting adult couples conducted in Quebec in the late 1980s in which 80% reported engaging in oral sex in the preceding year (Samson et al., 1993). Laumann et al. (1994), in discussing their findings, suggest that "If there has been any basic change in the script for sex between women and men, it is the increase in the incidence and frequency of fellatio and cunnilingus" (p. 102). Given that oral sex has become a common, normative aspect of adult sexual behaviour, it should not come as a complete surprise that as they become sexually active, some teens will also engage in these behaviours. These statistics on oral sex can be evaluated and interpreted in a range of ways but it is probably accurate to say that while the incidence and frequency of oral sex among teens and adults alike has been increasing, albeit gradually, declarations of an "epidemic of oral sex in middle school" are probably an exaggeration.

The Current Discourse and Its Implications for Sexual Health Education

There was once a time when the urgency to provide widespread HIV/AIDS prevention education to youth and adults alike included the idea of reducing risk through "non-intercourse sex" or "non-penetrative sex" or "outercourse." These terms seem to have fallen out of the vernacular of sexual health educators but it is somewhat ironic looking back on them that the current awareness that some teens engage in oral sex should cause such apparent shock and anxiety, particularly among media commentators. There is no doubt that some of this anxiety is well placed. Clearly, as with all sexual behaviours, some teens will become involved in oral sex through manipulation or peer pressure or because they made ill-advised decisions. But it is also worth speculating about whether there is something in particular about oral sex among teens that sparks anxiety among parents, educators, and the media. And it is here that perhaps we find the silver lining in the uproar over teens and oral sex. In educating youth about sex we have tended overwhelmingly to focus on the bio-physiological aspects of sexuality and reproduction. What we have tended not to talk about so much with youth, maybe because we are not so comfortable doing so, is sexual pleasure. Oral sex has nothing to do with reproduction so charts are not very helpful. In some basic respects, oral sex is about pleasure. And maybe this is at least part of what has disturbed so many people about oral sex and teens. It forces us to acknowledge that pleasure is a part of teen sexuality and the decisions that teens make about their relationships and their behaviour. Perhaps all the recent attention paid to oral sex and teens will force the issue onto the table of school-based sexual health education and parent-child discussions of sexuality. This is a good thing. Once we have calmed everybody down about the myth of an epidemic of oral sex in the middle schools we can move forward in addressing the issue of oral sex openly and honestly. This will involve a greater acknowledgement of the role of pleasure in teen sexuality. But at the same time this more holistic approach will allow us to do a much better job of helping youth make sound judgements about what is right for them, increase their skills in resisting peer pressure, and minimize their risks if and when they may choose to engage in oral sex.

Oral Sex and Pregnancy/STI/HIV Risk

Quite rightly, much of the concern around teens and oral sex relates to the potential emotional, psychosocial, and developmental consequences of young people's involvement in oral sex (Barrett, 2004). In addition, however, concern has been expressed regarding the potential health risks of oral sex. It is apparent and realistic to assume that part of the attraction to oral sex among young people is that this is a sexual behaviour that confers no risk of pregnancy. Educators need to acknowledge this as a component in teen decision-making about sexual behaviour. There is an often expressed concern that teens consider oral sex risk free and that educators need to emphasize that oral sex does carry a risk of STI transmission. However, it is not sufficient, and potentially counterproductive, to simply say that oral sex is risky. We must provide information about the STI/HIV risks of oral sex that is comprehensive and consistent with current medical knowledge. At present this suggests that we inform students that oral sex confers a lower risk of HIV and other STI infection than unprotected penile-vaginal or penileanal intercourse but that it is not risk free. Unprotected oral sex does present some level of risk for transmission of bacterial and viral STI as well as HIV (Edwards, 1998a; Edwards, 1998b; Hawkins, 2001). Students should also be informed that the use of condoms and oral dams can reduce the risk of infection from oral sex. Sexual health educators can offer further risk reduction strategies by indicating that mutual masturbation confers virtually no risk of STI/HIV transmission. These risk reduction strategies will be of particular relevance for gay, lesbian, and bisexual youth for whom oral sex may play a central role in their sexual expression.

References

Barrett, A. (2004). Teens and oral sex: A sexual health educator's perspective. *SIECCAN Newsletter, 39(1–2), in The Canadian Journal of Human Sexuality, 13,* 197-200.

Boekeloo, B.O., & Howard, D.E. (2002). Oral sexual experience among young adolescents receiving general health examinations. *American Journal of Health Behavior, 26,* 306-314.

Boyce, W., Doherty, M., Fortin, C., & MacKinnon, D. (2003). *Canadian Youth, Sexual Health and HIV/ AIDS Study.* Toronto, ON: Council of Ministers of Education.

Edwards, S., & Carne, C. (1998a). Oral sex and the transmission of viral STIs. *Sexually Transmitted Infections, 74,* 6-10.

Edwards, S., & Carne, C. (1998b). Oral sex and the transmission of non-viral STIs. *Sexually Transmitted Infections, 74,* 95-100.

Hawkins, D.A. (2001). Oral sex and HIV transmission. *Sexually Transmitted Infections, 77,* 307-308.

Laumann, E.O., Gagnon, J.H., Michael, R.T., & Michaels, S. (1994). *The Social Organization of Sexuality: Sexual Practices in the United States.* Chicago, IL: The University of Chicago Press.

Sampson, J.M., Levy, J.J., Dupras, A., & Tessier, D. (1994). Active oral-genital sex among married and cohabiting heterosexual adults. *Sexological Review, 1,* 143-156.

Warren, W.K., & King, A.J. (1994). *Development and Evaluation of an AIDS/STD/ Sexuality Program for Grade 9 Students.* Kingston, ON: Social Program Evaluation Group, Queens University.

POSTSCRIPT

Is There a Cause for Concern About an "Oral Sex Crisis" for Teens?

One of the ironies of the oral sex concern debate is that, in the past, sex educators who have taken a "harm reduction" approach or who have spoken with youth about the riskiness of various sexual behaviors for HIV and sexually transmitted infections (STIs) have lauded "outercourse" as a good alternative to "intercourse" (Barrett, 2004). Thus, there is a subset of teens who have engaged in oral sex but not intercourse (see Mosher et al., 2005, who report that approximately 12 percent of teens fit in this category). Indeed, there is research to suggest that oral sex is only a theoretical risk for some sexually transmitted infections.

What is missing from the literature is a more complete understanding of why some teens engage in oral sex but not intercourse. Some may engage in oral sex because they believe (correctly) that this is a lower pregnancy risk sexual activity. Others may engage in oral sex over intercourse as an STI risk reduction activity (which is what sex educators have been espousing since the beginning of the HIV/AIDS era). According to a representative poll of teens aged 13-16 years conducted by Princeton Survey Research Associates International in 2004 (http://www.msnbc.msn.com/id/6839072), the major reasons for engaging in oral sex included because the other person wanted to have oral sex, because the teen had met the right person, and because the teen wanted to satisfy a sexual desire. Other, less important, reasons for engaging in oral sex included pregnancy prevention, curiosity, and remaining a virgin (i.e., treating oral sex as a form of abstinence).

Some theorists and thinkers in this area are concerned that the oral sex phenomenon is gender biased (e.g., Tolman, interviewed in Remez, 2000). The idea of the "rainbow party" does tend to support this contention—that it is girls fellating boys rather than boys performing cunnilingus. Research by Boekeloo and Howard (2002) suggests that heterosexual oral-sexually active boys and girls are not experiencing a disparity in receiving and giving oral sex. In their sample of 12–15 year olds who were surveyed in their physician's office, 17 percent of boys and 20 percent of girls had engaged in oral sex (giving and/or receiving).

Another concern that has been raised about the practice of oral sex by teens is that this sexual behavior is treated cavalierly, which may impede intimate relationships in the future—a point raised in the Jayson selection. A study by Halpern-Felsher, et al. (2005) found that teens had a more permissive attitude toward casual oral sex than they did toward casual intercourse. However, it is noteworthy that the teens in this study disagreed with both casual oral sex and casual vaginal intercourse as permissible; they simply disagreed *more* strongly with casual vaginal intercourse.

Participation in oral sexual activities by teens is not well understood and has not been well-researched. Some camps argue that this is a serious problem, an epidemic that adults must address as a serious concern. Other parties approach the teen oral sex issue as an opportunity to further the sex education of teens. Both sides agree that more conversations between adults and teens about sexuality will be beneficial for the teens.

References/Further Readings

Barrett, A. (2004). Oral sex and teenagers: A sexual health educator's perspective. *Canadian Journal of Human Sexuality*, 13(3–4), 197–200.

Boekelloo, B., & Howard, D. (2002). Oral sexual experience among young adolescents receiving general health, examinations. *American Journal of Health Behavior, 26*, 306–314.

Boyce, W., Doherty, M., Fortin, C., & MacKinnon, D. (2003). *Canadian Youth, Sexual Health & HIV/AIDS Study: Factors Influencing Knowledge, Attitudes and Behaviours.* Toronto: Council of Ministers of Education, Canada.

Halpern-Felsher, B., Cornell, J., Kropp, R., & Tschann, J. (2005). Oral versus vaginal sex among adolescents: Perceptions, attitudes, and behavior. *Pediatrics*, 115(4), 845–851.

King, A., Beazley, R., Warren, W., Hankins, C., Robertson, A., & Radford, J. (1988). *Canada youth and AIDS study.* Kingston, ON: Queen's University.

Mosher, W., Chandra, A., & Jones, J. (2005). Sexual behavior and selected health measures: Men and women 15–44 years of age, United States, 2002. Centers for Disease Control and Prevention. National Center for Health Statistics. *Vital and Health Statistics, 362*, 1–22.

Prinstein, M., Meade, C., & Cohen, G. (2003). Adolescent oral sex, peer popularity, and perceptions of best friends' sexual behavior. *Journal of Pediatric Psychology*, 28(4), 243–249.

Remez, L. (2000). Special report: Oral sex among adolescents: Is it sex or is it abstinence? *Family Planning Perspectives*, 32(6), 298–304.

Ruditis, P. (2005). *Rainbow Party.* New York: Simon and Schuster.

ISSUE 8

Is Comprehensive Sex Education for Adolescents Too Liberal?

YES: Aida Orgocka, from "Perceptions of Communication and Education About Sexuality Among Muslim Immigrant Girls in the US," *Sex Education* (October 2004)

NO: John Santelli et al., from "Abstinence and Abstinence-Only Education: A Review of U.S. Policies and Programs," *Journal of Adolescent Health* (vol. 38, 2006)

ISSUE SUMMARY

YES: Aida Orgocka, a gender and development expert at the University of Illinois, presents a qualitative study of Illinois mothers' and daughters' perceptions of the sexual health school curriculum from a Muslim perspective. The participants tended to find the sex education curriculum at odds with Muslim values such that many of the girls opted to forgo the school-based sexual health classes.

NO: John Santelli, a professor of clinical population, family health, and clinical pediatrics at the Mailman School of Public Health in Columbia University, and colleagues review current U.S. policies encouraging abstinence-only sexual health education and discuss the potential negative impact and ethical considerations arising from these policies on adolescent sexual practices.

In recent years, the U.S. federal government has substantially increased funding for abstinence-based education while simultaneously placing more restrictions on what other sexual health topics are covered by this funding. If a sex education curriculum discusses other options (e.g., the benefits of using condoms or other forms of birth control), the program would not be eligible for funding under these policies and programs. While sex educators agree that abstinence is the most effective means of preventing pregnancy, sexually transmitted infections (STIs), and HIV/AIDS, they acknowledge that a substantial proportion of youth engage in sexual activity during their teen years and that much of this occurs prior to marriage. Thus, sex educators tend to promote the use of comprehensive sex education curricula; this is sometimes called "abstinence plus." That is, abstinence is a part of the curriculum, but discussion of what methods students can use to prevent STIs and pregnancy *if* they become or are sexually active are also presented.

Sex education researchers conclude that comprehensive sexuality education programs sometimes have no impact on students' sexual behavior. However, when these programs do have an effect, research tends to find that participants are more likely to postpone first sexual intercourse to a later date, reduce frequency of intercourse and the number of sexual partners, increase contraceptive use, and have a lower teen pregnancy rate (Kirby, 1997, 2001). Thus, when comprehensive sex education programs have an effect, it is in the desirable direction.

In contrast, there has been little empirical evidence to support the efficacy of abstinence-only programs (Hauser, 2004). Also, the Waxman Report (December 2004), prepared for the U.S. House of Representative Committee on Government Reform, investigated 13 commonly used abstinence-only sexual health education curricula and concluded that 11 out of 13 programs contained unproven claims, subjective conclusions, or factual inaccuracies.

Advocates of abstinence-only programs come from a more morally based viewpoint. That is, North American societies are pluralistic, and different perspectives may not be represented in the relatively more permissive sexuality education programs (i.e., comprehensive sex education curricula). Abstinence-only proponents fear that moral ideologies informing sexuality ideologies might be discounted by the more liberal curricula. For example, if the dominant sex education culture within a school curriculum endorses behaviors such as oral sex and masturbation as acceptable, this may be at odds with the moral and sexual teachings of a particular religious group. Thus, the sex education curriculum is seen as contradicting the particular religious value system and might be characterized as attempting to "indoctrinate" students into accepting an ideological system contravening the ideologies taught at home. In particular, Muslim students and parents often find the sex education curriculum dominated by Judeo-Christian ideology and values that are often deemed as culturally inappropriate (see Sanjakdar, 2004).

Santelli and colleagues present an analysis of abstinence and abstinence-only education policies in the United States. They present a variety of health-based reasons as to why comprehensive sex education—including abstinence discussions—is preferable to abstinence-only initiatives. They discuss the ethics of abstinence-only programs: (1) that abstinence-only violates students' rights to accurate sexual health information; (2) that they hold sexual minority (e.g., gay) students to a higher standard than heterosexual students; and (3) that they violate free choice and informed consent principles. Orgocka represents a somewhat opposing viewpoint by presenting a study of Muslim mothers and daughters who find that North American sex education is ideologically incompatible with their religious teachings regarding sexuality. As a result, these students may feel marginalized, and many elect to opt out of the school-based sex education.

YES

Aida Orgocka

Perceptions of Communication and Education About Sexuality Among Muslim Immigrant Girls in the U.S

Introduction

For the past three decades, issues of sexuality education for adolescents have occupied the agendas of researchers and policy makers alike. And although one in five children in the US live in an immigrant-headed household, we know surprisingly little about the challenges these youths face in obtaining information about sexuality, including biological reproduction, sexual intercourse, and sexual pleasure. This is particularly so for young immigrant girls who, through their sexual behavior, bear the brunt of maintaining family honor and ethnic and religious integrity. Parental perceptions that knowledge about sexuality leads to promiscuous sexual activity create obstacles for young immigrant girls wanting to obtain information about reproductive health.

This . . . study [investigated] how the interaction between Muslim immigrant mothers and their daughters shaped the daughters' agency in negotiating decisions about sexual conduct. It examines sexuality communication and education among Muslim immigrant girls in the US as mediated by their mothers and school-based sexuality education (SBSE) classes.

Exploring the link between these two channels of information is particularly interesting if not essential. Among Muslims, parents are a main source for teaching youths about sexuality and moral values regarding sexual conduct. Because education about sexuality is gender segregated, mothers teach their daughters, and fathers teach their sons. For Muslim immigrant families, in particular, educating activities at home are considered a necessity to counter the dominant information children receive at school, through their peers and the media. Because Muslim mothers are considered responsible for girls' sexual conduct, discussion of issues related to sexuality takes the form of moral interdiction and limits on outside influences, including SBSE programs.

Among religious Muslims, learning about sex in the school curriculum is viewed as part of a belief system that condones premarital sexuality rather than as a subject in the school curriculum. Although SBSE programs provide useful information regarding sexual health, skill-building and independent

From *Sex Education,* vol. 4, no. 3, October 2004, pp. 255–271. Copyright © 2004 by Taylor & Francis, Ltd. Reprinted by permission. Note: The complete text of this article contains many references to specific studies described. The interested individual should refer to the original publication for these extensive citations. These references have been omitted here in the interest of brevity.

decision-making information pertaining to sexual conduct, they may be perceived as propagating information that contradicts what youths are taught at home. Giving youths the tools to have 'safe' premarital sex is contrary to Islam and Muslim code of behavior. Parents perceive that these classes particularly challenge transmission of Islamic values to young girls by teaching them to conceptualize decision-making regarding sexual conduct as a personal rather than a family matter. As a result, most Muslim immigrant parents object to their children participating in SBSE classes. Some mothers may favor sending girls to SBSE classes, but all feel particularly responsible for countering information that challenges the moral values learnt at home.

Because sexuality education for Muslim families is closely connected to heterosexual partnership and marriage, the study's assumption was that girls participating in this research were heterosexual and would eventually marry. Focus group and individual semi-structured interviews were used to explore [the question,] What are the perceptions of mothers and daughters regarding school-based sexuality education classes?

Methods

Participants

Thirty mothers (mean age = 43.17 . . .) and their 38 daughters (mean age = 16.59, . . .) were recruited through snowball sampling techniques and by frequently visiting the local mosques and Islamic centers in Illinois. Over 83% of the mothers had been in the US for more than 10 years. About 47% had received a college education and about 53% were homemakers. All mothers were married. Daughters were predominantly US born (76%) with the rest having migrated with their parents when they were very young (24%). One attended middle school and another was home schooled (6%), 71% attended high school (53% in local public high schools and 47% local private high schools), and 23% attended college. Praying was central to most mothers and daughters. Seventy-seven per cent of the mothers and 68% of the daughters prayed at least three times a day. More mothers than daughters wore *hijab* (veil) (63% vs. 32%). Both mothers and daughters engaged in other aspects of being Muslim including wearing modest clothing, reading the *Qur'an*, and participating in activities of Muslim community. In addition to extended family, schools, and individual reading and exploration, both mothers and daughters identified their parents as important sources of Muslim education.

Data Collection Strategies

. . . The main body of data for this paper is based on focus groups and semi-structured interviews. In addition to helping elicit sensitive and rich contextual information, these were considered as empowering strategies that allowed Muslim mothers and daughters to express and reflect upon their own personal perspectives. . . . [The] wording of questions was kept almost the same for both mothers and daughters.

Focus groups were used to gain research insights and increase understanding of group perspectives on communication and education about sexuality. They also served as a preliminary tool to help develop the semi-structured guide for the individual interviews that were conducted afterwards. . . . To gauge their perceptions about SBSE classes, both mothers and daughters initially rated how often girls should attend SBSE classes on a five point scale of '1 = never' to '5 = always', and then were asked to elaborate on the answer.

Procedure

. . . Four group discussions with the mothers and six group discussions with the daughters were conducted separately in English. Up to five participants participated in each group. They were homogeneously grouped in terms of socio-economic status, age, marital status, place of residence, religiousness, country of origin and length of stay in the USA (especially for the mothers). . . .

The individual semi-structured interviews were also conducted separately with each of the mothers and daughters in English. For those few participants who were not fluent in English, at their request, a key informant who was fluent in Arabic and English attended the interview sessions. In a few other instances the mothers requested that their daughters be part of the interview process to translate for them in case they did not understand. . . .

The recorded material was transcribed *verbatim*. The analysis focused on representing mothers' and daughters' perceptions through their accounts. . . . Codes were oriented toward participants' understandings of communication with each other, as well as their perceptions of SBSE classes. . . . Upon coding, I identified the themes that permeated the group discussions and the interviews. . . .

[In] this study I looked for convergence in emergent themes across a sample of group discussions rather than across participants within a group. Perspectives of individual mothers and daughters were the focus of analysis in the interview material. The expectation for this part of the analysis was that both mothers and daughters would see communication and education about sexuality differently due to different immigration, age and education experiences.

Results

Perceptions of School-Based Sexuality Education

[More] daughters [29%] than mothers [3%] were of the opinion that they should 'rarely' attend SBSE classes. In addition, more mothers [30%] than daughters [11%] agreed that daughters should 'always' attend these SBSE classes. Group discussions and individual interviews shed light on some of the reasons for these answers.

Mothers' perceptions.   A common concern for mothers was that the dominant socio-cultural environment was very suggestive and conductive to unregulated and unrestricted sexual activity. In the mothers' words, 'unbridled sexuality' is so pervasive in the US that they 'can't even realize it,' 'the ads, kissing, hugging, whatever you call it, sex.' Given this socio-cultural environment, mothers often commented that their daughters should attend SBSE classes to obtain the 'correct information.' While they did not approve whole-heartedly of their daughters' participation in SBSE classes because they thought the family should provide the sexuality education, mothers were concerned that the alternative source of information could be their daughters' peers whose knowledge, in their opinion, was usually cloaked in misinformation and age-related curiosity:

> I would rather them know that in a clinical manner than what they hear in the hallways. I personally would not like the school to play any role in sex education at all, but I know realistically that the people she is around are sexually active, some as early as the age of eight. I don't want her to be totally ignorant of what's going on, and unfortunately because of the society we live in she needs to be aware.

Some mothers agreed that SBSE classes provided important information, especially when this information was worded in a technical and scientific fashion. Mothers reported that sexuality education facilitated information that they otherwise would not have been able to give because they were never given such information and they did not have the proper knowledge and skills to discuss these issues. A mother recalled that 'even when I was having a baby, I didn't know what was happening to me, and my husband didn't know anything either.' Other mothers thought that it was useful that SBSE classes focused on the diseases that resulted from unprotected sex because 'if she [knows] and if she [learns] in school, she will not do it.'

Despite the usefulness of SBSE classes, mothers perceived that some of the contents of the classes were problematic. Mothers perceived that these classes, by discussing dating and premarital sexual relations, encouraged a lifestyle that was un-Islamic. Pointing to this concern, some of the mothers did not consent to their daughters attending sexuality education classes.

> She doesn't have to take a sex class. I didn't take any sex class and I am fine. So it is a natural thing, you catch up with the stuff . . . I still remember one of my friends, her kids, in school they teach about sex in fifth grade and I heard that her daughter came and told her mom they showed something about banana and how to give oral sex and stuff. I don't want them to know all that . . . Like the next thing they will say is 'OK, mom, I want to take a class where they can teach you different positions!' I don't want that.

Mothers also reported that the means through which sexuality information was shared was inappropriate. Mothers objected to the use of videos as didactic materials on account that showing these videos could lead to girls wanting to experiment with sex.

That mothers perceived SBSE classes to be pushing an un-Islamic lifestyle was a main motivator for mothers to counter the information that was given in these classes. A few mothers reported that they sat in the classes to ascertain that the material was 'decent.' They also engaged in additional conversations with their teenage daughters and countered material presented in SBSE classes with Islamic views on premarital sexuality.

Daughters' perceptions. Daughters echoed the mothers' concern that in the environment they live in 'whether you want it or not you get all the information about sex.' They learnt about sex in public school, on the street, through friends—both female and male—who carried condoms in their pockets and bragged that they were 'cool' because 'they are not virgin.' While the girls did not intend to engage in premarital sex, they agreed that SBSE classes provided them with information that they could use in the future. Rather than battle with the changes in their bodies, they learned to understand and interpret these changes. Furthermore, these classes taught girls how to deal with any consequences that came from surprise situations such as attacks from a sex offender.

A few girls reported that SBSE classes, by being informative, helped them challenge the value-laden information they received at home. Bringing a book home helped daughters facilitate a more open discussion with mothers who attempted to teach about sex and sexuality through scare tactics.

> You get some good information in these classes. All my mother would tell me, she would tell me like myths . . . hypothetical things, things that old ladies from generation to generation will tell her. Like 'Mom, that's not even true!' Like women born without a hymen . . . I told my mom, 'The nurses came in and they showed us how to put on the condom.' And she was like, 'Why are they teaching you how to do that?' Like 'Because there's girls that are already doing that mom!' She doesn't realize.

Despite the usefulness of these classes, some girls, like their mothers, perceived that some of the contents of the classes were problematic. A few girls perceived that SBSE classes were not sensitive to the religious and cultural differences of students attending those classes. By concentrating on students who planned to be involved in sexual activities before graduating from high school, these classes marginalized the experiences of those students that did not intend to involve in such activities:

> Maybe a sex education class should take into account that not everybody sitting there and watching the videos cares nothing about them. I think it was mostly geared towards Americans, maybe the Christian point of view, and not take into account some people don't like to talk about it and don't know much about it. The levels of experience are different. But it was a kind of shock when I first had it, 'cause my parents didn't tell me. Most of my peers knew almost everything . . . They don't think it was a big deal and I did.

SBSE classes that discussed sexual relationships, also covered the consequences of unprotected sexual intercourse. However, girls perceived that these classes focused more than was necessary on warnings about diseases, infections and teenage pregnancy. Since Muslim girls participating in this study did not intend to engage in premarital sex, they found the material not only irrelevant but also distasteful. Three girls in the study defined sex as 'sick' and 'disgusting' and more had decided to not take SBSE classes.

Some girls suggested that the SBSE classes would be more useful if they were taught in gender-segregated classes. These would allow both male and female students to ask questions and not feel embarrassed because the other sex was present. SBSE classes had to also be age appropriate. Invariably, daughters recalled that they felt uncomfortable when their classmates giggled at the information being presented in class.

In the end, it is important to point out yet another observation. Muslim immigrant mothers and daughters participating in the study were not against sexuality education in principle. A few girls considered learning about sex and sexuality as part of their duty of being Muslim women. Learning about sex within the framework of Islam was for them, first and foremost, a religious requirement. An 18-year-old girl expressed this succinctly when she commented that 'as a Muslim, I should not be ashamed to discuss sex, or marriage, or issues of menstruation or anything, because we have the religious obligation to know this.'

Discussion

While the findings discussed here are restricted only to the researched group of Muslim immigrant mothers and daughters, themes may be extrapolated for work with Muslim and non-Muslim immigrant youth and their parents. Discussion of the study results focuses on [these] areas: . . . [a] sensitizing SBSE programs to the diversity of US populations; [b] implications for cooperation between parents and schools; and [c] implications for involvement of the community in youth's sexuality education. . . .

Sensitizing School-Based Sexuality Education

A good majority of the girls that had or were currently attending SBSE classes agreed that these classes were informative, especially when focusing on the anatomy of the female body. Topics such as body changes associated with biological maturity and menstruation were well explained. In fact, obtaining this information facilitated communication about sexuality between mothers and daughters and helped girls frame sexuality education as necessary within a larger perspective of premarital teenage pregnancy. Some mothers agreed that these classes were helpful to the daughters, since they did not have the scientific knowledge or the skills to talk to their daughters about sexuality. In fact, they indicated that as long as the SBSE classes were restricted to providing technical information through books they did not object.

While the SBSE classes provided useful information, some mothers had withdrawn their daughters from SBSE classes and some girls themselves did not express interest in attending these classes. Both mothers and daughters were dissatisfied with some of the contents and the way the classes were conducted. The majority of the girls that had attended SBSE classes perceived these classes to provide information in such a way that the choice to engage in sex was predetermined or assumed. As such, Muslim girls felt that these classes marginalized their experiences and decision to abstain from premarital sexual relationships. In fact, a few girls considered classes taught in this way a waste of time and energy. Mothers echoed these concerns and either prevented girls from attending these classes, or provided supplementary information within the Islamic framework to distance girls from experiences that these classes portrayed as normative for adolescents.

The other major dissatisfaction was that SBSE classes at times were a long series of warnings and diseases that came from unprotected sex. Muslim girls found unappealing such conceptualization of classes, and a few of them thought that they would engage in sex out of necessity to have babies only. Furthermore, both mothers and daughters agreed that most of this information was imparted at too early an age for girls. That some mothers and daughters disapproved of placing too much emphasis on unplanned pregnancies and sexually transmitted infections and diseases does not imply that SBSE classes should not cover these topics. The high rate of adolescent pregnancies and STDs makes imparting such information necessary. Furthermore, even if a person only has one partner, that partner may have had other experiences and that makes knowing the signs of an STI or STD imperative. However, it is possible that because these classes may have overemphasized the risks that came from unprotected sexual intercourse, they may have failed to describe sexuality as an integral part of developmental experience.

The objections mentioned here are not unique to Muslim immigrant populations. Aarons and Jenkins (2002) reported that Latino and African-American youth preferred clinics to schools for sex education and related services because the latter did not fit the reality of youths' lives. Ward and Taylor (1994) found that immigrant and minority youths perceived that SBSE classes failed to incorporate the reality that emotions related to sexuality are framed by cultural values and beliefs, that instructors were insensitive to youths' experiences and made assumptions about these youths based upon cultural stereotypes. While these findings may be skewed because only the perceptions of immigrant youths are reported, they suggest that sex educators face a challenging task in accomplishing the goal of reaching the diverse youths of America.

Fostering Collaboration Between Parents and Schools

Findings indicated that mothers were open to schools helping with education about sexuality. Most had reviewed and signed permission slips required for girls' participation in SBSE classes. Few took the initiative to reach out to schools and review the materials presented in these classes. That overwhelmingly mothers perceived that SBSE classes challenged the values imparted at home may evidence that mothers had a limited understanding of the contents and the manner in which information regarding sexuality was imparted in these classes.

To be sure, mothers play an active role in sexuality education and schools may help bridge the education experiences at home and school for immigrant youths. Sexuality educators may want to borrow from the experience of projects that address issues of achievement and English proficiency for immigrant youths. For example, Pecoraro and Magnuson (2001) suggest, among other strategies, that in order to better involve parents in school efforts to teach immigrant youths, schools need to build on what people already know from their experiences as parents and teachers in their home countries and create opportunities for parents to explore similarities and differences between new and native countries and to build bridges that will link the two experiences. Helping parents actively participate in the design of the sexuality education curricula as well as organizing classes for these parents may be two strategies for bringing parents closer to school and thus acquitting SBSE classes often perceived as challenging the transmission of family values.

Implications for Involvement of the Muslim Community

Muslim immigrant girls may have little knowledge about sexuality and may often be unprepared to deal with issues regarding sexuality and reproductive health. That girls may not be able to get information about sexuality through communication with mothers and/or sexuality education classes requires an exploration of other information venues. Two additional sources of information for Muslim girls and their parents could be registering/attending Islamic private schools and using resources offered by Islamic centers. Islamic schools shape their curricula within the parameters of Islam. Sexuality education is part of these curricula. A few girls in the study attended local private Islamic schools. They related that the classes were sex segregated and the curriculum was tailored to the students' ages. For example, actual explanations of intercourse within the framework of marriage were given to girls at the age of 17, the assumption being that these girls would soon marry. Although Islamic private schools address concerns of Muslim communities, only a fraction of Muslim families can afford to enroll their daughters in these schools.

Because most students attend public schools, the weight of supplementary sexuality education rests with the Islamic centers that overwhelmingly provide alternative education through Sunday schools. However, informal conversations with a few of the study's key informants suggested that no curriculum is in place to educate the young girls on issues of sexuality and marriage or to help parents discuss these issues. Islamic centers with such curricula have the potential to help both youth and their parents talk and learn about sexuality. Apart from brochures and booklets, these centers may help mothers become better sexuality educators by providing them with the information and skills necessary to talk not only about the technicalities but also the cognitive and affective dimensions of sexuality. Evaluation research on community efforts among other populations has shown that parent-training programs can significantly increase parents' knowledge and frequency of communicating with their adolescent children.

Islamic centers' efforts to serve Muslim youths have to be coupled with finding ways to attract these youths to their programs. About 40% of the girls participating in the study felt that they did not receive any information at the local Islamic center. Of the 50% who reported that they received information regarding women's duties and responsibilities at the Center, 30% were of the opinion that they received some instruction on how a woman dresses and behaves. Only 3% said they received information on spousal relationships.

This is consistent with findings from other research that shows that one of the major complaints is that most Islamic centers just teach the *Qur'an*, but not about life or social values (Husain & O'Brien, 1999).

To attract more girls, Islamic centers may work with primarily non-governmental organizations (NGOs) that have gained experience from tackling issues of sexuality education. For example, Girls Incorporated, a nationally recognized NGO, has developed age-appropriate curricula (Preventing Adolescent Pregnancy) that help girls aged 9–18 and their parents deal with issues of learning about sexuality and making decisions accordingly. A three-year evaluation found that girls who had attended this program regularly were half as likely to have sex as girls who had participated less or not at all in the program. While not everything presented in this program has relevance for Muslim immigrant girls it should be borne in mind that these girls live in the US and are exposed to sexuality-related issues with the same intensity as their non-Muslim peers. Programs developed by Girls Incorporated can throw in relief concerns about how contemporary information about sexuality should be. Because such programs are well-versed in the challenges that US girls face regarding dealing with their own sexuality, they may be combined with Islamic tenets and be used to design curricula and didactic materials (brochures, videos) that provide supplementary information for young Muslim girls.

Future Directions

While this study focused on Muslim immigrant girls and their mothers, research also needs to target how Muslim immigrant adolescent boys obtain information regarding sexuality. Research shows that Muslim adolescent males may be more sexually active than Muslim adolescent females (Kulwicki, 1989). Therefore, learning about sexuality is an imperative for better sexual and reproductive health for them, too. Moreover, although fathers are supposed to serve as conduits of information regarding sexuality, they may play this role minimally. Research with other populations has shown that this task is particularly daunting for fathers since talking about sexuality requires establishing an intimate bond and that challenges the principles of traditional masculinity (Kirkman *et al.*, 2001). These remarks warrant the importance of future studies in the field of understanding sexuality communication and education among immigrant male youths.

This research is not intended as a critique and/or evaluation of any particular sexuality education program. Its findings are based on perceptions of mothers and daughters and should be interpreted cautiously and not serve to dismiss the usefulness of SBSE classes. Worldwide, these programs aim to prevent and/or lower teenage pregnancy, inform about and reduce the chances of infection with STDs including HIV/AIDS, teach about the relationships between the sexes, provide an ethical framework for the expression of sexuality, and provide examples of healthy lifestyles, including a discussion of marriage relationships. These programs address biological, socio-cultural, psychological and spiritual dimensions of sexuality. Thus, it is imperative that the perceptions of educators and policy analysts should be taken into consideration.

Conclusion

This research explored Muslim immigrant girls' communication and education about sexuality as mediated by their mothers and SBSE classes. . . . The study . . . found that while SBSE classes were informative to girls, in participants' perceptions they marginalized Muslim immigrants girls' decisions and experiences to not engage in premarital sex by assuming that most adolescents engage in sex. This study's recommendation is that in order for SBSE programs to be effective they need to be characterized by cultural sensitivity to the diverse youth that need to obtain this information. Although SBSE may be attempting to address the various needs of immigrant youths, findings indicated that they have not yet adequately reached the Muslim community. Findings also showed that mothers and daughters were more open to sexuality education than indicated in the literature. Thus, further dialogue between schools and parents could be useful. Although surveying Islamic community efforts in educating young Muslim girls and their mothers was not part of this study, the limited sexuality-related knowledge girls received from communicating with their mothers and SBSE classes suggests that Islamic centers may be a potential venue through which girls and their mothers may obtain information about sexuality within the Islamic framework.

References

Aarons, S. J. & Jenkins, R. R. (2002) Sex, pregnancy, and contraception-related motivators and barriers among Latino and African-American youth in Washington, DC, *Sex Education*, 2, 5–30.

Husain, F. & O'Brien, M. (1999) *Muslim families in Europe: social existence and social care* (London, University of North London).

Kirkman, M., Rosenthal, D. A. & Feldman, S. S. (2001) Freeing up the subject: tension between traditional masculinity and involved fatherhood through communication about sexuality with adolescents, *Culture, Health & Sexuality*, 3, 391–411.

Kulwicki (1989) *Adolescent health needs assessment survey: executive summary* (Office of Minority Health, Michigan Department of Public Health).

Pecoraro, D. & Magnuson, P. (Eds) (2001) *LEP parent involvement: a guide for connecting immigrant parents and schools* (St. Paul, MN, Minnesota State Department of Children, Families and Learning).

Ward, J. V. & Taylor, J. M. (1994) Sexuality education for immigrant and minority students: developing a culturally appropriate curriculum, in: J. M. Irvine (Ed.) *Sexual cultures and the construction of adolescent identities* (Philadelphia, PA, Temple University Press).

John Santelli et al.

 **NO**

Abstinence and Abstinence-Only Education: A Review of U.S. Policies and Programs

This [paper] reviews key issues related to understanding and evaluating abstinence-only (AOE) or abstinence-until-marriage policies. We use the term AOE programs and policies to describe those that adhere to federal requirements (Table 1). We begin with background information on definitions of abstinence, initiation of sexual intercourse and marriage, physical and psychological health outcomes from these behaviors, and public support for abstinence and comprehensive sexuality education. Next, we review current federal policy and evaluations of abstinence education, including approaches to program evaluation and concepts of efficacy in preventing pregnancy and sexually transmitted infections (STIs). We then turn to the impact of AOE on other programs and the implications of AOE for specific populations such as youth who are sexually active (i.e., currently engaging in intercourse) and gay,

Table 1

Federal Definition of Abstinence-Only Education

Under Section 510 of the 1996 Social Security Act abstinence education is defined as an educational or motivational program which:

(A) has as its exclusive purpose, teaching the social, psychological, and health gains to be realized by abstaining from sexual activity

(B) teaches abstinence from sexual activity outside marriage as the expected standard for all school-age children

(C) teaches that abstinence from sexual activity is the only certain way to avoid out-of-wedlock pregnancy, sexually transmitted diseases, and other associated health problems

(D) teaches that a mutually faithful monogamous relationship in the context of marriage is the expected standard of human sexual activity

(E) teaches that sexual activity outside of the context of marriage is likely to have harmful psychological and physical effects

(F) teaches that bearing children out-of-wedlock is likely to have harmful consequences for the child, the child's parents, and society

(G) teaches young people how to reject sexual advances and how alcohol and drug use increases vulnerability to sexual advances

(H) teaches the importance of attaining self-sufficiency before engaging in sexual activity

From *Journal of Adolescent Health,* vol. 38, 2006, pp. 72–81. Copyright © 2006 by Elsevier Health Sciences. Reprinted by permission. Note: The complete text of this article contains many references to specific studies described. The interested individual should refer to the original publication for these extensive citations. These references have been omitted here in the interest of brevity.

lesbian, bisexual, transgender, and questioning (GLBTQ) youth. Finally, we explore critical human rights issues raised by AOE, including the right to health information and the ethical obligations of health care providers and health educators. . . .

Definitions of Abstinence

Abstinence, as the term is used by program planners and policymakers, is often not clearly defined. Abstinence may be defined in behavioral terms, such as "postponing sex" or "never had vaginal sex," or refraining from further sexual intercourse if sexually experienced, i.e., ever had sexual intercourse. Other sexual behaviors may or may not be considered within the definition of "abstinence," including touching, kissing, mutual masturbation, oral sex, and anal sex. Self-identified "virgins" engage in a variety of non-coital genital activities. Sexual behavior among adolescents is often sporadic, and "secondary abstinence" is common.

Abstinence, as used in government policies and local programs, is also frequently defined in moral terms, using language such as "chaste" or "virgin" and framing abstinence as an attitude or a commitment. One study of abstinence-only program directors, instructors, and youth found that all groups defined abstinence in moral terms, such as "making a commitment" and "being responsible," as well as in more behavioral terms, such as not engaging in coitus.[1] Federal regulations for domestic AOE funding also adopt a moral and culturally specific definition of abstinence, requiring that abstinence education "teaches that a mutually faithful monogamous relationship in context of marriage is the expected standard of human sexual activity."

In understanding the ongoing debates about abstinence education, it is important to understand that although health professionals generally view abstinence as a behavioral issue or as a health issue, many advocates of AOE programs are primarily concerned with issues such as character and morality, based on their specific religious or moral beliefs. In this review, we have defined abstinence as abstinence from sexual intercourse and focused on abstinence as a public health issue, recognizing that many people view abstinence as a moral or religious issue.

Initiation of Sexual Intercourse and Marriage

Although abstinence until marriage is the goal of many abstinence policies and programs, few Americans wait until marriage to initiate sexual intercourse. Most Americans initiate sexual intercourse during their adolescent years. Recent data indicate that the median age at first intercourse for women was 17.4 years, whereas the median age at first marriage was 25.3 years. . . .

[Health] Outcomes for Adolescent Sexual Behaviors

Initiation of sexual intercourse in adolescence is accompanied by considerable risk of STIs and pregnancy. Adolescents have the highest age-specific risk for many STIs, and the highest age-specific proportion of unintended pregnancy in the United States. . . . Long-term sequelae of STIs can include infertility, tubal pregnancy, fetal and infant demise, chronic pelvic pain, and cervical cancer. A significant proportion of human immunodeficiency virus (HIV) infections appear to be acquired during adolescence. . . .

Although federal AOE funding language requires teaching that sexual activity outside of the context of marriage is likely to have harmful psychological effects, there are no scientific data suggesting that consensual sex between adolescents is harmful. . . . We are aware of no reports that address whether the initiation of adolescent sexual intercourse itself has an adverse impact on mental health. We also know little about whether purposively remaining abstinent until marriage promotes personal resiliency or sexual function or dysfunction in adulthood. . . .

Public Support for Abstinence and Comprehensive Sexuality Education

Public opinion polls suggest strong support for abstinence as a behavioral goal for adolescents.[2-3] These polls also indicate strong support for education about contraception and for access to contraception for sexually active adolescents.

Data from a recent nationwide poll of middle school and high school parents found overwhelming support for sex education in school; 90% believed it was very or somewhat important that sex education be taught in school, whereas 7% of parents did not want sex education to be taught.[3] Only 15% wanted an abstinence-only form of sex education. Parents thought it was appropriate to provide high school and middle school youth with broad information on sexual issues. . . . In these polls, most parents and most adolescents do not see education that stresses abstinence while also providing information about contraception as a mixed message.[2-3]

Current Federal Policy and Local Programs

Although the federal government began supporting abstinence promotion programs in 1981 via the Adolescent Family Life Act (AFLA), since 1996 there have been major expansions in federal support for abstinence programming and a shift to funding programs that teach only abstinence and restrict other information. These expansions include Section 510 of the Social Security Act in 1996, which was part of welfare reform, and Community-Based Abstinence Education projects in 2000, funded through an earmark in the maternal child health block grant for Special Projects of Regional and National Significance (SPRANS) program. The SPRANS program bypasses the 510 program's state approval processes and makes grants directly to community-based organizations. Eligible applicants include faith-based organizations. Both 510 and SPRANS programs prohibit disseminating information on contraceptive services, sexual orientation and gender identity, and other aspects of human sexuality. Section 510 provides an eight-point definition of abstinence-only education (Table 1) and specifies that programs must have as their "exclusive purpose" the promotion of abstinence outside of marriage and may not in any way advocate contraceptive use or discuss contraceptive methods except to emphasize their failure rates.

Since fiscal year (FY) 1997, programs funded under the AFLA have been required to comply with these Section 510 requirements. The initial implementation of 510 has allowed funded programs to emphasize different aspects of these eight points as long as the program did not contradict any of them. The Congressional intent of the SPRANS program was more rigid: to create "pure" abstinence-only programs, in response to concerns that states were using funds for "soft" activities such as media campaigns instead of direct classroom instruction and were targeting younger adolescents. Programs funded under SPRANS must teach all eight components of the federal definition, they must target 12–18-year-olds, and, except in limited circumstances, they cannot provide young people they serve with information about contraception or safer-sex practices, even with their own non-federal funds. Three states, including, most recently, Maine, have refused federal AOE funding given federal restrictions on providing information about contraception.

Federal funding for abstinence-only programs has increased from $60 million in FY 1998 to $168 million in FY 2005. Section 510 requires funded states to match three state dollars for every four federal dollars. Virtually all the growth in funding since FY 2001 (to $105 million in FY 2005) has come in the SPRANS program. In 2004, the administration of the 510 program and SPRANS program was moved administratively within the Department of Health and Human Services (DHHS), from the health-focused Maternal and Child Health Bureau (MCHB) to the Administration of Children and Families, the federal agency that promotes marriage and responsible fatherhood, reportedly in order "to enhance and coordinate similar youth programs within HHS." This move may also have reflected some Congressional dissatisfaction with MCHB's flexible implementation of the program.

Evaluations of Abstinence-Only Education and Comprehensive Sexuality Education Programs in Promoting Abstinence

To demonstrate efficacy, evaluations of specific abstinence promotion programs must address methodological issues including (1) clear definitions of abstinence. . . , (2) appropriate research design, (3) measurement issues including social desirability bias, and (4) the use of behavior changes as outcomes. Evaluations should also consider the use of biological outcomes such as STIs, in addition to behavioral measures. Experimental and quasi-experimental research designs can be used to avoid self-selection bias and to isolate program effect from changes in the individual due to increasing age or maturation. Biological outcomes such as STI incidence or prevalence may significantly improve the validity of program evaluations.

Two recent systematic reviews examined the evidence supporting abstinence-only programs and comprehensive sexuality education programs designed to promote abstinence from sexual intercourse.[4–5] These reviews employed similar scientific criteria in selecting studies for evaluation. Program evaluations had to have been conducted since 1980, conducted in the United States or Canada, targeted teens under age 18, used an experimental or quasi-experimental design, and measured behavioral effects such as timing of first intercourse. Kirby also included studies that measured impact on pregnancy or childbearing but did not measure sexual behavior.

Both reviews demonstrated that comprehensive sexuality education effectively promoted abstinence as well as other protective behaviors. Among 28 studies of comprehensive programs evaluated in the Kirby review, nine were able to delay initiation of sexual intercourse, 18 showed no impact, and one hastened initiation of sex. Manlove et al identified three different types of comprehensive sexuality programs, and found that six of nine sex education programs delayed the onset of sex, compared with a control group, five of seven HIV/STI prevention programs delayed the onset of sex, and all four youth development programs delayed the onset of sex.

In contrast to the positive impact in delaying sexual intercourse seen with some comprehensive sexuality programs, Kirby found no scientific evidence that abstinence-only programs demonstrate efficacy in delaying initiation of sexual intercourse. Kirby found only three studies evaluating the impact of five different abstinence-only curricula that met minimal criteria for inclusion in the systematic review. No new study results have changed this conclusion (personal communication with Doug Kirby, November 2004). The more recent (2004) review by Manlove, reviewing many of the same studies, reached similar conclusions. Both Manlove and Kirby identified the lack of rigorously evaluated programs as a major problem in evaluating the effectiveness of abstinence-only education.

Non-peer-reviewed studies provide little support for the current federal support for abstinence-only programs. A review by Robert Rector identified 10 evaluations of AOE programs that appeared to demonstrate behavior change as a result of program participation.[6] However, few of these evaluations met the minimum scientific criteria listed above, and all contained flaws in methodology or interpretation of the data that could lead to significantly biased results. A review of 10 state program evaluations by Advocates for Youth found no evidence of an impact on adolescent sexual behavior.[7]

A rigorous national evaluation of abstinence-only education is currently being conducted by Mathematica Policy Research, Inc. with support from the DHHS's Office of the Assistant Secretary for Planning and Evaluation (OASPE). The second report from the Mathematica evaluation of first-year impacts of the programs did not include information on behavioral outcomes, reportedly given the short duration of follow-up. First-year impacts did include an increase in abstinence intentions (i.e., pledging to abstain from sex until marriage) and small effects on both norms supportive of abstinence and perceived consequences of teen and non-marital sex. No impacts were found for self-efficacy, self-esteem, or perceived self-control. A report on behavioral outcomes [was] planned . . . in 2005.

The minority staff of the Committee on Government Reform of the U.S. House of Representatives reviewed commonly used abstinence-only curricula for evidence of scientific accuracy. This report found that 11 of the 13 curricula contained false, misleading, or distorted information about reproductive health, including inaccurate information about contraceptive effectiveness, the risks of abortion, and other scientific errors. These curricula treat stereotypes about girls and boys as scientific fact and blur religious and scientific viewpoints.

Although counseling about abstinence is recommended as part of the American Medical Association's Guidelines for Adolescent Preventive Services, we found no published evaluations of clinical counseling to promote abstinence.

Concepts of Efficacy for Abstinence in Preventing Pregnancy and STIs

Abstinence from sexual intercourse has been described as fully protective against pregnancy and sexually transmitted infections. This is misleading and potentially harmful because it conflates theoretical effectiveness with the actual practice of abstinence. Abstinence is not 100% effective in preventing pregnancy or STIs as many teens fail in remaining abstinent. Moreover, some STIs may be spread via other forms of sexual activity, such as kissing or manual or oral stimulation. In addition to the program evaluations described above, attempts have been made to calculate the efficacy of abstinence in preventing pregnancy or STIs.

One approach has relied on notions from contraceptive efficacy research such as *method failure* or *perfect use* (i.e., theoretical or best use efficacy when a method is used perfectly, i.e., consistently and correctly) and *user failure* or *typical use* (i.e., effectiveness of a method as it is commonly used). However, efficacy trials of abstinence as a method of contraception that are comparable to contraceptive efficacy trials have not been conducted. The most useful data in understanding the efficacy of abstinence come from examination of the virginity pledge movement in the National Longitudinal Survey of Youth (Add Health) [49, 50]. Virginity pledgers, like contraceptive users, are a self-selected group.

Add Health data suggest that many teens who intend to be abstinent fail to do so, and that when abstainers do initiate intercourse, many fail to protect themselves by using contraception.[8-9] Bearman and colleagues have examined the virginity pledge movement; they estimate that over 2.5 million adolescents have taken public "virginity pledges." They found that pledgers were more likely to delay initiation of intercourse, 18 months on average for adolescents aged 12–18 years. However, those pledgers who failed at abstinence were less likely to use contraception after they did initiate sexual intercourse. At six-year follow-up, the prevalence of STIs (chlamydia, gonorrhea, trichomoniasis, and human papillomavirus [HPV]) was similar among those taking the abstinence pledge and non-pledgers.[9] Although pledgers tended to marry earlier than non-pledgers, if married, most pledgers had vaginal intercourse before marriage (88%). Virtually all non-pledgers who had married had sex before marriage (99%). Although pledgers had fewer sexual partners compared to non-pledgers, they were less likely to report seeing a doctor for an STI concern and were less likely to receive STI testing.

Robert Rector of the Heritage Foundation has reanalyzed the Add Health data and severely criticized the Bruckner study in a recent presentation.[10]

However, the Rector study has not undergone peer review and it, in turn, has been severely criticized for manipulating statistical norms for significance.[11] A serious flaw in this analysis was the use of self-reported STIs, instead of laboratory-reported infections as used in the Bruckner study. This is problematic given that many STIs are asymptomatic and pledgers were less likely to be tested for STIs.

Based on our review of the evaluations of specific AOE curricula and research on virginity pledges, user failure with abstinence appears to be very high. Thus, although theoretically completely effective in preventing pregnancy, in actual practice the efficacy of AOE interventions may approach zero.

Impact of Abstinence-Only Policies on Comprehensive Sexuality Education

. . . Although comprehensive sexuality education is broadly supported by health professionals, increasingly, abstinence-only education is replacing more comprehensive forms of sexuality education. In Texas, for example, the Texas Board of Education has decided to remove most information about contraception from new health education textbooks. Recent reports describe teachers and students being censured for responding to questions or discussing sexuality topics that are not approved by the school administrators, as well as restricting access to HIV/AIDS experts from the classroom, and censoring what experts and teachers can say in the classroom. The cancellation of Programs that Work from the Division of Adolescent and School Health at the Centers for Disease Control and Prevention, is another example. Programs that Work used a rigorous peer-reviewed process to identify programs that were effective in changing adolescent sexual risk behaviors; this cancellation is believed to be the result of the Center for Disease Control and Prevention's (CDC) failure to identify any abstinence-only programs as effective. Likewise, Rep. Henry Waxman in a July 2005 letter to DHHS Secretary Michael Leavitt criticized an abstinence-inspired DHHS website (4parent.gov) as inaccurate and ineffective, promoting misleading and inaccurate information on STIs and condoms, and providing a narrow focus on abstinence. The website used content from the National Physicians Center for Family Resources, a supporter of AOE, instead of scientists from the National Institutes of Health (NIH) or CDC or physicians from leading professional organizations such as the American Academy of Pediatrics or Society for Adolescent Medicine.

Surveys on health educational practice in the United States provide further evidence of an erosion of comprehensive sexuality education. Data from the School Health Policies and Programs Study in 2000 found that 92% of middle and junior high schools and 96% of high schools taught abstinence as the best way to avoid pregnancy, HIV, and STDs. Only 21% of junior high and 55% of high school teachers taught the correct use of condoms. Between 1988 and 1999, sharp declines occurred in the percentage of teachers who supported teaching about birth control, abortion, and sexual orientation, and in the percentages who actually taught these subjects. For example, in 1999, 23% of secondary school sexuality education teachers taught abstinence as the only way to prevent pregnancy and STDs, compared with only 2% who had done so in 1988. In 1999, one-quarter of sex education teachers said they were prohibited from teaching about contraception.

Impact of Federal Abstinence Policies on Pregnancy and HIV Prevention Programs

Federal and state governments provide support for family planning programs, which are available to adolescents through Title X of the Public Health Service Act. Title X program guidelines stress that abstinence should be discussed with all adolescent clients. Starting in the FY 2004 service delivery grant announcements, Office of Population Affairs announced that program priorities for Title X grantees would include a focus on extramarital abstinence education and counseling, increasing parental involvement in the decisions of minors to seek family planning services, the reporting of statutory rape, and working with faith-based organizations. Thus, Title X grantees are now expected to focus on these new priorities, while continuing to provide condoms and other contraceptive services, STI and HIV prevention education, cancer screening, and other reproductive health services. These changes may weaken efforts to promote effective reproductive health services for adolescents and unmarried individuals who are sexually active.

Language stressing abstinence has also appeared in drafts of the CDC's Interim HIV Content Guidelines for AIDS-Related Materials. These Guidelines require that "all programs of education and information receiving funds under this title shall include information about the harmful effects of promiscuous sexual activity and intravenous drug use, and the benefits of abstaining from such activities."

Abstinence-only policies by the U.S. government have also influenced global HIV prevention efforts. The President's Emergency Plan for AIDS Relief (PEPFAR), focusing on 15 countries in sub-Saharan Africa, the Caribbean, and Asia that have been severely affected by AIDS, requires grantees to devote at least 33% of prevention spending to abstinence-until-marriage programs. Human rights groups find that U.S. government policy has become a source for misinformation and censorship in these countries. U.S. emphasis on abstinence may also have reduced condom availability and access to accurate information on HIV/AIDS in some countries.

Abstinence-Only Education and Sexually Active Youth

Programs geared to adolescents who have not yet engaged in coitus systematically ignore sexually experienced adolescents, a group with specific reproductive health needs and who often require more than abstinence education. Sexually experienced teens need access to complete and accurate information about contraception, legal rights to health care, and ways to access reproductive health services, none of which are provided in abstinence-only programs.

Abstinence-Only Education and GLBTQ Youth

Abstinence-only sex education may have profoundly negative impacts on the well-being of gay, lesbian, bisexual, transgender and questioning (GLBTQ) youth. An estimated 2.5% of high school youth self-identify as gay, lesbian or bisexual, and more may be uncertain of their sexual orientation. However, as many as 1 in 10 adolescents struggle with issues regarding sexual identity. Abstinence-only sex education classes are unlikely to meet the health needs of GLBTQ youth, as they largely ignore issues surrounding homosexuality (except when discussing transmission of HIV/AIDS), and often stigmatize homosexuality as deviant and unnatural behavior. Homophobia contributes to health problems such as suicide, feelings of isolation and loneliness, HIV infection, substance abuse, and violence among GLBTQ youth.

Under Section 510 requirements, emphasis must be placed on heterosexual marriage as the only appropriate context for sexual relationships. Federal law and regulations limit the definition of marriage within the meaning of federally funded abstinence-only programs to exclude same-sex couples. With the exception of Massachusetts, no states offer legal marriage to gay and lesbian couples, and recently, 11 states have passed laws specifically barring same-sex marriage. Lifelong abstinence as an implied alternative holds GLBTQ youth to an unrealistic standard markedly different from that of their heterosexual peers.

The Human Right to Sexual Health Information

Paradoxically, although abstinence is often presented as the moral choice for adolescents, we believe that the current federal approach focusing on AOE raises serious ethical and human rights concerns. Access to complete and accurate HIV/AIDS and sexual health information has been recognized as a basic human right and essential to realizing the human right to the highest attainable standard of health. Governments have an obligation to provide accurate information to their citizens and eschew the provision of misinformation; such obligations extend to government-funded health education and health care services.

International treaties provide that all people have the right to "seek, receive and impart information and ideas of all kinds," including information about their health. The U.N. Committee on the Rights of the Child, the U.N. body responsible for monitoring implementation of the Convention on the Rights of the Child, and which provides authoritative guidance on its provisions, has emphasized that children's right to access adequate HIV/AIDS and sexual health information is essential to securing their rights to health and information.

Article 12 of the International Covenant on Economic, Social and Cultural Rights (ICESCR) specifically obliges governments to take all necessary steps for the *"prevention, treatment and control of epidemic . . . diseases,"* such as HIV/AIDS. The Committee on Economic, Social and Cultural Rights, the U.N. body responsible for monitoring implementation of the ICESCR, and which provides authoritative guidance on its provisions, has interpreted Article 12 to require the *"the establishment of prevention and education programmes for behaviour-related health concerns such as sexually transmitted diseases, in particular HIV/AIDS, and those adversely affecting sexual and reproductive health."*

The United Nations Guidelines on HIV/AIDS and Human Rights provide guidance in interpreting international legal norms as they relate to HIV and AIDS. These guidelines similarly call on states to *"ensure that children and adolescents have adequate access to confidential sexual and reproductive health services, including HIV/AIDS information, counseling, testing and prevention measures such as condoms,"* and to *"ensure the access of children and adolescents to adequate health information and education, including information related to HIV/AIDS prevention and care, inside and outside school, which is tailored appropriately to age level and capacity and enables them to deal positively and responsibly with their sexuality."* Access to accurate health information is a basic human right that has also been described in international statements on reproductive rights such as the Programme of Action of the International Conference on Population and Development—Cairo, 1994.

Overall, these international treaties and statements clearly define the important responsibility of governments to provide accurate and complete information on sexual health to their citizens.

Ethical Obligations of Health Care Providers and Health Educators

We believe that patients have rights to accurate and complete information from their health care professionals and that health care providers have ethical obligations to provide accurate health information. Health care providers may not withhold information from a patient in order to influence their health care choices. Such ethical obligations are part of respect for persons and are operationalized via the process of providing informed consent. Informed consent requires provision of all pertinent information to the patient. Similar ethical obligations apply to health educators. . . .

[We] believe that it is unethical to provide misinformation or to withhold information from adolescents about sexual health, including ways for sexually active teens to protect themselves from STIs and pregnancy. Withholding information on contraception to induce them to become abstinent is inherently coercive. It violates the principle of beneficence (i.e., do good and avoid harm) as it may cause an adolescent to use ineffective (or no) protection against pregnancy and STIs. We believe that current federal AOE is ethically problematic, as it excludes accurate information about contraception, misinforms by overemphasizing or misstating the risks of contraception, and fails to require the use of scientifically accurate information while promoting approaches of questionable value.

Summary and Authors' Commentary

Although abstinence from sexual intercourse represents a healthy behavioral choice for adolescents, policies or programs offering "abstinence only" or "abstinence until marriage" as a single option for adolescents are scientifically and ethically flawed. Although abstinence from vaginal and anal intercourse is theoretically fully protective against pregnancy and disease, in actual practice, abstinence-only programs often fail to prevent these outcomes. Although federal support of abstinence-only programs has grown rapidly since 1996, existing evaluations of such programs either do not meet standards for scientific evaluation or lack evidence of efficacy in delaying initiation of sexual intercourse.

Although health care is founded on ethical notions of informed consent and free choice, federal abstinence-only programs are inherently coercive, withholding information needed to make informed choices and promoting questionable and inaccurate opinions. Federal funding language promotes a specific moral viewpoint, not a public health approach. Abstinence-only programs are inconsistent with commonly accepted notions of human rights.

In many communities, AOE has been replacing comprehensive sexuality education. Federally funded AOE programs censor lifesaving information about prevention of pregnancy, HIV and other STIs, and provide incomplete or misleading misinformation about contraception. The federal government's emphasis on abstinence-only approaches may also be harming other public health efforts such as family planning programs and HIV prevention efforts—domestically and globally. Federally funded abstinence-until-marriage programs discriminate against GLBTQ youth, as federal law limits the definition of marriage to heterosexual couples.

Schools and health care providers should encourage abstinence as an important option for adolescents. "Abstinence-only" as a basis for health policy and programs should be abandoned.

References

1. Goodson P, Suther S, Pruitt BE, Wilson K. Defining abstinence: views of directors, instructors, and participants in abstinence-only-until-marriage programs in Texas. J Sch Health 2003;73(3):91–6.

2. Albert B. American Opinion on Teen Pregnancy and Related Issues 2003. Washington, DC: National Campaign to Prevent Teen Pregnancy, 2004.

3. Dailard C. Sex education: politicians, parents, teachers and teens. Issues Brief (Alan Guttmacher Inst) 2001(2):1–4.

4. Kirby D. Emerging Answers: Research Findings on Programs to Reduce Teen Pregnancy. Washington, DC: National Campaign to Prevent Teen Pregnancy, 2001.

5. Manlove J, Romano-Papillo A, Ikramullah E. Not Yet: Programs to Delay First Sex among Teens. Washington, DC: National Campaign to Prevent Teen Pregnancy, 2004.

6. Rector RE. The Effectiveness of Abstinence Education Programs in Reducing Sexual Activity Among Youth. The Backgrounder #1533. Washington, DC: The Heritage Foundation, 2002.

7. Hauser D. Five Years of Abstinence-Only-Until-Marriage Education: Assessing the Impact. Washington, DC: Advocates for Youth, 2004.

8. Bearman PS, Bruckner H. Promising the future: virginity pledges and first intercourse. Am J Sociol 2001;106:859–912.

9.   Bruckner H, Bearman PS. After the Promise: the STD consequences of adolescent virginity pledges. J Adolesc Health 2005;36:271–8.

10. Rector RE, Johnson KA. Adolescent virginity pledges, condom use, and sexually transmitted diseases among young adults. Presented to the National Welfare Research and Evaluation Conference of the Administration of Children and Families, Washington, DC, June 14, 2005.

11. Ellenberg J. Sex and significance: how the Heritage Foundation cooked the books on virginity [cited 2005 Jul 29]. Available from: http://slate.msn.com/id/2122093/

POSTSCRIPT

Is Comprehensive Sex Education for Adolescents Too Liberal?

While there is little argument among practitioners, educators, and researchers about the importance of teaching abstinence as a viable, important component of school-based sexual health education, what other topics are to be taught—and in what framework they are to be presented—remains controversial. For example, condoms can be presented as highly effective—when used properly and consistently, condoms are 97 percent effective at preventing pregnancy (ideal or theoretical effectiveness rate; based on what is called "method failure"—condoms, as a method, fail only 3 percent of the time). On the other hand, condoms can be presented as having a high failure rate of 14 percent (i.e., only 86% effective). This is based on "typical" use rates—meaning that people may not use condoms correctly so that 14 out of 100 couples who report that they use condoms as their birth control method become pregnant within a year. This figure is based on "user failure"; people who do not use the method correctly introduce "user" error into the effectiveness of the birth control device. Thus, an educator can put her/his personal slant on the device by being either overly optimistic (i.e., condoms are extremely effective) or overly pessimistic (i.e., condoms are incredibly unreliable). Quite simply, the perspective of the educator colors the presentation of the information.

Morality is integrally linked to sex education—there is no sex education that is amoral or without a moral perspective. Where the difference lies is in the overarching framework. Theorists Shweder, Much, Mahapatra, and Park (1997) discuss different moral models to which people subscribe. Those who are in favor of comprehensive sexual health education might be considered as adopting an "ethic of autonomy," where the independence of the individual is highly respected. From this ethical perspective comes the "harm reduction" model. An example of a harm reduction intervention is needle exchange programs for intravenous drug users. The idea behind this is that an individual makes his/her own decisions—in this case to inject drugs—and that others cannot proscribe their behavior. What one can do is to make the behavior, as undesirable and/or repugnant as we find it, as safe as possible for the individual. Thus, by offering to exchange dirty needles for new, clean ones, we are reducing the harm the individual is doing to her/himself while respecting the individual's autonomy.

Another moral framework is the "ethic of divinity," whereby there is a "right" and a "wrong" way of behaving or acting. The wrong way is considered as contravening "natural law" or the way things *should* be. Sometimes natural law is viewed as going against nature, while other times it is viewed as going against the way God meant it to be. This is often shaped by the particular religious perspectives to which one subscribes. Using the intravenous drug use example, a person who subscribes to an ethic of divinity might argue that needle exchange programs subtly condone drug use and that "Just Say No" campaigns are more congruent with their ethical belief system. Drug use violates a natural law principle that one needs to treat the body "as a temple" (i.e., with respect). Using drugs violates this law; thus, one must do all that is possible to have the drug user discontinue the behavior.

Santelli and colleagues clearly come from an ethic of autonomy. They refer to misinformation or withholding of information as violating the *principle of beneficence* (i.e., do good and avoid harm). They clearly view comprehensive sex education curricula as congruent with their ethical framework. While Orgocka does not argue against comprehensive sex education, per se, her participants may represent people who oppose some of the comprehensive sexual education curricula that are viewed as contradicting, challenging, or even violating traditional family values (be these Islamic or those of other conservative religious minority groups). The family values perspective clearly fits within the "ethic of divinity" of Islam. For example, rules about sexual health have a strong impact on many areas of life in Islamic culture (e.g., prayers, bathing, marriage), and sexual health education is considered part of the purview of a correct religious upbringing (Sanjakdar, 2004).

Is there such a thing as a sexual health curriculum that satisfies all of these different ethical "camps"? Certainly, a curriculum will garner less objection with various facets if it can represent some aspect of all of the moral perspectives such that it respects autonomy but also demonstrates cultural sensitivity. A codicil: It should be noted that people rarely subscribe to one ethical framework "purely" without incorporating some ideology based on the other ethical perspectives.

References/Further Readings

Hauser, D. (2004). *Five years of abstinence-only-until-marriage education: Assessing the impact*. Washington, D.C.: Advocates for Youth.

Kirby, D. (1997). *No easy answers: Research findings on programs to reduce teen pregnancy*. Washington, D.C.: National Campaign to Prevent Teen Pregnancy.

Kirby, D. (2001). *Emerging answers: Research findings on programs to reduce teen pregnancy*. Washington, D.C.: National Campaign to Prevent Teen Pregnancy.

Sanjakdar, F. (2004) The critical role of schools and teachers in developing a sexual health education curriculum for Muslim students. Paper presented at the Australian Association for Research in Education, Melbourne, Victoria, Australia. (ISSN 1324-9339). Available on the Web at: http:// www.aare.edu.au/04pap-san04188.pdf.

Shweder, R.A., Much, N.C., Mahapatra, M., & Park, L. (1997). The "big three" of morality (autonomy, community, divinity) and the "big three" explanation of suffering. In A.M. Brant & P. Rozin (Eds.), *Morality and Health* (pp. 99–169). Florence, KY: Taylor & Frances/Routledge.

The Waxman Report. (2004, December). "The content of federally funded abstinence-only education programs." Prepared for Representative Henry A. Waxman, US House of Representatives Committee on Government Reform. Minority Staff Special Investigations Division. Retrieved June 23, 2006 from: http://www.democrats.reform.house.gov/Documents/20041201102153-50247.pdf.

ISSUE 9

Does Sex on TV Negatively Impact Adolescent Sexuality?

YES: Rebecca L. Collins, et al., from "Watching Sex on Television Predicts Adolescent Initiation of Sexual Behavior," *Pediatrics* (September 3, 2004)

NO: Rebecca L. Collins, et al., from "Entertainment Television as a Healthy Sex Educator: The Impact of Condom-Efficacy Information in an Episode of *Friends*," *Pediatrics* (November 5, 2003)

ISSUE SUMMARY

YES: Rebecca Collins and colleagues from the RAND Corporation present evidence from a longitudinal survey that adolescents who viewed more sexual content at baseline were more likely to initiate intercourse and progress to more advanced sexual activities during the subsequent year.

NO: Collins and colleagues in an earlier study suggested that entertainment television can also serve as a healthy sex educator and can work in conjunction with parents to improve adolescent sexual knowledge.

Although parents, schools, and the church play an important role in guiding and educating children and adolescents, the mass media, particularly television, has a very important influence on socialization. The negative effects of violence on television have long been studied with consistent findings indicating that exposure to violence is a risk factor for engaging in violent behaviours. More recently, the impact of sex on television has emerged as a "hot topic" in research. Why is that so? Two reasons come to mind: first, our understanding of the relationship between the media and behaviour, and second, the increase in sexual content on television.

The Kaiser Family Foundation (*Sex on TV 4,* 2005) reports that sexual content currently appears in 70 percent of all television programs. This rate increased from 56 percent in 1998 and 64 percent in 2002. Gone are the Mary Tyler Moore days of single beds and casual touching. Sexual content today is defined as talk about sex such as virginity and love; sexual behaviours such as flirting, kissing, and oral sex; and sexual intercourse—either implied or depicted. Of the programs with sexual content, 68 percent include talk about sex (up from 54 percent in 1998), 35 percent include sexual behaviours (versus 23 percent in 1998), and the remaining 11 percent include scenes in which sexual intercourse is either depicted or strongly implied (up from 7 percent in 1998). Primetime shows in particular have very high rates of sexual content, and these rates also continue to rise (77 percent in 2005 versus 68 percent in 1998 and 71 percent in 2002).

With these alarming statistics, concerns arise as to the type of information adolescents are getting about sex, especially with respect to safe sex and risky sexual behaviours. The Kaiser Foundation reports that of the 20 most popular shows for teens, only 10 percent of those with sexual content include information about risks (e.g., emotional/physical consequences) and/or responsibilities (e.g., contraception). Two-thirds of these messages have been interpreted by the Kaiser Foundation as minor or inconsequential, and of the shows that involve adolescent characters, only 23 percent include messages about sexual risks or responsibility. On a positive note, the majority (89 percent) of sexual intercourse acts involve characters age 25 or older who have an established relationship with their partner. Does all this sex on TV affect adolescent sexuality and sexual activity? Before addressing this question, an examination of adolescent sexual behaviours warrants attention.

Nearly two-thirds of adolescents in North America will have had sexual intercourse before graduating from high school. More than a third of sexually active adolescents report not using a condom the last time they had sexual intercourse, and one-third of all females under the age of 20 become pregnant. An alarming 4 million teens contract a sexually transmitted infection (STI) each year, and adding to this, approximately 50 percent of all new HIV infections occur among adolescents under the age of 25 (Centers for Disease Control and Prevention, 2002). Although intercourse is common among today's youth, most report they wish they had waited before having sex. This could indicate that many are having sex before they are ready (Martino et al., 2005). What factors contribute to early initiation? This brings us back to the question stated above: Is the media and in particular television a contributing factor?

According to the Kaiser report, 83 percent of parents believe sex on TV contributes to early sexual behaviour. Interestingly, the majority of adolescents surveyed agree. Given that television is an important source of information, it is imperative that we understand the effects the messages have on sexual behaviours. Does the exposure have a positive or negative influence on sexual socialization? Does sex on TV shape an adolescents conception of reality? Does sex on television teach our youth that sexual intercourse comes before love? Does it teach them risks and responsibilities? Does sex on TV essentially shape adolescent sexuality?

In the selections that follow, a group of researchers from the RAND Corporation present two sides to this argument. In the first study, they found that watching high levels of sex on television doubled the next-year likelihood of initiating intercourse. In the second selection, the same authors argue that sex on TV can serve as a healthy sex educator and can work in conjunction with parents to improve adolescent sexual knowledge.

YES

Rebecca L. Collins et al.

Watching Sex on Television Predicts Adolescent Initiation of Sexual Behavior

A key period of sexual exploration and development occurs during adolescence. During this time, individuals begin to consider which sexual behaviors are enjoyable, moral, and appropriate for their age group. Many teens become sexually active during this period; currently, 46% of high school students in the United States have had sexual intercourse.[1] Although intercourse among youths is common, most sexually active teens wish they had waited longer to have sex,[2] which suggests that sex is occurring before youths are prepared for its consequences. . . . [Furthermore, unplanned] pregnancies and STDs are more common among those who begin sexual activity earlier.[3]

Therefore, early sexual initiation is an important health issue. This raises the question of why individuals become sexually involved at younger ages. What factors hasten sexual initiation, and what factors delay its onset? There are many well-documented predictors of age of intercourse initiation, both social and physical. However, 1 factor commonly cited by parents and policy makers as promoting sex among teens has received little systematic scientific investigation, namely, television (TV). There is good scientific reason to think that TV may be a key contributor to early sexual activity. Sexual behavior is strongly influenced by culture,[4] and TV is an integral part of US teen culture. . . . [Sexual] messages [on TV] are commonplace, according to a scientific content analysis of a representative sample of programming from the 2001–2002 TV season. Sexual content appears in 64% of all TV programs; those programs with sexual content average 4.4 scenes with sexually related material per hour. Talk about sex is found more frequently (61% of all programs) than overt portrayals of any sexual behavior (32% of programs). Approximately 1 of every 7 programs (14%) includes a portrayal of sexual intercourse, depicted or strongly implied.[5]

This high-dose exposure to portrayals of sex may affect adolescents' developing beliefs about cultural norms. TV may create the illusion that sex is more central to daily life than it truly is and may promote sexual initiation . . . , a process known as media cultivation.[6] Exposure to the social models provided by TV also may alter beliefs about the likely outcome of engaging in sexual activity. Social learning theory predicts that teens who see characters having

From *Pediatrics*, vol. 114, no. 3, September 3, 2004, pp. e280–e289. Copyright © 2004 by American Academy Of Pediatrics. Reprinted by permission. Note: The complete text of this article contains many references to specific studies described. The interested individual should refer to the original publication for these extensive citations. These references have been omitted here in the interest of brevity.

casual sex without experiencing negative consequences will be more likely to adopt the behaviors portrayed.[7] Although televised sexual portrayals can theoretically inhibit sexual activity when they include depictions of sexual risks (such as the possibility of contracting an STD or becoming pregnant), abstinence, or the need for sexual safety, this type of depiction occurs in only 15% of shows with sexual content. In other words, only ~1 of every 7 TV shows that include sexual content includes any safe sex messages, and nearly two-thirds of these instances (63%) are minor or inconsequential in their degree of emphasis within the scene.[5] As a result, sexual content on TV is far more likely to promote sexual activity among US adolescents than it is to discourage it. . . .

Previous work demonstrated links between viewing of sexual content on TV and attitudes toward sex, endorsement of gender stereotypes likely to promote sexual initiation, and dissatisfaction with virginity, as well as a wide range of perceptions regarding normative sexual behavior.[8] In addition to these studies, 2 groundbreaking articles published in the early 1990s examined the question of whether exposure to sex on TV influences adolescent sexual behavior. The studies found positive associations between any lifetime intercourse and TV viewing among adolescents, but methodologic limitations rendered the results inconclusive.[9, 10] . . .

[The present study was] designed to [further] test the effects of TV sexual content on adolescent sexual initiation [while correcting previous methodologic problems.] We examined the effects of exposure to TV sexual content overall, exposure to TV depictions of sexual risks or sexual safety, and exposure to TV portrayals of sexual behavior versus talk about sex. Although TV producers and the general public have expressed concern regarding both sexual talk and sexual behavior, portrayals of behavior have typically been the focus of such attention. Given the potential applications of our research, we considered it important to determine whether this emphasis is well placed. Social learning theory predicts that observation of either sexual talk or sexual behavior will influence teens to have sex, as long as the portrayed consequences are not negative, but the theory does not address whether the magnitudes of these effects will differ.[7] Finally, we examined the effects of hours spent viewing TV, independent of content. Some theory and research argue that any time spent watching TV affects sexual behavior,[6, 10] whereas other research suggests that only programs with known sexual content have an influence.[7, 9] . . .

We hypothesized that adolescents exposed to greater amounts of sexual content on TV would initiate intercourse sooner and would progress more quickly to higher levels of noncoital activity. However, we expected that exposure to portrayals of sexual safety or the risks that accompany sexual activity would be associated with a delay in sexual advancement. . . .

Methods

Procedure

We conducted a national telephone survey in spring 2001 and reinterviewed the same group 1 year later, in spring 2002. The survey measured TV viewing habits, sexual knowledge, attitudes, and behavior, and a large set of demographic and psychosocial variables shown to predict sexual behavior or TV viewing habits in previous research. . . .

Enrolling adolescents in a telephone survey that assesses sexual behavior requires care and sensitivity. All households were sent a letter describing the study before telephone contact, so that they could carefully consider their participation. At the time of the baseline telephone interview, we briefly surveyed the parents, to determine the household composition and to measure the parents' sexual attitudes. An adolescent participant was then randomly selected from among all household members in the age range of 12 to 17 years. Parental consent for the adolescent's participation and then the adolescent's assent were obtained before the interview. . . .

Sample

. . . [A] sample of 1762 adolescents, 12 to 17 years of age, . . . participated in both interviews. This longitudinal sample was 48% female, 77% white, 13% African American, 7% Hispanic, and 4% Asian or other race. . . . Seventeen percent had ever had intercourse at baseline and 29% at the follow-up assessments. . . .

Measures

Exposure to Sexual Content on TV

Three measures reflected the content of TV viewed at baseline, ie, exposure to sexual content, exposure to portrayals of sexual risks or the need for safety, and relative exposure to sexual behavior versus talk about sex. These measures were based on a set of 23 programs. . . . After eliminating movies, sports, game shows, and specials (1-time airings), we included 15 of the 20 programs on the top 10 list for 1 of the 4 groups. Five additional broadcast programs and 3 cable programs that were known (on the basis of prior content analyses) or expected (on the basis of reviews in the popular press) to contain high levels of sexual content were also included in the list. The final list included programs appearing on broadcast networks and basic and premium cable channels and encompassed animated and live action shows, reality shows, sitcoms, and dramas. As part of the baseline survey, teens indicated the frequency with which they watched these 23 programs during the previous TV season ("since school started last fall") on a 4-point scale, ranging from "never" to "every time it's on." We derived the exposure measures by multiplying the self-reported viewing frequency for each program by 1 of 3 indicators of the average content in an episode of that program and summing across programs.

Methods developed by Kunkel et al,[5] as part of a much larger study of TV sexual content, were used to determine the sexual content in a sample of episodes for the 23 programs. . . . Coders unitized the episodes into distinct scenes, indicating the presence of any of the following: 1) sexual behavior: physical flirting, passionate kissing, intimate touch, intercourse implied, or intercourse depicted; 2) sexual talk: talk about own/others' plans or desires, talk about sex that has occurred, talk toward sex, expert advice, or other; or 3) talk or behavior depicting risks or the need for safety in regard to sexual activity: abstinence, waiting to have sex, portrayals mentioning or showing condoms or birth control, and portrayals related to acquired immunodeficiency syndrome, STDs, pregnancy, or abortion. . . .

For each TV series studied, the amount of sexual content was calculated as the average number of scenes per episode containing a major focus on sexual behavior plus the average number of scenes containing a major focus on talk about sex. . . . The proportion of sexual content that included sexual behavior was measured by dividing the average number of scenes that contained a major focus on sexual behavior by the average number of scenes with any sexual content for each episode. Risk and safety content was calculated as the average number of scenes per episode containing any such portrayal, whether the focus was major or minor. . . .

Average Hours of TV Viewing

We measured time spent watching TV with a set of 5 items assessing hours of viewing on various days of the week and at different times of day. Responses were averaged to create a continuous indicator of average viewing time.

Sexual Behavior

Questions assessed behavior with someone of the opposite sex. Intercourse experience at both the baseline and follow-up assessments was measured with the item "Have you ever had sex with a boy/girl? By sex we mean when a boy puts his penis in a girl's vagina" (yes/no). . . . We measured lifetime levels of noncoital experience with a scale developed for this study. . . . Adolescents indicated whether they had ever 1) kissed,* 2) "made-out" (kissed for a long time), 3) touched a breast/had their breast touched,* 4) touched genitals/had their genitals touched, or 5) given or received oral sex. Items with an asterisk were asked of all youths, and the others were asked only if the response to the item listed immediately before it was yes. . . .

Covariates

[A number of covariates were measured as part of the baseline interview. These included gender, race/ethnicity, age, educational expectations, overall mental health, religiosity, self-esteem, deviance, and sensation seeking. In addition, indicators of social environment known to predict initiation of coitus were also measured. These included age of friends, living arrangements, parents' education, parental monitoring, mother's work status, and parental discipline norms.]

Analyses

Preliminary Analyses

. . . Our preliminary analyses tested simple associations between the baseline TV viewing variables and sexual behavior. Because youths who see more sex on TV are also youths who watch more TV overall and who therefore see more sexual risk and safety content, the TV variables are best understood in the context of one another. We thus examined all 4 TV variables simultaneously in these tests. We also tested whether other respondent characteristics might explain any relationship between viewing sexual content and behavior, by examining bivariate associations between these characteristics and sex-heavy TV viewing at the baseline evaluation, intercourse initiation by the follow-up interview, and advancement in the level of noncoital behavior by the follow-up interview.

Our key analyses were a pair of multivariate regression equations including all TV viewing variables and all covariates as predictors of changes in sexual behavior from the baseline assessment to the follow-up assessment. A final pair of equations incorporated interaction terms, to test for differences in the associations between TV exposure and sexual behavior change as a function of age (<15 years vs ≥15 years of age), gender (male versus female), and race/ethnicity. . . .

Results

Before controlling for other variables, a diet of TV high in sexual content at baseline was strongly related to initiation of intercourse and advancement of noncoital activity levels in the following year. TV exposure to relatively more depictions of sexual behavior than talk were unrelated to either behavior, and although higher levels of overall viewing were negatively correlated with sexual advancement, these relationships did not reach statistical significance. However, TV exposure to the risks of sex was related to less progression in noncoital behavior. . . .

The factors that were positively associated with initiation of intercourse among virgins were older age, having older friends, getting low grades, engaging in deviant behavior, and sensation-seeking. Those associated with a lower probability of intercourse initiation were parental monitoring, parent education, living with both parents, having parents who would disapprove if the adolescent had sex, being religious, and having good mental health. Only 1 additional variable predicted changes in noncoital activity; exposure to risk or safety portrayals was related to a lower level of noncoital activity. Variables that were not predictive of either outcome were gender, race, self-esteem, educational aspirations, and mother's work outside the home.

[Most] of the variables predictive of later sex were also correlated at baseline with a sex-heavy TV diet, and most correlations were in the same direction as those observed for sexual activity. These variables could potentially account for the relationships between exposure to sexual content and sexual activity observed. To test for TV effects independent of such factors, we entered all of the bivariate predictors of intercourse initiation or noncoital stage into our models as covariates. We also included the gender and race variables in multivariate analyses, because they were central to planned tests for subgroup differences. The resulting models were excellent predictors of the outcome variables. A concordance or c statistic, scaled so that 50% corresponds to chance and 100% corresponds to perfect prediction, indicated that respondents' initiation of intercourse was correctly predicted 79% of the time and their advances in noncoital behavior were correctly predicted 90% of the time. . . .

The significant coefficient for sexual content in these models indicates that, after more than a dozen other predictors of sexual behavior were taken into account, exposure to TV sexual content remained a strong predictor of intercourse initiation among those who were virgins at the first interview. Exposure to sexual content was also strongly predictive of progressing noncoital activity. . . . [The] likelihood of intercourse initiation [was] approximately double for the high-exposure group, across all ages studied. . . . The probability of initiating breast touching was ~50% higher and the probability of initiating genital touching was almost double in the high-exposure group. . . .

After other factors were controlled statistically, greater relative exposure to behavior remained unassociated with later sexual behavior. We also found no significant association between exposure to portrayals of sexual risk and/or safety and later sexual behavior and no association between average hours of TV viewing and sex in these multivariate models.

Many of the other respondent characteristics that were bivariate predictors of intercourse initiation remained significant in the multivariate model, including older age, having mostly older friends, lower parent education, not living with both parents, less parental monitoring, less religiosity, poor mental health, sensation-seeking personality, deviant behavior, and low school grades. Only a small subset of these factors predicted noncoital activity in the multivariate model. Other than viewing sexual content, older age and less parental monitoring predicted advancing noncoital activity.

The effects of TV viewing were largely similar across demographic groups, with a few key exceptions. . . . African Americans with high levels of exposure to sexual risk and safety portrayals were less likely to have intercourse, whereas the sexual behavior of individuals from all other races combined was not related to such exposure. . . . This race interaction was also significant for noncoital activity. . . . African Americans were less likely to advance their noncoital activity level with exposure to sexual risk and safety portrayals, whereas changes in the activity levels of other races were not related to such exposure. . . .

The model predicting noncoital sex also produced a significant interaction between gender and total hours of TV viewing. . . . More time spent watching TV delayed noncoital activity among male subjects but had no effect among female subjects. . . .

Discussion

We observed substantial associations between the amount of sexual content viewed by adolescents and advances in their sexual behavior during the subsequent year. Youths who viewed 1 SD more sexual content than average behaved sexually like youths who were 9 to 17 months older but watched average amounts of sex on TV. This effect is not insubstantial. Predicted probabilities showed that watching the highest levels of sexual content effectively doubled the next-year likelihood of initiating intercourse and greatly increased the probability of advancing 1 level in noncoital activity. In other words, after adjustment for other differences between high and low viewers of sexual content, 12-year-olds who watched the highest levels of this content among youths their age appeared much like youths 2 to 3 years older who watched the lowest levels of sexual content among their peers. The magnitude of these results are such that a moderate shift in the average sexual content of adolescent TV viewing could have substantial effects on sexual behavior at the population level.

It is noteworthy that the association between viewing sexual content and intercourse initiation appeared to be much stronger before our introduction of covariates to the model. The finding that these factors reduce the effects of TV viewing on behavior demonstrates the importance of including such controls in future research. The majority of factors we examined in our work predicted both viewing of sexual content and advances in sexual behavior. Nonetheless, when we controlled statistically for these associations, the relationship between exposure to TV sex and later sexual behavior remained substantial, indicating that it could not be explained by any of the variables in our study. Relationships between viewing sexual content and advancing sexual behavior were not attributable to the effects of developing sexual behavior on selective viewing of sexual content. Our analyses controlled for adolescents' level of sexual activity at baseline, rendering an explanation of reverse causality for our findings implausible.

This result replicates and extends the findings of Brown and Newcomer.[9] Those authors found the same pattern of association with a sex-heavy TV diet in their research, but they could not clearly eliminate third-variable and reverse-causality explanations. We also extend their result by showing that it holds for noncoital sexual behaviors, across an age span of 5 years.

We did not find an association between sexual behavior and average hours of TV viewing. . . . Our result . . . undercuts cultivation theory, which suggests that TV content is homogeneous enough that overall viewing should predict sexual outcomes. Although the process of media cultivation may well take place, content is not as uniform as it was when the theory was proposed, which perhaps explains why the prediction was not supported. We observed a nonsignificant but suggestive negative coefficient for hours of viewing predicting noncoital sex (with other variables controlled). This would be consistent with a "babysitter effect" often attributed to TV, in which youths who spend more time viewing have less time to engage in problem behaviors.

We obtained the predicted relationship between exposure to portrayals of sexual risk or the need for sexual safety and delay of sexual behavior, but only among African American youths. . . . It may be that African Americans are more likely to use TV as a source of sexual information than are other groups. Other studies suggested that African Americans watch more TV and interpret sexual content differently.[11] However, we know of no theory that explains those findings, or our own, and we think that this is an important area for future research.

Portrayals of sexual talk and sexual behavior appear to have similar effects on youths. This is not surprising from a theoretical standpoint. Social learning theory posits that information is gleaned from what others say about a behavior as well as what they do, because both indicate social approval or disapproval of the activity in question. It apparently makes little difference whether a TV show presents people talking about whether they have sex or shows them actually having sex. Both affect perceived norms regarding sex, and thus sexual behavior.

Finally, we found that a number of factors were predictors of the transition to intercourse, consistent with previous work. However, there were fewer multivariate predictors of noncoital sex. This indicates the need for greater study of such behaviors, which may be increasingly common among adolescents as they struggle to become sexually active in a way that they perceive to be safe and/or preserving of virginity.

A limitation of this research was our inability to control for adolescent interest in sex or sexual readiness before TV viewing. Youths who are considering coital or noncoital activities that they have not yet enacted may watch more sex on TV (eg, to get information or to satisfy desires). They may subsequently engage in these sexual activities sooner but as a result of their higher levels of interest, not as a result of their TV exposure. . . .

Other limitations appear to be based on the sensitive nature of our research topic. Although rates of intercourse were within the expected range at the follow-up evaluation, they were somewhat low at the baseline evaluation, which suggests that some participants were not initially honest about their sexual experience. . . .

Finally, although TV accounts for more of children's time than any other medium, the sexual content in films, music, and magazines is also likely to hasten sexual advancement. Therefore, it will be important to address these other contributions to sexual socialization in both future research and interventions. Indeed, we should note that, because TV viewing of sexual content is probably related to exposure to sex in other media, our results may reflect at least partially the influence of music, magazines, or movies. . . .

With these limitations in mind, our findings have clear implications. Reducing the amount of sexual talk and behavior on TV or the amount of time that adolescents are exposed to this content is likely to appreciably delay the initiation of both coital and noncoital sexual activities. Increasing the percentage of portrayals of sexual risk and safety, relative to other sexual content, might also inhibit early sexual activity, particularly among African American youths. However, reducing exposure to sexual content on TV may be difficult. An option that does not require altering TV content or adolescents' viewing habits has met with some success in other areas. Parents who view violent programs with their children and discuss their own beliefs regarding the behavior depicted may be able to reduce the effects of positively portrayed aggressive content on their children's behavior.[12] This process may also help limit the negative effects of sexual portrayals that do not contain risk information. . . .

References

1. Centers for Disease Control and Prevention. Trends in sexual risk behaviors among high school students: United States, 1991–2001. *MMWR Morb Mortal Wkly Rep.* 2002;51:856–859.

2. National Campaign to Prevent Teen Pregnancy. *With One Voice* 2002: America's Adults and Teens Sound Off About Teen Pregnancy. Washington, DC: The National Campaign to Prevent Teen Pregnancy; 2002.

3. Koyle P, Jensen L, Olsen J. Comparison of sexual behaviors among adolescents having an early, middle and late first intercourse experience. *Youth Soc.* 1989;20:461–476.

4. Nathanson C. *Dangerous Passage: The Social Control of Sexuality in Women's Adolescence.* Philadelphia, PA: Temple University Press; 1991.

5. Kunkel D, Eyal K, Biely E, et al. *Sex on TV3: A Biennial Report to the Kaiser Family Foundation.* Menlo Park, CA: The Henry J. Kaiser Foundation; 2003. Available at: www.kff.org/entmedia/loader.cfm?url=/commonspot/security/getfile. cfm&PageID=14209. Accessed July 20, 2004.

6. Gerbner G, Gross M, Morgan L, Signorielli N. Living with television: the dynamics of the cultivation process. In: Bryant J, Zillman D, eds. *Perspectives on Media Effects.* Hillsdale, NJ: Lawrence Erlbaum Associates; 1986:17–40.

7. Bandura A. *Social Foundations of Thought and Action: A Social Cognitive Theory.* Englewood Cliffs, NJ: Prentice Hall; 1986.

8. Buerkel-Rothfuss N, Strouse J. Media exposure and perceptions of sexual behaviors: the cultivation hypothesis moves to the bedroom. In: Greenberg B, Brown J, Buerkel-Rothfuss N, eds. *Media, Sex and the Adolescent.* Cresskill, NJ: Hampton Press;1993.

9. Brown JD, Newcomer SF. Television viewing and adolescents' sexual behavior. *J Homosex.* 1991;21:77–91.

10. Peterson JL, Moore KA, Furstenberg FF Jr. Television viewing and early initiation of sexual intercourse: is there a link? *J Homosex.* 1991;21:93–118.

11. Brown JD, Schulze L. The effects of race, gender, and fandom on audience interpretations of Madonna's music videos. *J. Commun.* 1990;40:88–102.

12. Donnerstein E, Slaby R, Eron L. The mass media and youth aggression. In: Eron LD, Gentry JH, Schlegel P, eds. *Reason to Hope: A Psychosocial Perspective on Violence and Youth.* Washington, DC: American Psychological Association; 1994:219–250.

Rebecca L. Collins et al.  **NO**

Entertainment Television as a Healthy Sex Educator: The Impact of Condom-Efficacy Information in an Episode of *Friends*

Forty-six percent of all high school students in the United States have had sex, and rates of sexually transmitted diseases and unintended pregnancy are high among these youth.[1] One factor thought to contribute to adolescent sexual risk is television.[2] It has been argued that television has become a sex educator to America's children, usurping the role of parents. Seven of ten primetime network programs contain sexual content, and the average primetime show with such content contains six scenes with sex per hour.[3] This high prevalence of sexual content has raised concern, in part, because of fear that the lessons taught by television are inaccurate and that, even when it is accurate, television is providing information more appropriately conveyed by parents. However, the same reasoning that supports these concerns can be used to argue that television is sometimes a healthy sex educator and may aid parents rather than usurp their roles.

The idea that television presents a distorted picture of sexuality is strongly supported by content analyses. Sex is largely portrayed on television as a casual activity, without health or other life consequences. The vast majority of scenes with sexual content fail to depict the responsibilities concomitant with sexual activity or to note the risks of pregnancy and contraction of sexually transmitted diseases.[3] Nonetheless, portrayals of sexual risk and responsibilities are sometimes present on television. Such portrayals were included in 15% of programs with sexual content in the 2001 to 2002 season and in 34% of shows with sexual content that involve teen characters.[3] This raises the possibility that television can be a healthy sex educator, teaching valuable lessons to adolescent audiences by modeling responsible behavior or pointing out the consequences that can result from careless sexual activity.[4] Consistent with this notion, 60% of teens participating in a recent survey said that they learned about how to say "no" to a sexual situation by watching television, and 43% said they learned something from television about how to talk to a partner about safer sex.[5]

From *Pediatrics,* vol. 112, no. 5, November 2005, pp. 1115–1121. Copyright © 2005 by American Academy Of Pediatrics. Reprinted by permission. Note: The complete text of this article contains many references to specific studies described. The interested individual should refer to the original publication for these extensive citations. These references have been omitted here in the interest of brevity.

Clearly, parents are able to put information about sexuality in a context appropriate to family beliefs, values, and culture, which may differ from the television mainstream. However, the concern that television is usurping parents' role as sex educators can also be countered. Rather than substituting for parents, television may act as a catalyst to conversation, giving parents and their children an entrée to topics they find difficult to broach with one another. Thirty-three percent of 15- to 17-year-olds report that they have had a conversation about a sexual issue with one of their parents because of something they saw on television.[5] These conversations not only give parents a chance to provide their own input on sexual health issues, but also give them an opportunity to challenge any negative media messages and to reinforce positive messages. Thus, television may promote the role of parents as sex educators, rather than undermine it.

This article explores these positive opportunities for sex education via the entertainment media by studying the impact of one episode of the sitcom *Friends* that contained information about sexual risk. . . . The episode focuses on a pregnancy resulting from condom failure. It was part of the season's main story line, in which . . . Rachel experiences an unplanned pregnancy as a result of a single night of sex with Ross . . . (her former boyfriend). In the episode, Rachel tells Ross about the pregnancy for the first time. Ross responds with disbelief and exclaims "but we used a condom!" A statement that "condoms are only 97% effective" appears in this scene and also a subsequent one, reinforcing the condom use and condom failure elements of the story. Thus, the possibility of condom failure and the resulting consequence of pregnancy . . . could potentially have had a powerful effect on young people's sexual knowledge.

Other studies of health information contained in entertainment programming (sometimes termed "edu-tainment") suggest that this may have occurred. . . . For example, information about family planning was conveyed to large numbers of Africans as part of existing entertainment programming and apparently changed health behavior as a result[6]. . .

These studies show . . . that it is possible to deliver health messages to a very large audience through edu-tainment. They also indicate a potential for influencing health-related awareness, knowledge, and beliefs in this manner. We expected to observe such effects for the *Friends* episode. We hypothesized that adolescent *Friends* viewers would demonstrate enhanced awareness of condom failure. . . . We also expected a substantial percentage of viewers to report learning something about condoms as a result of the episode. . . .

[We] expected to find that many adolescents changed their beliefs about condom efficacy as a result of the episode, because the events portrayed might provide new information, inspire a search for information, or spur discussion regarding the issue of condom efficacy. Because the information conveyed in the *Friends* episode was fairly complex, we did not expect viewers' condom-efficacy beliefs to be changed in a single direction. Like much information regarding sexual health, the condom message in the episode communicated that the outcome of condom use is uncertain. It (accurately) indicated that condoms are very effective and should be used if one has sex, and also that condoms cannot be relied on with absolute certainty, so even protected sex should involve a careful decision. . . . [We] expected the *Friends* episode to have a mixed effect on perceptions of condom efficacy among adolescents, precipitating changes toward both enhanced and reduced perceived efficacy. . . .

We also hypothesized that the *Friends* episode would provoke conversation about the show between adolescent viewers and their parents, and result in discussions of pregnancy and condom efficacy that might not otherwise have occurred. . . .

We expected any interactions with parents that occurred to moderate the impact of the *Friends* episode. Previous research indicates that children who watch programming with their parents are differentially influenced by the content they see, as are children who discuss media content with their parents.[7] This process, termed mediation, sometimes counteracts media effects and sometimes enhances them, depending on whether parents agree with the media message. We expected the *Friends* condom-efficacy episode to more strongly affect adolescents who watched with their parents, who discussed the episode with their parents, or who discussed condom efficacy with their parents as a result of seeing the episode. . . .

Finally, although we expected the aforementioned effects, we also anticipated that many teens exposed to the episode would fail to process or retain the sexual health information it contained. . . . [We] hypothesized and tested for a few additional moderators that might determine who is most strongly affected. First, we predicted that all program effects (on condom awareness, condom beliefs, and talking to parents) would be stronger for more regular *Friends* viewers. Regular viewers are more likely to attend closely to the program, identify with the characters, and think later about its content. Second, we predicted that effects of the *Friends* episode would be greater among younger and sexually inexperienced adolescents, because they would have less real-life experience on which to draw. . . .

Methods

Sample

Respondents were drawn from the larger group of [adolescents (12–17 years)] in the Rand Television and Adolescent Sexuality study (TAS). . . . The TAS surveys asked about television-viewing habits, demographic and psychosocial characteristics, sexual attitudes, beliefs, knowledge, and behavior.

. . . For this study, we sampled all 648 respondents who were regular *Friends* viewers at TAS baseline, defined as teens who watch *Friends* "a lot" or "every time." . . . [of the 648, 506 were available for interviews. . . . completion rate of 78%]. . . . Most analyses for this study focused on the 323 adolescents who reported seeing the episode and a subset of 155 of adolescents whose viewership could be confirmed with an additional question about the episode's content. . . . In one additional statistical test, the analysis sample consisted of the 472 *Friends* survey participants (305 self-reported and 150 confirmed viewers) who were surveyed at the TAS follow-up.

The TAS sample slightly underrepresented Hispanics, and slightly overrepresented two-parent households, compared with the nation as a whole. . . .

[Confirmed] viewers were more likely to be female, to come from somewhat more educated families, and to be current regular viewers of *Friends*.

Procedures

... Fifty percent of participants were interviewed within 3 weeks of the air date ..., and the remainder were interviewed within 4 weeks of the air date.... Median time between TAS baseline and the *Friends* survey was 6 months, as was the median time from the *Friends* survey to TAS follow-up.

Measures

Viewership of *Friends* and of the episode of interest were established at the outset of the *Friends* interview. We began with a short introduction informing respondents that we were interested in their responses to a recent episode of *Friends*. We then repeated the item from the TAS survey that was used to select our sample: "How often do you watch the television show *Friends*? (never, once in a while, a lot, every time it's on)." To assess whether respondents saw the key episode, we asked two questions: "Did you see the episode a few weeks ago when Rachel told Ross she's pregnant?" and "Did you see the episode where Phoebe and Joey got the fire department to break down Monica and Chandler's door?" The latter event took place during the condom-efficacy episode, but was unrelated to the plot. Respondents who reported seeing the pregnancy episode were classified as self-reported viewers. The subset who also reported seeing the fire department episode were classified as confirmed viewers. ...

Among both self-reported and confirmed viewers, we assessed interpretation and recall of the key reproductive health information with a set of three items: "According to the episode, did Ross and Rachel use a condom when they had sex?," "What percent of the time did the *Friends* episode say condoms work in preventing pregnancy, from zero to 100%?," and "Which comes closer to the main message you took from this episode: lots of times condoms don't prevent pregnancy, or condoms almost always prevent pregnancy?".... There was a wide range of responses to the percent-effectiveness question. Based on the distribution, we recoded it to a dichotomous measure reflecting responses of >95% but <100% versus all other responses.... Responses to the question about whether Ross and Rachel used a condom were coded to reflect "yes" versus all other responses.

We assessed the effects of the episode on condom beliefs with three measures, based on two items in the *Friends* survey. To tap perceived learning, we asked, "In thinking about that episode, did you learn anything new about condoms that you didn't know before? ... To measure changes in perceived condom efficacy we asked, "In real life, how effective are condoms for preventing pregnancy?".... This same item had been asked in the earlier TAS survey. We derived a dichotomous variable that reflected any change in condom-efficacy beliefs versus no change from a comparison of responses to the item at these 2 time points. Using the same repeated item, we also assessed the direction of belief change among those with any change, creating a dichotomous indicator of reduced perceptions of condom efficacy (less effective versus more effective).

Parental mediation surrounding the episode was tapped with a set of four items. Coviewing was assessed with, "When you watched the *Friends* episode in which Rachel told Ross she was pregnant, were you with a parent or other adult?" Parental discussion was assessed with three items: "Did you talk with a parent or another adult about that episode?," "Because of that episode, did you talk to a parent or another adult about how effective condoms are in preventing pregnancy?," and "Did you talk with a parent or another adult about whether it's good or bad that Rachel is pregnant, or did you not talk about this?"

We drew some additional data from the Rand TAS survey. For comparison with the *Friends* survey item concerning discussions of condom effectiveness, we drew responses to the baseline item: "Have you talked with a parent about condoms in the last 12 months (yes/no)?" Respondent gender, race/ethnicity, age in years, and experience with sexual intercourse (yes/no) were also measured with the TAS baseline survey and used in the present analyses. Finally, we asked respondents to the TAS follow-up, "What percent of the time do you think condoms work in preventing pregnancy, from zero to 100%?" . . .

Results

The pregnancy episode may have reached more than half of teen *Friends* watchers in our sample of frequent viewers: Sixty-four percent recalled seeing the episode where Rachel told Ross she is pregnant. However, we could confirm viewership among only 27% of those surveyed (ie, this percentage also reported seeing the fire-department episode). Most of those who saw the episode (59% of self-reported and 54% of confirmed viewers) interpreted its message as "lots of times, condoms don't prevent pregnancy.". . . A substantial minority of self-reported viewers (32%) remembered that the episode described Ross and Rachel as having used a condom when they had sex. The majority of confirmed viewers (65%) recalled this information. Fifteen percent of self-reported and 31% of confirmed viewers recalled that the episode said condoms were between 95% and 100% effective.

From 10% to 17% of viewers said they learned something new about condoms from the episode. About half of adolescents in both viewer groups rated the effectiveness of condoms differently than they had in the TAS survey 6 months before. Among these individuals, perceptions of condom effectiveness changed in both directions (more or less effective) about equally often. This was true regardless of how viewership was defined. . . . When asked as part of our earlier survey, most adolescents saw condoms as very or somewhat effective, and this was still true after the *Friends* episode.

Forty percent of those who reported watching the episode said they watched with an adult. From 16% to 24% of viewers talked with an adult about the episode, ≈10% talked with an adult about Rachel's pregnancy, and ≈10% talked with a parent or other adult about condom effectiveness because of the episode. Reactions to the episode were modified by viewing or discussing it with an adult. We tested for these effects among both confirmed and self-reported viewers; results were very similar. For simplicity, we present only confirmed-viewer effects. In this group, we found that teens who watched the condom episode with an adult (versus those who watched alone or with another youth) were twice as likely to recall that condoms were said to be between 95% and 100% effective. . . . Those who watched with an adult were also far more likely to talk to an adult about the episode. . . . Coviewing was not related to changes in condom beliefs or self-reports of learning something new about condoms. . . . Almost half (47%) of adolescents who discussed the episode with an adult recalled that condoms were described as >95% effective, nearly twice the number who remembered this information among those who did not talk with an adult. . . . Many adolescents who talked about the episode with an adult reported talking about condom effectiveness (31%), and many (33%) talked about Rachel's pregnancy. These percentages were substantially higher than those observed among adolescents who didn't specifically discuss the *Friends* episode with adults. . . .

Participants who had a condom-effectiveness discussion with an adult as a result of watching *Friends* were more than twice as likely to say they learned something new about condoms from the episode. . . . This was the only group in the study who may have experienced a directional change in their condom beliefs. Among those who changed their perceptions of condom efficacy after the episode, 75% of teens who talked to an adult about condom efficacy came to see condoms as more effective, whereas only 35% of those who did not discuss condoms with adults came to see condoms as more effective. . . . Surprisingly, discussions of condom effectiveness were unrelated to the likelihood of remembering that condoms were described as between 95% and 100% effective. . . .

To test whether the episode had enduring effects on viewers' condom-related knowledge, we examined responses to the condom efficacy item in the TAS follow-up survey. At TAS follow-up, 24% of self-reported and 30% of confirmed viewers rated condoms as 95% to 100% effective. In comparison, only 18% of the *Friends* sample who did not see the condom episode (before the *Friends* survey) rated condoms as 95% to 100% effective at follow-up. . . .

To explore the generalizability of the effects observed, we tested for differences between frequent and occasional viewers within our sample. . . . [We] found that 72% of frequent viewers versus 21% of occasional viewers recalled that Ross and Rachel used a condom, . . . and that frequent viewers who changed their condom beliefs were less likely than occasional viewers to view condoms as less effective than they had 6 months previously. . . .

Discussion

. . . Entertainment television is often presumed to have an exclusively negative influence on America's adolescents and is sometimes blamed for high rates of sexual activity, sexually transmitted disease, and unplanned pregnancy in this group. The jury is still out on whether television has such effects. Clearly, television is saturated with sexual content but empirical evidence that such content affects adolescent sexual behavior is still preliminary. [8,9] Although sexual content may eventually prove to affect sexual behavior, this study suggests that television can also be a positive force in the sex education of youth and has the potential to affect a broad cross section of teens. Television can teach the risks and responsibilities that accompany sexual activity in a way that books, pamphlets, and classroom instruction cannot, by portraying the experiences of sexually active individuals with whom adolescents identify. This vivid illustration of sexual consequences is hard to come by in other ways, because information about specific individuals' condom use is rarely available in real life. Entertainment television also has the advantage of being able to model socially responsible behavior without explicitly advocating it. Advocacy messages can produce resistance among adolescents.

A second key set of findings addresses the role of parents in this educational process. Forty percent of adolescent viewers watched the episode with an adult, and from 16% to 24% discussed it with an adult. Both of these factors served to reinforce the educational value of the show's content, helping teens to retain the information about how often condoms work. The 10% of viewers who were catalyzed by the episode into having a discussion of condom efficacy with an adult were also more likely to say they learned something new from the show. These interactions with adults apparently emphasized the effectiveness of condoms, more so than condom failure, because adolescents who reported them were the only group to see condoms as more effective than they had previously. The role of parents in altering television's impact is noteworthy and is consistent with research showing that parents and adults can enhance learning from educational programming.[10]

Although it would certainly be a bad idea for television to substitute entirely for traditional sources of sex education, television may supplement and enhance the effects of information from other sources. In this study, television served this role by instigating discussions of condom efficacy between teens and their parents, opening the door for sex education within the family. Analyses exploring whether conversations resulting from the episode were occurring among adolescents and parents who had already talked about condom use revealed that discussions of condom efficacy as a result of viewing were unrelated to prior conversations on the topic. This suggests that the program reopened some existing channels of communication, providing the opportunity for reinforcement of prior education by parents, and also helped some families to broach the topic for what may have been the first time. We assume that more discussion is positive, especially from parents' perspective, although we recognize this may not be true in all cases.

We observed few effects of the *Friends* episode on participants' condom-efficacy beliefs. Approximately 40% of viewers changed their beliefs from what they had been a few months earlier, when we last surveyed them. These changes could be real effects of viewing the condom episode if the program led to a search for more information about condom efficacy, or questioned adolescents' preexisting beliefs. However, these changes could also reflect instability in beliefs or their measurement over time that would have been observed regardless of episode viewing. We also observed little directional change in beliefs. Here we expected to find little change, because the complexity of the condom efficacy message could lead some adolescents to see condoms as more effective, and others as less. There was, however, a single exception to this null result: those who talked with parents about condom efficacy because of the *Friends* episode apparently came to see condoms as more effective. As noted, the episode accurately indicated both that condoms are effective and that condoms occasionally fail. Thus, parents could use the presented information to reinforce either or both of these messages. Although the episode itself did not sway teens either way on the issue, our finding concerning discussions with adults suggests that parents who talked to their kids may have emphasized condom effectiveness, rather than fallibility. This finding also reinforces the point that television may assist parents in their roles as sex educators, rather than substitute for them. Parents appear to have used the episode as a springboard for expression of their own views.

Although we did not observe strong effects of the *Friends* episode on condom beliefs, this should not be taken to indicate that television has little influence on sexual knowledge. Although the show we studied is one with which adolescents strongly identify, we looked at only one episode, and, as we have noted, the information it contained was ambiguous in its implications. Our finding that many young viewers retained the basic message about condoms and the more specific condom facts presented, even after 3 to 4 weeks, suggests that if sexual risk and responsibility portrayals were more prevalent on television and addressed subjects where the facts are less complex, the effects observed might well be powerful. A number of organizations are currently working to achieve this. The National Campaign to Prevent Teen Pregnancy and the Henry J. Kaiser Family Foundation currently work with television writers and producers to help them embed health messages in their entertainment programming.[4] . . .

Conclusions

The American Academy of Pediatrics has recommended that the broadcast industry adopt guidelines for responsible sexual content. The *Friends* episode studied herein would almost certainly meet these guidelines because of its portrayal of condom use. And our findings indicate that exposure to the program did have important educational effects. . . . Our results [also] suggest that families should . . . watch and discuss television together. . . . Finally, pediatricians should be notified by producers of entertainment programming when educational material is going to air on programs popular with youth. This would allow them to discuss the content with their patients and their parents.

References

1. Trends in sexual risk behaviors among high school students: United States, 1991–2001. *MMWR Morb Mortal Wkly Rep.* 2002;51:856–859.

2. Steyer JP. *The Other Parent: The Inside Story of the Media's Impact On Our Children.* New York, NY: Atria Books; 2002.

3. Kunkel D, Eyal K, Biely E, et al. *Sex on TV3: A Biennial Report to the Kaiser Family Foundation.* Santa Barbara, CA: Kaiser Family Foundation; 2003.

4. Brown JD, Keller SN. Can the mass media be healthy sex educators? *Fam Plann Perspect*. 2000;32;255–256.

5. Kaiser Family Foundation. *Teens, Sex and TV*. Menlo Park, CA: Kaiser Family Foundation; 2002.

6. Piotrow P, Rimon JG, Winnard K, et al. Mass media family planning promotion in three Nigerian cities. *Stud Fam Plann*. 1990;21:265–274.

7. Desmond RG, Singer JL, Singer DG, Calam R, Colimore K. Family mediation patterns and television viewing: young children's use and grasp of the medium. *Hum Commun Res*. 1985;11:461–480.

8. Brown JD, Newcomer SF. Television viewing and adolescents' sexual behavior. *J Homosex*. 1991;21:77–91.

9. Peterson JL, Moore KA, Furstenberg FF Jr. Television viewing and early initiation of sexual intercourse: is there a link? *J Homosex*. 1991;21:93–118.

10. Austin EW. Exploring the effects of active parental mediation of television content. *J Broadcast Electronic Media*. 1993;37:147–158.

POSTSCRIPT

Does Sex on TV Negatively Impact Adolescent Sexuality?

It is interesting that research conducted by the RAND Corporation found conflicting evidence for the effects of sex on TV. On the one hand, they present evidence that adolescents who viewed high levels of sexual content were more likely to initiate intercourse and progress to more advanced sexual activities during the subsequent year. They also reported that exposure to "talk about sex" on TV was associated with the same risks as exposure to sexual behaviour. In the second selection, however, the same researchers argued that sex on television could work in conjunction with parents to improve adolescent sexual knowledge and behaviours. Specifically, youth who watched sexual content on television with an adult and later discussed the content with an adult were more likely to benefit from the information than youth who did not watch with an adult or discuss the content with an adult. Why the conflicting reports? Upon examining the articles in more detail, one can find possible explanations.

In the first study, African American youths who watched content that included risks and responsibilities were less likely than other ethnic groups to initiate intercourse in the subsequent year. In the second selection, the content focused predominantly on risk factors, specifically contraception failure. In combining the findings from these two articles, it could be argued that when risk and responsibility factors are addressed in the sexual content, positive outcomes are possible. When sexual content involves sexual behaviours and intercourse without addressing risk and responsibility, negative outcomes result. In other words, adolescents with still-developing cognitive capacities may not be able to go beyond " the immediate messages" in the content. If sex is portrayed as irresponsible and enjoyable, adolescents process it as such and have a desire to imitate. On the other hand, when risks are addressed, they recognize the importance of safe sex. Furthermore, having an adult present during the program (i.e., a mature perspective) further enhances the adolescent's ability to interpret the messages effectively. Given that only 10 percent of popular teen programs include sexual content addressing risks and responsibilities might explain the negative outcomes in some studies. The positive outcomes may be explained in terms of specific content (i.e., risks and responsibilities) as well as the presence of an adult to support understanding. Further research is needed to clarify this issue.

References/Further Readings

Brodie, M., Foehr, U., Rideout, V., Baer, N., Miller, C., Flournoy, R., & Altman, D. (2001). Communicating health information through the entertainment media. *Health Affairs*, 20, 192–199.

Brown, J. D., & Keller, S. N. (2000). Can the mass media be healthy sex educators? *Family Planning Perspectives*, 32, 255–256.

Brown, J. D., & Witherspoon, E. M. (2002). The mass media and American adolescents' health. *Journal of Adolescent Health*, 31, 153–170.

Centers for Disease Control and Prevention. (2002). Trends in sexual risk behaviors among hig school students—United States, 1991–2001. *Morbidity and Mortality Weekly Report*, 51, 856–859.

Kaiser Family Foundation Report. (2005). *Sex on TV* 4. The Henry J. Kaiser Family Foundation. Menlo Park, CA. http://www.kff.org.

Martino, S. C., Collins, R. L., Kanouse, D. E., Elliott, M., & Berry, S. H. (2005). Social cognitive processes mediating the relationship between exposure to television's sexual content and adolescents' sexual behaviour. *Journal of Personality and Social Psychology*, 89, 914–924.

ISSUE 10

Does a Traditional or "Strong" Double Standard with Respect to Sexual Behavior Exist Among Adolescents?

YES: Mary Crawford and Danielle Popp, from "Sexual Double Standards: A Review and Methodological Critique of Two Decades of Research," *Journal of Sex Research* (February 2003)

NO: Michael J. Marks and R. Chris Fraley, from "The Sexual Double Standard: Fact or Fiction?" *Sex Roles* (February 2005)

ISSUE SUMMARY

YES: Mary Crawford, a psychology professor at the University of Connecticut, and her graduate student Danielle Popp present evidence suggesting the double standard that males are socially rewarded and females socially derogated for sexual activity exists among adolescents as it does among adults.

NO: Researchers Michael Marks and Chris Fraley oppose the above claim and suggest that there is little evidence that the traditional double standard exists among adolescents or even among adults.

"What do you call a girl with many sexual partners? A slut. What do you call a guy with many sexual partners? A stud." This quote, taken directly from students in a Psychology of Gender class, illustrates how easily young people can identify the key constructs involved in the sexual double standard. The sexual double standard, put simply, is that the same heterosexual behavior is judged differently depending on whether a male or a female is engaging in the behavior. That is, boys who are sexual are celebrated or rewarded for their behavior while girls who are similarly sexual are censured or punished for their behavior. While the "line" is arguable for what sexual behaviors by girls is acceptable, across times and social groups, girls and boys can identify what is and is not permissible vis-a-vis girls' sexual activity. For example, in the 1950s, a Catholic school girl whose skirt was too short and showed "too much leg" would have been branded as "loose." In contrast, sexual intercourse may be permissible for a girl of the 2000s *if* she is in a romantic relationship with a boy; otherwise, she may still be labeled as "loose" (i.e., in today's language, a slut, whore, etc.). In 2002, Canadian television aired a news piece documenting the double standard in adolescents—showing a teenage boy who was labeled a "player" and was admired by his peers for dating many young women while two teenage girls were tearfully interviewed about the negative emotional impact of being labeled "loose."

Sociologist Ira Reiss was one of the first people to write about the sexual double standard from an academic viewpoint. In his classic 1967 work, *The Social Context of Premarital Sexual Permissiveness,* Reiss discussed the double standard in relation to premarital intercourse and divided the double standard into "orthodox" and "transitional" categories. The orthodox standard viewed premarital intercourse as permissible for males but not for females under *any* circumstance, while the transitional double standard viewed premarital intercourse as permissible for males under any circumstance and permissible for females but only if they were engaged or deeply in love. In the 1960s, Reiss optimistically predicted that North American society would move toward increasing sex-role equality and decreasing sexual double standards.

Research on the double standard continued into the 1970s and beyond. A meta-analysis by Oliver and Hyde (1993) found a gender difference in the endorsement of the sexual double standard. Reiss's 1960 studies found that men were more likely than women to endorse the double standard (while women were more likely to endorse total abstinence for all). In contrast, Oliver and Hyde found that women were more likely to endorse the double standard than men. This gender effect became stronger across the years. Thus, both men and women were becoming more permissive in their sexual attitudes, *but* men were dropping their endorsement of the double standard while women were moving from an abstinence-only attitude to a more double standard–based attitude. It is noteworthy that this gender difference in double standard endorsement was only moderate to small, which is not surprising as there is strong and consistent research that men are more sexually liberal than women (i.e., if we consider the double standard as a form of sexist sexual conservatism). Many different types of studies today seem to suggest that the sexual double standard was and is alive and well in the 1980s, 1990s, and 2000s, as is documented in the selection by Crawford and Popp.

In contrast, other researchers maintain that, while lay people believe that the sexual double standard exists and they are able to articulate the double standard easily, a sexual double standard does not exist in terms of its application to the evaluation of others. In their selection, Marks and Fraley interpret the existing research as failing to support the sexual double standard. Even in considering Reiss's 1967 data, students did not endorse the double standard to any great extent. In fact, only 25 percent endorsed a double standard (either orthodox or transitional; almost half (42 percent) endorsed abstinence from sexual intercourse for all). While reading the following selections, consider whether the evidence presented can be interpreted as supporting or refuting the existence of the sexual double standard.

YES  Mary Crawford and Danielle Popp

Sexual Double Standards: A Review and Methodological Critique of Two Decades of Research

Traditionally, men and women have been subjected to different "rules" guiding sexual behavior. Women were stigmatized for engaging in any sexual activity outside of heterosexual marriage, whereas for men such behavior was expected and rewarded. Boys had to "sow their wild oats," but girls were warned that a future husband "won't buy the cow if he can get the milk for free." Women were faced with a Madonna-whore dichotomy: They were either pure and virginal or promiscuous and easy. . . .

What follows is a review of evidence from a variety of research methods including experimental designs, ethnographies, interviews, focus groups, and linguistic analyses. . . .

Experimental Research

Experimental research has been used to examine individuals' preferences for partners and their beliefs about acceptable levels of sexual activity for males and females at varying relationship stages. Experimental methods have been used to examine both individual double standards and perceptions of societal double standards. Individual double standards have been examined using within-subject designs, in which participants are asked to answer questions or make judgments about the sexual behavior of either male or female targets and are immediately asked the same questions about targets of the other sex. Perceptions of societal double standards have been examined directly by asking participants whether or not societal double standards exist. Sexual double standards also can be inferred from experiments using between-subjects designs, in which one group of participants is asked about male targets, and another group is asked the same questions about female targets.

Within-Subject Designs: Measures of Individual Double Standards

Within-subject designs provide the purest test of double standards because the same participants respond to the same set of questions for each target. We found

From *Journal of Sex Research*, vol. 40, no. 1, February 2003, pp. 13–26. Copyright © 2003 as conveyed via Copyright Clearance Center. Reprinted by permission. Note: The complete text of this article contains many references to specific studies described. The interested individual should refer to the original publication for these extensive citations. These references have been omitted here in the interest of brevity.

only two within-subject experimental studies in our search of the literature. . . . Six hundred ninety Scottish teenagers . . . were asked to estimate how many sexual partners most 20-year-old women or men have had and to rate a hypothetical young woman or man who changes sex partners a number of times during the year. Respondents predicted that women would have had significantly fewer sexual partners than men. Further, for both religious men and nonreligious women, sexually active women were considered less popular among both sexes than sexually active men. Finally, women who changed sex partners a number of times during the year were rated as more irresponsible and as having less self-respect than men who engaged in the same behaviors.

Sprecher and Hatfield (1996) found that men endorsed a double standard for women and men who were dating casually (. . . dating less than one month) but not for women and men who were dating seriously (. . . almost one year) or who were pre-engaged (had seriously discussed the possibility of getting married). In the U.S., . . . undergraduates . . . completed a premarital sexual permissiveness scale for themselves, "a male," and "a female." The permissiveness scale asked participants to rate the acceptability of sexual intercourse at each of five dating stages (first date, casually dating, seriously dating, pre-engaged, and engaged). Male participants held significantly more permissive attitudes for a male (the total score for items referring to a male) than for a female. Men's endorsement of a double standard was strongest at the first date but also existed for intermediate dating stages. Overall, U.S. men reported greater endorsement of double standards than did U.S. women.

This study was part of a cross-cultural comparison of double standards in the U.S., Japan, and Russia. Of note in the Japanese and Russian samples, which also consisted entirely of [undergraduates], Russian students were more likely than U.S. students to show what the researchers termed a *traditional* double standard, especially at the first date, casual, and serious dating levels. Additionally, the greater endorsement of double standards by male participants than by female participants found in the U.S. sample was not found in the Russian and Japanese samples.

Between-Subjects Designs: Measures of Societal Double Standards

In between-subjects designs, each participant is presented with only one target; therefore, a direct measure of the double standard within the individual cannot be obtained. However, by comparing responses across participants by target sex, it is possible to determine whether, overall, women and men are judged differentially for engaging in the same behavior. . . .

Person-perception tasks allow researchers to examine the consequences of double standards on evaluations of males and females engaging in identical behavior. Evidence of double standards exists if women are evaluated differently than men for engaging in comparable levels of sexual activity under the same conditions.

Sprecher, McKinney, and Orbuch (1987) had . . . undergraduates . . . read a questionnaire ostensibly completed by another student. The questionnaire included manipulations for target sex, age at first coitus (16 or 21), and relationship stage at first coitus (a steady dating relationship that had lasted almost a year or a casual one that had lasted one week). Participants rated the fictional student on 23 bipolar scales that composed four factors: Sexual and Other Values (e.g., sexually experienced, sexually liberal, liberal in sex-roles), Maturity and Intelligence (e.g., responsible), Positive Personality (e.g., likable), and Dominance (e.g., dominant, active, masculine). There was a main effect for target sex such that female targets received higher scores on the Sexual and Other Values scale and lower scores on the Maturity and Intelligence, Positive Personality, and Dominance scales. There were also significant interactions between target sex and relationship stage at first coitus (Positive Personality and Dominance) and between target sex and age at first coitus (Maturity and Intelligence, Positive Personality, Dominance). Although having first coitus in a noncommitted relationship or at a young age had a negative effect on how both males and females were evaluated, the negative effect was greater for females. These results suggested that women were perceived more negatively than men for being more sexually experienced.

In a series of two studies, Oliver and Sedikides (1992) examined mate-selection preferences. . . . In Study 1, . . . undergraduates . . . were asked to complete a sexual permissiveness scale as they would want either a blind date or spouse to complete it. Both male and female participants preferred low levels of sexual permissiveness in both blind dates and spouses. Male participants preferred lower levels of sexual permissiveness in a spouse than in a blind date; there were no significant differences for female participants. In Study 2, . . . undergraduates read a sexual permissiveness scale ostensibly filled out by an opposite sex student who was either sexually permissive or sexually nonpermissive. Participants then rated the target on . . . Evaluation (e.g., morality) and Attraction (e.g., sexual attractiveness). Although the permissive target received lower evaluation ratings overall, female participants rated the male permissive target significantly more negatively than males rated the female permissive target. Male participants rated the female target as significantly more attractive when she was permissive than nonpermissive. Females rated the permissive male target as less desirable as both a spouse and a blind date. However, males rated the permissive female target as significantly less desirable for a spouse and significantly more desirable for a blind date than they rated the nonpermissive female target.

Milhausen and Herold's (1999) . . . female undergraduate participants . . . completed a questionnaire measuring both perceptions of a societal double standard and personal endorsement of double standards. . . . Findings indicated that participants overwhelmingly . . . believed that there is "a double standard for sexual behavior (a standard in which it is more acceptable for a man to have had more sexual partners than a woman)" (p. 363). Similarly, 93% of participants . . . believed that "women who have had many sex partners are judged more harshly than men who have had many sex partners" (p. 363). When asked to explain their answers, 49% of respondents mentioned women's being penalized for their sexual behavior, and 48% mentioned men's being rewarded for theirs. Additionally, 42% of participants believed that it is women who "judge women who have had sex with many partners more harshly" (p. 363). Personal endorsement of double standards was measured by asking participants to indicate on a 5-point scale whether they would encourage or discourage a male or female friend from dating someone who has had intercourse with more than 10 different partners. Results showed that women were more likely to discourage a female friend from dating a man who had 10 previous sexual partners than to discourage a male friend from dating a woman who had 10 previous partners.

A smaller group of studies . . . showed little or no support for double standards. Jacoby and Williams (1985) presented . . . undergraduates with five "sexual profiles" of opposite sex persons consisting of sets of answers to questions about sexual ideology and experience. Participants rated the dating and marriage desirability of the target in each profile. Findings indicated that there was no difference in the kinds of relationships in which sex was seen as acceptable for men and women and that no more than moderate sexual experience was desirable in either a male or female dating or marriage partner. . . .

Mark and Miller (1986) asked . . . undergraduates . . . to read a supposed transcript of an interview with another student whose sex and sexual permissiveness (virgin, relationship sex, casual sex) were varied. After reading the transcript, participants rated the target on . . . [ten] factors: Poor Adjustment, Unconventional, Likable, Agreeable, Caring, Assertive, Immoral, Conforming, . . . Trusting [, and] Sexual (chaste-promiscuous, modest-immodest, non-seductive-seductive, moral-immoral). . . . Participants also completed . . . evaluations and mental health [questions]. Results indicated little support for sexual double standards. The only significant results were on the sexual and agreeable scales. Male participants judged female targets as more sexual than male targets if they engaged in casual sex. Liberal males and traditional females rated females who had had casual sex as marginally less agreeable than they rated males who had had casual sex.

Sprecher (1989) asked . . . undergraduates . . . to answer a premarital sexual permissiveness scale for 1 of 20 targets. Targets varied in gender, age, and relationship to the participant (i.e., a female or sister). The permissiveness scale asked participants to rate the acceptability of three sexual behaviors (heavy petting, sexual intercourse, and oral-genital contact) at four different relationship stages (first date, casually dating [dating less than 1 month], seriously dating [dating almost 1 year], and engaged). Although the findings did not support sexual double standards, they suggested that age (regardless of target sex) is important when evaluating sexual standards.

O'Sullivan (1995) had . . . undergraduate students . . . read a vignette about a target who varied in sex, number of past partners (low [2 for males and 1 for females] or high [13 for males and 7 for females]), and type of relationship (committed or noncommitted). . . . Male targets were rated somewhat less positively than female targets overall. Sexually experienced targets received the least positive evaluations, and targets in noncommitted sexual relationships were rated as [more negative. Little] evidence of double standards was found. Women did not receive more negative evaluations than men did when described as having had high numbers of past sexual partners in noncommitted relationships. . . .

Sprecher, Regan, McKinney, Maxwell, and Wazienski (1997) asked . . . undergraduate . . . students . . . to complete one of three versions of a mate-selection preference list consisting of 18 partner traits. The target's sexual experience was manipulated using three versions of the sexuality items: sexual chastity (no previous sexual partners), some sexual experience (few sexual partners), or considerable sexual experience (several previous partners). Sprecher et al. found no evidence of a heterosexual double standard, with participants reporting no differences in preference for level of sexual experience based on target sex.

Gentry (1998) asked participants . . . to read a portion of an interview with a fictional heterosexual . . . student focusing on relationships and sexuality. The target's sex, number of relationships (either an exclusive, monogamous sexual relationship or sexual relations with multiple partners), and level of sexual activity (above average, below average, or average) were manipulated. . . . Results showed that participants based their judgments about the targets on information about number of relationships and level of sexual activity rather than the target's sex.

Summary and Critique of Experimental Studies

Of the 11 studies reported in detail, 5 found evidence of sexual double standards. Only 2 of the 11 studies used within-subject designs; both of these found evidence of double standards.

Studies varied in the possible moderating variables they assessed. Only one study reported analyses based on target age; both target age and its interaction with target sex were significant (Sprecher et al., 1987). Seven reported analyses based on relationship stage; of these seven, three reported overall evidence of double standards. Additionally, all three found significant main effects of relationship stage and interactions between target sex and relationship stage. Two studies found that sexually active men were judged more harshly than were sexually active women. . . .

Experimental designs have several advantages for studying sexual attitudes. They allow the researcher to manipulate or control variables believed to influence double standards, such as relationship stage. Unlike any other method, they permit causal inferences to be drawn. Because they typically present participants with hypothetical scenarios and use paper-and-pencil measures of dependent variables, they are relatively easy to use with large samples, which yield more statistical power. Their decontextualized scenarios also allow participants to reflect on their attitudes without personal emotional involvement.

Offsetting these theoretical and practical advantages are several limitations. An intrinsic problem with statistical comparisons is that the null hypothesis of similarity can never be taken as proven, whereas hypotheses of differences can be assessed probabilistically. The statistical emphasis on significant differences may foster the "file drawer problem" in which studies reporting similarities in attitudes toward a target's behavior regardless of target sex may remain unpublished, leading to an overestimate of double standards.

Other limitations of experimental methods are not intrinsic but occur frequently in practice. For example, virtually all the experimental studies described in this review relied on convenience samples of North American . . . students. This is a serious limitation, not just because these samples are unrepresentative of the general population, but because they are unrepresentative in particular ways that are rarely discussed or even acknowledged by researchers. . . .

In designing experimental studies of double standards, researchers have occasionally confounded target sex and participant sex. . . . If women's evaluations of men differ from men's evaluations of women, the difference could be due to either participant sex or target sex. Participants might be endorsing different standards for women and men, or they might be endorsing a single standard, but one that is different for female and male participants. The former fits our definition of a double standard; the latter does not. However, even if individual women and men each hold a single standard, if the standard held by women is different from the standard held by men, heterosexual women and men could still be evaluated differently by potential partners. These complexities can be teased out by systematically varying, both participant sex and target sex.

Another theoretical and practical issue in experimental designs is that the conceptual and linguistic categories used to measure double standards are preformed by the experimenter. . . . [The] response categories available to participants may be inadequate to represent the variable under consideration. [Even] when the categories seem adequate, the method assumes that they have the same meaning to all participants and that the meaning ascribed to the category by participants is the same as that ascribed by the experimenter. . . .

Qualitative and Interpretive Designs

In contrast to experimental methods, qualitative studies more readily lend themselves to contextually sensitive phenomena. The questions they can address are more open-ended and diffuse, less abstract and hypothetical. Here we review studies using ethnographic, interview, focus group, and linguistic analyses.

Ethnographic Studies

Ethnographic researchers, by definition, attempt to capture the belief systems of a community through close and sustained observation. Therefore, individuals' accounts of their communities' norms and their own beliefs about sexuality may emerge as part of broader ethnographic studies not specifically focused on double standards.

Heterosexual double standards are salient in ethnographies of adolescent culture in U.S. middle schools. In a 3-year study, Eder, Evans, and Parker (1995) used a variety of data sources: They observed lunchtime activity, attended extracurricular activities, conducted individual and small group interviews, and recorded audio and video tapes of students' spontaneous conversations with peers. Within the middle school peer culture, girls (but never boys) sometimes were negatively labeled simply because they showed interest or assertiveness with respect to sexuality. Girls who initiated any kind of sexual overture (e.g., "making a pass") were labeled "bitches," "sluts," and "whores." The sanction against female sexual agency extended to wearing attractive clothing or makeup, which also could earn the label of whore. The routine use of sexual insults aimed at girls by boys, and to a lesser extent by girls, suggested that middle school students "do not believe that girls should be sexually active or have a variety of boyfriends, while such behaviors are viewed as normal and acceptable for boys" (p. 131). Eder et al. (1995) concluded, "labeling young girls in this manner becomes part of a continual attempt to limit their sense of sexual autonomy and identity" (p. 153).

Focusing on girls, Orenstein (1994) conducted a yearlong ethnographic study of two middle schools, one suburban, White, and affluent, the other urban, largely ethnic minority, and poor. Girls' accounts described their fear of the slut label and their shamed silence around sexual desire. Orenstein vividly captured how double standards can be communicated even in a sex education class. The teacher, Ms. Webster, is trying to illustrate the risk of sexually transmitted diseases:

> "We'll use a woman," she says, drawing the Greek symbol for woman on the blackboard. "Let's say she is infected, but she hasn't really noticed yet, so she has sex with three men."
>
> (As she draws symbols for men on the board) a heavyset boy in a Chicago Bulls cap stage whispers, "What a slut," and the class titters.
>
> "Okay," says Ms. Webster, who doesn't hear the comment. "Now the first guy has three sexual encounters in six months." She turns to draw three more women's signs, her back to the class, and several of the boys point at themselves proudly, striking exaggerated macho poses.
>
> "The second guy was very active, he had intercourse with five women." As she turns to the diagram again, two boys stand and take bows.
>
> During the entire diagramming process, the girls in the class remain silent. (p. 61)

Double standards have emerged in ethnographies of college students as well. Moffat (1989) studied peer culture on a university campus, focusing on sexual beliefs and attitudes and using a variety of methods. He conducted participant observation while "passing" as a student living in a men's dormitory, and he analyzed sexual autobiographies written by students in sexuality classes. He reported that the majority of students believed in heterosexual double standards and classified women into dichotomous categories of "good" women or sluts. Moffat characterized the attitudes of the male students he studied as follows:

> Men have the right to experiment sexually for a few years. There are a lot of female sluts out there with whom to so experiment. And once I have gotten this out of my system, I will then look for a good woman for a long-term relationship (or for a wife). (1989, p. 204)

Interview and Focus Group Studies

Individual interviews and focus group discussions are open-ended methods of self-report. In these settings, participants can express beliefs and attitudes in their own terms and provide contextual information to justify or explain their positions. One such study relied on interviews conducted with 55 adolescents, both boys and girls, with a mean age of 16 years (Martin, 1996). Participants were students at three high schools, one working-class public and two upper-middle-class private institutions. They were interviewed privately in the school setting for about an hour each. Questions assessed identity, self-esteem, and body image, as well as experiences with the physical changes of puberty, intimate relationships, and sexual intercourse. . . .

Both girls and boys distinguished between girls they called sluts, "hos," or "Sally off the street" and girls they called "regular" or "normal" girls, those who could become someone's girlfriend. Distinctions such as these were not made for boys. However, having sex was not enough to earn the label of slut. Instead, peers' distinctions were made based on whether the girl was "too young" or had "too many" partners. Martin concluded that "the double standard in sex is still firmly rooted in teenage culture" (pp. 85–86).

In addition to the double standards of peers, many girls perceived parental double standards. For example, one respondent who expressed confusion and guilt about her sexual activity reported that her boyfriend's mother categorized any girl who "slept with" a boyfriend or even used a tampon during menstruation as a slut. Martin's female participants appeared to "take the distinction of slut to heart and fear it." She concluded, "Regardless of its particular contextual meaning, the word slut holds a lot of power. Being called a slut or a ho—or feeling like one—is to feel degraded and dirty" (pp. 86–87).

In a study of attitudes toward condom use among 105 young (median age 18) drug users in Western Australia, both male and female participants were asked "What do young men think of young women who carry condoms?" and "What do young women think of young men who carry condoms?" (Loxley, 1996). Results showed discrepancies between participants' reports of the attitudes of people of their own sex and the other sex. Participants of each sex believed that those of the other sex held more negative attitudes than were actually reported (e.g., women thought men had more negative attitudes toward women than men actually reported having). This mismatch suggests that perceptions of societal double standards may influence behavior. However, the transparent within-subject design, with each participant being asked about both sexes' attitudes, may have induced unknown biases in responding. . . .

Other studies, using single-sex samples, also show that adolescents perceive and are affected by sexual double standards. Thompson (1995), using a snowball sampling technique and open-ended interviews, gathered stories from 400 girls representing a variety of geographical locations, class backgrounds, and ethnicities. . . . Thompson concluded that the heterosexual double standard remains "virulently alive and well" (p. 31) but that it is less absolute and more contextually negotiated than in the past. Girls described innumerable fine lines as to what constituted good and bad sexual behavior, lines that mapped local and individual constructions of sex and gender. They appeared to use these maps to define and orient themselves as "good girls," as opposed to "easy" girls or sluts.

A smaller study of 17 male college students (ages 18–22) used . . . transcripts from interviews (Fromme & Emihovich, 1998). These respondents endorsed a double standard that divided women into two groups. "Good women" were those who say no to casual sex or to intercourse early in a relationship; these women were seen as acceptable for longer term relationships. "Bad women" were those who had sex on a first date or sex with many partners. The authors noted that their respondents did not seem to recognize that they derogated women for behaviors they accepted for themselves, as in this comment:

> If I met a woman in a bar and had sex with her chances are I wouldn't call her because I wouldn't have any respect for her. Because if she did something like that . . . would I want someone like that for the rest of my life? No, of course not. (p. 174)

One other source of first-person accounts deserves mention. Espin (1997), drawing on her knowledge of Hispanic/Latin culture and on experiences as a therapist with Latina clients, notes that Hispanics in the U.S. continue to attribute a great deal of importance to female sexual purity. Particularly among the upper social classes, women's virginity before marriage is a cultural imperative, and women's sexual behavior is an important marker of a family's honor. Married women are expected to remain completely monogamous while accepting their husbands' extramarital sexual affairs. Indeed, experiencing sexual pleasure and gratification, even in marriage, may be interpreted as evidence of a lack of purity and virtue in women.

Using a focus group technique, Fullilove, Fullilove, Haynes, and Gross (1990) recruited low-income urban African American women to participate in small-group discussions of sexuality. The researchers reported data from six homogeneous groups, some comprised of adolescents and some of adult women. Participants spontaneously described a dichotomy of sexual roles for women: the "good girl/madonna" role and the "bad girl/whore" role. A comparable dichotomy did not exist for men. For the participants in this study, sexual intercourse outside marriage did not necessarily relegate a woman to the bad girl/whore category. Rather, bad women were those who engaged in casual sex or offered sex in return for money or drugs.

Ward and Taylor (1994), in a study of sexuality education for minority students, conducted homogeneous focus groups with urban adolescent boys and girls of six ethnic or cultural groups: Vietnamese, Portuguese, African American, White, Haitian, and Hispanic. Each group was facilitated by an adult from the relevant cultural background. Without exception, groups from all ethnic backgrounds described heterosexual double standards that were "limiting and oppressive to females" (p. 63). There were some variations across ethnic groups. For example, some groups stressed premarital chastity more than others did. However, contrasting expectations for females and males, with more restrictions on females' behavior, were clearly expressed in all groups.

The importance of local community norms is echoed in a study of 512 high school students (ages 15–19) from rural Australian small towns (Hillier, Harrison, & Warr, 1998). Using a combination of survey and focus group methods, participants' attitudes about safe sex were explored. Fourteen single-sex focus groups were conducted in seven towns, each led by a same-sex facilitator. Analyses of content and themes were conducted and "cross-verified by project members" (p. 18).

Participants judged many of the risks of having sex to be greater for young women than for young men. Chief among these was the "sullied reputation" risk, a pervasive concern expressed in every female focus group. Loss of one's reputation was perceived to lead to sexual harassment, loss of both female and male friends, shame, and alienation. Respondents made clear their belief that losing one's good reputation could happen quickly and easily in a small town where everyone's activities were known and talked about. The risk of a bad reputation was perceived by both sexes to apply only to girls. Such double standards were clearly captured in these remarks from two focus groups:

> Girl: They (boys) have a one-night stand and nothing happens. We're more in fear of getting labeled like a tart or a slut or something. Whereas the boys if they have it they don't get labeled . . . and we're more ashamed of it if we do.
> Boy: You do it for the feeling and to brag about it afterwards. (Hillier et al., 1998, p. 26)

The researchers concluded that when young women in these small towns had sexual intercourse, or even when others wrongly believed that they did, they risked losing friends, family, and the opportunity for future relationships. These risks were exacerbated by the fact that females were more socially defined through their relationships than males were. Therefore, the young women were unequally positioned with their sexual partners with respect to their power to negotiate.

Attitudes toward sexual risk taking also provided the impetus for a study of U.S. inner city youth (Stanton, Black, Kaljee, & Ricardo, 1993). The primary method was focus groups, conducted with young people in two age groups (9–10 and 13–14), supplemented by interviews with parents and ethnographic background study. The focus group sample was drawn from patients at an urban pediatric clinic serving a largely low-income African American population.

Attitudes about girls' and boys' sexual activity seemed to be more similar than different in this population. High levels of sexual activity were perceived as normative for both sexes. One difference that did emerge was that sexual activity for even very young boys was socially accepted by peers and adults, whereas attitudes toward girls' sexual activity were more variable. Although some girls chose to abstain from sexual intercourse and reported that peers respected their choice, others reported a great deal of pressure to become sexually active. Moreover, participants agreed that girls who became pregnant received considerable positive attention and acceptance. Thus, these results suggest that peer pressure on boys strongly discouraged abstinence from intercourse. Although there was similar peer pressure on girls, at least some girls perceived abstinence as a viable option.

Taken together, these analyses of diverse ethnic and cultural groups suggest that contemporary sexual double standards are local and subcultural constructions rather than a universal mandate.

Language and Discourse Analyses

Language both reflects and reinforces social reality. Studies of terms for sexually active women and men show that such terms differ in frequency and connotation. The English language has many more terms describing women than men in specifically sexual ways, and the great majority of these are negative. In a study of slang from a U.S. university, almost 90% of the words for women and only 46% of the words for men had negative connotations. Many negative words for women described them as being very sexually active ("turboslut," "roadwhore," "skag," "wench"). There was only one term for very sexually active men ("Mr. Groin"), and it was not seen as unambiguously negative (Munro, 1989). In a language corpus from another university, Sutton (1995) found that students generated many negative words for women when asked simply to collect 10 slang terms that they and their friends used often. By far the largest category was terms denoting sexually active women: "bait," "beddy," "ho," "hooker," "hootchie," "scud," "skank ho," "slag," "slut," "tramp," and "whore" are examples. Sexually active women were also denoted by their genitals: "pelt," "slam hole," "stimey hole," and "tuna." The only comparable male term offered by students was "hoebuck" (a parallel to "hobag" but less negative in connotation). Thus, the linguistic resources available to assess the sexual behavior of women and men differ considerably and define women's (more than men's) morality and desirability in terms of their sexuality.

The only experimental study to include an open-ended question about language and sexuality was conducted by Milhausen and Herold (1999). Participants were asked what words they would use to describe a man or woman who has had many sexual partners. Two raters independently coded responses into categories. Virtually all the words listed for highly experienced men and women were deemed negative. Terms for men most often connoted sexual predation ("player") and promiscuity ("sleazy"). Terms for women most often connoted promiscuity ("slut") and psychological dysfunction ("insecure"). Milhausen and Herold tallied the number of negative terms applied to female and male targets. Finding no difference, they concluded that their linguistic analysis provided no support for double standards. All the participants in this study were women. . . .

Another recent study of language use showed that men are more likely to be portrayed positively and agentically in everyday talk about sex. Weatherall and Walton (1999) studied college students' metaphors for sexual activity by asking students to keep daily diaries of their sex talk for a week. Common types of metaphors were food and eating, animals, sport and games, and war and violence. Although most of these metaphors would seem to be potentially gender neutral, males were two and a half times more likely to be the actor in mundane talk about sexual activity. These linguistic data may reflect the double standard in agency and initiation that is a frequently recurring theme in qualitative and quantitative studies that assess attitudes about sexuality. . . .

Summary and Critique of Qualitative Studies

The majority of the ethnographies, interview and focus group studies, and linguistic analyses reviewed here found evidence for double standards, and sometimes indicated the influence of some of the same contextual factors shown in quantitative studies. As a group, the qualitative studies used a much more varied spectrum of participants with respect to ethnicity, race, social class, age, and social position than did the quantitative studies. Although there is no intrinsic reason that quantitative studies could not draw from diverse populations, this has not been the case in practice.

Qualitative researchers' use of diverse samples yields some benefits. It adds to the limited database of quantitative studies using college students and potentially can correct for some of the developmental and social biases introduced by over-relying on college sample. By drawing on participants from varying social positions, this research also helps portray the variety of socially constructed double standards. Open-ended methods have the potential to show the dynamic aspects of double standards: how they are conveyed in interaction and actively employed as a means of social control for both sexes. In the middle school sex education class described by Orenstein (1994), . . . both boys and girls were provided with models that might encourage them to incorporate sexual double standards into their value systems. Some boys engaged in macho posturing about high levels of male sexual activity, and some voiced negative labels for females who behaved similarly. These behaviors occurred without sanction from an authority figure and with approval from other students.

Of course, interpretive methods have their drawbacks, too. They are costly in terms of time. They require researchers who are members of the group being studied and/or highly trained in developing rapport and trust. Finally, unlike laboratory studies, they cannot manipulate variables to establish causality, and they cannot systematically examine the interaction of several factors.

There is potential for selection bias in choosing interpretive studies for a review, and this review is no exception. Because interpretive methods such as ethnographies may be very broad in scope, with the goal of capturing the ethos of a community, a narrow topic such as sexual double standards may be embedded in the (often book-length) report but not accessible by keyword or index searches. Another potential selection bias is that interpretive studies that look for but do not find evidence of double standards may not mention the topic in their reports, so that the published literature overrepresents the incidence of double standards. This is analogous to the file-drawer problem in quantitative studies. In this review, our criteria for including a qualitative study were necessarily less precise than our criteria for including a quantitative study. . . .

References

Eder, D., Evans, C. C., & Parker, S. (1995). *Gender and adolescent culture.* New Brunswick, NJ: Rutgers University Press.

Espin, O. M. (1997). *Latina realities: Essays on healing, migration and sexuality.* Boulder, CO: Westview Press.

Fromme, R. E., & Emihovich, C. (1998). Boys will be boys: Young males' perceptions of women, sexuality and prevention. *Education and Urban Society, 30,* 172–188.

Fullilove, M. T., Fullilove, R. E., Haynes, K., & Gross, S. (1990). Black women and AIDS prevention: A view towards understanding the gender rules. *The Journal of Sex Research, 27,* 47–64.

Gentry, M. (1998). The sexual double standard: The influence of number of relationships and level of sexual activity on judgments of women and men. *Psychology of Women Quarterly, 22,* 505–511.

Hillier, L., Harrison, L., & Warr, D. (1998). "When you carry condoms all the boys think you want it": Negotiating competing discourses about safe sex. *Journal of Adolescence, 21,* 15–29.

Jacoby, A. P., & Williams, J. D. (1985). Effects of premarital sexual standards and behavior on dating and marriage desirability. *Journal of Marriage and the Family, 47,* 1059–1065.

Loxley, W. (1996). "Sluts" or "sleazy little animals"?: Young people's difficulties with carrying and using condoms. *Journal of Community & Applied Social Psychology, 6,* 293–298.

Mark, M. M., & Miller, M. L. (1986). The effects of sexual permissiveness, target gender, subject gender, and attitude toward women on social perception: In search of the double standard. *Sex Roles, 15,* 311–322.

Martin, K. A. (1996). *Puberty, sexuality, and the self: Girls and boys at adolescence.* London: Routledge.

Milhausen, R. R., & Herold, E. S. (1999). Does the sexual double standard still exist? Perceptions of university women. *The Journal of Sex Research, 36,* 361–368.

Moffat, M. (1989). *Coming of Age in New Jersey.* New Brunswick, NJ: Rutgers University Press.

Munro, P. (1989). *Slang U.* New York: Harmony Books.

Oliver, M. B., & Sedikides, C. (1992). Effects of sexual permissiveness on desirability of partner as a function of low and high commitment to relationship. *Social Psychology Quarterly, 55,* 321–333.

Orenstein, P. (1994). *Schoolgirls: Young women, self-esteem, and the confidence gap.* New York: Doubleday.

O' Sullivan, L. F. (1995). Less is more: The effects of sexual experience on judgments of men's and women's personality characteristics and relationship desirability. *Sex Roles, 33,* 159–181.

Sprecher, S. (1989). Premarital sexual standards for different categories of individuals. *The Journal of Sex Research, 26,* 232–248.

Sprecher, S., & Hatfield, E. (1996). Premarital sexual standards among U.S. college students: Comparison with Russian and Japanese students. *Archives of Sexual Behavior, 25,* 261–288.

Sprecher, S., McKinney, K., & Orbuch, T. L. (1987). Has the double standard disappeared? An experimental test. *Social Psychology Quarterly, 50,* 24–31.

Sprecher, S., Regan, P. C., McKinney, K., Maxwell, K., & Wazienski, H. (1997). Preferred level of sexual experience in a date or mate: The merger of two methodologies. *The Journal of Sex Research, 34,* 327–337.

Stanton, B. F., Black, M., Kaljee, L., & Ricardo, I. (1993). Perceptions of sexual behavior among urban early adolescents: Translating theory through focus groups. *Journal of Early Adolescence, 13,* 44–66.

Sutton, L. A. (1995). Bitches and skankly hobags: The place of women in contemporary slang. In K. Hall & M. Bucholtz (Eds.), *Gender articulated: Language and the socially constructed self* (pp. 279–296). New York: Routledge.

Thompson, S. (1995). *Going all the way: Teenage girls' tales of sex, romance, and pregnancy.* New York: Hill and Wang.

Ward, J. V., & Taylor, J. (1994). Sexuality education for immigrant and minority students: Developing a culturally appropriate curriculum. In J. M. Irvine (Ed.), *Sexual cultures and the construction of adolescent identities* (pp. 51–68). Philadelphia: Temple University Press.

Weatherall, A., & Walton, M. (1999). The metaphorical construction of sexual experience in a speech community of New Zealand university students. *British Journal of Social Psychology, 38,* 479–498.

Michael J. Marks and R. Chris Fraley

 **NO**

The Sexual Double Standard: Fact or Fiction?

In contemporary society it is widely believed that women and men are held to different standards of sexual behavior. As [many have] noted, "a man who is successful with many women is likely to be seen as just that—successful . . . [whereas] a woman known to have 'success' with many men is . . . likely to be known as a 'slut.'" The view that men are socially rewarded and women socially derogated for sexual activity has been labeled the *sexual double standard.*

The sexual double standard has received a lot of attention from contemporary critics of Western culture. Tanenbaum (2000), for example, has documented the harassment and distress experienced by adolescent girls who have been branded as "sluts" by their peers. Other writers have critiqued the way the media help to create and reinforce negative stereotypes of sexually active women and how these stereotypes may contribute to violence against women. Given the attention the sexual double standard has received in contemporary discourse, one might assume that behavioral scientists have documented the double standard extensively and elucidated many of the mechanisms that generate and sustain it. Despite much systematic research, however, there is virtually no consistent evidence for the existence of this allegedly pervasive phenomenon.

We have three objectives in this [paper]. Our first is to review briefly the empirical literature on the sexual double standard. As we discuss, research findings concerning the double standard do not strongly support its existence. Next, we discuss several methodological reasons why previous researchers may not have been able to document a double standard even if one exists. Finally, we report a study that was designed to determine whether the sexual double standard exists by rectifying the methodological limitations of previous studies.

Empirical Research on the Sexual Double Standard

The sexual double standard seems to be a ubiquitous phenomenon in contemporary society; one recent survey revealed that 85% of people believe that a double standard exists in our culture. The double standard is frequently publicized by the media. For example, MTV, a popular cable television channel that specializes in contemporary culture, recently aired a program called "Fight for Your Rights: Busting the Double Standard" that was designed to

From Sex Roles: A Journal of Research, vol. 52, no. 3/4, February 2005, pp. 175–186. Copyright © 2005 by Springer Journals (Kluwer Academic). Reprinted by permission. Note: The complete text of this article contains many references to specific studies described. The interested individual should refer to the original publication for these extensive citations. These references have been omitted here in the interest of brevity.

convey the idea that a sexual double standard exists and that people should try to transcend it by exhibiting more egalitarian thinking.

Although the sexual double standard seems pervasive, empirical research does not necessarily show that people evaluate sexually active men and women differently. In fact, much of the literature reveals little or no evidence of a double standard. O'Sullivan (1995), for example, conducted a person perception study in which individual participants read vignettes of a male or female target who reported a high or low number of past sexual partners. Participants then evaluated the targets in domains such as likeability, morality, and desirability as a spouse. Although men and women who engaged in casual intercourse were evaluated more negatively than those whose sexual experiences occurred in committed relationships, a double standard was not found. Gentry (1998) also employed a person perception task and found that raters judged both male and female targets who had relatively few past sexual partners and who were in monogamous relationships more positively than targets who had a high number of partners and had frequent casual sex. Again, no evidence of a double standard was found. Sprecher et al. (1988) examined how appropriate certain sexual acts were for men and women of various ages. Although older targets received more permissive responses (i.e., they were allowed more sexual freedom), there were few differences in the standards used for men versus women for any age group.

Researchers have also documented many characteristics of respondents that influence attitudes toward sexuality, but few, if any, of these findings are consistent with a double standard. For instance, Garcia (1982) found that respondents' degree of androgyny was related to the sexual stereotypes they held. Androgynous participants (i.e., people who possess high levels of both masculine and feminine psychological traits) displayed a single standard, whereas gender-typed respondents (i.e., masculine men and feminine women) displayed a slight preference for female targets in the low-sexual experience condition. However, a preference for high-experience male targets over low-experience male targets was not found.

The number of sexual partners respondents have had also appears to influence their judgments of targets. Milhausen and Herold (1999), for example, found that women with many sexual partners were more tolerant of highly sexually active men than were women with few sexual partners. However, the interaction between target gender, target experience, and participant experience was not tested. The gender of the respondent has also been shown to influence views on sexuality. Women tend to hold sexual standards that are stricter than those of men, but do not necessarily apply those standards differently as a function of the gender of the person being evaluated.

In summary, although it appears that people *do* evaluate others with respect to the number of sexual partners those people have had, research does not consistently show that those evaluations differ for male and female targets. Even in situations in which men and women are evaluated differently, the associations usually vary only in magnitude, not in sign. In other words, there are some situations in which both women and men may be evaluated more negatively as the number of sexual partners they report increases, but this association is only slightly stronger for women than it is for men. As we will explain below, this pattern can be characterized as a "weak" rather than "strong" double standard. If the sexual double standard is as pervasive and powerful as many people believe, empirical research should reveal cross-over interactions such that the association between sexual experience and evaluations is negative for women but positive for men.

Sexual Double Standard Research Methodology

Although the empirical literature would seem to suggest that the sexual double standard is not in operation, it may be the case that behavioral scientists have failed to tap it properly. Commonly used paradigms for studying the sexual double standard may have methodological limitations that prevent the double standard from emerging. If this is the case, changes are needed in the methodology used in sexual double standard research.

One limitation of past research is the likely existence of demand characteristics. For example, if a study explicitly requires participants to rate the appropriateness of certain sexual behaviors for men, immediately followed by identical questions regarding women, participants may try to answer either in an egalitarian manner or in a manner that is consistent with what they believe to be the norm. Given that many people have preconceived notions about the sexual double standard, it is important to minimize demand characteristics when researching attitudes toward sexuality.

A second limitation of past research involves the presentation of sexual activity in a valenced fashion. For example, some researchers have used materials that imply that premarital sexual intercourse "is just wrong" or have described a target as having a number of past sexual partners that is "a lot above average." This kind of language implies that there is something abnormal or inappropriate about the target's activity. Describing sexual activity with value-laden terms or implying that a person is involved in *any* behavior to an excess may lead to biased evaluations of that person, regardless of whether that person is male or female. If a sexual double standard exists, the use of these kinds of descriptors may occlude researchers' ability to document it clearly.

Finally, much of the past double standard research has not differentiated between attitudes and evaluations. *Attitudes* toward sexual behavior may include general beliefs about the norms of the culture, personal decisions about when sex is permissible, and the perceived appropriateness of certain sexual behaviors. *Evaluations* concern real judgments made about specific people who engage in sexual activity. Attitudes may be independent of the way people actually evaluate one another. Because of this, results concerning attitudinal differences (e.g., women hold less permissive sexual standards than men do) as evidence of the double standard's existence may conflict with results concerning evaluations of others' behavior. We believe that at the core of popular interest in the sexual double standard is the notion that men and women are evaluated differently depending on their sexual experience. Although the general attitudes that people hold about sexuality are of interest to psychologists, these attitudes may not be reflected in the actual evaluations that people make about one another. Therefore, it is imperative to focus on the evaluations that people make about specific individuals.

Overview of the Present Study

The objective of the present experiment was to determine whether people evaluate men and women differently based on the number of sexual partners they have had. To do this, we asked participants to rate a target on a number of evaluative dimensions. We manipulated both (a) the sex of the target and (b) the number of sexual partners reported by the target. This experiment was explicitly designed to rectify some of the limitations of previous research on the sexual double standard. For example, we focused on the evaluations people made about specific targets rather than general perceptions of social norms. We did not include valenced or biased descriptions of sexual activity (e.g., "promiscuous," "above average number of partners"). Moreover, we employed a between-subjects design to reduce potential demand characteristics. These features enabled us to draw attention away from the sexual focus of the study and allowed us to tap the way people evaluate others who vary in gender and sexual experience. . . .

Competing Hypotheses

If a traditional or "strong" sexual double standard exists, then as the number of sexual partners reported increases, male targets would be evaluated more positively and female targets more negatively. . . .

It is also possible that a "weak" double standard exists, such that both men and women are derogated for high levels of sexual experience, but to different degrees. . . . Finally, if there is no sexual double standard, then we would observe equivalent slopes for male and female targets. . . .

Method

Participants

. . . The . . . sample consisted of 144 undergraduates from a large midwestern university (44 men, 100 women) who participated in fulfillment of partial course credit. The mean participant age in this sample was 19.66 ($SD = 3.14$, range 18–30 years). . . .

Design

We employed a 2 (target sex) × 6 (number of partners: 0, 1, 3, 7, 12, or 19) between-subjects design. . . .

Procedure

A page (constructed by the experimenters) that contained five questions and the answers to those questions was given to the participants to read. Participants were told that the page was a section from a general public survey that had been completed by an anonymous individual. The page contained answers to questions such as "What are your hobbies?" and "How do you see yourself?" Information about the target's sexual experience was conveyed in response to the question "What is something not many people know about you?" The key phrase in the response was "I've had sex with [number] [guys/girls]. I don't really have much to say about it. It's just sort of the way I've lived my life."

After reading the page that contained the target's answers, participants were asked to rate 30 evaluative statements about the target. Participants rated each item on a *Disagree* [to] *Agree* [scale]. These items . . . power, intelligence, likeability, morality, quality as a date, quality as a spouse, physical appeal, and friendship [comprised] four evaluative factors: *values* . . . , *peer popularity* . . . , *power/success* . . . , and *intelligence*. . . .

Results

. . . [A statistical technique, called multiple regression was used to analyse the results.]

In the values domain, there was a main effect of number of sexual partners. . . . Targets with more partners were evaluated more negatively. . . . There was no main effect of target sex and no . . . interaction [of number of sexual partners and target sex.]

In the domain of peer popularity, there was a main effect of number of sexual partners. . . . Targets with more partners were evaluated more negatively. . . . There was no main effect of target sex and no . . . interaction [of number of sexual partners and target sex].

In the domain of power/success, there were no main effects of target sex or number of sexual partners, although there was a tendency for participants to evaluate targets with many partners more negatively. . . . There was no . . . interaction [of number of sexual partners and target sex].

In the domain of intelligence, again there was a main effect of number of sexual partners. . . . Targets with more partners were evaluated more negatively. . . . There was no . . . interaction [of number of sexual partners and target sex].

Discussion

To date, there has been little evidence that women are evaluated more negatively than men for having many sexual partners. However, if the double standard exists, methodological limitations of previous research may have prevented it from emerging clearly. In the present research, we sought to provide a rigorous test of whether or not the sexual double standard exists by rectifying methodological limitations of previous studies. Our data reveal virtually no evidence of a traditional, or "strong," sexual double standard. . . .

These results . . . suggest that although the double standard may not operate in overall evaluations of persons, it may play a role in shaping perceptions of sexually active people in specific domains. Concerning the domain of intelligence, for example, engaging in frequent casual sex may not be a "smart" thing to do in light of the dangers of sexually transmitted diseases (especially AIDS). . . .

These results suggest that even after addressing some of the methodological limitations of previous research, traditional accounts of the sexual double standard do not appear to characterize the manner in which sexually active men and women are evaluated. This raises the question of whether the sexual double standard is more a cultural illusion than an actual phenomenon. If the double standard does not accurately characterize the manner in which people evaluate sexually active others, why does belief in it persist?

One possibility is that people are sensitive to our culture's "sexual lexicon." Many writers have observed that there are more slang terms in our language that degrade sexually active women than sexually active men. On the basis of such observations, people may conclude that a sexual double standard exists. However, one must be cautious when citing sexual slang as evidence of a double standard. It may be more valuable to consider the relative frequency of the use of slang terms than to consider solely the number of slang terms that exist. When Milhausen and Herold (2001) analyzed the frequency of sexual slang used to describe men and women in actual discourse, they found that the majority of men and women used negative terms to describe both sexually experienced men *and* women. They reported that a minority of men (25%) and women (8%) actually used words such as "stud" to describe sexually active men. Moreover, sexually active men were frequently described with words that fall into the category of *sexual predator* (e.g., "womanizer") or *promiscuous* (e.g., "slut," "dirty"). So although a difference exists in the *number* of sexual slang terms to describe men and women, it is not nearly analogous to the difference in the frequency of their *use* for men and women.

The confirmation bias may also help to explain why people believe that the sexual double standard exists. Confirmation bias refers to a type of selective thinking in which one tends to notice evidence that confirms one's beliefs and to ignore or undervalue evidence that contradicts one's beliefs. Confirmation biases may lead people to notice cases that are consistent with the double standard (e.g., a woman being referred to as a "slut") and fail to notice cases inconsistent with the double standard (e.g., a man being referred to as a "whore"). Because the vast majority of people believe that a sexual double standard exists, it is likely that people will process social information that seemingly corroborates the sexual double standard and will ignore information that refutes it. In short, although men and women may have an equal probability of being derogated (or rewarded) for having had many sexual partners, people may tend to notice only the instances in which women are derogated and men are rewarded. Attending to cases that are consistent with the double standard while ignoring cases inconsistent with it may create the illusion that the sexual double standard is more pervasive than it really is.

Limitations of the Present Study

Although we sought to correct some limitations of past research, other limitations remain. First, the statistical power of the student sample was low because of the relatively small sample size. . . .

Second, the results reported here may not generalize to populations outside of Western culture. Culture can be a powerful sculptor of sexual attitudes and behavior; the double standard may exist in one culture, but be absent from another. For instance, a review of the anthropological literature on sex and sexuality in Africa reveals much evidence of a double standard in African culture.

Third, this study, like much previous research, employs an experimental person perception paradigm. Studying the double standard in more naturalistic settings may reveal dynamics not otherwise tapped by more artificial methodologies. For example, observing "hot spots" where social interactions are possibly centered on sex (e.g., bars, locker rooms) may offer insight to the kinds of attitudes expressed concerning the sexual activity of men and women.

Finally, the present research is relatively atheoretical, partly because we believe that it is necessary to document the phenomenon of the double standard systematically (if it exists) before bringing theoretical perspectives to bear on it. Nonetheless, there may be theoretical perspectives that would help guide us in a more effective search for this phenomenon. For example, social psychological theory suggests that people tend to conform to social norms in the presence of others. Because there are strong gender norms concerning the appropriate sexual behavior of men and women, people may behave in accordance with these norms in social situations. Our study, like other studies on the double standard, only focused on individuals in nongroup situations. Social psychological theory suggests that social interaction in group contexts may be a necessary precondition for the emergence of the double standard.

Conclusions

In an effort to denounce the sexual double standard, contemporary authors, critics, and the media may actually be *perpetuating* it by unintentionally providing confirming evidence for the double standard while ignoring disconfirming evidence. Most accounts from these sources cite numerous cases of women being derogated for sexual activity, perhaps in an effort to elicit empathy from the audience. Empathy is a commendable (and desirable) goal, but these writings may also serve to embed the double standard in our collective conscious. Suggesting that a societal double standard is the basis of the derogation of women shifts focus away from those who are truly at fault—

those who are engaging in or permitting sexual harassment and other forms of derogation.

In closing, we believe that it may be beneficial to shift the emphasis of sexual double standard research from the question of *whether* the double standard exists to *why* the double standard appears to be such a pervasive phenomenon when it really is not. By addressing this question, future researchers should be able to elucidate the disparity between popular intuitions and the research literature and open doors to novel avenues for our understanding of attitudes toward sexuality.

References

Garcia, L. T. (1982). Sex-role orientation and stereotypes about male-female sexuality. *Sex Roles, 8,* 863–876.

Gentry, M. (1998). The sexual double standard. The influence of number of relationships and level of sexual activity on judgments of women and men. *Psychology of Women Quarterly, 22,* 505–511.

Milhausen, R. R., & Herold, E. S. (1999). Does the sexual double standard still exist? Perceptions of university women. *Journal of Sex Research, 36,* 361–368.

Milhausen, R. R., & Herold, E. S. (2001). Reconceptualizing the sexual double standard. *Journal of Psychology and Human Sexuality, 13,* 63–83.

O'Sullivan, L. F. (1995). Less is more: The effects of sexual experience on judgments of men's and women's personality characteristics and relationship desirability. *Sex Roles, 33,* 159–181.

Sprecher, S., McKinney, K., Walsh, R., & Anderson, C. (1988). A revision of the Reiss Premarital Sexual Permissiveness Scale. *Journal of Marriage and the Family, 50,* 821–828.

Tanenbaum, L. (2000). *Slut!* New York: Harper Collins.

POSTSCRIPT

Does a Traditional or "Strong" Double Standard with Respect to Sexual Behavior Exist Among Adolescents?

The selections presented here both provide compelling cases for the existence of the double standard and the non-existence of the double standard. How a particular study is conducted seems to have an impact on whether a double standard effect is documented (or not). Could researchers be incorrectly measuring the sexual double standard or missing important components of how the double standard is conveyed? Both Marks and Fraley as well as Crawford and Popp would agree that classic social science research, whereby an experiment is conducted holding as many other variables constant as possible, may fail to capture a true double standard effect. It seems as if participants in these types of studies are not judging males and females differentially; participants seem to like "sexually permissive" individuals less, regardless of their gender. The double standard seems to be more evident in the qualitative research (e.g., ethnographies, interviews) reviewed by Crawford and Popp. When observing people in a more naturalistic setting, the double standard seems to be alive and well (e.g., the classroom example cited in Crawford and Popp is particularly compelling).

Another clever qualitative study was published recently that attempted to document subtle or covert sexual messages consistent with the sexual double standard. Aubrey (2004) content analyzed sexual messages conveyed in television dramas that were aimed at adolescents (e.g., Gilmore Girls, Dawson's Creek) and found that there was a trend that supported the sexual double standard such that women tended to be more likely to receive negative consequences (e.g., guilt, rejection) of sexual behavior. Also related to the double standard is the idea that "good girls" will not initiate sexual behavior. Aubrey assessed the results of female sexual initiation and found negative consequences were the more likely outcome when a woman initiated sex relative to when a man initiated sex. This conveys messages to both women and men: Women—do not initiate sex or bad things will ensue; and men—when women initiate sex, it may be dangerous for either or both of you. Also, this study found that men initiated sex much more often than women did; the message to youth may be that men are expected to be more sexually active and women are expected to be passive recipients. This is also an indirect sexual double standard-type message.

Whether a sexual double standard exists or not, people believe it exists. Milhausen and Herold (1999) found that 93 percent of their sample of university women agreed that the double standard exists. Does this belief have any potential impact on the sexuality of youth—particularly young women—in our society? Indeed, it is possible that women will be less prepared to have sex if they believe in the existence of the double standard. For example, one study cited by Crawford and Popp found that if a woman believed her male partner endorsed the double standard, she was less likely to provide a condom during intercourse. The belief in the double standard existence may also have an adverse effect on young women's views of themselves. They may evaluate their own sexual desires as undesirable and in conflict with societal standards. As a result, they may experience ambivalence about their sexuality (see Welles, 2005). It is possible that this contributes to women's greater negativity about sex relative to men.

The belief in the existence of the sexual double standard may be more important than the actual existence of the double standard. That is, maybe we do not evaluate others by the double standard but perhaps we adjust our behavior and assess ourselves in relation to our belief in this perceived "norm." In fact, Marks and Fraley (2005) conducted a follow-up study where they found evidence that people pay more attention to information that is consistent with their belief in the double standard and ignore information that contradicts the double standard. Thus, our own "confirmation bias" (i.e., the tendency to pay closer attention to social information that is consistent with our belief system and discount information that is inconsistent) may perpetuate the belief in the sexual double standard. Further, media such as television, news sources, and magazines may further endorse the existence of the sexual double standard (see Aubrey, 2004). If we make people aware of these personal and systemic biases, we may be able to counteract the effects of these beliefs—particularly when these effects may be detrimental to youth.

References/Further Readings

Aubrey, J. S. (2004). Sex and punishment: An examination of sexual consequences and the sexual double standard in teen programming. *Sex Roles, 50,* 505–514.

Double Standard, (DVD) (2002). CTV. Product information available at: http://www.mcintyre.ca/cgi-bin/search/productsview.asp?ID=495.

Marks, M. & Fraley, R.C. (2005). Confirmation bias and the sexual double standard. *Sex Roles, 52*(3–4), 19–26.

Milhausen, R.R., & Herold, E. S. (1999). Does the sexual double standard still exist? Perceptions of university women. *The Journal of Sex Research, 36,* 361–368.

Oliver, M.B., & Hyde, J.S. (1993). Gender differences in sexuality: A meta-analysis. *Psychological Bulletin, 114,* 29–51.

Reiss, I. (1967). *The social context of premarital sexual permissiveness.* New York: Holt, Rinehart, and Winston.

Welles, C.E. (2005). Breaking the silence surrounding female adolescent sexual desire. *Women & Therapy, 28*(2), 31–45.

White, E. (2001). *Fast girls: Teenage tribes and the myth of the slut.* New York: Scribner.

ISSUE 11

Is Female Sexual Orientation More Fluid than Male Sexual Orientation During Adolescence?

YES: Lisa M. Diamond, from "Was It a phase? Young Women's Relinquishment of Lesbian/Bisexual Identities Over a 5-Year Period," *Journal of Personality and Social Psychology* (vol. 84, no. 2, 2003)

NO: Margaret Rosario et al., from "Sexual Identity Development Among Lesbian, Gay, and Bisexual Youths: Consistency and Change Over Time," *The Journal of Sex Research* (February 2006)

ISSUE SUMMARY

YES: Lisa Diamond, an assistant professor of psychology and women's studies at the University of Utah, presents evidence from a 5-year study that young women tend to be more fluid in terms of sexual preference than adolescent males.

NO: Researchers Rosario and colleagues oppose the hypothesis that females are more sexually fluid than males. They argue that female youth were less likely to change their sexual identity than males.

Often adults dismiss adolescent same-sex romantic or sexual relationships as "just a phase." This "phase" concept is reinforced in popular television shows where it is not uncommon to hear a joke about a woman who "tried it" in college—meaning she had sexual relations with another woman. In the following selection, Diamond makes a similar reference to this with the term "LUG" (lesbian until graduation). Within the lesbian community, one might hear jokes about "tourists visiting the Isle of Lesbos"—referring to women who are curious about sex with other women but who do not adopt a sexual minority identity label (e.g., lesbian, bisexual, or part of the women's community). These anecdotal accounts illustrate the controversy surrounding women's sexual fluidity. The flexibility of women's—especially young women's—sexuality has been a question of interest since the sexual revolution; men's sexuality, in contrast, appears to be more stable.

Roy Baumeister's theory of erotic plasticity (2000, 2004) condends that women's sexuality is more plastic (i.e., can be more easily shaped by cultural, social, and environmental factors) and is more reactive to such external factors as historical events, socialization and peer influence, and other cultural determinants. In contrast, Baumeister contends that there is substantial evidence of the invariability of men's sexuality. As an example, Baumeister cites that the sexual revolution had a greater impact on women's sexuality—which changed a lot—than on men's sexuality—which changed very little. Thus, women's sexuality changed as a consequence of their social environment. Hypotheses can be derived from his theory, such as women who are exposed to positive gay/lesbian/bisexual environments would be more likely to consider or to engage in same-sex behavior while men would not be as likely to do so.

There are a number of explanations as to why this gender difference in erotic plasticity might exist. For example, differences in erotic plasticity may be based on power differences: Women tend to be in lower positions of social power, so flexibility is more adaptive (i.e., to please their more powerful male partners). Alternatively, men may have a stronger sex drive than women; a milder sex drive is more easily molded. Therefore, gender differences in erotic plasticity may be explained by either nature or nurture.

In his extensive review and theoretical paper, Baumeister (2000) considers studies of the bisexual behavior of women and men as evidence of women's greater erotic plasticity. In the following selection, Diamond applies Baumeister's theory by investigating adolescent women who initially identify as a sexual minority (i.e., as a lesbian or bisexual woman) and then relinquish that label (i.e., identifying as heterosexual or *not* as lesbian or bisexual). Rosario et al.'s study challenges the gender plasticity hypothesis by comparing both young men's and women's sexual minority label relinquishment longitudinally.

YES

Lisa M. Diamond

Was It a Phase? Young Women's Relinquishment of Lesbian/Bisexual Identities Over a 5-Year Period

When an individual "comes out" as lesbian, gay, or bisexual, the transition is typically presumed to be permanent. Yet there are numerous cases—described in memoirs, media reports, and retrospective studies—of individuals who come out as lesbian, gay, or bisexual and then relinquish these identities later on. One recent and widely publicized example is Anne Heche, an actress who began identifying as lesbian when she became romantically involved with the comedian Ellen Degeneres. After their relationship dissolved, she stopped openly identifying as lesbian and became engaged to a man. In many college communities, women that come out as lesbian during their college years, only to drop this identification after graduating, are jokingly called "LUGs," or "lesbian until graduation."

What accounts for such cases? Although one might suspect that individuals who relinquish sexual-minority (i.e., nonheterosexual) identities are retreating from the stigma attached to same-sex sexuality, many such individuals had openly embraced their sexual-minority status. A more provocative possibility is that such individuals were never "really" gay to begin with, and that their temporary lesbian/gay/bisexual identification stemmed from confusion or curiosity rather than an intrinsic same-sex orientation. This interpretation is premised on the widely acknowledged distinction between sexual orientation and sexual identity. Sexual orientation is generally understood as an essential, early-developing, stable predisposition to experience sexual attractions for persons of the same sex, the other sex, or both sexes. Sexual identity, in contrast, refers to the self-concept an individual organizes around this predisposition, typically labeled (in this culture) "heterosexual," "gay," "lesbian," or "bisexual."

Identity and orientation do not always coincide, and this accounts for the aforementioned notion of the "false lesbian." As research on sexual orientation has increasingly emphasized its potential developmental antecedents, a set of implicit developmental criteria has gradually emerged by which "true" sexual minorities (i.e., those with same-sex orientations) might be distinguished from "false" ones (i.e., those without such orientations). Specifically,

From *Journal of Personality and Social Psychology*, vol. 84, no. 2, 2003, pp. 352–364. Copyright © 2003 by American Psychological Association. Reprinted by permission. Note: The complete text of this article contains many references to specific studies described. The interested individual should refer to the original publication for these extensive citations. These references have been omitted here in the interest of brevity.

the former are presumed to have experienced the onset of their same-sex sexuality at an early age, independent of external influences, and to have more exclusive same-sex attractions and behavior. If these are, in fact, markers of an essential and enduring same-sex orientation, then sexual minorities with these characteristics should be unlikely to relinquish their sexual minority identities over time. The current study provides the first systematic test of this hypothesis, using a sample of young women who first identified as sexual minorities in their teens and early 20s, and who have undergone three structured interviews about their sexual identity over a 5-year period.

Relinquishing a Sexual-Minority Identity

The notion that individuals who relinquish lesbian/gay/bisexual identities were never authentically gay does not imply that such individuals never experienced same-sex attractions or enjoyed same-sex behavior. Rather, such experiences are presumed to have been triggered by temporary situational factors, such as exposure to an unusually gay-positive environment. The resulting differentiation between sexual minorities whose same-sex sexuality is an enduring sexual predisposition and those for whom it is situational (and hence transitory) has a long history in the scientific and popular literature on sexual orientation. Some of the factors suggested to precipitate situational same-sex sexuality include . . . play, exploration, lack of opposite-gender partners, hazing, initiation rituals, intoxication, sexual frustration, prostitution, boredom, opportunism, curiosity, and mistakes. . . . Developmental stage is also presumed important: Situational same-sex sexuality is thought to be particularly likely during adolescence and young adulthood, partly because of a greater social tolerance for experimentation. Ideological dissatisfaction with the institution of heterosexuality also plays a role, yielding the phenomenon of the "political lesbian." Another precipitating factor is the formation of an unusually close same-sex friendship that unexpectedly gives rise to sexual feelings. There appears to be greater preoccupation with the enduring/situational dichotomy as it applies to women than to men, reflecting tacit acknowledgment that women's same-sex desires and behaviors appear to be more sensitive than men's to situational and contextual factors.

Sexual Minorities' Developmental Histories

[Both] researchers and laypeople have gravitated toward a set of implicit developmental criteria for distinguishing enduring from situational same-sex sexuality. Specifically, authentic lesbians are presumed to have first experienced same-sex attractions at earlier ages, to have had childhood indicators of homosexuality such as gender atypicality, and to have initially questioned their sexuality on the basis of internal same-sex desires rather than situational factors. These criteria derive from the widespread conceptualization of sexual orientation as an early developing, fixed trait.

Yet there is extensive variability among sexual minorities regarding these developmental factors, particularly among women. Fewer sexual-minority women than men report an early onset of same-sex attractions or behavior, or recall gender-atypical ideation or behavior. More sexual-minority women than men report that their sexual questioning was not initially triggered by same-sex desires, but by ideological factors, social reference groups, and a rejection of or commitment to particular social–political roles. Because such experiences are inconsistent with the notion of sexual orientation as an early-developing, intrinsic trait, many women with such experiences express ambivalence about the true nature of their sexuality. As writer Minnie Bruce Pratt articulated, "Was I heterosexual in adolescence only to become lesbian in my late twenties? Was I lesbian always but coerced into heterosexuality? Was I a less authentic lesbian than my friends who had 'always known' that they were sexually and affectionally attracted to other women?"

The only nonanecdotal evidence for the presumed link between one's developmental history and one's future identity comes from [a] study of heterosexual, gay/lesbian, and bisexual adults [that] found that the sexual profile that individuals eventually settled into generally concorded with their earliest recollected desires and experiences. In other words, men and women that ended up considering themselves gay or lesbian were those whose earliest sexual desires were experienced for the same sex, whereas those who ended up considering themselves heterosexual reported that their earliest sexual desires were experienced for the other sex. Of course, these data are subject to retrospective distortion: Because it is widely believed that sexual orientation expresses itself at an early age, sexual-minority individuals reflecting on their childhoods often selectively attend to events and experiences that are consistent with their current identity, attractions, and behavior. One way to minimize this bias is to assess sexual minorities' developmental trajectories far in advance of assessing later changes in sexual identity, as in the current study.

Nonexclusive Attractions and Behavior

Historically, models of sexual identity development have focused only on individuals with exclusive same-sex attractions. This pattern reflects the long-standing assumption that lesbian/gay individuals are the most common and representative "types" of sexual minorities. Yet when it comes to women, this is not the case. In [a] national, representative sample of American adults, the majority of American women who reported experiencing same-sex attractions also reported experiencing other-sex attractions. Also, two thirds of the adult women who reported a female sexual partner in the previous 5 years also reported having a male partner during the same time period. Of importance, many surveys have found that these patterns of nonexclusive attractions and behavior are found even among women who considered themselves lesbian (rather than bisexual).

Of course, the key question is whether such women were *always* somewhat attracted to men, despite identifying as lesbian, or whether their overall pattern of attractions (and, hence, their underlying orientation) has actually changed over time. There is more empirical support for the former scenario than the latter, given that prior studies have detected few large-scale changes over time in self-reported ratios of same-sex to other-sex attractions. Yet, the question of change deserves continued investigation, particularly among women who relinquish their sexual-minority identities. If these women's attractions have actually changed, then identity relinquishment might represent a straightforward "updating" of identity. If their attractions have not changed, then identity relinquishment might instead represent a new *interpretation* of one's attractions. The current research examines both of these possibilities (which, importantly, are not mutually exclusive) by comparing the 5-year trajectories of same-sex and other-sex attractions in women who relinquished versus maintained their sexual-minority identities, and by assessing women's own explanations for identity changes.

The Current Study

. . . With regard to developmental histories, it is hypothesized that women who have relinquished their sexual-minority identities will have reported (5 years previously) a later age of first same-sex attractions, sexual questioning, same-sex sexual contact, and/or sexual-minority identification. It is also hypothesized that these women will be less likely to have reported (5 years previously) that their sexual questioning was prompted by generalized same-sex attractions, and more likely to have reported that their questioning was prompted by situational factors such as exposure to sexual minority ideas/individuals or by the formation of an unusually close same-sex friendship. With regard to attractions and behavior, it is expected that women who have relinquished their sexual minority identities will have reported smaller ratios of same-sex to other-sex sexual and emotional attractions across the entire 5 year assessment period, and that their same-sex attractions and behavior have declined over time. Finally, content analyses of women's narrative explanations of their sexual identity trajectories will be conducted to determine how they experience and interpret the process of identity relinquishment.

Method

Participants.   Participants were 80 nonheterosexual women between the ages of 18 and 25 years who were initially interviewed [(T1)] as part of a longitudinal study of sexual identity development among young women. Two follow-up interviews were conducted . . . 2 years after [(T2)] and . . . 5 years [(T3)] after the initial assessment. . . .

At the beginning of each interview, each woman was asked, "How do you currently label your sexual identity to yourself, even if it's different from what you might tell other people? If you don't apply a label to your sexual identity, please say so." Lesbian- and bisexual-identified women were categorized according to their chosen identity labels. Women who declined to attach a label to their sexuality were classified as *unlabeled*. . . .

Procedures.   . . . T1 interviews assessed the age at which participants first consciously questioned their sexual identity, first experienced a same-sex attraction, first engaged in same-sex contact, and first openly adopted a sexual-minority identity. Women also described the specific context in which they first questioned their sexual identity, and these responses were coded into three categories by independent raters. The context of first questioning was coded as *exposure to facilitating environment* if the participant reported that her sexual questioning was precipitated by one of the following events: meeting, hearing about, or otherwise learning about lesbian/gay/bisexual people, discovering that a friend had same-sex attractions, discussing issues related to sexual orientation with friends, dating a bisexual man, or becoming the object of another woman's sexual interest. The context of first questioning was coded as *same-sex attractions* if the participant reported that her questioning was precipitated by an awareness of sexual desires for women, unusual closeness to women, fascination with women's bodies or women's beauty, intentional sexual contact with another woman, or distinct disinterest in men. The context of first questioning was coded as *single emotional bond* if a woman reported that the same-sex feelings that precipitated her sexual questioning were limited to a singular emotional same-sex friendship that did not (at least at that time) generalize to other women. . . .

Childhood indicators were coded as present if the participant reported any of the following experiences prior to the age of 13: same-sex attractions, fascination with women's bodies or women's beauty, gender atypicality, feelings of differentness, or a notable disinterest in boys. . . .

To assess same-sex attractions, women were asked at each interview to report the percentage of their total attractions that were directed toward the same sex on a day-to-day basis; separate estimates were provided for sexual versus emotional attractions. This yields an estimate of the relative frequency of same-sex versus other-sex attractions, regardless of the intensity of these attractions or the total number of sexual attractions experienced on a day-to-day basis. Such ratios of same-sex to other-sex attractions are generally taken to represent one's underlying sexual predisposition for women, men, or both, and are commonly represented as "Kinsey ratings" between 0 (*exclusive other-sex attractions*) and 6 (*exclusive same-sex attractions*). . . . To assess sexual behavior, participants were asked to report the total number of men and women with whom they engaged in sexual contact (defined as any sexually motivated intimate contact) between T1 and T2 and between T2 and T3. This information was translated into percentages, so that 100% represents exclusive same-sex behavior and 0% represents exclusive other-sex behavior.

During T3 interviews, women were prompted to describe how they currently perceived their sexual identity and how they interpreted any changes they had undergone. [Responses were coded] for the following themes . . . *ambivalence about labeling, uncertainty about the future, love depends on the person and not the gender, labels are limiting,* and *sexuality is fluid.* . . .

Results

. . . Forty-eight percent of women changed their sexual identity label between T1 and T3. . . . Altogether, 22 women (27% of the sample) relinquished their lesbian/bisexual identities for heterosexual or unlabeled identities between T1 and T3. . . .

It should also be noted that the relinquishment group contains two sub-groups: women who gave up sexual minority identities for heterosexual identities ($n = 10$) and women who gave up sexual minority identities for unlabeled identities ($n = 12$). Although both of these transitions qualify as relinquishments, it is not known whether they represent the same type of experience and whether they are motivated by similar factors. . . .

[It] bears noting that women who identified as lesbian at T1 or T2 were less likely to relinquish their identities than women who had identified as bisexual or unlabeled at T1 or T2 (17% vs. 38%). . . .

Identity relinquishment and developmental histories. [Analyses] were conducted to test whether women who relinquished their sexual-minority identities had, at T1, reported later ages of first same-sex attractions, sexual questioning, same-sex sexual contact, or sexual-minority identification. None of these analyses detected significant effects of relinquishment status. . . . [Women] who maintained their sexual-minority identities underwent these developmental milestones at approximately the same ages as women who relinquished their sexual-minority identities by T3. . . . It should be noted that the largest effect detected—the age of first same-sex sexual contact—was actually in the opposite direction than predicted: Women in the relinquish group had slightly younger rather than older ages of first same sex contact. . . .

Next, [an] analysis was conducted to test whether the context of first questioning (same-sex attractions, reported by 46% of women; exposure to a facilitating environment, reported by 38%; or a single emotional same-sex bond, reported by 16%) was significantly related to relinquishment. There was no association between these variables. . . . Of women who maintained their identities, 51% questioned as a result of same-sex attractions, 36% because of a facilitating environment, and 14% because of a single emotional bond. These percentages were 32%, 45%, and 23%, respectively, among women who relinquished their identities. . . .

Finally, [an] analysis was conducted to test whether women who maintained their identities were more likely than women who relinquished their identities to have reported, at T1, childhood indicators of same-sex sexuality (attraction to or fascination with the same sex, feelings of "differentness," or gender-atypicality). Altogether, 57% of the sample reported at least one of these indicators. Women who maintained their identities were not disproportionately likely to have reported these indicators. . . .

Identity relinquishment and sexual/emotional attractions. . . . [Women] who relinquished their identities started out with lower percentages of same-sex sexual attractions at T1 and maintained those lower levels throughout the entire study. . . . As with sexual attractions, women who relinquished their identities started out with lower percentages of same-sex emotional attractions at T1 and maintained those lower levels throughout the entire study. . . .

Identity relinquishment and sexual behavior. An analysis . . . was conducted to test whether women who relinquished their sexual-minority identities engaged in less frequent same-sex sexual contact between T1 and T3 than women who maintained their sexual-minority identities. . . . The first analysis focused on the relative frequency of same-sex to other-sex behavior, represented as the percentage of sexual partners from T1 to T3 that were of the same sex. . . . The results demonstrated that women who relinquished their sexual minority identities had significantly smaller ratios of same-sex to other-sex sexual contact than women who maintained their identities, even after adjusting for ratios of same-sex to other-sex attractions. . . .

Themes in narrative descriptions of sexual identity.   . . . Women in the relinquish group were significantly more likely to report ambivalence about labeling . . . and less likely . . . to report perceiving their sexuality as fluid. . . . Examples of these responses and their relevance for interpreting long-term sexual identity development are addressed in greater detail below.

Discussion

This study confirms that not all women who claim sexual minority identities during adolescence and young adulthood continue to do so indefinitely. In this sample of predominantly White, well-educated women, over one fourth relinquished their lesbian or bisexual identities over a 5-year period. Half of these women returned to heterosexual identifications; the other half stopped labeling their sexuality altogether. Women who relinquished their sexuality-minority identities reported significant declines in their same-sex behavior over the 5-year assessment period, yet their attractions did not significantly change. Notably, women who ended up reidentifying as heterosexual had reported disproportionately small percentages of sexual and emotional attractions to women from the very beginning of the study.

   Contrary to expectation, identity relinquishment was not related to the timing and context of a woman's initial sexual identity development. There were no significant differences between women who relinquished versus maintained their sexual-minority identities with regard to the age at which they reported having first experienced same-sex attractions, first questioned their sexual identities, first experienced same-sex sexual contact, or first identified as sexual minorities. Women who relinquished their identities were not disproportionately likely to have initially questioned their sexuality as a result of environmental factors (such as taking a women's studies class) or singular relationships (i.e., falling in love with one specific woman) rather than generalized attractions for the same sex. Also, they were just as likely as women who maintained their identities to have recollected childhood "indicators" of same-sex sexuality such as early gender atypicality.

   Although findings of "no association" are often dismissed as uninterpretable, this study exemplifies a case in which null findings communicate important information about the phenomenon of interest. Specifically, these results challenge the long-standing assumption that women whose same-sex sexuality expresses itself at an early age, and whose sexual questioning is prompted by internal versus external cues, are more "authentically" gay and therefore more likely to maintain a sexual-minority identity over time.

Regardless of whether she became aware of same-sex attractions at age 10 versus age 20, and regardless of whether she questioned her identity because of same-sex fantasies or because of taking a women's studies class, the best way to predict the long-term course of her sexual-minority identification is to examine her attractions and behavior, not her developmental history.

Clearly, these findings require replication before reliable generalizations can be made to the overall population of female sexual minorities. . . . Another concern is that only 10 women reported the most extreme cases of relinquishment—giving up sexual-minority identities for heterosexual identities—making it difficult to draw robust conclusions about this phenomenon. Of course, this is an inevitable byproduct of the fact that such transitions appear to be fairly atypical (although their actual prevalence remains unknown). To capture a substantially larger and more representative sample of such women, future longitudinal research would have to begin with a much larger and more diverse sample of female sexual minorities, which obviously poses logistical problems. Thus, although the current study is limited by its small and nonrepresentative sample, it is nonetheless valuable for providing the first empirical observations of sexual-minority identity relinquishment as it occurs.

The relevance of developmental trajectories.   Although this study found that the timing and context of a woman's sexual identity development was a poor predictor of identity relinquishment over a 5-year period, this does not indicate that developmental factors are irrelevant for understanding interindividual differences in the long-term course of sexual attraction, behaviors, and identities. Rather, the present findings highlight the need for future research to more rigorously model the hypothetical relationship between an individual's sexual-developmental trajectory and his or her pattern of same-sex and other-sex sexuality. [Variables] such as "age of first attractions" are the subject of frequent investigation in studies of interindividual variability in sexual-minority populations, but the rationale for this focus is rarely explicitly specified.

Clearly, future theory and research must strive to identify the specific mechanisms through which particular patterns of sexual identity development might be associated with the nature and long-term course of sexual attractions, behaviors, and identities. Furthermore, researchers must attend to a broader set of developmental variables. [One suggestion is] that the subjective quality of an individual's same-sex versus other-sex attractions and relationships might be more predictive of later identity outcomes than their timing, yet few studies of sexual identity development collect data appropriate for exploring this possibility.

Current and prior patterns of attractions and behavior.   In contrast to the findings regarding developmental trajectories, women's current and prior attractions and behavior were associated with identity relinquishment. As expected, women that eventually relinquished their sexual-minority identities had been pursuing less and less same-sex behavior over the 5-year period of the study. . . . Yet their same-sex attractions did not show similar declines. These findings are consistent with the notion that identity relinquishment does not represent a fundamental change in sexual orientation itself, but rather a change in how women interpret and act on their sexual orientation. Specifically, it appears that women with sexual and emotional attractions to both sexes often find it difficult to maintain a sexual-minority identity in the face of increasing and/or predominant other-sex behavior. . . .

Identifying as bisexual did not seem to provide a ready solution to this problem: Bisexuality is frequently misinterpreted or denigrated by both heterosexuals and sexual minorities as promiscuity, indecisiveness, or immaturity. As one respondent in the current study said, "I feel sort of uncomfortable calling myself bisexual because if I'm talking to a guy, it's the usual thing: 'Oh, so do you do this and that and the other thing?' And if I'm talking to a gay woman, then she's like, 'Oh, really. I can't trust you.' " Another noted, "A lot of people that I talk to say 'Well, you know bisexuality is just one step up from one or the other, so you're not actually bisexual, you're actually on your way to becoming either straight or gay.'" Researchers have long noted that contemporary sexual identity labels oversimplify the nature and experience of same-sex sexuality; clearly, this leaves many women with nonexclusive attractions with few options other than relinquishing lesbian/bisexual labels when they perceive that their experiences contradict lesbian/bisexual norms.

Of course, contemporary notions of sexual orientation also oversimplify (or more commonly, simply ignore) the phenomenon of heterosexuality, and the findings of this study suggest that traditional models of heterosexual development also require revision. Given the prevalence of nonexclusivity and plasticity in women's sexuality, the meaning and implications of same-sex attractions and behavior within the normative female heterosexual life course deserve further scrutiny. For example, should we view the T3 heterosexuals—who had disproportionately small percentages of same-sex attractions throughout the entire study—as "marginal" bisexuals or open-minded and experimental heterosexuals? The impossibility of definitively answering this question illustrates the importance of supplementing quantitative analyses of attractions and behavior with qualitative analyses of women's own interpretations of the links and distinctions between their attractions, behaviors, and identities.

Women's interpretations of sexual identity change.   One notable finding of the content analyses of women's sexual identity narratives was that women who relinquished their identities were disproportionately less likely to endorse a notion of sexuality as inherently fluid. This suggests that acknowledging and accepting one's capacity for diverse, fluctuating desires and experiences might actually promote stability in sexual identification by eliminating the implicit pressure to jettison one's identity label once it is contradicted by novel feelings or behaviors. This perspective is reflected in many women's responses: "I think I've become more comfortable in looking at [sexuality] as a continuum. . . . all of my life I have been attracted to both men and women, and I have come to a comfortable place of calling myself a lesbian in spite of that." Another noted, "I have this male friend I sleep with, like once a year. It doesn't bother me, I don't feel like anybody is going to take my 'lesbian license' away or anything."

In contrast, women with more rigid notions of sexuality found that the only way to reconcile mismatches between behavior and identity was to switch identities. As one woman said, "I think I still have the same orientation, but things are different because now I'm in a heterosexual relationship, and it's pretty serious and I guess that's what basically forms my identity." Another noted, "[My gay friends] have never really been comfortable with me identifying as bisexual, considering all the relationships that I've been having with men. So in order to appease them, I'm coming out as heterosexual."

Notions of sexual fluidity also appear important for understanding distinctions between women who relinquished sexual-minority identities for heterosexual versus unlabeled identities. The main quantitative difference between these groups was that the heterosexual women reported disproportionately lower same-sex attractions and behavior throughout the study; however both groups had similar developmental histories, and both reported drops in same sex behavior between T1 and T3. Yet the qualitative analyses demonstrated that they interpreted their experiences differently. [Women] in the unlabeled subgroup were disproportionately likely to report ambivalence about labeling, to describe their sexuality as fluid, to report uncertainty about the future, and to report that labels were limiting. This suggests that whereas women in the heterosexual subgroup perceived heterosexual identification as a viable solution to the problem posed by their nonexclusive attractions and behavior, this was not the case for women in the unlabeled subgroup. As one of these women remarked, "I don't really think that labels adequately or accurately describe anybody. I think you can be with a man your whole life and still be a lesbian and I think you can be with a man and a woman, back and forth, and still *not* be bisexual."

Another important finding that emerged from women's responses was the fact that relinquishing lesbian and bisexual identification did not entail relinquishing same-sex sexuality. Rather, all of the women in the sample acknowledged the possibility for future same-sex attractions and/or behavior. As one heterosexually identified woman said, "I never found another [girl] that made me want to be her girlfriend. So I started to think that maybe I'm not as gay as I thought I was. But I'm still completely open. If I meet another woman, then fine." Another remarked, "I'm mainly straight, but I'm one of those people who, if the right circumstance came along, would change my viewpoint. The only thing constant is change." These are important observations given the ongoing debate over whether it is possible (or ethical) to change individuals' sexual orientations through "conversion therapy." The fact that all of the women in the relinquish group continued to experience same-sex attractions, coupled with the overall longitudinal stability of attractions in the sample as a whole, suggests that same-sex desires are far less amenable to (conscious or unconscious) change than are behavior and identity. This mitigates against the success of therapies aimed at altering sexual minorities' predispositions for same-sex partners.

These findings also suggest that it is inappropriate to interpret identity relinquishment as an admission that one's previous sexual minority identity was "wrong." Only one woman in the sample interpreted her prior sexual-minority identification as a phase, and even *she* acknowledged the possibility of same-sex sexuality in the future. The remaining women spoke in more complex terms about subtle changes and reassessments in other-sex and same-sex feelings and behaviors, and many expressed concern that their personal transformations might be misinterpreted as "proof" that most self-identified lesbian/gay/bisexual youth are just confused about their sexuality. As one woman said, "It's my own individual process I'm going through. I don't talk about it much, because I don't want straight people to think that all bisexuals will 'grow out of it' or that they will eventually want to marry a man." Another noted, "Even though I don't call myself a lesbian anymore, I totally cringe when people say 'Oh, was that a phase,' ugh! That's not it at all, and I'm still attracted to women." Thus, the results of this study highlight the extent to which nonexclusivity and plasticity in women's attractions and behaviors potentiate multiple transitions in identification and behavior over the life course. Clearly, we require more extensive longitudinal research on the nature, prevalence, and relevance of such transitions, and how individuals with different backgrounds and different environments integrate such changes into their self-concepts. . . .

Conclusion

This study is certainly not the first to document patterns of change and fluidity in same-sex sexuality that contradict conventional models of sexual orientation as a fixed and uniformly early-developing trait. Historically, such cases have been considered exceptional rather than normative, and consequently have received little systematic study. However, . . . such cases represent more than just idiosyncratic variation. Rather, they have important implications for understanding the nature, development, and longterm course of same-sex sexuality. This study represents an important preliminary step toward subjecting "exceptional" patterns of sexual-minority identification to the sort of systematic analysis that will hopefully reveal how and why certain individuals experience diverse, changing, and conflicting patterns of sexual attraction, behavior, and identification over the life course.

Margaret Rosario, et al.  **NO**

Sexual Identity Development Among Lesbian, Gay, and Bisexual Youths: Consistency and Change Over Time

The development of a lesbian, gay, or bisexual (LGB) sexual identity is a complex and often difficult process. Unlike members of other minority groups (e.g., ethnic and racial minorities), most LGB individuals are not raised in a community of similar others from whom they learn about their identity and who reinforce and support that identity. Rather, LGB individuals are often raised in communities that are either ignorant of or openly hostile toward homosexuality. Because sexual identity development is a process for which LGB individuals have been unprepared and which is contextually unsupported and stigmatized, it would seem that the process would be characterized by inconsistency or incongruence among its affective, cognitive, and behavioral components, such that behavior may not always coincide with affect or identity. However, psychological theory has long maintained that individuals seek to achieve congruence among affect, cognitions, and behaviors because incongruity generates psychological tension. Thus, same-sex oriented affect and behavior may lead individuals to adopt an identity consistent with such sentiments and behavior (e.g., as gay or lesbian). Similarly, identification as gay or lesbian may lead individuals to engage in sexual behaviors consistent with that identity. Indeed, the incongruence among gay identity and heterosexual behavior has been used to explain the eventual transition from heterosexual to homosexual behavior, so as to eliminate dissonance between identity and behavior. In this article, we examine consistency and change in LGB sexual identity, as well as the congruence between changes in identity and other aspects of sexuality (e.g., behavior, affect, and attitudes).

Sexual identity development for LGB individuals, also known as "the coming-out process," has received considerable attention, resulting in numerous theoretical models. These theoretical models, taken together, describe a process of identity formation and integration as individuals strive for congruence among their sexual orientation (i.e., sexual attractions, thoughts, and fantasies), sexual behavior, and sexual identity. Identity formation consists of becoming aware of one's unfolding sexual orientation, beginning to question whether one may be LGB, and exploring that emerging LGB identity by becoming involved in gay-related social and sexual activities.

From *Journal of Sex Research,* vol. 43, no. 1, February 2006, pp. 46–57. Copyright © 2006 as conveyed via Copyright Clearance Center. Reprinted by permission. Note: The complete text of this article contains many references to specific studies described. The interested individual should refer to the original publication for these extensive citations. These references have been omitted here in the interest of brevity.

Identity integration involves incorporating and consolidating a LGB identity. This is evident by the individual coming to accept a LGB identity, resolving internalized homophobia by transforming negative attitudes into positive attitudes, feeling comfortable with the idea that others may know about the unfolding identity, and disclosing that identity to others. Identity formation and integration are involved in a reciprocal process. They share some common components, such as gay-related social activities, that serve as both a facilitator and an outcome of identity development over time.

Research on Identity Formation and Integration

Research on the sexual identity development of LGB individuals has focused primarily on the age of various developmental milestones associated with identity formation. Although the studies generally support an overall linear trend from sexual attractions to sexual activity to self-identification as LGB at the group level, they also highlight considerable variability at the individual level. However, the studies are limited because they utilize retrospective reports that may bias results, given the tendency of people both to craft narratives consistent with their current condition and to minimize past fluctuations or changes. Thus, the retrospective design may overestimate the linear nature or consistency of the data. Developmental researchers have argued that LGB sexual identity development should be studied longitudinally and prospectively.

Only two longitudinal and prospective studies have examined changes in sexual identity over time, both of which were conducted among young women. Although no comparable studies exist on the sexual identity development of males, three longitudinal studies of young men have examined changes in sexual attractions. Taken together, the studies have found considerable consistency, as well as change, in sexual self-identification and attractions over time. For example, among 80 female youths, . . . Diamond (2000; 2003) found that 70% were consistent in their self-identification as lesbian, bisexual or unlabeled after two years, and 50% were consistent after five years. An additional 15% transitioned to a lesbian or bisexual identity after two years, as did 14% after five years. Few youths transitioned from a lesbian, bisexual, or unlabeled identity to a straight identity. Among 216 behaviorally bisexual men (ages 18–30 years). Stokes and colleagues (1997) found that over the course of one year, 49% reported no changes in sexual orientation, 34% became more homosexually oriented, and 17% became more heterosexually oriented. Clearly, the consistency and change documented by these research studies must now be understood.

Prospective changes in LGB sexual identity would be expected to be influenced by aspects of earlier sexual identity formation, such as time since the occurrence of sexual developmental milestones. Sexual identity formation takes time because many LGB youths go through a period of sexual questioning, experimentation, and conflict before assuming and consistently self-identifying as LGB. Thus, we hypothesized that youths for whom more time has passed since reaching various sexual developmental milestones are more likely to report a sexual identity that is consistently LGB than youths who reached the milestones more recently. One study examining this hypothesis

(Diamond, 2003) may have had too little statistical power to detect differences in the age of sexual developmental milestones between female youths maintaining an identity as lesbian or bisexual and those youths who changed to a straight or unlabeled identity.

Changes in LGB sexual identity would also be expected to correlate with other aspects of sexuality more broadly—specifically, sexual orientation and sexual behavior. Given congruence theory, we hypothesized that youths with a consistent gay/lesbian identity would have a sexual orientation that is more same-sex centered and would be more likely to report same-sex behaviors, but less likely to report other-sex behaviors than youths who, for example, recently transitioned from a bisexual identity to a gay/lesbian identity. Indeed, Diamond (2003) found that female youths who were consistent in their lesbian or bisexual identity reported more same-sex sexual attractions than peers who transitioned from a lesbian or bisexual identity to a heterosexual or unlabeled identity. Similarly, sexual behavior (e.g., number of female sexual partners) differed between those with a consistent sexual identity and those who relinquished their lesbian/bisexual identity. Unfortunately, no comparisons were made between the consistently lesbian and bisexual youths. Regardless, research among adults has not found a high level of congruity among aspects of sexuality. Perhaps external constraints, such as living in potentially hostile communities (e.g., rural settings) as compared with more supportive communities (e.g., urban environments), retard or impede congruence.

Finally, we hypothesized that changes in sexual identity would influence aspects of identity integration, given the need for congruence. . . . Although research has not examined this hypothesis longitudinally, cross-sectional research has found that differences in sexual identity were associated with differences in aspects of identity integration. In an earlier report on our sample, we found that youths who self-identified as gay/lesbian, as compared with bisexual, were involved in more gay-related social activities, endorsed more positive attitudes toward homosexuality, were more comfortable with other individuals knowing about their same-sex sexuality, and disclosed their sexual identity to more individuals. However, this past report neither examined changes in sexual identity nor investigated the longitudinal relations between changes in sexual identity and aspects of identity integration.

Gender

The individual variability in the age of sexual developmental milestones mentioned earlier has led researchers to critique linear models of development, particularly for women. Theorists have suggested that women are more likely than men to self-identify as bisexual and that women are more "fluid" or "plastic" in their sexual identity than men, although others dispute these claims because they consider the research inconclusive. The available evidence is mixed. Several studies have found that more female than male youths identified as bisexual. However, a large national study found that female youths were no more likely than male peers to identify as bisexual. In addition, studies have found some gender differences in the average age and order of various sexual developmental milestones, but not in all instances. Despite these findings, the potential role of gender on changes in sexual identity remains unexamined because the studies examining longitudinal changes in sexual identity development have been based on single-sex samples (e.g., Diamond, 2000; Stokes et al., 1997).

This Study

[We] examine consistency and change in sexual identity over time among LGB youths. Further, we examine how LGB youths who remain consistent in their sexual identity differ from those who have changed their sexual identity with respect to sexual identity formation (i.e., sexual developmental milestones, sexual orientation, and sexual behavior) and identity integration (i.e., comfort and acceptance of LGB identity, involvement in gay social activities, positive attitudes toward homosexuality, comfort with others knowing about their sexuality, and self-disclosure of identity to others). We hypothesized that youths who were consistent over time in a gay/lesbian identity would have been aware of their same-sex sexual orientation, been sexually active with the same sex, and been involved in gay-related social activities for a longer period of time than youths who had changed sexual identities. We also hypothesized that consistently-identified gay/lesbian youths would have a current sexual orientation that is more same-sex centered, report a higher prevalence of recent sexual behavior with the same sex but a lower prevalence of recent sexual behavior with the other sex, and report higher levels of identity integration than youths who had changed sexual identities or consistently identified as bisexual. We also expected differences between consistently bisexual youths and those who had changed identities: we hypothesized that youths who had transitioned from a bisexual to a gay/lesbian identity were more likely than consistently bisexual youths to have a current sexual orientation that is more same-sex centered, report a higher prevalence of recent sexual behavior with the same sex but a lower prevalence of recent sexual behavior with the other sex, and evidence higher levels of identity integration. In addition, we examined potential gender differences in consistency and change in sexual identity, given the hypothesis in the literature that female youths are more fluid in their sexual identity than male peers.

Method

Participants

Male and female youths, ages 14 to 21 years, were recruited from organizations that serve LGB youths. . . . The final sample consisted of 156 youths (51% male) with a mean age of 18.3 years ($SD = 1.65$). . . .

Procedure

. . . Youths were administered a questionnaire by [a same-sex] interviewer at baseline and subsequent assessments 6 and 12 months later. . . .

Measures of Sexual Identity and Identity Formation

Sexual identity, sexual developmental milestones, sexual orientation, and sexual behaviors were assessed using the Sexual Risk Behavior Assessment—Youth (SERBAS-Y) for LGB youths. . . .

Sexual identity. . . . asking, "When you think about sex, do you think of yourself as lesbian/gay, bisexual, or straight?" . . . Items also assessed whether youths had ever thought they were really gay/lesbian or bisexual prior to the baseline assessment.

Psychosexual developmental milestones. . . . Youths were asked the ages when they were first attracted to, fantasized about, and were aroused by erotica focusing on the same sex. The mean age of these three milestones was computed to obtain a mean age of awareness of same-sex sexual orientation. . . .

Youths also were asked about the age when they first thought they "might be" gay/lesbian, when they first thought they "might be" bisexual, when they first thought they "really were" gay/lesbian, and when they first thought they "really were" bisexual. Finally, youths were asked about the age when they first engaged in any one of a several specific sexual activities (i.e., manual, digital, oral, anal-penile, vaginal-penile, and analingus) with the same sex and with the other sex. . . .

Sociosexual developmental milestones. [We] asked youths at baseline for the age when they first spoke or wrote to anyone (e.g., peer, counselor, teacher, coach, adult, switchboard) about homosexuality or bisexuality. We asked a similar series of questions with respect to ages when they first participated in various social or recreational gay-related activities (e.g., going to a gay bookstore or coffee house). . . .

Current sexual orientation. . . . Youths were asked the extent to which their recent sexual attractions, thoughts, and fantasies were focused on the same or the other sex (a) when in the presence of other individuals, (b) while masturbating, dreaming, or daydreaming, and (c) when viewing erotic material in films, magazines, or books. . . .

Recent sexual behaviors. [We] focused on whether youths reported any sexual activity (i.e., manual, digital, oral, anal-penile, vaginal-penile, and analingus) with the same sex or other sex.

Measures of Identity Integration

Involvement in gay-related activities. The prevalence of lifetime involvement in gay/lesbian-related social activities was assessed at baseline using [an 11-item] scale (e.g., going to a gay bookstore, gay coffee house, gay pride march, gay fair, gay club or bar). . . . At subsequent assessments, youths were asked about their involvement in the past 6 months (i.e., since their last assessment). . . .

Attitudes toward homosexuality.   . . . eleven items (e.g., "My [homosexuality/bisexuality] does not make me unhappy") . . . assessed attitudes toward homosexuality. The mean of these items was computed at each assessment. . . .

Comfort with homosexuality.   . . . twelve items (e.g., "If my straight friends knew of my [homosexuality/bisexuality], I would feel uncomfortable") . . . assessed comfort with others knowing the youth's sexuality. The mean of these items was computed for each time period. . . .

Self-disclosure of sexual identity to others.   Youths were asked at baseline to enumerate "all the people in your life who are important or were important to you and whom you told that you are (lesbian/gay/bisexual)." At subsequent assessments, youths were asked about the number of individuals to whom the youth had disclosed during the past six months (i.e., since the last assessment). The number of individuals reported was used as the indicator of self-disclosure to others. . . .

Certainty about, comfort with, and self-acceptance of sexuality.   At the 6-month and 12-month assessments, [we] asked youths who had self-identified as gay/lesbian, "How certain are you about being lesbian/gay at this point?" and asked the bisexual youths, "How certain are you about being bisexual at this point?" . . . "How comfortable are you with your lesbianism/gayness?" and asked the bisexual youths, "How comfortable are you with your lesbian/gay side?" [We] asked the gay/lesbian youths, "How accepting of your lesbianism/gayness are you?" and asked the bisexual youths, "How accepting are you of your lesbian/gay side?" We coded the prevalence of being very certain/comfortable/accepting (1) as compared to being less than very certain/comfortable/accepting (0) for each variable. . . .

Results

Sample-Level Sexual Identity Over Time

. . . Prior to the baseline assessment, nearly 40% of youths had self-identified only as gay/lesbian, an equal number had identified as gay/lesbian and bisexual, and one fifth identified exclusively as bisexual. Over the three subsequent assessments, the number of youths identifying as gay/lesbian increased, while the number of youths identifying as only bisexual decreased.

The examination of sexual identity over time ignores potential changes within youths of different sexual identities. . . . In general, youths either maintained their sexual identity or assumed a gay/lesbian identity over time. Youths who had identified as gay/lesbian at earlier times consistently identified as such at later times. Youths who had identified as both gay/lesbian and bisexual prior to baseline were approximately three times more likely to identify as gay/lesbian than as bisexual at subsequent assessments. Of youths who had identified only as bisexual at earlier assessments, 60–70% continued to identify as bisexual, while approximately 30–40% assumed a gay/lesbian identity over time.

Individual-Level Changes in Sexual Identity Over Time

As valuable as the aforementioned data may be, they are limited because the level of analysis is the sample rather than the individual. Sample-level data fail to address the critical issue of individual change in sexual identity. Therefore, at the individual-level of analysis, we created profiles for each youth of the change in sexual identity over the four longitudinal times, resulting in three major groups composed of youths who (a) consistently self-identified as gay/lesbian, (b) transitioned from bisexual to gay/lesbian identities, or (c) consistently self-identified as bisexual. [Few youths demonstrated] other patterns of change in sexual identity. . . .

Change in Sexual Identity: Univariate Relations

We [compared] the three LGB sexual identity groups (i.e., consistently gay/lesbian, consistently bisexual, and transitioned to gay/lesbian) with respect to the time since the youths experienced various psychosexual and sociosexual milestones of identity formation. The youths generally did not differ significantly on the time since reaching various psychosexual milestones, contrary to hypothesized expectations. However, as hypothesized, the youths did differ on time since reaching sociosexual milestones. Consistently gay/lesbian youths had their first discussion about same-sex sexuality with another individual and were involved in a gay-related social activity for at least a year longer than either of the other two groups of youths. . . .

As hypothesized, youths who consistently identified as gay/lesbian differed from consistently bisexual and transitioned youths on current sexual orientation and sexual behaviors. Consistently gay/lesbian youths reported both sexual orientation and sexual behaviors that were more same-sex centered than peers who transitioned to a gay/lesbian identity, and both of these groups of youths differed from peers who consistently identified as bisexual. Youths who consistently identified as gay/lesbian were more certain about, comfortable with, and accepting of their LGB identity than were peers who transitioned to a gay/lesbian identity or who consistently identified as bisexual. Furthermore, consistently gay/lesbian youths were involved in more gay-related social activities, endorsed more positive attitudes toward homosexuality, and were more comfortable with other individuals knowing about their homosexuality.

Gender and Age

. . . [Female] youths were over three times more likely than male youths . . . to identify consistently as gay/lesbian than to transition from a bisexual to a gay/lesbian identity. . . . Female youths also were less likely than male youths . . . to have transitioned from a bisexual to a gay/lesbian identity as compared with maintaining a bisexual identity. . . . Furthermore, female youths were no more likely than male youths to identify as consistently bisexual as compared with consistently gay/lesbian. . . . Youths who were consistently gay/lesbian were significantly older than youths who had transitioned to a gay/lesbian identity. . . .

Discussion

Although changes in sexual identity are possible over time, very little research has examined such changes—and none among both male and female youths. [We] found evidence of both considerable consistency and change in LGB sexual identity over time. Youths who identified as gay/lesbian prior to baseline were overwhelmingly consistent in this identity. In contrast, many youths who identified as bisexual or as both gay/lesbian and bisexual prior to baseline later identified as gay/lesbian. These findings suggest that, although there were youths who consistently self-identified as bisexual throughout the study, for other youths, a bisexual identity served as a transitional identity to a subsequent gay/lesbian identity.

[We] found three patterns of sexual identity over time: consistently gay/lesbian, transitioned from bisexual to gay/lesbian, and consistently bisexual. Of the youths, 72% consistently identified as gay/lesbian or bisexual over time. This finding of consistency is similar to past research (Diamond, 2000: 70%). . . .

Youths who changed sexual identities were hypothesized to report experiencing psychosexual and sociosexual milestones of identity formation more recently than youths whose sexual identity remained consistently gay/lesbian. For the psychosexual milestones, we found no support for this hypothesis. . . . One explanation for the null findings is that psychosocial factors (e.g., a family with strong anti-gay attitudes, experiences of ridicule, greater internalized homophobia) may delay some youths from developing a consistent LGB identity or may lead some youths to adopt a bisexual identity before identifying as gay/lesbian. For the sociosexual milestones, however, we found, as hypothesized, that among the consistently gay/lesbian youths, more time had passed since they experienced sociosexual milestones than was the case among consistently bisexual youths or youths who transitioned from a bisexual to gay/lesbian identity.

Consistent with social psychological theory regarding congruence among affect, cognition, and behavior, and as hypothesized, we found that changes in sexual identity were significantly and strongly associated with current sexual orientation and sexual behaviors. The differences in sexual orientation and sexual behavior between consistently gay/lesbian youths and youths who transitioned to a gay/lesbian identity suggest that, even after adopting a gay/lesbian identity, youths continued to harbor discrepancies between the new identity and subsequent sexual orientation and behavior. Indeed, the observed decrease in the magnitude of these differences over time suggests that even after the adoption of a gay/lesbian identity, transitioned youths continue to change their orientation and behavior to match their new sexual identity. The findings of congruence between sexual identity, orientation, and behavior appear, at first, to contrast with previous research on adults that has found that many individuals with same sex attractions and behavior do not identify as LGB. . . .

Changes in sexual identity were hypothesized to be associated with corresponding changes in aspects of the identity integration process. Indeed, we found that consistently gay/lesbian youths differed from youths who transitioned from bisexual to gay/lesbian identities. The differences indicated that even after youths self-identify as gay/lesbian, a great deal of change may continue to take place in many aspects of sexuality. Thus, acceptance, commitment, and integration of a gay/lesbian identity is an ongoing developmental process that, for many youths, may extend through adolescence and beyond.

As hypothesized, consistently bisexual youths scored significantly lower than consistently gay/lesbian youths on most markers of identity integration. These data may indicate that consistently bisexual youths take a longer period of time to form and integrate their sexual identity than do consistently gay/lesbian youths. The data also may indicate that consistently bisexual youths experience more cognitive dissonance than consistently gay/lesbian youths. Clearly, more research into the similarities and differences between bisexual and gay/lesbian youths is needed, with follow-up of samples through adolescence and perhaps into adulthood.

Considerable interest has been expressed in potential gender differences in sexual identity development. . . . [Female] youths were significantly more likely than male peers to identify consistently as gay/lesbian than to change identities. These findings challenge past research suggesting that the sexual identity of females is more fluid than that of males. . . . However, because studies of change in sexual identity have been conducted among single-sex samples of females (e.g., Diamond, 2000; 2003), any observed changes may have generated an impression of plasticity, when such a hypothesis could not be tested without comparable data on males. Another indicator of the fluidity hypothesis would be a higher prevalence of bisexuality among female than male youths. However, we found that female youths were no more likely to self-identify as consistently bisexual than were male youths. This finding, although at odds with some cross-sectional findings, is consistent with other cross-sectional findings. In addition, we found no gender differences in the relations between sexual identity and aspects of sexual identity formation or integration. These findings indicate a similar process of sexual identity development between male and female youths. Because this study is the first, to our knowledge, to have data on changes in sexual identity over time among both male and female youths, we advocate for more longitudinal research on gender differences in sexual identity.

The study findings are tempered by potential study limitations. First, our sample was recruited from gay-focused organizations and, therefore, the extent to which the findings generalize to a more heterogenous sample of LGB youths is unknown. However, given that the youths in the current sample were no more consistent in their sexual identity than lesbian and bisexual youths recruited from both gay and non-gay venues (Diamond, 2000), we do not believe this to be a major limitation. Second, the size of the sample was modest. However, it had sufficient power to detect a medium effect, and it was much larger than past research studies on changes in sexual identity. . . . Finally, we followed the youths prospectively for a single year. However, because the developmental task of adolescence is identity formation and integration and because adolescence extends through approximately age 25 in the

United States, we advocate that future research follow individuals through their twenties, allowing researchers to obtain a more thorough understanding of the process of sexual identity development. Our data, although limited to a one-year follow-up period, lend support and provide a rationale for the importance of longitudinal assessments of sexual identity development.

References

Diamond, L. M. (2000). Sexual identity, attractions, and behavior among young sexual-minority women over a 2-year period. *Developmental Psychology, 36,* 241–250.

Diamond, L. M. (2003). Was it a phase? Young women's relinquishment of lesbian/bisexual identities over a 5-year period. *Journal of Personality and Social Psychology, 84,* 352—364.

Stokes, J. P., Damon, W., & McKirnan, D. J. (1997). Predictors of movement toward homosexuality: A longitudinal study of bisexual men. *The Journal of Sex Research, 34,* 304-312.

POSTSCRIPT

Is Female Sexual Orientation More Fluid than Male Sexual Orientation During Adolescence?

The gendered theory of erotic plasticity suggests that women are more sexually flexible than men and that this flexibility would extend to sexual orientation. A hypothesis derived from Baumeister's theory is women would be more fluid than men in terms of their sexual orientation and/or their sexual behavior (with same-sex and other-sex partners). For example, in the Kinsey surveys, it was found that lesbian women were more likely to have had sexual intercourse with men than gay men were to have had sexual intercourse with women. Several more recent studies have found this same pattern with lesbians exceeding gay men in terms of sexual behavior with other-sex partners. Also, more women than men identify as bisexual than exclusively homosexual, according to Baumeister.

Diamond extended this theory by hypothesizing that bisexual women would be more erotically plastic in their sexual orientation labeling than lesbian women would be. In studying women longitudinally over 5 years, Diamond found that almost 30 percent of her sample of women renounced a sexual minority identity label at the end of her longitudinal study. Also, more bisexual or "unlabelled" women changed their sexual orientation label relative to those who self-identified as lesbians at the beginning of the study. These findings can be interpreted in a number of ways: First, they can be seen as supporting Baumeister's theory of the erotic plasticity of females. Young women who were more "sexually flexible" at the beginning of the study (i.e., bisexuals) were more likely to change self-labels, consistent with the plasticity theory. In contrast, Diamond suggests that women do not endorse the idea of sexual fluidity, but are changing their self-labels to be more consistent with their sexual behaviors and desires. With this interpretation, identity change would not be due to plasticity at all; rather, it would result from trying to resolve psychological discomfort (dissonance) associated desires and sexual behaviors incongruent with sexual self-labels—it is easier to change the label.

Rosario et al.'s study speaks more directly to the hypotheses set out by Baumeister. Contrary to the idea that women are more erotically plastic than men, Rosario et al. found that female youth were less likely to change identities over the year-long longitudinal study than were the male youth who participated. Also contrary to Baumeister's theory, the girls were no more likely than the boys to self-identify as bisexual as opposed to lesbian/gay. Their results suggest that males and females have similar sexual identity developmental processes, and women may not be more flexible than men.

Do these findings mean that the erotic plasticity theory should be discounted? There are a number of considerations that must be taken into account before we prematurely dismiss this theory. Diamond's results can be interpreted to support Baumeister's theory. However, her study involved older participants than those in the Rosario et al. study. Further, Diamond's longitudinal analysis lasted 5 years while Rosario et al.'s consisted of a 1-year follow-up. Perhaps female and male youth are equally erotically plastic, but once we head into emerging adulthood (e.g., early-to-mid 20s), women remain more sexually flexible, and men become more erotically fixed. Certainly, these two studies speak to the gendered theory of erotic plasticity; however, many more studies need to be conducted before we can accept or reject this theory. Another noteworthy point is that we know very little about the sexuality of bisexual individuals; in research studies, bisexual women tend to be categorized with lesbian women. As a result, our knowledge of the unique sexual development and processes of bisexual youth and adults is quite limited.

References/Further Readings

Baumeister, R.F. (2000). Gender differences in erotic plasticity: The female sex drive as socially flexible and responsive. *Psychological Bulletin*, 126(3), 347–374.

Baumeister, R.F. (2004). Gender and erotic plasticity: Sociocultural influences on the sex drive. *Sexual and Relationship Therapy*, 19(2), 133–139.

Russell, S.T., & Seif, H. (2002). Bisexual female adolescents: A critical analysis of past research, and results from a national survey. *Journal of Bisexuality*, 2(2), 73–94.

On the Internet . . .

Future of Children

Future of Children is an organization that promotes effective policies and programs for children.

http://www.futureofchildren.org

Advocates for Youth

Advocates for Youth is a youth-serving organization that creates programs and advocates for policies that provide information on reproductive and sexual health.

http://www.advocatesforyouth.org

National Youth Violence Prevention Resource Center

This Web site, operated by the National Youth Violence Prevention Resource Center, features information on youth violence and teen dating abuse.

http://www.safeyouth.org

eNotAlone

eNotAlone is a Web-based organization that provides information on cyber-relationships. It provides tips on meeting people online and has different articles and testimonials by people with experiences in online dating.

http://www.enotalone.com/41-1.html

Faith Trust Institute

Faith Trust Institute is an international organization working to end sexual and domestic violence. This Web site provides training, consultation, and educational materials regarding teen relationships, child abuse, sexual violence, and domestic violence.

http://www.faithtrustinstitute.org

Egale Canada

Egale Canada is a national organization dedicated to lesbian, gay, bisexual, and trans-identified people and their families.

http://www.egale.ca/index.asp?lang=E&menu=33

Pew Internet and American Life Project

The Pew Internet and American Life Project examines the impact of the Internet on families, communities, work and home, daily life, education, health care, and civic and political life.

http://www.pewinternet.org/

PART 3

Relationships

Social relationships are critical in the growth, development, and behaviour of adolescents. There are many different types of relationships that are important to teens, including family ties, friendships, and romantic relationships. The following three issues address some aspect of the social relations of youth and the impact that these relationships have on adolescent development.

- Does Divorce or Disruption in Family Structure During Adolescence Have a Detrimental Effect on Development?

- Does Dating Impede Developmental Adjustment for Adolescents?

- Do Cyber-Friendships Hinder Healthy Adolescent Development?

ISSUE 12

Does Divorce or Disruption in Family Structure During Adolescence Have a Detrimental Effect on Development?

YES: Paul R. Amato, from "The Impact of Family Formation Change on the Cognitive, Social, and Emotional Well-Being of the Next Generation," *The Future of Children* (Fall 2005)

NO: Eda Ruschena et al., from "A Longitudinal Study of Adolescent Adjustment Following Family Transitions," *Journal of Child Psychology and Psychiatry* (vol. 46, no. 4, 2005)

ISSUE SUMMARY

YES: Sociology professor Paul Amato presents evidence that children growing up in stable, two-parent families are less likely to experience cognitive, emotional, and social problems than those who do not.

NO: Eda Ruschena, a psychologist at the Catholic Education Office in Melbourne, and her colleagues from the University of Melbourne claim that adolescents do not necessarily experience negative social, emotional, or psychological outcomes during family transitions.

Family structure has undoubtedly changed in the past 60 years. Marriage, for example, has become a less permanent institution, resulting in more divorces, more children of divorce, and subsequently more blended families. Just a few decades ago, most children in North America grew up in intact, two-parent families. This has changed, however, with increasing divorce rates. Since 1950, the divorce rate has almost doubled. In Canada, more than 70,000 divorces were granted in 2003 (Statistics Canada, 2006). In the United States, this number is considerably larger, with more than 950,000 divorces granted every year. The U.S. divorce rate in 2005 was 0.36 percent divorces per capita (National Vital Statistics Report, 2005). Predictions of first marriages ending in divorce are currently at 50 percent, and with 75 percent of these divorced people remarrying, blended families are becoming common. It is estimated that 40 percent of children will experience family divorce, and many will find themselves in blended families (Hetherington & Elmore, 2003).

Over the years, these changes in family structure have influenced the direction of research on this topic. Prior to the 1970s, the few studies that existed focused on the negative effects of family disruption, stating that children in such families and more specifically in families of divorce were at greater risk for maladjustment and delinquency. It was only when divorce rates started to climb at alarming rates in the late sixties and early seventies (i.e., increasing 113 percent between 1966 and 1976) that researchers began examining divorce in greater detail (Kelly, 2003). The focus, however, was still on divorced families as flawed families. There were no studies at the time comparing children of divorced families to children of never-divorced families. As a result, there was no evidence to support the argument that children of divorce were in fact worse off. Furthermore, longitudinal studies did not exist, making it impossible to distinguish between short-term and long-term outcomes.

In the 1980s, research on divorce continued to increase rapidly, addressing some of the limitations from the past. Researchers began examining children's overall adjustment, both short term and long term; however, studies remained one-sided and heavily focused on the negative effects. By the late 1980s, strides were finally being made toward identifying the risks and protective factors associated with both positive and negative outcomes. In addition, researchers began expanding the research on risk and resilience to identify environmental situations and circumstances that placed some children at greater risk for psychosocial maladjustment while protecting others from the long-term negative effects. The fact that some children and adolescents functioned well after divorce confirmed the importance of examining psychosocial well-being as well as environment.

What are the effects of divorce? Perhaps if children are not involved, divorce can be seen as a way of setting adults free from unhappy and/or abusive marriages. However, when a marriage dissolves and children are involved, there are consequences. Parent-child relationships change, living arrangements change, and financial situations change (Wallerstein & Lewis, 2004). For adolescents, these changes can be difficult, especially moving neighborhoods or schools. But, do these adjustments have a detrimental effect on all adolescents? Many researchers report negative outcomes for all children but adolescents in particular, finding they are affected behaviourally, academically, emotionally, and socially. Others find that a disruption to family structure does not pose a threat to healthy adolescent development and that the majority of adolescents do not have long-term psychological adjustment problems. Opposing views continue to exist. Is the divorced or disrupted family a happy family with well-adjusted adolescents? Are adolescents from long-term, stable families better off emotionally and socially? These questions are addressed in the selections that follow.

Amato reports that while chronic conflict is damaging to children and adolescents, two-parent families are usually better. He argues that children growing up in stable, two-parent families are less likely to experience cognitive, emotional, and social problems than those who do not. Opposing this view, Ruschena and her colleagues claim that adolescents do not necessarily experience negative social, emotional, or psychological outcomes during family transitions.

YES

Paul R. Amato

The Impact of Family Formation Change on the Cognitive, Social, and Emotional Well-Being of the Next Generation

Perhaps the most profound change in the American family over the past four decades has been the decline in the share of children growing up in households with both biological parents. Because many social scientists, policymakers, and members of the general public believe that a two-parent household is the optimal setting for children's development, the decline in such households has generated widespread concern about the well-being of American children. . . .

My goal in this article is to . . . [address two] questions. First, how do children in households with only one biological parent differ in terms of their cognitive, social, and emotional well-being from children in households with both biological parents? Second, what accounts for the observed differences between these two groups of children? . . .

Research on the Effects of Family Structure on Children

The rise in the divorce rate during the 1960s and 1970s prompted social scientists to investigate how differing family structures affect children. Their research focus initially was on children of divorced parents, but it expanded to include out-of-wedlock children and those in other nontraditional family structures.

Parental Divorce

Early studies generally supported the assumption that children who experience parental divorce are prone to a variety of academic, behavioral, and emotional problems. In 1971, . . . Wallerstein and Kelly began an influential long-term study of 60 divorced families and 131 children. According to the authors, five years after divorce, one-third of the children were adjusting well and had good relationships with both parents. Another group of children (more than one-third of the sample) were clinically depressed, were doing poorly in

From *The Future of Children Journal*, vol. 15, no. 2, Fall 2005, pp. 75–96. Copyright © 2005 by Brookings Institution Press. Reprinted by permission. Note: The complete text of this article contains many references to specific studies described. The interested individual should refer to the original publication for these extensive citations. These references have been omitted here in the interest of brevity.

school, had difficulty maintaining friendships, experienced chronic problems such as sleep disturbances, and continued to hope that their parents would reconcile.[1]

Despite these early findings, other studies in the 1970s challenged the dominant view that divorce is uniformly bad for children. For example, . . . Hetherington [et al. found that the] children with divorced parents exhibited more behavioral and emotional problems than did the children with continuously married parents. Two years after divorce, however, children with divorced parents no longer exhibited an elevated number of problems (although a few difficulties lingered for boys). Despite this temporary improvement, a later wave of data collection revealed that the remarriage of the custodial mother was followed by additional problems among the children, especially daughters.[2]

Trying to make sense of this research literature can be frustrating, because the results of individual studies vary considerably: some suggest serious negative effects of divorce, others suggest modest effects, and yet others suggest no effects. Much of this inconsistency is due to variations across studies in the types of samples, the ages of the children, the outcomes examined, and the methods of analysis. To summarize general trends across such a large and varied body of research, social scientists use a technique known as meta-analysis.

In 1991, . . . Keith and I published the first meta-analysis dealing with the effects of divorce on children.[3] Our analysis summarized the results of ninety-three studies published in the 1960s, 1970s, and 1980s and confirmed that children with divorced parents are worse off than those with continuously married parents on measures of academic success (school grades, scores on standardized achievement tests), conduct (behavior problems, aggression), psychological well-being (depression, distress symptoms), self-esteem (positive feelings about oneself, perceptions of self-efficacy), and peer relations (number of close friends, social support from peers). . . . Moreover, children in divorced families tend to have weaker emotional bonds with mothers and fathers than do their peers in two-parent families. These results supported the conclusion that the rise in divorce had lowered the average level of child well-being.

Our meta-analysis also indicated, however, that the estimated effects of parental divorce on children's well-being are modest rather than strong. We concluded that these modest differences reflect widely varying experiences within both groups of children. Some children growing up with continuously married parents are exposed to stressful circumstances, such as poverty, serious conflict between parents, violence, inept parenting, and mental illness or substance abuse, that increase the risk of child maladjustment. Correspondingly, some children with divorced parents cope well, perhaps because their parents are able to separate amicably and engage in cooperative co-parenting following marital dissolution.

In a more recent meta-analysis, based on sixty-seven studies conducted during the 1990s, . . . children with divorced parents, on average, scored significantly lower on various measures of wellbeing than did children with continuously married parents.[4] As before, the differences between the two groups were modest rather than large. Nevertheless, the more recent meta-analyses revealed that children with divorced parents continued to have lower average levels of cognitive, social, and emotional well-being, even in a decade in which divorce had become common and widely accepted. . . .

Children Born Outside Marriage

[Like] children with divorced parents, children who grow up with a single parent because they were born out of wedlock are more likely than children living with continuously married parents to experience a variety of cognitive, emotional, and behavioral problems. Specifically, compared with children who grow up in stable, two-parent families, children born outside marriage reach adulthood with less education, earn less income, have lower occupational status, are more likely to be idle (that is, not employed and not in school), are more likely to have a nonmarital birth (among daughters), have more troubled marriages, experience higher rates of divorce, and report more symptoms of depression.

A few studies have compared children of unmarried single parents and divorced single parents. Despite some variation across studies, this research generally shows that the long-term risks for most problems are comparable in these two groups. . . .

Although it is sometimes assumed that children born to unwed mothers have little contact with their fathers, about 40 percent of unmarried mothers are living with the child's father at the time of birth.[5] If one-third of all children are born to unmarried parents, and if 40 percent of these parents are cohabiting, then about one out of every eight infants lives with two biological but unmarried parents. Structurally, these households are similar to households with two married parents. And young children are unlikely to be aware of their parents' marital status. Nevertheless, cohabiting parents tend to be more disadvantaged than married parents. They have less education, earn less income, report poorer relationship quality, and experience more mental health problems.[6] These considerations suggest that children living with cohabiting biological parents may be worse off, in some respects, than children living with two married biological parents.

Consistent with this assumption, . . . Brown found that children living with cohabiting biological parents, compared with children living with continuously married parents, had more behavioral problems, more emotional problems, and lower levels of school engagement.[7] . . . Parents' education, income, psychological well-being, and parenting stress explained most—but not all—of these differences. . . .

The risk of relationship dissolution also is substantially higher for cohabiting couples with children than for married couples with children. For example, the Fragile Families Study indicates that about one-fourth of cohabiting biological parents are no longer living together one year after the child's birth. [8] . . .

Death of a Parent

Some children live with a single parent not because of divorce or because they were born outside marriage but because their other parent has died. Studies that compare children who experienced the death of a parent with children separated from a parent for other reasons yield mixed results. The Amato and Keith meta-analysis found that children who experienced a parent's death scored lower on several forms of well-being than did children living with continuously married parents. Children who experienced a parent's death, however, scored significantly *higher* on several measures of well-being than did children with divorced parents. McLanahan and Sandefur found that children with a deceased parent were no more likely than children with continuously married parents to drop out of high school. Daughters with a deceased parent, however, were more likely than teenagers living with both parents to have a nonmarital birth.[9] . . . [In summary,] these studies suggest that experiencing the death of a parent during childhood puts children at risk for a number of problems, but not as much as does divorce or out-of-wedlock birth.

Discordant Two-Parent Families

Most studies in this literature have compared children living with a single parent with a broad group of children living with continuously married parents. Some two-parent families, however, function better than others. Marriages marked by chronic, overt conflict and hostility are "intact" structurally but are not necessarily good environments in which to raise children. Some early studies compared children living with divorced parents and children living with two married but discordant parents. In general, these studies found that children in high-conflict households experience many of the same problems as do children with divorced parents. . . .

A more recent generation of long-term studies has shown that the effects of divorce vary with the degree of marital discord that precedes divorce. When parents exhibit chronic and overt conflict, children appear to be better off, in the long run, if their parents split up rather than stay together. But when parents exhibit relatively little overt conflict, children appear to be better off if their parents stay together. In other words, children are particularly at risk when low-conflict marriages end in divorce. In a twenty-year study, Alan Booth and I found that the majority of marriages that ended in divorce fell into the low-conflict group. Spouses in these marriages did not fight frequently or express hostility toward their partners. Instead, they felt emotionally estranged from their spouses, and many ended their marriages to seek greater happiness with new partners. Although many parents saw this transition as positive, their children often viewed it as unexpected, inexplicable, and unwelcome. Children and parents, it is clear, often have different interpretations of family transitions.

Stepfamilies

Although rates of remarriage have declined in recent years, most divorced parents eventually remarry. Similarly, many women who have had a nonmarital birth eventually marry men who are not the fathers of their children. Adding a stepfather to the household usually improves children's standard of living. Moreover, in a stepfamily, two adults are available to monitor children's behavior, provide supervision, and assist children with everyday problems. For these reasons, one might assume that children generally are better off in stepfamilies than in single-parent households. Studies consistently indicate, however, that children in stepfamilies exhibit more problems than do children with continuously married parents and about the same number of problems as do children with single parents. In other words, the marriage of a single parent (to someone other than the child's biological parent) does not appear to improve the functioning of most children.

Although the great majority of parents view the formation of a stepfamily positively, children tend to be less enthusiastic. Stepfamily formation is stressful for many children because it often involves moving (generally to a different neighborhood or town), adapting to new people in the household, and learning new rules and routines. Moreover, early relationships between stepparents and stepchildren are often tense. Children, especially adolescents, become accustomed to a substantial degree of autonomy in single-parent households. They may resent the monitoring and supervision by stepparents and react with hostility when stepparents attempt to exert authority. Some children experience loyalty conflicts and fear that becoming emotionally close to a stepparent implies betraying the nonresident biological parent. Some become jealous because they must share parental time and attention with the stepparent. And for some children, remarriage ends any lingering hopes that the two biological parents will one day reconcile. Finally, stepchildren are overrepresented in official reports of child abuse. . . .

Variations by Gender of Child

Several early influential studies found that boys in divorced families had more adjustment problems than did girls.[2] Given that boys usually live with their mothers following family disruption, the loss of contact with the same-gender parent could account for such a difference. In addition, boys, compared with girls, may be exposed to more conflict, receive less support from parents and others (because they are believed to be tougher), and be picked on more by custodial mothers (because sons may resemble their fathers). Subsequent studies, however, have failed to find consistent gender differences in children's reactions to divorce.

The meta-analyses on children of divorce provide the most reliable evidence on this topic. The Amato and Keith meta-analysis of studies conducted before the 1990s revealed one significant gender difference: the estimated negative effect of divorce on social adjustment was stronger for boys than girls. In other areas, however, such as academic achievement, conduct, and psychological adjustment, no differences between boys and girls were apparent.[3] In my meta-analysis of studies conducted in the 1990s, the estimated effect of divorce on children's conduct problems was stronger for boys than for girls, although no other gender differences were apparent.[4] Why the earlier studies suggest a gender difference in social adjustment and the more recent studies suggest a gender difference in conduct problems is unclear. Nevertheless, taken together, these meta-analyses provide some limited support for the notion that boys are more susceptible than girls to the detrimental consequences of divorce. . . .

Why Do Single-Parent Families Put Children at Risk?

Researchers have several theories to explain why children growing up with single parents have an elevated risk of experiencing cognitive, social, and emotional problems. Most refer either to the economic and parental resources available to children or to the stressful events and circumstances to which these children must adapt.

Economic Hardship

For a variety of reasons, . . . most children living with single parents are economically disadvantaged. It is difficult for poor single parents to afford the books, home computers, and private lessons that make it easier for their children to succeed in school. Similarly, they cannot afford clothes, shoes, cell phones, and other consumer goods that give their children status among their peers. Moreover, many live in rundown neighborhoods with high crime rates, low-quality schools, and few community services. Consistent with these observations, many studies have shown that economic resources explain some of the differences in well-being between children with single parents and those with continuously married parents.[9] Research showing that children do better at school and exhibit fewer behavioral problems when nonresident fathers pay child support likewise suggests the importance of income in facilitating children's well-being in single-parent households.[10]

Quality of Parenting

Regardless of family structure, the quality of parenting is one of the best predictors of children's emotional and social well-being. Many single parents, however, find it difficult to function effectively as parents. Compared with continuously married parents, they are less emotionally supportive of their children, have fewer rules, dispense harsher discipline, are more inconsistent in dispensing discipline, provide less supervision, and engage in more conflict with their children. Many of these deficits in parenting presumably result from struggling to make ends meet with limited financial resources and trying to raise children without the help of the other biological parent. Many studies link inept parenting by resident single parents with a variety of negative outcomes among children, including poor academic achievement, emotional problems, conduct problems, low self-esteem, and problems forming and maintaining social relationships. Other studies show that depression among custodial mothers, which usually detracts from effective parenting, is related to poor adjustment among offspring.[9] . . .

Exposure to Stress

Children living with single parents are exposed to more stressful experiences and circumstances than are children living with continuously married parents. . . . This results in feelings of emotional distress, a reduced capacity to function in school, work, and family roles, and an increase in physiological indicators of arousal.[11] Economic hardship, inept parenting, and loss of contact with a parent . . . can be stressful for children. Observing conflict and hostility between resident and nonresident parents also is stressful. Conflict between nonresident parents appears to be particularly harmful when children feel that they are caught in the middle, . . . and when one parent attempts to recruit the child as an ally against the other. Interparental conflict is a direct stressor for children, and it can also interfere with their attachments to parents, resulting in feelings of emotional insecurity.

Moving is a difficult experience for many children, especially when it involves losing contact with neighborhood friends. Moreover, moves that require changing schools can put children out of step with their classmates in terms of the curriculum. Children with single parents move more frequently than other children do, partly because of economic hardship . . . and partly because single parents form new romantic attachments. . . . Studies show that frequent moving increases the risk of academic, behavioral, and emotional problems for children with single parents.[9] For many children, . . . the addition of a stepparent to the household is a stressful change. And when remarriages end in divorce, children are exposed to yet more stressful transitions. . . .

Conclusion

. . . Research clearly demonstrates that children growing up with two continuously married parents are less likely than other children to experience a wide range of cognitive, emotional, and social problems, not only during childhood, but also in adulthood. Although it is not possible to demonstrate that family structure is the cause of these differences, studies that have used a variety of sophisticated statistical methods, including controls for genetic factors, suggest that this is the case. This distinction is even stronger if we focus on children growing up with two *happily married* biological parents.

. . . Compared with other children, those who grow up in stable, two-parent families have a higher standard of living, receive more effective parenting, experience more cooperative co-parenting, are emotionally closer to both parents (especially fathers), and are subjected to fewer stressful events and circumstances. . . .

[In summary, the] importance of increasing the number of children growing up with two happily and continuously married parents and of improving the well-being of children now living in other family structures is self-evident. Children are the innocent victims of their parents' inability to maintain harmonious and stable homes. . . .

Endnotes

1. Judith S. Wallerstein and Joan B. Kelly, *Surviving the Breakup: How Children and Parents Cope with Divorce* (New York: Basic Books, 1980).

2. E. Mavis Hetherington, "Divorce: A Child's Perspective," *American Psychologist* 34 (1979): 851–58; E. Mavis Hetherington, Martha Cox, and R. Cox, "Effects of Divorce on Parents and Children," in *Nontraditional Families,* edited by Michael Lamb (Hillsdale, N.J.: Lawrence Erlbaum, 1982), pp. 233–88.

3. Paul R. Amato and Bruce Keith, "Consequences of Parental Divorce for Children's Well-Being: A Meta-Analysis," *Psychological Bulletin* 10 (1991): 26–46.

4. Paul R. Amato, "Children of Divorce in the 1990s: An Update of the Amato and Keith (1991) Meta-Analysis," *Journal of Family Psychology* 15 (2001): 355–70.

5. Larry L. Bumpass and Hsien-Hen Lu, "Trends in Cohabitation and Implications for Children's Family Contexts in the United States," *Population Studies* 54 (2000): 29–41; Sara McLanahan and others, "Unwed Parents or Fragile Families? Implications for Welfare and Child Support Policy," in *Out of Wedlock: Causes and Consequences of Nonmarital Fertility,* edited by Lawrence L. Wu and Barbara Wolfe (New York: Russell Sage Foundation, 2001), pp. 202–28.

6. Susan Brown, "The Effect of Union Type on Psychological Well-Being: Depression among Cohabitors versus Marrieds," *Journal of Health and Social Behavior* 41 (2000): 241–55; Susan Brown and Alan Booth, "Cohabitation versus Marriage: A Comparison of Relationship Quality," *Journal of Marriage and the Family* 58 (1996): 668–78; Judith Seltzer, "Families Formed outside of Marriage," *Journal of Marriage and the Family* 62 (2000): 1247–68.

7. Susan Brown, "Family Structure and Child Well-Being: The Significance of Parental Cohabitation," *Journal of Marriage and the Family* 66 (2004): 351–67. For a general review of this literature, see Wendy Manning, "The Implications of Cohabitation for Children's Well-Being," in *Just Living Together: Implications of Cohabitation for Families, Children, and Social Policy,* edited by Alan Booth and Ann Crouter (Mahwah, N.J.: Lawrence Erlbaum Associates, 2002), pp. 21–152.

8. M. Carlson, Sara McLanahan, and Paula England, "Union Formation and Dissolution in Fragile Families," Fragile Families Research Brief, no. 4 (Bendheim-Thoman Center for Research on Child Wellbeing, Princeton University, January 2003); see also Sara McLanahan, "Diverging Destinies: How Children Are Faring under the Second Demographic Transition," *Demography* 41 (2004): 606–27.

9. Sara McLanahan and Gary Sandefur, *Growing Up with a Single Parent: What Hurts, What Helps* (Harvard University Press, 1994).

10. Valarie King, "Nonresident Father Involvement and Child Well-Being: Can Dads Make a Difference?" *Journal of Family Issues* 15 (1994): 78–96; Sara McLanahan and others, "Child Support Enforcement and Child Well-Being: Greater Security or Greater Conflict?" in *Child Support and Child Well-Being,* edited by Irwin Garfinkel, Sara McLanahan, and Philip K. Robins (Washington: Urban Institute Press, 1996), pp. 239–56.

11. L. I. Pearlin and others, "The Stress Process," *Journal of Health and Social Behavior* 22 (1981): 337–56; Peggy A. Thoits, "Stress, Coping, and Social Support Processes: Where Are We? What Next?" *Journal of Health and Social Behavior,* extra issue (1995): 53–79.

Eda Ruschena, Margot Prior,
Ann Sanson, and Diana Smart

 **NO**

A Longitudinal Study of Adolescent Adjustment Following Family Transitions

Divorce has become considerably more common in the West over the recent decades. The Australian Bureau of Statistics (2002) has projected that for a group of present-day newborn babies and based on 1997–1999 divorce rates, 32% of their future marriages will end in divorce. . . . Concomitant with these family changes there has been an increase in research focused upon adjustment outcomes for children. The overall picture remains unclear, however, with reviews of the large body of literature in this field finding inconsistent outcomes that are largely dependent upon methodological characteristics of individual studies. There is little doubt, though, that divorce brings a number of important stressors for children (Emery, 1999). The process of separation, of learning to alternate between households, of perhaps moving homes or schools, can be very challenging. Contact with the non-residential parent can be sporadic and may diminish over time (Emery, 1999). Whether children are survivors, winners, or losers, after their parents' divorce or remarriage, depends upon a large number of interconnected variables (Hetherington, 1989).

A majority of researchers focusing upon the effects of family transitions have examined behavioural, emotional and academic outcomes, with the reported outcomes appearing largely negative (Amato & Keith, 1991). . . .

Another central focus for research is how family structure and functioning affects and is affected by transitions. There is agreement that the relationship between the residential parent and the child can be a protective factor in terms of children's adjustment after divorce, but in reality there is often a decline in parenting quality after a family transition, with more inconsistent discipline and affection. A decline in post-divorce relationships between fathers and their children is common, although problems may also have been present prior to the divorce (Amato & Booth, 1996; Zill, Morrison, & Coiro, 1993) so a causal relationship should not be assumed.

Another theoretical stance contends that it is not the divorce per se which leads to poorer outcomes for children, but the influence of inter-parental conflict. Indirectly, conflict may diminish parents' emotional energy and interfere with their ability to respond sensitively to their children's emotional needs.

From *Journal of Clinical Psychology*, vol. 46, no. 4, 2005, pp. 353–363. Copyright © 2005 by John Wiley & Sons. Reprinted by permission. Note: The complete text of this article contains many references to specific studies described. The interested individual should refer to the original publication for these extensive citations. These references have been omitted here in the interest of brevity.

Parents in high conflict marriages engage in more erratic disciplinary practices and are more likely to use anxiety or guilt-inducing techniques to discipline their children than parents in low-to-moderate conflict marriages, according to Kelly (1998). Further, the very structure of the post-transition family can lead to poorer outcomes for children, with the absence of a biological parent (usually the father) and the attendant loss of resources (financial, emotional) being the most influential factors. Studies comparing children and adolescents from families that have experienced either parental death or divorce (Kiernan, 1992) have shown lower well-being for children affected by divorce compared to those who have lost a parent through death, suggesting an additional adverse mechanism operating in divorced families, other than simply parent loss.

Divorce often leads to deterioration in financial circumstances for families and this is associated with poorer outcomes for children (Emery, 1999; Rodgers, 1996). This may be partly due to the flow-on effects of economic losses, such as having to move schools or suburbs and losing contact with peers and familiar environments, further taxing the coping resources of children and adolescents already suffering emotional strain. In addition to being a predictor variable in adjustment outcomes, income can also be seen as a confounding variable, hence many studies of post-divorce outcomes controlling for the influence of income find differences between married and single-parent families reduced by about half, for measures such as school attainment, and by a lesser amount for internalising and externalising behaviour problems. However, considerable variance in children's adjustment between the two groups remains unexplained.

Additional family transitions such as remarriage of one or both parents and/or the addition of step-siblings can affect children's functioning. Number of marital transitions was associated with behavioural difficulties in longitudinal studies by . . . Hetherington and Clingempeel (1992), and difficulties were apparent in the stepfather–stepchild relationship and also in sibling relationships.

Gender and age of the child have also been implicated in variable outcomes in the family transitions literature. Many studies have observed significantly worse outcomes for boys rather than girls (Hetherington, Stanley-Hagan, & Anderson, 1989). Alternatively Zill et al. (1993) found no reliable interactions with gender on any of the measured variables in their study. . . . In terms of age at transition, developmental psychologists generally believe that the limited understanding of pre-school children leaves them more vulnerable to the effects of parental conflict and family disruption . . . (Hetherington & Clingempeel, 1992; Zill et al., 1993). On the other hand, later divorces may be more deleterious than earlier ones, perhaps because the developmental challenges of adolescence and young adulthood can compound the stress of family disruption. . . .

Temperament is another influential factor in terms of the impact of stressful life events upon children and adolescents. . . . [A] number of studies have uncovered associations between positive, outgoing, flexible temperamental attributes and improved outcomes after a family transition (Hetherington et al., 1989). . . .

Rationale for the Study

Few major research studies of outcomes after divorce have emanated from Australia. . . . A review of 25 Australian studies conducted from the 1970s until the 1990s (Rodgers, 1996) showed that as with international findings, many Australian researchers have found divorce to be associated with a range of adverse social and psychological outcomes, for adolescents and adults. However, research seemed patchy, . . . and many studies had problems related to a lack of statistical power. . . .

Longitudinal data offers many advantages for [the] research. The availability of data from the Australian Temperament Project (ATP) from 1983 to 2000 allowed us to examine two key questions using this approach. Firstly, we examined group differences between children who had experienced a family transition, that is, a parental separation, divorce or death, and those who had not, on outcome measures such as degree of family attachment, level of educational attainment, and behavioural measures of social competence and psychosocial maladjustment. We hypothesised that children experiencing separation and divorce would be at risk for poorer outcomes. Secondly, for those experiencing family transitions, we tested the potency of key variables identified in the literature . . . to predict better or worse adjustment.

Method

Participants

. . . This project began in 1983 when the mother of every infant aged four to eight months, who attended selected infant Welfare Centres in a specific two-week period, was invited to participate in the project. The total number of families recruited at the first stage of the research was 2,443. . . . From infancy onwards, at roughly 15–18-month intervals, families were contacted . . . with requests to complete questionnaires (13 data waves in all). . . .

By 2000, when the target participants were 17–18 years old, . . . 1,310 parents and 1,260 adolescents responded to the surveys. . . .

The data bank from the 18 years of this study was used to explore predictors of outcome for young people who at 17–18 years of age reported that their family had undergone a family transition during the child's lifetime.

Procedure

The ATP data bank was accessed for data on the sample from infancy to 17–18 years of age. In the year 2000, a separate questionnaire, independent of the main ATP survey, was also sent to a sub-sample of the ATP cohort (aged 17–18 years), relating to their experiences of family transitions. This sub-sample [($n = 151$)] was chosen by selecting those adolescents who answered affirmatively to questions in the ATP year 2000 survey about their experience of a marital separation, divorce, remarriage, or parental death during their lifetime. . . . One hundred and forty-nine participants from the general ATP database, whose families *had not* been through a transition (that is, a divorce, separation or death), provided the comparison group. . . .

Measures

Demographic information. These data, collected at 17–18 years, via both the general ATP questionnaire and the separate Family Transitions Questionnaire, included information about the participant adolescent's gender, birth order, number of children in the family, living arrangements and geographic location. Participants were asked about transitions occurring over the ATP adolescent's lifetime, including whether parents had separated, divorced, died, or remarried, presence of step-siblings in the family, number of house and school moves over the ATP adolescent's lifetime, and the level of contact with the non-residential parent. Overall socioeconomic status (SES) was available for every data . . . using the mean of both parents' occupational and educational status. . . .

Behaviour problems. A number of measures had been used to assess behaviour problem. . . . The Behar Pre-school Behaviour Questionnaire provided information on parent-reported problem behaviour at child age of three to four years. . . . Across ages five to twelve years, the Rutter Problem Behaviour Questionnaire was used to identify problem behaviours via parent ratings. . . . During the adolescent years, (ages 13–14 and 17–18) the Revised Behaviour Problem Checklist was used to measure parent perceptions of behaviour problems, including different aspects of internalising and externalising behaviours. An adolescent self-report measure, with parallel sub-scales to the parent form, was adapted from the RBPQ by the ATP team. . . . At age 17–18, the Short Mood and Feelings Questionnaire was used to measure self-reported depressive symptoms, . . . and a short form of the Revised Manifest Anxiety Scale was used to measure self-reported anxious behaviours. . . .

Academic measures. Total School Problems was a five-item . . . scale measuring both academic and behaviour problems at school at 17–18 years, as reported by parents. . . .

Measures of temperament. Parents rated their ATP adolescent (at 17–18) on a number of temperament dimensions using the School Age Temperament Questionnaire. . . .

Family measures (at age 17–18). The *Parent's Overall Temperament Rating scale* was an ATP measure that comprised one question, reflecting the parent's perception of how easy or difficult the child was when compared to other children of the same age. . . . The *Sibling Relationship scale* comprised ten questions . . . that rated intimacy and support, as well as conflict between the ATP adolescent and up to two siblings. . . . *Attachment to parents* was an adolescent-reported short form of the . . . Inventory of Parent Attachment that assessed the quality of the parent–adolescent relationship. . . . The *Parent–Adolescent Conflict scale* was a parent-completed short-form of the Prinz

Conflict Behaviour Questionnaire covering aspects of the parent–adolescent relationship. . . . A *Parental Marital Conflict scale* was a retrospective parent-reported measure of inter-parental conflict over two time periods: between birth and twelve years, and from twelve years to the present. . . .

Peer relationship measure.   Antisocial Peer Associations was a six-question scale, . . . which measured parental reports of the degree to which their adolescent associated with substance-using and/or anti-social peers. The 15–16-year-old data were used for this study.

Social skills measures.   When the children were 11–12 and 13–14 years of age, parents and children completed the Social Skills Rating System. . . .

Family transition information.   The Family Transitions questionnaire . . . sought information about post-transition living arrangements, social support during and after the transition, contact with the non-residential parent, and details of further family changes that may have occurred since the original transition. This questionnaire also assessed the adolescent's feelings of regret, relief, and ambivalence in relation to the parents' separation. . . .

Results

1. *Descriptive characteristics of the groups*

The transitions group comprised those adolescents who at 17–18 years of age reported that their family had experienced a transition during the child's lifetime. They were compared with comparison group participants on a number of demographic variables. . . . On most factors, the two groups were found to be similar, although a greater number of transition group members lived independently from parents (7% versus 1% respectively).

Transitions experienced by participants included parental death, separation and divorce, remarriage of one or both parents, the addition of step-parents and/or step-siblings, as well as house moves and school changes directly resulting from these family transitions, with some respondents experiencing multiple transitions of the same type. . . . A one-way ANOVA showed the mean number of house moves to be significantly lower for those adolescents who did not experience a family transition. . . . A majority (63%) of those having experienced family transitions did not have step-siblings. The mean . . . age at which the transition occurred was eleven years old and almost half the sample experienced their transition during adolescence.

Data from the concurrent 17–18 years questionnaire . . . showed that almost half the respondents still saw their non-residential parent at least fortnightly. . . . Finally, respondents were asked about their satisfaction with their level of contact with the non-residential parent. Responses were split between those who indicated contact was insufficient and those who felt it to be satisfactory. Only a small number of respondents indicated that the degree of contact was too great.

2. *Between-group differences: Transitions groups versus comparison group participants*

Behaviour problems.   The first analysis examined whether negative conse-quences of family transitions were detectable in late adolescence (17 to 18 years of age). . . . Analyses of variance comparing groups on a composite score of parent- and teen-reported problem behaviours, and on internalising and externalising problems separately, showed no main effect of group type nor interaction effects between group and gender. Gender differences were found, however, in terms of overall problem behaviours . . . and internalising prob-lems, [with girls reporting] greater difficulties. . . .

An ANOVA using the longitudinal data (from age 3–4 to 17–18) examined whether rates of problems were higher among those who came from a family that *would* experience a transition at some time over the course of the ATP. . . . There was no significant difference found between the transitions and comparison groups on this analysis at any point in time.

Differences in family factors.   Further analyses examined group differences in relation to: parents' evaluations of their relationship with the ATP adolescent, parental rating of the adolescent's overall ease or difficulty compared to peers, parent–child conflict, inter-parental conflict, and quality of the ATP adolescent's relationship with siblings. A MANOVA revealed no significant effects of gender alone or gender and group combined, but there was a significant main effect for group type. . . . Transitions group parents reported more conflict with their adolescent than comparison group parents. . . . Com-parison adolescents also reported a better quality relationship with their reporting parent than transitions group adolescents, in terms of factors such as communication, trust, and lack of alienation. . . .

Differences in social skills.   No significant main effect of group type or inter-active effect of group type and gender were found on the measures of social skills . . . from age 11 to 14. However, . . . [females] reported themselves to have significantly more empathy than their male counterparts, . . . and females were reported by both themselves and their parents to be significantly more cooperative. . . .

Academic differences.   There was no significant difference between groups on an overall school problems score measured at age 17–18. . . .

3. *Between group differences: Divorce group, parental death group and comparisons*

Thirty-one participants in the sample had experienced a parental death. They were compared with 50 randomly selected subjects whose parents had divorced and 50 randomly selected subjects who were still in their original families, to investigate the effect of type of family transition compared to no transition. . . . No significant differences were found between the three groups, on the following: overall behaviour problems and specific internalising or externalising problems at 17–18 years, composite behaviour problems across the ages from 3–4 to 17–18, family factors, and school problems at 17–18 years. . . .

4. *Predictors of outcomes: Analyses within the transitions group*

A number of linear regression analyses were performed within the transitions group to explore predictors of outcomes at age 17–18. Predictor variables included the following: gender, number of transitions during the participant's lifetime, number of years since the transition occurred, socioeconomic status, parent's overall rating of the ease or difficulty of the ATP adolescent, inter-parental conflict, parent-teen conflict, the adolescent's tendency to associate with antisocial peers, and concurrent temperament dimensions of reactivity, approach-withdrawal and persistence. . . .

Three separate regression analyses were performed predicting overall behaviour problems, externalising problems and internalising problems in the transitions group. Of all the variables listed above, the parent's overall rating of their adolescent as easy or difficult, the tendency to associate with antisocial peers, gender, and two dimensions of temperament (all at age 17–18) were significant predictors of more behaviour problems. . . .

5. *Analyses within the comparison group*

In order to explore whether these predictors of problem behaviour were unique to transition group adolescents, similar regression analyses (again at age 17–18) were repeated with the comparison group. As items such as years since tran-sition and number of transitions clearly did not apply to this group, the regres-sion analyses had fewer predictor variables, but were otherwise similar. Again, parent's overall rating and dimensions of temperament were significant pre-dictors of behaviour problems. Socioeconomic status was also a predictor of higher internalising behaviour problems for the comparison group. . . .

6. *Comparisons with other ATP participants who were potential members of the transitions group*

Given that relatively few group differences were found between transitions and comparison group participants, it was important to check that the transi-tions group was representative of a community sample of adolescents who had experienced a family transition. Although the original ATP participants at 4–8 months old were carefully shown to be a representative community sam-ple, there has been some attrition over time. Analyses were performed on a sample of data from 1983 (age 4–8 months) comparing the entire transitions sample ($N = 262$) with children who did not later participate in the 17–18-year-old survey wave, but whose families had previously reported experiencing a transition at some point during the project ($N = 121$). . . .

T-tests revealed that the transitions group's families were of significantly higher socio-economic status (SES) in 1983 compared to the non-participating group. . . . There were no significant differences on the total behaviour problems composite; the approach, rhythmicity, cooperation, activity–reactivity and irritability temperament dimensions; or the easy–difficult temperament scale at 4–8 months of age. Thus while the transitions group appeared to be a higher SES group than the non-participating group, and this may have influenced their continuance in the study, the two groups were similar on all aspects of functioning assessed at enrolment in the study.

Discussion

Using a large, longitudinal database, this research aimed to test the hypothesis that Australian adolescents whose families had experienced a family transition would have poorer outcomes in behaviour, well-being and family processes compared with adolescents living in their original families. . . .

Group Differences

Contrary to our hypothesis, there were no group differences on internalising, externalising and overall behaviour problems at 17–18 years, findings that contrast with those of many researchers in this field who have found that children and adolescents who have experienced transitions are significantly worse off in terms of behavioural adjustment (Amato & Keith, 1991). Longitudinal analyses did not reveal group differences in either overall or extreme problem behaviour scores. . . . For problem behaviour scores from age 3 to 18 years, transitions group participants scored similarly to their peers from intact families.

Most published studies in the family transitions literature tend to focus upon negative behavioural outcomes. In this study, positive behaviours in the domain of social competence were also examined. The two groups were again comparable on such dimensions as responsibility, cooperativeness, selfcontrol and empathy.

Although the literature repeatedly points to a decline in academic functioning after family transition (Rodgers, 1996), the lack of significant differences between the ATP groups on this variable was also supported by qualitative interview data used in another, unreported part of this study. Most interviewees were dismissive of notions that their schoolwork was affected by parental divorce. Hence, overall, it appeared that the young people from the ATP were developing well both across time and at late adolescence. . . .

One possible reason for the lack of significant differences between the transitions and comparison groups could be that the transitions group was a particularly well-functioning one. Comparison of the current transitions group with another ATP subgroup which had earlier reported a family transition but had not participated in the 17–18-year data collection revealed modest but significant differences between the groups on family socio-economic background, but no differences on any of the measured aspects of child functioning. Thus it did not seem that this transitions group was an especially high-functioning one. . . .

It may also be that distinctive characteristics of Australian society are contributing to successful outcomes for these adolescents, although Rodgers

(1996) dismissed the notion that Australia was somehow dissimilar from other countries in contributing to better adjustment outcomes after divorce, since the majority of Australian findings actually supported the concept of group differences. However, in Dunlop and Burns' work (1988) and now in this study, adolescents from families that have experienced transitions and those still in their original families appear to be functioning in very similar ways. Particular Australian factors such as the provision of social security benefits and legal enforcement of child maintenance payments may mitigate some of the more extreme financial hardship and life stress that can ensue after a family breakdown. Given that few significant differences were found between the transitions and intact groups, it is not surprising that the adolescents who had experienced a parental death were not differentiated from their peers on behavioural, academic, family and coping variables (Kiernan, 1992). . . .

Most of the significant main effects in this study involved gender. Girls experienced higher overall levels of behaviour problems and specifically, more internalising problems including anxiety and depression. These findings are consistent with much of the research into overall gender differences in psychological symptomatology. . . . Girls were also found to be more socially competent than boys in late childhood to early adolescence, which is also a normative finding (Prior et al., 2000). However, since there were no interactions between gender and group status, this effect cannot be ascribed to the effects of separation and divorce.

Predictors of Functioning

Parental rating of the ATP child's ease or difficulty compared to his or her peers consistently predicted higher problem behaviours. Over the years, this ATP-devised measure has been predictive for a variety of outcomes (Prior et al., 2000) and rather than being a measure of temperament as originally formulated, it appears to represent the level of ease and harmony in the parent–child relationship. Consistent with the findings of researchers such as Hetherington (1989), dimensions of temperament have proved significant in predicting behavioural outcomes in this study, as they have in much previous ATP research (Prior et at., 2000), with a lack of persistence or attentional self-regulation associated with externalising problems, and withdrawal, or shyness, associated with internalising problems, Despite the traditional emphasis placed on factors such as age at transition, years since transition, and contact with the non-residential parent, these factors did not contribute to the functional outcomes experienced by the adolescent. Of all the specifically transitions-related variables, only number of transitions experienced was (weakly) predictive of overall behaviour problems in the transitions group. . . .

The identified, significant predictors of behavioural outcomes were not unique to the transitions group. Personality factors such as dimensions of temperament and parent's overall ease/difficulty rating, rather than external, structural factors, were also associated with problem behaviour in the comparison group. The child's temperament would clearly have a powerful effect upon the type of relationship he or she has with a parent, which would in turn affect adjustment outcomes for the child. Dunlop and Burns (1988) showed that regardless of whether parents are together or apart, adolescents who have a warm and supportive relationship with at least one parent show better adjustment on a variety of measures than those who do not. For example, possessing the trait of persistence, i.e., the ability to follow through on a task even when circumstances are difficult, may enable a person to trial different coping strategies, if one proved to be unsuccessful, or to just keep persevering. Being able to approach others for help or to allow the approach of others is likely to be another factor involved in optimal coping. Social and personal networks can allow young people to access help during hardship. Moreover, children and adolescents with positive temperamental styles are more likely to have developed warm, supportive parental relationships that would be invaluable during any period of difficulty. . . .

Conclusion

. . . [The] current research is useful in portraying children and adolescents from transitions families as functioning in similar ways to their peers from intact families. For this large Australian adolescent sample, the family transition has not necessarily negatively impacted on current social, emotional or psychological outcomes, although relationships with parents may have been negatively affected. For those with poorer behavioural outcomes, the most prominent contributing factors were dimensions of temperament and parent–child relationship quality, rather than structural determinants related to the transition itself. Although many studies in the literature have found significant negative effects, the results are often tempered by small effect sizes. That is, while a small group of children from disrupted families are often found to be functioning more poorly than peers from intact families, the vast majority are developing into competent human beings, functioning satisfactorily in most domains. This study highlights the resilience of many young people faced with personal and social upheaval.

References

Amato, P.R., & Booth, A. (1996) A prospective study of divorce and parent–child relationships. *Journal of Marriage and the Family*, 58, 356–365.

Amato, P.R., & Keith, B. (1991). Parental divorce and the well-being of children: A meta-analysis. *Psychological Bulletin*, 110, 26–46.

Australian Bureau of Statistics. (2002). *Marriages and divorces Australia*. Catalogue No. 3310.0. Canberra.

Dunlop, R., & Burns, A. (1988). *Don't feel the world is caving in: Adolescents in divorcing families*. Melbourne: Australian Institute of Family Studies.

Emery, R.E. (1999). *Marriage, divorce and children's adjustment* (2nd edn). Thousand Oaks, CA: Sage.

Hetherington, E.M. (1989). Coping with family transitions: Winners, losers, and survivors. *Child Development, 60, 1–14.*

Hetherington, E.M., & Clingempeel, W.G. (1992). Coping with marital transitions: A family systems perspective. *Monographs of the Society for Research in Child Development, 57* (2–3, Serial No. 227).

Hetherington, E.M., Stanley-Hagan, M., & Anderson, E.R. (1989). Marital transitions: A child's perspective. *American Psychologist, 44,* 303–312.

Kelly, J.B. (1998). Marital conflict, divorce and children's adjustment. *Child and Adolescent Psychiatric Clinics of North America, 7,* 259–271.

Kiernan, K.E. (1992). The impact of family disruption in childhood on transitions made in young adult life. *Population Studies, 46,* 213–234.

Prior, M., Sanson, A., Smart, D., & Oberklaid, F. (2000). *Pathways from infancy to adolescence: Australian Temperament Project 1983–2000.* Melbourne: Australian Institute of Family Studies.

Rodgers, B. (1996). Social and psychological wellbeing of children from divorced families: Australian research findings. *Australian Psychologist, 31,* 174–182.

Zill, N., Morrison, D.R., & Coiro, M.J. (1993). Long-term effects of parental divorce on parent–child relationships, adjustment, and achievement in young adulthood. *Journal of Family Psychology, 7,* 91–103.

POSTSCRIPT

Does Divorce or Disruption in Family Structure During Adolescence Have a Detrimental Effect on Development?

In examining the research on family structure, Amato argues that children growing up in a stable long-term two-parent family are less likely to have psychosocial problems both during childhood and adulthood. He concludes that the children who have stable family structures have a higher standard of living, receive better parenting, have stronger and more secure attachments to parents, and are exposed to fewer stressful events. Ruschena and colleagues, on the other hand, examined family transitions such as separation, divorce, remarriage, and death on children and adolescents and found no significant differences between groups on measures of behavioral and emotional adjustment, academic outcomes, and social competence. In other words, adolescents from disruptive family structures functioned the same as adolescents from intact families.

Supporting Amatos' argument, Sun and Li (2002) also found that children of divorce have lower scores on measures of well-being (i.e., academic functioning, locus of control, and self-esteem) compared to children of intact families. Although they reported that family resources could mediate the negative effects of disruption over time, the process essentially affected children continuously both before and after divorce.

Mavis Hetherington, on the other hand, supports the arguments of Ruschena and her colleagues, stating that 75–80 percent of children from divorced homes are coping well and certainly functioning in the normal range 20 years later (Hetherington & Kelly, 2002). Although Hetherington states, "Divorce is usually brutally painful to a child," she argues that "negative long-term effects have been exaggerated to the point where we now have created a self-fulfilling prophecy" (p. 7). An important point that Hetherington raises is that many children of divorce are "uncommonly resilient, mature, responsible, and focused."

So, which is it: Do adolescents suffer continuously, or do they fare well over time? Wallerstein and Lewis take a "middle of the road approach to this argument." They view divorce not so much as an acute stress from which the child recovers but instead a life-transforming experience that can have both positive and negatives outcomes. From this perspective, instead of debating whether or not adolescents suffer, researchers should focus on finding ways to ensure the life experience is positive. What are the risk factors for a negative experience, and what are the protective factors leading to a positive experience? For example, Wallerstein and Lewis identified grandparents as a protective factor, stating that children from divorced homes faired better if they had close stable grandparents. Children felt comforted by the models that the grandparents provided. On the other hand, a risk factor identified was mood and affect of the parents. Children who continued to suffer during adulthood often reported that it was difficult to move on if one parent remained lonely and unhappy.

Additional risk factors identified in the research include the initial separation such as the abrupt departure of one parent, continuing parent conflict after separation, ineffective or neglectful parenting, loss of important relationships such as extended family members, and financial/economic changes (Kelly, 2003). Protective factors identified by Kelly are competent custodial parents, effective parenting from the non-residential parent, and amicable versus high conflict relationship between the divorced parents. In summary, the outcomes for children and adolescents appear to be complex and dependent on many factors that can either have a detrimental effect on development or contribute to a positive outcome.

References/Further Readings

Hetherington, E. M., & Elmore, A. M. (2003). Risk and resilience in children coping with their parents' divorce and remarriage. In S. S. Luthar (Ed.), *Resilience and vulnerability: Adaptation in the context of childhood adversities* (pp. 183– 212). Cambridge: Cambridge University Press.

Hetherington, E. M., & Kelly, J. (2002). *For better or for worse: Divorce reconsidered*. New York: Norton.

Kelly, J. B. (2003). Changing perspectives on children's adjustment following divorce: A view for the United States. *Childhood*, 10, 237-254.

National Vital Statistics Report, 2005, Volume 54. National Centre for Health Statistics, Hyattsville, MD. http://www.cdc.gov/nchs/products/pubs/pubd/nvsr/54/54-pre.htm.

Peris, T. S., & Emery, R. E. (2004). A prospective study of the consequences of marital disruption for adolescents: Predisruption family dynamics and postdisruption adolescent adjustment. *Journal of Clinical Child and Adolescent Psychology*, 33, 694-704.

Statistics Canada. (2006). Divorces by province and territory. CANSIM, table 053-0002, http://www40.statcan.ca/101/cst01/famil02.htm.

Sun, Y., & Li, Y. (2002). Children's well-being during parents' marital disruption process: A pooled time-series analysis. *Journal of Marriage and Family*, 64, 472-488.

Wallerstein, J. S., & Lewis, J. M. (2004). The unexpected legacy of divorce: Report of a 25-year study. *Psychoanalytic Psychology*, 21, 353-370.

ISSUE 13

Does Dating Impede Developmental Adjustment for Adolescents?

YES: Deborah P. Welsh, Catherine M. Grello, and Melinda S. Harper, from "When Love Hurts: Depression and Adolescent Romantic Relationships," in Paul Florsheim, ed., *Adolescent Romantic Relations and Sexual Behavior* (Lawrence Erlbaum, 2003)

NO: Wyndol Furman and Laura Shaffer, from "The Role of Romantic Relationships in Adolescent Development," in Paul Florsheim, ed., *Adolescent Romantic Relations and Sexual Behavior* (Lawrence Erlbaum, 2003)

ISSUE SUMMARY

YES: Researchers Welsh, Grello, and Harper, while not arguing that all teen romantic relationships are detrimental, demonstrate how such relationships can be a catalyst for teens who are at-risk to develop depression.

NO: Wyndol Furman, a child clinical psychologist at the University of Denver, and Laura Shaffer make the case for areas where romantic relationships can impact teen development. While many of their arguments are speculative or supported only by correlational research, they make a compelling case for the benefits of teenage romances.

When should teens be allowed to date? Is this just inconsequential "puppy love"? Are these relationships good or bad for adolescents? Should adults attempt to dissuade teens from dating? These are questions that capture the debate about adolescent romantic relationships.

Dating is a key process for adolescents. Much of teens' time is spent attempting to date, talking about dating, actually dating, and recovering from dating relationships. Thus, teen romantic relationships seem like a normal part of adolescent development. Early developmental theorists in the 1950s, such as Harry Stack Sullivan and Erik Erikson, argued that dating in early and middle adolescence prepares the teen for developing mature, functional adult interpersonal relationships. However, little research has addressed the impact of romantic relationship on adolescent development. Rather, most research in the area of close adolescent relationships has focused on relationships with peers or parents.

Much of the research that does exist seems to focus on adolescent romantic relationships as a negative outcome; that is; romantic relationships are often viewed as part of a constellation of problem behavior such as early initiation of intercourse and other sexual activities, alcohol and substance use, parental defiance, and delinquency. Romantic relationships have been linked to stress experiences for adolescents. For example, research suggests that teens sometimes enter into romantic relationships for undesirable motivations such as to elevate their social status, to prove their "maturity," or to help them separate from their family. Teen romance can add to stress levels by interfering with friendships and parental relationships as well as perhaps distracting the adolescent from his/her academic achievement. Also, teen romantic relationships have been investigated as contributing to negative emotions that may lead to depression. Breaking up, in particular, can have a variety of negative effects on youth, including having a negative impact on the adolescent's self-image and self-worth, feeling undesirable, feelings of betrayal, and general sadness.

Less attention is focused on the many benefits of teen romantic relationships. For example, romantic partners are a significant source of social support for the adolescent, relationships are a source of strong positive emotions, and dating helps the adolescent become more autonomous. Romantic relationships can also be a means of developing better interpersonal skills and competencies, gaining status and popularity, and helping to solidify various social identities. Intrapersonally, the teen may develop a positive sense of self through dating (i.e., feel desirable, wanted, intimate) and positive self-regard. Research seems to suggest that affiliation, companionship, and friendship are critical components of romantic relationships for adolescent development.

Welsh, Grello, and Harper discuss what they call the "dark side" of adolescent romance. While these authors acknowledge the potentially positive aspects of teen romantic relationships, they present many of the potential pitfalls of such relationships and how these may lead at-risk individuals to depression, which can have an adverse impact on adolescent development. Furman and Shaffer, while acknowledging the potential pitfalls of teen romantic relationships, discuss the potential positive impact that such relationships can have, including facilitating identity development, enhancing peer and family relationships, providing positive sexual development, and encouraging academic achievement.

YES

Deborah P. Welsh, Catherine M. Grello, and Melinda S. Harper

When Love Hurts: Depression and Adolescent Romantic Relationships

The pervasiveness of depression along with the extremely serious psycholog-ical, social, and economic consequences it wreaks in our society makes it one of the most pressing mental health concerns of our time. Depression in adoles-cents is associated with detrimental consequences, including social impair-ment in family, peer, and romantic relationships, academic problems, suicide, and risk for future depressive episodes. Adolescence, particularly early to middle adolescence, is considered the pivotal time period during which overall rates of depression rise and gender differences in depressive symptoms emerge. Inter-estingly, this is also the time during which adolescents typically begin romantic relationships. Although romantic relationships clearly play a normative, healthful role in adolescent development for most adolescents . . ., this [paper] focuses on the dark side of adolescent romance. That is, we examine when romantic relationships may be detrimental to adolescent development and may be associated with the rise of depressive symptomatology as well as with the gender difference in depression that emerges during adolescence.

[We] first present . . . theoretical models explaining the etiology of adoles-cent depression and . . . theoretical models of adolescent romantic relationships. We attempt to integrate these perspectives in an effort to explain the link between romantic relationships and depressive symptomatology in adolescents. Our inte-grative model posits that a variety of individual characteristics may place certain adolescents at risk for developing depressive symptoms when exposed to the stres-sors inherent in romantic relationships. Second, we examine some of these stres-sors or challenges associated with different developmental stages of adolescents' romantic relationships. Finally, we [conclude with] practical implications. . . .

Models of Adolescent Depression

Most contemporary models of adolescent depression are multifaceted and include cognitive, interpersonal, socio-cultural, and biological components. . . . Some people respond to distressing feelings with a passive, ruminative style of cop-ing that tends to promote further depressive symptoms while others use more

From ADOLESCENT ROMANTIC RELATIONS AND SEXUAL BEHAVIOR: THEORY, RESEARCH, AND PRACTICAL IMPLICATIONS, Paul Florsheim, ed. by Deborah P. Welsh, Catherline M. Grello, and Melinda S. Harper, pp. 185–211. Copyright © 2003 by Lawrence Erlbaum Associates. Reprinted by permission. Note: The complete text of this article contains many references to specific studies described. The interested individual should refer to the original publication for these extensive citations. These references have been omitted here in the interest of brevity.

active, distracting types of strategies that are more effective in interfering with the positive feedback cycle of depressive symptoms. Girls and women are more likely to ruminate in response to depressive feelings, while boys and men are more likely to use the more active, and adaptive, coping styles . . . [The] challenge of mastering the new domain of developing and maintaining sexual/romantic relationships is the most prominent new hurdle experienced by adolescents.

Global interpersonal styles have also been suggested as an important component in developmental models of depression. . . . Interpersonally vulnerable individuals are preoccupied with the affection of others, with feelings of loneliness and helplessness, fear abandonment, desire intense closeness, and they have difficulty in expressing anger overtly. [When] individuals with this pattern of interpersonal vulnerability experience stressful events involving other people, intense feelings of interpersonal vulnerability are potentiated, and internalizing psychological disorders result. Once again, the role of adolescent romantic relationships is likely to serve as one of the most significant stressors for adolescents in this etiological model of depression. . . .

[Difficulties] in achieving individuation within parent–adolescent relationships may be reflected in later romantic relationships. These differences are manifested in maladaptive interpersonal behaviors that maintain and increase depressive symptoms in adolescents by exacerbating physiological stress responses to interpersonal conflict. . . . [One] style, wherein girls engage in interpersonal conflict but give up and concede to others, is [called agitated submission]. In contrast, boys with higher levels of depressive symptoms exhibit a behavioral pattern that is highly submissive, but low in conflict and more distancing [passive submission]. . . .

Adolescent romantic relationships play a significant role in these three models of adolescent depression. They provide the context in which precipitating ineffective cognitive coping strategies (e.g., rumination), potentiating feelings of interpersonal vulnerability, and/or ineffective behavioral coping are likely to manifest and be maintained.

Models of Adolescent Romantic Relationships

. . . Furman and Wehner (1994, 1997) . . . proposed a developmental theory of adolescent romantic relationships that builds upon attachment theory. A fundamental component of their theoretical model is the concept of "views," which refers to the preconceptions, beliefs, and expectations held by individuals about particular types of relationships. Furman and Wehner postulated that individual couple members' views of romantic relationships influence their patterns of interaction in their romantic relationships as well as the way they *interpret* the interactions that occur within those relationships. Thus, two members of the same dating couple may be involved in the same interaction and, due to differences in their views of romantic relationships, may interpret and respond to that interaction very differently. Furman and Wehner (1994, 1997) conceptualized individuals' views of romantic relationships as either *secure, dismissing,* or *preoccupied* in nature, similar to the categorization scheme used by attachment theorists. They asserted that individuals' views of romantic relationships are affected by romantic experiences and, in turn, affect adolescents' perceptions of their romantic experiences. Therefore, a correlation is expected between individuals' views of romantic relationships and their perceptions of the interaction occurring in their romantic relationships. In fact, empirical evidence [supports this].

. . . [One] of the key ways in which internal working models of past relationships influence adolescents' current romantic relationships is via their impact on expectations of attaining acceptance and avoiding rejection. [Adolescents develop] anxious or angry expectations of rejection as a result of a history of experiencing rejection from parents, peers, and romantic partners. These "rejection-sensitive" individuals possess a cognitive-affective processing system that becomes activated in social situations where rejection is possible, and influence the interpretation and course of their interactions in ways that confirm and maintain their rejection expectations. One way rejection-sensitive individuals may try to avoid rejection is by exercising self-silencing behaviors, including the suppression of their opinions, thus submerging their individual identity within the context of the romantic relationship. In our current project of high-school-aged adolescents, the Study of Tennessee Adolescent Romantic Relationships (STARR), we found that girls who reported the greatest loss of their sense of self in their romantic relationships were significantly more likely to report depressive symptoms when compared to all other adolescents. Interestingly, adolescent boys were twice as likely as girls to lose their sense of self in their romantic relationships. However, losing their sense of self in their romantic relationships did not seem to be problematic for the adolescent boys in the sample. There was no correlation between loss of self and depressive symptoms in boys.

In summary, . . . recent models of romantic relationship development highlight the importance of understanding the lenses that individual adolescents bring to their romantic relationships and the ways in which these lenses impact couple members' own perceptions of their interpersonal relationships and interactions. These models predict that individual qualities that adolescent couple members bring to their romantic relationships (i.e., their beliefs and expectations of relationships formed from their prior experiences of relationships) will be related to the nature of their current romantic relationships, their interactions within the context of these current romantic relationships, and their subjective understanding of these interactions. In a cyclical and self-fulfilling manner, adolescents' subjective understanding of their interactions impacts the nature of their interactions with their romantic partners which, in a recursive loop, further impacts their subjective understanding of those interactions.

Although these models were formulated to understand the normative development of adolescent romantic relationships, they have clear implications for the development of depression, especially when integrated with the models of depression discussed previously. For example, adolescents who transition to romantic relationships with insecure models of relationships and are highly sensitive to relational rejection will be likely to interpret their partners' behaviors in more negative ways, which will result with these individuals responding to their partners in less effective ways, such as self-silencing. . . .

Developmental Considerations of Romantic Relationships

. . . [The] similar timing between the increase in rates of depression, the emergence of gender differences in depression, and the onset of adolescent romantic relationships is probably not coincidental. Rather, theoretical and empirical evidence suggest that adolescent dating relationships may serve as a stressor facilitating depression, an interpersonal context in which maladaptive coping styles develop and are maintained, as well as a context in which symptoms of psychological distress become manifest. Our integrative model posits that a variety of individual characteristics may place certain adolescents at risk for developing depressive symptoms when exposed to the stressors inherent in romantic relationships. Some of the key individual characteristics differentiating deleterious romantic relationships from healthy normative development include gender (female), a ruminative cognitive style of coping, an interpersonally vulnerable style, an agitated submissive (girls) or passive submissive (boys) pattern of interpersonal behavioral coping, an insecure internal working model of relationships, rejection sensitivity, self-silencing behavior, and developmental level (e.g., premature commitment, premature transition to sexual intercourse). We argue that these elements gleaned from theories of depression and theories of romantic relationship development fit together to provide a framework for understanding the intersection between adolescents' romantic relationships and the emergence of adolescent depressive symptoms. We . . . now . . . [discuss] . . . specific aspects of romantic relationships that are particularly problematic for adolescents who . . . may be more vulnerable to the developmental challenges of romantic relationships.

Stressors Associated with the Romantic Relationship Context

Romantic relationships are the most affectively charged domain for adolescents, and, thus, are the single largest source of stress for adolescents. . . . In a high school sample, . . . girls attributed 34% of their strong emotions to real and fantasized romantic relationships and boys attributed 25% of their strong emotions to romantic relationships (Wilson-Shockley, 1995). The suggestion that romantic relationships accounted for between a quarter and a third of all middle teens' strong emotional states was quite impressive and far greater than any other single domain including school, family, or same-sex peer relationships. . . . Although the majority of these strong emotions attributed to romantic relationships were positive, a substantial minority (42%) were negative, including feelings of depression. . . .

In a recent empirical investigation of over 12,000 nationally representative adolescents between 12 and 17 years of age, Joyner and Udry (2000) examined the association between change in depressive symptoms over a 1-year period and involvement in a romantic relationship. They found that adolescents who became romantically involved during the year between data collection points showed more depressive symptoms than adolescents who were not romantically involved during the year. . . . [Females may be] more vulnerable to the detrimental impact of romantic relationships. Romantic relationships are a new domain for adolescents in which they must struggle to gain competence. It is probably not surprising that they occupy a disproportionately large portion of adolescents' thoughts and create more stress (both positive and negative) than any other domain. These studies provide strong and compelling empirical data to suggest that aspects of romantic relationships are stressful and related to depression in adolescents.

Adolescent romantic relationships have three developmental stages. There are different challenges associated with each stage of relationship development. In the first stage, *infatuation,* adolescents are concerned with whether or not the object of their attraction reciprocates their interest. . . . In the following sections, we examine [the] specific struggles associated with each of the developmental stages of adolescent dating: infatuation (stressor = unreciprocated love), dyadic dating stage (stressors = sexual behavior decision-making and infidelity), and the termination stage (stressor = breaking-up).

I. Infatuation Stage

Unreciprocated Love

Adolescents are clearly capable of experiencing romantic love. However, quite frequently, these feelings are one-sided and unreciprocated. The feelings of love for another can exist even when the adolescent has rarely or never spoken to the admired one [or] when the admired individual shows no interest in return. Fantasy can be strong, as many adolescents believe that the admired one returns the same feelings of admiration. When the fantasy is potent, adolescents frequently misinterpret signals from the admired individual. These misinterpretations can increase the adolescents' vulnerability to disappointment when the adolescent eventually discovers that the individual does not return the admiration.

Although adolescents typically report positive feelings during the pursuit of a relationship, when the rejection from unreciprocated adolescent love occurs, the rejected adolescent frequently reports decreased self-esteem and despair, increased humiliation and feelings of inferiority, and decreased feelings of desirability and attractiveness. These negative emotions are reportedly devastating and often enduring, as the adolescent not only has to deal with the personal rejection but the abandonment of the fantasy. Individuals who enter an unrequited love relationship who are rejection sensitive, have insecure attachment models, tend to ruminate, are interpersonally vulnerable, or have agitated submissive interpersonal patterns of interaction would be expected to be particularly prone to depressive symptoms following the rejection of an unreciprocated love relationship.

II. Dyadic Dating Stage

[If the interest is reciprocated, adolescents may move to the second stage of romantic relationships.]

Sexual Decision Making

Sexual behaviors are an important aspect of adolescents' romantic relationships. In fact, the incorporation of sexuality into relationships is the primary element that distinguishes romantic relationships from adolescents' other close relationships. Sexual intercourse, the primary and almost exclusive sexual behavior examined by researchers, has become a statistically normative behavior among adolescents. . . . Sexual activity is clearly prevalent in adolescent romantic relationships. The decision about what sexual activities should and will occur within the context of any given adolescent's romantic relationships and the sequella of those decisions, however, are often associated with a great deal of turmoil.

Adolescents report that peer pressure is one of the strongest motivations for engaging in sexual behavior, and peer group rejection or acceptance of sexual intercourse is very much related to adolescents' decisions to abstain or transition to sexual intercourse. The decision to have sexual intercourse is experienced differently by adolescent males and females, with females experiencing first intercourse significantly more negatively than males. It is likely that adolescents who are more vulnerable to depression, particularly interpersonally vulnerable adolescents and less securely attached or rejection sensitive adolescents, are especially susceptible to the power of peer pressure. In addition, these high-risk adolescents may look to sexuality to compensate for poor past relationships. Attachment style has been empirically associated with adolescent sexual behavior[;] insecurely attached adolescents are more sexually promiscuous, have sex more frequently, and engage in sexual behaviors at an earlier age. . . .

Sexual behaviors have been strongly linked with depression, especially in adolescent females. . . . This link is strongest in younger adolescents, suggesting that sexual intercourse may be a clearer marker of psychological distress when it occurs early or off-time rather than when it occurs at a more normative time. . . . Tubman, Windle, and Windle (1996) found evidence that premature sexual debut was associated with depression and that late transition to intercourse was associated with decreased self-esteem and poor social relationships. . . .

In an earlier project from our lab, we observed and interviewed 61 middle- to late-adolescent heterosexual couples in an intensive study of their communication processes, their relational and psychological functioning, and their sexual behavior. We found that distinct sexual behaviors were related in very different ways to the couple members' individual and relational functioning. Specifically, we found that the more affectionate sexual behaviors of hand-holding, kissing, and light petting were associated with more committed and more intimate relationships. Whether or not couples were engaging in sexual intercourse was not related to their individual or relational functioning. However, sexual intercourse was associated with couple members' perceptions of higher levels of interpersonal conflict in their videotaped conversations. Additionally, we found that couple members' experience of having power or control in their sexual decision making was related to psychological well-being in the adolescent females. Female couple members who felt that they had less voice than their boyfriends in decisions about sex reported lower self-esteem. These findings suggest that sexual behaviors and decision-making are related to adolescents' mental health.

In summary, sexual behaviors are associated with depressive symptoms in what is probably a bi-directional or cyclic fashion. That is, depressed adolescents are more likely to engage in sexual behaviors, specifically sexual intercourse, and these behaviors are likely to further exacerbate adolescents' depression. However, it is important to keep in mind that most of the literature on adolescent sexuality has operated from a deficit model, in which sexual behaviors (intercourse) are assumed to be a marker or symptom of psychological distress in adolescents. Thus, research operating from this deficit paradigm has focused on comparing adolescents who have had sexual intercourse with those who have not. This sort of investigation prevents an understanding of the diversity of adolescents' experiences about their sexuality. Further, by focusing exclusively on heterosexual intercourse as the definition of sexuality, the current research literature fails to capture the diversity of sexual behaviors experienced by heterosexual as well as gay and lesbian adolescents and the mental health implications of these behaviors. It is important for future research in this area to explore adolescent sexuality from a normative, developmental position that allows us to understand the meanings that adolescents ascribe to sexual behaviors and to their decisions about whether to engage in particular sexual activities. This approach will allow researchers to differentiate the adolescents for whom sexual behavior is symptomatic of psychological disturbance from those for whom sexual behavior is associated with healthy, developmentally appropriate exploration.

Infidelity

Heterosexual adolescents' romantic relationships are typically characterized by mutual expectations for emotional and sexual fidelity. . . . Investigations of heterosexual adolescents' attitudes toward sexual betrayal reveal very low tolerance of infidelity from both males and females. Adolescents typically define infidelity in terms of sexual behaviors, especially petting and intercourse. . . . In spite of strong personal as well as cultural heterosexual prescriptions for exclusive dyadic romantic relationships, extra-dyadic romantic involvement is extremely common during adolescence among heterosexual and gay youth. . . .

[The] extremely high degree of sexual betrayal identified among adolescent romantic couples in spite of strong personal attitudes and cultural prescriptions about the unacceptability of infidelity may stem from competing and conflicting developmental demands of adolescence. Two of the most important developmental tasks of adolescence include identity development and intimacy development. Adolescents' search for identity is facilitated by exploration, including multiple romantic partners. To the extent that the perception of oneself as sexually and socially desirable is important to adolescents' developing identities, opportunities for greater sexual experiences that promote positive self-image will be difficult to resist. These developmental needs conflict, however, with adolescents' need to develop the capacity to maintain intimate, committed, enduring relationships. . . .

Unfaithfulness in a romantic relationship can be particularly devastating to adolescents who value exclusivity as they experience the violation as a loss of trust and loyalty in addition to the loss of the romantic partner. Adolescents express the belief that when a partner cheats, the relationship is irreparably damaged. Most adolescent romantic relationships do not survive infidelity and are typically terminated once the transgression is exposed, and both partners appear to experience a range of negative emotions. . . .

The guilt and confusion over violating one's personal values along with the feelings of excitement experienced in conjunction with the infidelity may lead certain unfaithful adolescents toward depression. Likewise, the loss of trust, loss of relationship, and the feelings of personal undesirableness experienced by the partner cheated on can also initiate a negative spiral of depression in vulnerable youth. . . .

III. Termination Stage

Breaking Up

Breaking up with a romantic partner is common. . . . The termination of these emotionally intense relationships is often traumatic for heterosexual as well as for gay and lesbian adolescents and clearly amplifies an adolescent's vulnerability for depression. Gay, lesbian, and heterosexual couples have not been found to differ in either their reasons for dissolving a relationship or on the levels of distress caused by the breakup. Several investigations have found that females are especially susceptible to depressive symptomatology immediately following the dissolution of a romantic relationship.

Most studies have found that initial distress following the breakup of a romantic relationship is high and then subsides as time passes. However, for some adolescents, especially female adolescents, the pain can endure. . . . Mearns (1991) . . . found evidence linking clinical depression with recent romantic relationship dissolution, particularly for females. . . .

Another explanation for the gender difference in the impact of romantic relationship termination may be a consequence of the intensity of emotion, commitment, and investment in the relationship. Although males report falling in love more frequently and at younger ages than females, females report experiencing more commitment and more passionate feelings towards their partners. Studies have consistently demonstrated that increased commitment leads to increased relationship investment. . . . [The] intensity of distress following the dissolution of a romantic relationship is dependent on the amount of investment the individual had in the relationship. Thus, females' tendency to be more committed and have more investment in their romantic relationships, possibly in conjunction with their greater tendency to use less adaptive cognitive and interpersonal coping strategies, may contribute to the greater incidence of depression they experience following the termination of their romantic relationships.

There is evidence that the impact of relationship termination may depend on who initiates the breakup as well as the availability of alternative resources and social support. The partner who initiates the termination of the relationship suffers less initial emotional distress following the breakup than the aggrieved partner. The initiator of a desired breakup has more control over the breakup and therefore, has had more time to mentally prepare for the loss of the relationship. The initiator of a desired breakup is also likely to be the less committed member of the couple and is more likely to have alternative options. The partner who feels responsible for the problems that led up to the breakup, especially when this partner is female, often experiences strong distress along with guilt and self-blame following the relationship termination. Psychological distress following relationship dissolution subsides when adolescents begin new romantic relationships. This may stem from the increased self-esteem adolescents experience as a result of feeling renewed desirability, from the reparation of adolescents' fragile developing sense of personal identity which may be located within a relational domain, or from the resumption of day-to-day interactions, goals, and plans that were interrupted by the breakup. Social support in general facilitates recovery and adjustment following romantic relationship dissolution in the long run, although social support does little to relieve the initial distress of breaking up.

Conclusion

Taken together, the available theoretical and empirical evidence supports a link between adolescent romantic relationships and the development of depressive symptomatology. Programs and policies designed to address the profound problem of adolescent depression should target adolescent romantic relationships as a key component. Intervention/prevention strategies need to be designed at multiple levels of influence including interventions focused on impacting adolescents directly as well as programs aimed at influencing those who work with and care for adolescents. . . .

We have argued for a link between developmental models of depression and developmental models of adolescent romantic relationships. We have provided . . . evidence that suggests that certain cognitive and interpersonal strategies utilized by some adolescents, particularly female adolescents, along with insecure internal representations of interpersonal relationships put these adolescents at risk for developing depressive symptoms during their adolescent years. This risk may be expressed in the form of depression when these at-risk adolescents are faced with certain relational challenges common to adolescents as they learn to develop and maintain mature romantic relationships. We have recommended that depression prevention and intervention programs incorporate developmental theories and findings regarding adolescent romantic relationships with interpersonal and cognitive theories of depression in an attempt to change the ways in which adolescents interact within their romantic relationships, how they view their relationships, and how they cope with the challenging aspects of those relationships in order to promote healthier individual and relational functioning.

References

Furman, W., & Wehner, E. A. (1994). Romantic views: Toward a theory of adolescent romantic relationships. In R. Montemayor, G. R. Adams, & T. P. Gullotta (Eds.), *Personal relationships during adolescence* (pp. 168–195). Thousand Oaks, CA: Sage.

Furman, W., & Wehner, E. A. (1997). Adolescent romantic relationships: A developmental perspective. In S. Shulman & W. A. Collins (Eds.), *New directions for child development: Romantic relationships in adolescence: Developmental perspectives* (pp. 21–36). San Franciso: Jossey-Bass.

Joyner, K., & Udry, R. (2000). You don't bring me anything but down: Adolescent romance and depression. *Journal of Health and Social Behavior, 41,* 369–391.

Mearns, J. (1991). Coping with a breakup: Negative mood regulation expectancies and depression following the end of a romantic relationship. *Journal of Personality and Social Psychology, 60*(2), 327–334.

Tubman, J. G., Windle, M., & Windle, R. C. (1996). The onset and cross-temporal patterning of sexual intercourse in middle adolescence: Prospective relation with behavioral and emotional problems. *Child Development, 67,* 327–343.

Wilson-Shockley, S. (1995). *Gender differences in adolescent depression: The contribution of negative affect.* Unpublished master's thesis, University of Illinois at Urbana-Champaign.

Wyndol Furman and
Laura Shaffer

 **NO**

The Role of Romantic Relationships in Adolescent Development

Most of us would characterize our adolescent romantic relationships as short-lived and superficial. In some respects, this description is correct. Most adolescent relationships only last a few weeks or months; it is unlikely that these relationships have the depth and complexity that characterize long-term committed relationships.

At the same time, the characterization of these relationships as short and superficial is incomplete. These relationships are central in adolescents' lives. They are a major topic of conversation among adolescents. Real or fantasized relationships are the most common cause of strong positive and strong negative emotions—more so than friendships, relationships with parents, or school. Moreover, adolescents are not the only ones who see these relationships as significant. The formation of romantic relationships is often thought to be one of the important developmental tasks of adolescence, and these relationships have significant implications for health and adjustment.

Not only are adolescent romantic relationships significant in their own right, but . . . they play an important role in shaping the general course of development during adolescence. In particular, adolescents face a series of tasks that include (a) the development of an identity, (b) the transformation of family relationships, (c) the development of close relationships with peers, (d) the development of sexuality, and (e) scholastic achievement and career planning. In the sections that follow, we describe how romantic relationships may play a role in each of these key developmental tasks.

Three caveats are warranted. First, the research primarily has been conducted with heterosexual adolescents in Western cultures, and we know little about gay, lesbian, and bisexual relationships or romantic relationships in other cultures. Second, even the existing literature on Western heterosexual romantic relationships is limited. The question of what impact they have on development has received almost no attention. Thus, our comments are often speculative and will need to be tested empirically. Finally, the effects of romantic relationships vary from individual to individual. As will be seen repeatedly, the specific impact they have is likely to depend heavily on the nature of the particular experiences.

Romantic Relationships and Identity Development

According to Erikson, the key developmental task of adolescence is the development of identity. During early adolescence, there is a proliferation of self representations that vary as a function of the social context. That is, early adolescents develop a sense of themselves with their mothers, fathers, friends, romantic partners, and others. Sometimes their different selves may contradict one another, but such contradictions are usually not acknowledged. In middle adolescence, they begin to recognize such seeming contradictions in their conceptions of themselves, and may be conflicted or confused. By late adolescence, many of them are able to integrate the seeming contradictions into a coherent picture.

Romantic experiences may play a role in the development of a sense of self or identity in two ways. First, adolescents develop distinct perceptions of themselves in the romantic arena. They do not simply have a concept of themselves with peers, but have different self-schemas of themselves with the general peer group, with close friends, and in romantic relationships. Romantic self-concept is related to whether one has a romantic relationship and to the quality of that relationship, suggesting that romantic experiences may affect one's sense of self in the romantic domain. Thus, adolescents who have had positive experiences may think of themselves as attractive partners, whereas those who have had adverse romantic experiences may have little confidence in their ability to be appealing partners or have successful relationships.

Second, romantic experiences and romantic self-concept may also affect one's global self-esteem. This effect is poignantly expressed in our of our teen's reflections about her romantic experiences, including those with an abusive partner. "Hum, what have I gained? (6 sec.pause). I feel I haven't gained like a lot, but I feel like I lost a lot. I lost my self-respect. I don't respect myself. It's like I feel like I have no self-esteem, no self-control, no nothing." Consistent with her comments, romantic self-concept has been empirically found to be substantially related to self-worth. Romantic self-concept is also related to one's self-concept in other domains, particularly physical appearance and peer acceptance.

Although global self-esteem and perceived competence in various domains are fundamental aspects of self-representations, the concept of identity entails more than these. In the process of developing an identity, adolescents acquire moral and religious values, develop a political ideology, tentatively select and prepare for a career, and adopt a set of social roles, including gender roles. Romantic relationships may facilitate the development of these facets of identity. . . . On the other hand, sometimes romantic relationships may hinder the identity development process. For example, parenthood—a potential consequence of romantic involvement—is thought to have a detrimental effect on adolescents' normative exploration of identity because of the constant demands and responsibilities it entails. Unfortunately, we can only speculate about how romantic relationships may facilitate or hinder identity development, as we have little empirical data about the role they may play. We know that peers and friends influence adolescents' attitudes and behaviors, but as yet, the specific influence of romantic relationships or romantic partners simply has not been examined.

One particularly promising domain to study is gender-role identity. According to the gender intensification hypothesis, early adolescence is a period in which gender-related expectations become increasingly differentiated. Girls are expected to adhere to feminine stereotypes of behavior, whereas boys are expected to adhere to masculine stereotypes. It is commonly thought that the emergence of dating may be one of the most powerful factors contributing to the intensification of conventional gender roles. Romantic partners, as well as other peers, may reinforce or punish different gender-related behaviors or roles; certainly adolescents are likely to act in ways that they think might make them more attractive to members of the other sex. Of course, different romantic partners are likely to have different expectations regarding gender roles, and one's own experiences in romantic relationships would be expected to affect one's concepts of gender roles.

The Transformation of Family Relationships

During adolescence, relationships with parents and other family members undergo significant changes. . . . Romantic relationships may play a role in these transformations of family relationships in several ways. At the most basic level, adolescents spend less time with family members and more time with the other sex or in romantic relationships as they grow older. Those who have romantic relationships spend less time with family members than those who are not currently involved with someone.

Romantic relationships are also a common source of conflict and tension in the family. . . . Dating and romantic relationships are topics in which parents and adolescents have different expectations and both are invested in exercising jurisdiction. . . . In other instances, . . . conflicts with family members may lead some adolescents to seek out romantic relationships to escape family problems. . . .

[Parents] may have ambivalent feelings about their children's romantic relationships. For example, mothers report being both joyful that their daughters are happy, and yet sometimes jealous and aware of the loss of an exclusive tie. Similarly, the satisfaction of seeing their sons mature can be counterbalanced by the realization that they are growing up and eventually leaving the household. . . . A serious relationship can be seen as an intrusion or threat to the family. . . .

Although conflict and ambivalent feelings about romantic relationships may occur commonly, these should not be overstated. In popular stereotypes, adolescence is thought of as period of great strife between parents and peers, but in fact, peer and parental influences are typically synergistic. We believe that the same synergism may be characteristic of romantic relationships and family relationships. . . .

The links between supportive behavior in relationships with romantic partners and parents are complicated. As adolescents grow older, they are more likely to turn to a boyfriend or girlfriend for support [and] less likely to seek support from their parents. The early phases of the transition from a parent as the primary attachment figure to a romantic partner may begin in adolescence, particularly in late adolescence. Specifically, adolescents may begin to turn to their partners or peers for a safe haven, although their parents are likely to remain as their primary secure base.

[The] amount of support in the two types of relationships at any particular age is positively correlated. Perhaps the ability to be supportive in one relationship carries over to the other relationship. Having a supportive romantic relationship (vs. just any romantic relationship) may also have a positive effect on one's general emotional state, which in turn may foster positive interactions in the home. Thus, although romantic relationships can be a source of strain on relationships with parents, they may have some positive effects on these relationships in other instances.

The Development of Close Relationships with Peers

Concomitant with the changes in the family throughout adolescence are significant changes in peer relationships. . . . Over the course of adolescence, they increasingly turn to their peers for support as these relationships become more intimate in nature. . . .

Adolescent romantic relationships may contribute to adolescents' peer relations in several ways. . . . [Adolescents] spend increasing amounts of time with their peers, and these changes in the sheer frequency of interaction primarily occur in interactions with the other sex or in romantic relationships. One function such interactions serve is affiliation. These affiliative interactions are both stimulating and utilitarian in nature. Such interchanges provide opportunities for reciprocal altruism, mutualism, and social play. Adolescents may develop their capacities to cooperate and co-construct a relationship. Moreover, the interactions are very rewarding in nature, as spending time with the other sex or having a romantic relationship is associated with positive emotionality.

The presence of such romantic relationships is also likely to influence the relationships one has with other peers. A boy/girlfriend becomes part of the adolescent's network and, in a significant minority of instances, remains part of the network even after the romantic element of the relationship has dissolved. He or she may introduce the teen to other adolescents. If the relationship becomes more serious, the social networks of the two overlap more as mutual friendships develop. . . .

Just as the impact on family relationships varies, romantic relationships' effects on peer relations do also. For example, three different patterns of relations between the peer group and romantic relationships [have been] identified. . . . In some cases the peer group became less salient as the romantic relationship was given priority. Sometimes, the choice between peers and romantic relationships was a source of conflict between the adolescent and the peers or partner. Finally, sometimes the peer group relations remained unchanged by the presence of the new relationship.

Romantic relationships can also affect one's standing in the peer group, as dating in Western cultures has traditionally served the functions of status grading and status achievement. Dating a particularly attractive or popular person could improve one's popularity or reaffirm that one is popular. . . .

Additionally, adolescents are likely to date those who share similar interests, attitudes, and values to theirs. Their dating selections may reinforce the reputation they have or identify the crowd they are seen as being part of. That is, their peers are likely to think they are similar to the individuals they are dating.

Finally, although double standards of sexual behavior are much less striking than they used to be, ethnographic work suggests that having sexual intercourse can still enhance boys' status in the peer group, whereas it may jeopardize the status of girls in at least some peer groups. Similarly, having a serious romantic relationship can lead to ridicule and jeopardize one's status in some peer groups where members of the other sex are simply seen as objects for sexual conquest.

[Romantic] relationships . . . can affect friendships in particular. . . . Often a romantic partner becomes the best friend, displacing the old friend.

Regardless of whether romantic relationships do or do not displace a friendship, it seems likely that the experiences in friendships and romantic relationships may influence each other. Both forms of relationships entail intimate disclosure, support seeking and giving, and mutuality. The skills that these require appear likely to carry over from one type of relationship to the other. . . .

Sexual Development

The development of sexuality is another key task in adolescence. As adolescents' bodies begin to mature in reproductive capacities, their sexual desires increase. Most adolescents begin to experiment with sexual behavior, and gradually develop some comfort with their sexuality. . . .

It almost seems unnecessary to say that romantic relationships play a key role in the development of sexuality. Certainly, sexual behavior often occurs in brief encounters, as adolescents "hook-up" with each other for an evening. Additionally, sexual behaviors, particularly mild forms of sexual behavior, commonly occur with friends with whom adolescents are not romantically involved. Nevertheless, casual or committed romantic relationships are primary contexts for sexual behavior and learning about sexuality. The majority of adolescents first have intercourse with someone they are going steady with or know well and like a lot. Moreover, most teenagers are selective about with whom they have intercourse. . . .

Aside from the idea that romantic relationships are a primary context for the development of sexuality, we know remarkably little about the specific role these relationships play. In fact, we know more about the influence of peers and parents than about romantic partners. Yet, it is difficult to believe that the partner and the nature of the relationship do not play critical roles in determining sexual behavior and in determining what is learned from the experiences.

Some descriptive information exists on the characteristics of sexual partners. For example, . . . [adolescents] are also more likely to have sexual intercourse for the first time with someone who is already sexually active than someone who is not. . . . [The] modal reason given for first having intercourse is to have the partner love them more. These findings suggest that the characteristics of the partner and one's feelings about the partner are critical determinants of sexual behavior, but we still know little about the particulars.

In part, the absence of information about the role of romantic relationships may reflect the field's focus on sexual intercourse, contraception, and pregnancy and their demographic correlates. The field has emphasized these components because of the significance they have for health. Yet, an understanding of adolescent sexuality requires a broader perspective. Bukowski, Sippola, and Brender (1993) proposed that the development of a healthy sense of sexuality includes: (a) learning about intimacy through interaction with peers, (b) developing an understanding of personal roles and relationships, (c) revising one's body schema to changes in size, shape, and capability, (d) adjusting to erotic feelings and experiences and integrating them into one's life, (e) learning about social standards and practices regarding sexual expression, and (f) developing an understanding and appreciation of reproductive processes. We believe that one's romantic relationships are likely to be one of the primary, if not the primary context, for learning about most of those facets of sexuality. Romantic relationships provide a testing ground not only for the *how* of sexual behavior but also for the *what* and *when*. They provide a context in which adolescents discover what is attractive and arousing. Adolescents learn what they like in their partners and what partners tend to like. They learn to reconcile their sexual desires, their moral values, and their partners' desires.

Finally, a critical facet of sexual development is the establishment or solidification of sexual orientation. Much of the existing research on adolescent sexuality and romantic relationships has focused on heterosexual adolescents, but current estimates indicate that approximately 10% of youth in the U.S. will consider themselves gay, lesbian, or bisexual at some point in their lives. Many sexual minority youth become aware of their same-gender attractions in early to mid-adolescence. . . . The majority . . . date heterosexually. Adolescents who are questioning their sexual orientation often find that these relationships help them determine or confirm their sexual preferences.

Scholastic Achievement and Career Planning

Around the beginning of adolescence, students in the United States make a transition from elementary school to middle school or junior high. In middle adolescence, they move on to high school. Some continue on to colleges or vocational schools in late adolescence, whereas others complete their formal education when they graduate from high school, and still others drop out of middle school or high school. Similar educational transitions occur in other Western societies. What is common across Western cultures, at least, is that the emphasis on academic learning increases with age, and students began to take increasingly different paths. . . .

[Early] involvement in romantic relationships has been linked with poorer scholastic achievement. In fact, romantic involvement and sexual behavior have been found to be negatively correlated with academic achievement throughout adolescence. Such associations could exist because those who are less academically oriented may be more likely to develop romantic relationships, or because romantic relationships may have an adverse effect on school achievement.

The time spent with a romantic partner could distract from schoolwork, but we suspect that any such effect may be highly dependent on the characteristics of the partner and the nature of the relationship. . . . That is, some partners may detract from school, but others may promote achievement by studying together, helping with homework, encouraging achievement, or providing support. . . .

Romantic partners may also influence career plans and aspirations. They can serve as comrades with whom to share ideas and dreams. They may encourage or discourage particular careers or educational plans. Developing a committed relationship, deciding to get married, or having a child is also likely to affect the plans for the future. . . . [Romantic] relationships may have either benefits or drawbacks for career plans, depending on the particular circumstances.

Clinical and Educational Implications

Our discussion of the role of romantic relationships in adolescent development has a number of implications for clinicians, educators, and parents. Perhaps the most obvious is how important romantic relationships can be in adolescents' lives. Not only are they central in the eyes of adolescents, but we have described the impact they may have on adolescent development.

Often, however, adults tend to downplay the significance of these relationships. Parents may tease their teens about a romantic relationship, or dismiss it as "only puppy love" and try to discourage them from getting too romantically involved as adolescent. In part, such reactions are understandable. . . . Romantic experiences entail a number of risks, such as pregnancy, sexual victimization, and violence. As valid as these parental concerns may be, however, they miss the point to some degree. Even if the relationships are relatively superficial, they are phenomologically quite important, and as we have suggested, may contribute to adolescent development. Thus, although parental monitoring of adolescent romantic experiences seems highly desirable, some sensitivity to the significance of the relationships for youth seems important as well. Disparaging or derogating a teen's relationship is not likely to be an effective parenting strategy. . . .

In general, those working with adolescents would want to consider the role romantic experiences play in different aspects of development. For example, sex education programs may want to consider the role relationships play in sexual behavior, and not just focus on anatomy and contraceptive practices. Similarly, because the romantic domain is an important one in identity development, clinicians working with adolescents who are struggling with identity issues may want to consider how these issues are enacted in relationships. Clinicians and parents should also be sensitive to the role romantic experiences may play in the process of redefining relationships with family members or peers. . . .

Conclusions

Although we have tried to make the case that romantic relationships may influence the course of adolescent development, . . . evidence is quite limited. Not only has relatively little research been conducted on these relationships in adolescence, but also the existing work has been guided primarily by models in which these relationships are treated as outcomes. For example, most research . . . seems to implicitly be guided by the idea that friendships or family relationships affect romantic relationships. The studies, however, are all correlational, and in most cases, the data are gathered at one time point. Thus, it is at least theoretically possible that the causal influences are in the other direction, or in both directions.

The limitations in our data bases cannot be corrected by simply recognizing that correlation does not imply causation. In designing our research, we need to consider deliberately how romantic relationships may impact other adolescent relationships or facets of development. This point is nicely illustrated in the literature on parental reactions to dating relationships. Some studies suggested that parental support is associated with increased or continued involvement in a dating relationship (Lewis, 1972), whereas other work suggested that romantic relationships could be enhanced by parental interference—the Romeo and Juliet effect (Driscoll, Davis, & Lipetz, 1972). The issue here is not that the findings are contradictory, however, but that the work had only considered the idea that parents may shape their offsprings' romantic relationships. Little consideration was given to the idea that late adolescents may also be attempting to shape their parents' impressions of the relationship and thus, may modify their own interactions with their parents. Leslie, Huston, and Johnson (1986), however, found that the vast majority of late adolescents monitor the information they provide about their romantic relationships, and have made multiple efforts to influence their parents' opinions about the romantic relationships. The parents, too, had often communicated either approving or disapproving reactions. Thus, by considering the idea that the paths of influence may be bi-directional, the investigators provided a better understanding of the process than if they had simply tested a unidirectional model.

It is also important to remember that the effects of romantic experiences may not be salutary. We have focused mainly on how romantic relationships may contribute to the normative developmental tasks of adolescence, but there are risks as well. Approximately 20% to 25% of young women are victims of dating violence or aggression. Adolescent romantic break-ups are one of the strongest predictors of depression, multiple-victim killings, and suicidal attempts or completions (Brent et al., 1993; Fessenden, 2000; Joyner & Udry, 2000; Monroe et al., 1999). Most incidents of sexual victimization are perpetrated by a romantic partner. The sexual activity that commonly co-occurs with romantic involvement places adolescents at risk for sexually transmitted diseases or becoming pregnant.

Perhaps the critical point is that the impact of romantic experiences is likely to vary from individual to individual. In the various sections . . . , we have tried to emphasize how not only the existence of a romantic relationship, but the quality of that relationship or the timing of the involvement may determine what the outcome of the experience will be. . . . [The] characteristics of the partner will also influence the nature of the romantic experience and its impact.

The emphasis on the variability of romantic experiences points out the need to identify the critical processes that are responsible for any impact that romantic experiences have. It may not be the simple presence of a relationship, but instead certain features or experiences that occur within the relationship that determine the outcome. . . .

Finally, in order to understand the impact of romantic relationships, we will need to understand the context in which they occur. The nature of these experiences vary as a function of the social and cultural context in which they occur. Conversely, we need to separate out the specific influence of romantic experiences from related experiences. . . . [It] had been shown that peer relationships in general had an impact on development, but as yet, nobody had examined the specific impact of romantic relationships. Although romantic relationships certainly share many features with other forms of peer relations, they also have some distinct features that may lead them to have a different impact than other peer relationships.

In summary, we have tried to discuss how romantic relationships may contribute to various facets of adolescent development, including the development of an identity, the transformation of family relationships, the development of close relationships with peers, the development of sexuality, and scholastic achievement and career planning. The evidence is consistent with the idea that romantic experiences may play a role in these various domains, but the evidence is still limited. . . .

References

Brent, D. A., Perper, J. A., Moritz, G., Baugher, M., Roth, C., Balach, L., & Schweers, J. (1993). Stressful life events, psychopathology, and adolescent suicide: A case control study. *Suicide and Life-Threatening Behavior, 23,* 179–187.

Bukowski, W. M., Sippola, L., & Brender, W. M. (1993). Where does sexuality come from? In H. E. Barbaree, W. L. Marshall, & D. R. Laws (Eds.), *The juvenile sex offender* (pp. 84–103). New York: Guilford.

Driscoll, R., Davis, K. E., & Lipetz, M. E. (1972). Parental inteference and romantic love: The Romeo and Juliet effect. *Journal of Personality and Social Psychology, 24,* 1–10.

Fessenden, F. (2000, April 9). They threaten, seethe, and unhinge, then kill in quantity. *New York Times,* p. 1.

Joyner, K., & Udry, J. R. (2000). You don't bring me anything but down: Adoescent romance and depression. *Journal of Health and Social Behavior, 41,* 369–391.

Leslie, L. A., Huston, T. L., & Johnson, M. P. (1986). Parental reactions to dating relationships: Do they make a difference? *Journal of Marriage and the Family, 48,* 57–66.

Lewis, R. (1972). A developmental framework for the analysis of premarital dyadic formation. *Family Process, 11,* 16–25.

Monroe, S. M., Rohde, P., Seeley, J. R., & Lewinsohn, P. M. (1999). Life events and depression in adolescence: Relationship loss as a prospective risk factor for first onset of major depressive disorder. *Journal of Abnormal Psychology, 108,* 606–614.

POSTSCRIPT

Does Dating Impede Developmental Adjustment for Adolescents?

Based on both readings, it is clear that adolescent romantic relationships are important to teens and their development. While these relationships typically lack the seriousness and commitment levels involved in many adult romantic relationships, they should not be dismissed as "puppy love." Well over half of teens have had a romantic relationship in the past year and a half (see Bouchey & Furman, 2003) and these relationships appear to be of critical importance in teens' social lives.

Based on Welsh, Grello, and Harper, it is possible that these relationships can have a detrimental impact on the development of teens—particularly those who are at risk of depression. For the at-risk teen, the relationship may be a causal factor in the depression because of the potential negative events that can occur within the dating scenario (e.g., cheating, breakups, rejection) coupled with dysfunctional interpersonal styles (e.g., submissive response to conflict). Alternatively, a depressed individual may enter a romantic relationship in an attempt to distract him/herself from other unpleasant environmental events (e.g., child-parent conflict). There are many stages within the relationship cycle that may be interpreted negatively and may trigger depression by the depression-prone individual.

Furman and Shaffer's article depicts a more optimistic perspective on teen dating and its potential impact on development. The romantic relationship may have a variety of positive effects on the adolescent's identity development, family relationships, peer relations, sexual development, and scholastic achievement. While acknowledging the potential risks of teen dating (e.g., violence, unexpected pregnancy, depression), there are many positive growth experiences inherent in teen dating both intra- and interpersonally. The developmental impact on an adolescent who is dating is likely very complex, depending on an interaction of the individual, the situation, and the environment in which the dating occurs. Sadly, we do not know a lot about these possible "normal" dating sequences.

Clinicians, educators, and researchers need to develop better explicated theories of the normal progress of adolescent romantic relationships. Simply knowing that an adolescent is involved in a romantic relationship tells us little about needed intervention (e.g., to help prevent negative outcomes such as depression or relationship violence). Being able to predict which types of teens and which types of romantic relationships have negative consequences for the adolescent seems imperative for efforts to help these youth have positive growth experiences rather than experience detrimental outcomes. This is an area of adolescence that is in dire need of further research.

Also, it is important not to draw conclusions about adolescent romances without adequate information. In an interview with the online publication, *Hypography: Science for Everyone,* where Wyndol Furman was asked to comment on a study that found that adolescents in romantic relationships were more depressed, more likely to engage in delinquency, and more prone to alcohol abuse than adolescents who did not date (Joyner & Udry, 2000). He was quoted as saying that "It's not like romantic relationships hold only danger for teens, without any benefits. . . . I don't buy that, any more than the idea that driving a car is only dangerous. There are risks, but are you going to give up your car?"

References/Further Readings

Adolescent lovers studied (14 February 2001). *Hypography: Science for Everyone.* http://www.hypography.com/article.cfm?id=29888.

Bouchey, H. A., & Furman, W. (2003). Dating and romantic experiences in adolescence. In G. R. Adams & M. D. Berzonsky (Eds.). *Blackwell handbook of adolescence* (pp. 313–329). Malden, MA: Blackwell.

Florsheim, P. (Ed.). (2003). *Adolescent romantic relations and sexual behavior: Theory, research, and practical implications.* Mahwah, NJ: Erlbaum.

Furman, W. (2002). The emerging field of adolescent romantic relationships. *Current Directions in Psychological Science,* 11(5), 177–180.

Joyner, K., & Udry, J. R. (2000). You don't bring me anything but down: Adolescent romance and depression. *Journal of Health and Social Behavior,* 41, 369–391.

ISSUE 14

Do Cyber-Friendships Hinder Healthy Adolescent Development?

YES: Lauren Donchi and Susan Moore, from "It's a Boy Thing: The Role of the Internet in Young People's Psychological Wellbeing," *Behavior Change* (vol. 21, no. 2, 2004)

NO: Elisheva F. Gross, Jaana Juvonen, and Shelly L. Gable, from "Internet Use and Well-Being in Adolescence," *Journal of Social Issues* (vol. 58, no. 1, 2002)

ISSUE SUMMARY

YES: Psychologists Lauren Donchi and Susan Moore suggest that adolescent boys who rate their on-line friendships as very important are more likely to have lower self-esteem and to be lonely. Those with more face-to-face friendships have more self-esteem and are less lonely.

NO: Elisheva Gross and colleagues, researchers of adolescent psychology, conclude that adolescents mainly engage in on-line communication with close others, and such communication is just as effective as face-to-face communication and is mainly devoted to ordinary yet intimate topics (e.g., friends, gossip, etc.).

In recent years, the Internet has increasingly assumed an important role in everyday life. In 2005 in Canada, 67.9 percent of households had at least one regular Internet user. This was up from 64 percent in 2003 and 59 percent in 2002 (Statistics Canada, 2004). In the United States, rates are similar with 68 percent of the population using the Internet on a regular basis (Pew Internet Report, 2005a). In both countries, usage is very dependent on children and adolescents. Homes with unmarried children under age 18 have the highest rates of Internet use, with more and more children and adolescents using it as a means of communication (e.g., e-mail, Instant Messenger, and chat rooms). More specifically, 87 percent of American adolescents between the ages of 12 and 17 have Internet access (Pew Internet Report, 2005b). Of these, more than 90 percent reported using e-mail on a regular basis, approximately 50 percent reported using Instant Messaging, and 22 percent reported participating in on-line chat rooms. Not surprisingly, these statistics are age dependent. In other words, adolescent use increases with age, such that 43 percent of 10–11-year-olds versus 86 percent of 16–17-year-olds use Instant Messenger programs such as MSN (Pew Internet Report, 2004).

Instant messaging and chat rooms are ways of sending instant real-time messages to other on-line users. It is a rapidly growing way of communicating, especially among today's adolescents. The text-based messages between two or more individuals who are simultaneously on-line are generally informal (i.e., without punctuation and often with grammatical errors). In addition to text messaging, users can view each other as they chat (e.g., using a webcam), send or receive files, and play games. Many youth are also using their cell phones to text message while away from their computer. With so many youth using MSN and other on-line communication programs, it seems pertinent to examine the effects on psychosocial development. Are these cyber-relationships healthy?

Past research has found that face-to-face communication and participation in social groups have a positive effect on levels of social support, probability of having fulfilling personal relationships, self-esteem, commitment to social norms, and overall psychological well-being. Because the Internet permits communication and social interaction, time spent on-line can facilitate communication with distant friends and relatives. It can also facilitate conversation with friends close by without having to plan for get-togethers (Parks & Roberts, 1998).

Although positive outcomes such as these have been reported, it has been argued that the benefits depend on the quality of the on-line relationships as well as what adolescents are giving up to spend time chatting on-line. In other words, cyber-friendships may not be of the same quality as face-to-face friendships, and time spent on-line is time not spent elsewhere, such as engaging in sports and social activities. Taking this argument further, one could worry that Internet communication encourages isolation as well as the formation of superficial relationships with strangers. There is also the danger that children and adolescents will become prey for Internet pornography and/or pedophiles who use the Internet to establish intimate relationships with children. This is undoubtedly a concern for parents. With the current statistics on adolescent Internet usage, it is the right time to examine these issues and ask the following questions: What exactly are the dangers of the Internet, and more specifically, on-line communications or cyber friendships on adolescent development? Are there benefits to this type of communication? Do males and females similarly experience the positive and negative effects of Internet communication use? And, finally, are cyber-relationships healthy relationships?

These important questions are addressed in the selections that follow. In the first, Lauren Donchi and Susan Moore suggest that adolescent boys who rate their on-line friendships as very important are more likely to experience the negative effects of cyber-relationships. In the second selection, Elisheva Gross and colleagues report that adolescents mainly engage in on-line communication with close others, and such communication is beneficial and as effective as face-to-face communication.

YES

Lauren Donchi and Susan Moore

It's a Boy Thing: The Role of the Internet in Young People's Psychological Wellbeing

. . . In Australia, 37% of all households currently have Internet access and this percentage is continuing to rise (Australian Bureau of Statistics, 2001). However, while the majority of Australians (61%) have some access to the Internet, the largest single grouping of users is teenage children. Males, particularly younger males, are more frequent users than females, although Odell, Korgen, Schumacher and Delucchi (2000) argue that the gender gap is closing quickly. Given these statistics, it would not be surprising to had that the Internet has a marked effect on social life. . . .

One way to assess the relationships between social wellbeing and Internet use among young people is to examine the role that online and offline (face-to-face) friendships play in the alleviation of loneliness and the maintenance or development of self-esteem. . . . While it is well known that friendship is important to wellbeing, is this importance specific to face-to-face friends? . . .

Another variable of importance in examining wellbeing in Internet-use relationships is the actual time spent online. Longer amounts of time could be interpreted as relatively antisocial, and may reduce possibilities for social learning and social reinforcement in 'real-life' situations. On the other hand, if the time is spent engaged in Internet relationships, social learning and social rewards may still be available. Thus, in this study, we investigated the associations between time spent on the Internet (in different pursuits including personal communication, entertainment and information-seeking), number and importance of online and offline friendships, and social wellbeing.

This study focuses on Internet use and social relationships of young people in the 15 to 21 years age group, . . . a time in which friendship and peer-group belongingness is particularly salient to psychosocial development. . . . Peer interactions present opportunities for adolescents to develop the social competencies and social skills required for participation in adult society. Research affirms that peer friendships are important for maintaining psychological health and that peer-relationship difficulties are likely to be a source of stress to young people that leads to feelings of loneliness (Demir & Tarhan, 2001; Parkhurst & Asher, 1992). . . .

While adolescent social relations typically take place in face-to-face settings, the introduction of communication applications on the Internet (e.g., email, chatrooms, Usenet newsgroups), . . . has led to the suggestion that Internet networks may also function as important social networks for users. Some support for this view is provided by Parks and Floyd (1996), who . . . found that nearly two-thirds of respondents had formed personal relationships with people they had met via an Internet newsgroup. . . . Further, a study by the Pew Internet and American Life Project (2001) . . . found that Internet communication was an essential feature of young people's social lives and had partially replaced face-to-face interactions. So while the Internet enables people to form online social networks, whether these online friendships can provide a substitute for face-to-face friendships in assisting development towards social maturity and psychological wellbeing is an open question. . . .

Disturbing signs that the Internet fosters loneliness in users first emerged in a longitudinal study conducted by Kraut and colleagues (Kraut et al., 1998; Kraut & Mukopadhyay, 1999) . . . [who] found that after controlling for initial-outcome variables, greater use of the Internet was associated with increased loneliness. They also found that teenagers used the Internet for more hours than adults and increases in Internet use were associated with larger increases in loneliness for teenagers than for adults. These findings were somewhat controversial, and the study was criticized for methodological reasons (small sample; no control group without access to the Internet). . . .

Since the publication of Kraut et al.'s (1998) . . . study that claimed 'using the Internet adversely affects psychological wellbeing' (p. 1028), social scientists have shown . . . interest in the Internet. However, much of the available research . . . has produced mixed results.

Some research has substantiated claims that Internet use is associated with reduced psychological wellbeing. For example, Armstrong, Phillips and Saling (2000) examined Internet use and self-esteem levels . . . [and found] that more time spent on the Internet was associated with lower self-esteem.

[On the other hand, a] recent longitudinal study conducted by Shaw and Gant (2002) [investigating] Internet use, loneliness and self-esteem . . . found that over the course of the study, during which subjects chatted anonymously on the Internet, participants' loneliness decreased and self-esteem increased.

Other research has [also] shed doubt on the association between Internet use and psychological wellbeing. Gross, Juvonen and Gable (2002) found that time online was not associated with loneliness. They surveyed 130 adolescents between the ages of 11 and 13 years. . . . Kraut and colleagues (2002) [in] . . . a second longitudinal study . . . found no overall relationship between Internet use and loneliness or self-esteem. However, they [did report] that Internet use was associated with better outcomes for extroverts (i.e., decreased loneliness and increased self-esteem) and worse outcomes for introverts (i.e., increased loneliness and decreased self-esteem). Hence in [their] study, individual characteristics served as important moderating variables between internet use and psychological wellbeing. . . . In sum, while much research has studied the relationship between Internet use and psychological wellbeing, the available data is equivocal.

One reason for the mixed findings regarding Internet use and loneliness may be that while evidence points to the importance of employing a multidimensional concept of loneliness, there is little available research which links more complex conceptions of loneliness to Internet use. Most studies have employed the UCLA Loneliness Scale, which has come to be viewed as the standard scale to assess loneliness, measuring it as a global construct. One exception was Weiss (1973), who distinguished between emotional loneliness and social loneliness. Emotional loneliness is characterised by a feeling of abandonment, emptiness and apprehension due to the absence of a close, intimate attachment. Social loneliness refers to the feeling of boredom and marginality due to the lack of belonging to a social network or community. Weiss argues that relief from emotional loneliness requires the formation of an attachment relationship that promotes a sense of emotional security, whereas remediation from social loneliness requires being accepted as a member of a friendship network that provides a sense of social integration.

The association between Internet use and Weiss's (1973) bimodal theory of loneliness was examined by Moody (2001), who compared 166 university students' self-reported Internet use to their social and emotional loneliness and to their friendship networks both on the Internet and on a face-to-face basis. Moody developed the Social Network Scale to assess the latter. His findings revealed that while students who spent more time on the Internet communicating with friends were likely to have higher rates of emotional loneliness, they were less like to experience social loneliness than those who spent less time on the Internet communicating with friends. Moody concluded that the psychological effects of Internet use are more complex than previous studies have indicated. His findings suggest that by limiting the face-to-face component of social interaction, emotional loneliness might occur despite high Internet use, providing some individuals with a sense of social integration and thus lowered social loneliness.

Following Moody's (2001) lead, the present study employed Weiss's (1973) distinction between emotional and social loneliness in studying the associations between Internet use, social networks and psychological wellbeing. Furthermore, in keeping with previous research, global loneliness (as measured by the UCLA scale) and self-esteem were also used as measures of psychological wellbeing. The study distinguished between time spent on different activities on the Internet, and used measures of social networks which included, but were not limited to, number of friends. . . . In short, this study examined the relationships between wellbeing, time spent on the Internet, and social networks, including online and offline (face-to-face) networks. Patterns of relationships were examined separately for the sexes because of previous research suggesting differences in the ways young men and young women use the Internet, even though differences in the amount of time spent on the Internet by males and females are closing (Odell et al., 2000).

Method

Participants

There were 336 participants, aged 15 to 21 years in the sample (114 males and 222 females). This included 110 [secondary school students (mean age 16.16) and] 226 university-based [students (mean age 18.55)]. . . .

Materials

The questionnaire consisted of sections designed to measure demographic variables (gender, age, education level), Internet use, social networks, loneliness and self-esteem.

Measuring Internet use In order to assess the amount of time young people spend on the Internet on an average day, respondents were presented with a list of Internet activities. Thirteen of the activities related to three categories of Internet use: interpersonal communication (4 items; e.g., 'visiting chat rooms'), entertainment (5 items; e.g., 'searching for things of personal interest') and information (4 items; e.g., 'finding articles and references'). For each Internet activity, participants were asked to indicate in minutes the time spent on each activity 'on an average day'. . . .

Measuring social networks Respondents use of the Internet and face-to-face relations for communicating with friends was measured using the 12-item Social Network Scale (Moody, 2001). . . . Respondents were asked to indicate how well each item described them on a 5-point Likert scale. . . .

In order to assess the number of friends young people regularly communicate with on the Internet and on a face-to-face basis, participants were asked to answer two questions: 'How many friends do you talk to regularly on the Internet?' and 'How many friends do you talk to regularly on a face-to-face basis?'

Measuring loneliness The UCLA Loneliness Scale was used to measure loneliness conceptualized as a global, unidimensional construct. . . . The 20-item scale has 10 descriptive feelings of loneliness and 10 descriptive feelings of satisfaction with social relationships. . . .

[The] . . . 10-item Emotional and Social Loneliness Scale . . . was used to measure loneliness conceptualized as a multidimensional construct. The scale comprises two 5-item subscales that distinguish between emotional loneliness (e.g., 'I don't have a special love relationship') and social loneliness (e.g., 'Mostly, everyone around me seems like a stranger'). . . .

Measuring self-esteem The measure used to obtain an assessment of self-esteem was Form A of the 16-item Texas Social Behaviour Inventory. . . .

Results

Gender Differences in Internet Use

. . . Males and females spent similar lengths of time on the Internet on an average day engaged in personal communication: female mean—65.4 minutes, male mean—68.7 minutes; and information-seeking: female mean—56.5 minutes, male mean—59.1 minutes. However, males spent significantly longer using the Internet for entertainment on an average day, in fact, about twice as much time as females: female mean—63.9 minutes, male mean—121.6 minutes. . . . In addition, males said they had more regular Internet friends than females. . . . For face-to-face regular friendships the trend was reversed, with females indicating more friendships. . . . The sexes did not differ on the importance they attached to either Internet or face-to-face friendships.

Relationships between Online and Face-to-Face Friendships

. . . The numbers of friends on- and offline were positively associated for both sexes; the more friends in one domain, the more in the other (they may indeed be an overlapping set). An interesting gender difference occurred for the scales measuring perceived importance of the two domains; for females these two scales were unrelated, suggesting that online and offline networks were not developed at the expense of one another. For males, these two scales were negatively associated, suggesting that the young men in this study tended to emphasise one domain over the other.

Network Group Differences on Wellbeing

The number of regular face-to-face friends (face-to-face friends) and number of regularly-communicated-with online friends (online friends) were divided at their respective medians into high and low face-to-face and high and low online friendship groups. A four-way multivariate analysis of variance was conducted with gender (male, female), education level (school, university), face-to-face friendship group (high, low) and online friendship group (high, low) as the independent variables. The dependent variables were the four measures of wellbeing: general loneliness (UCLA loneliness score), social loneliness, emotional loneliness and self-esteem.

The main effects of gender . . . and face-to-face friendship group . . . were significant; other main effects did not show significant group differences. . . .

Males were significantly more socially lonely than females, . . . and males were also significantly more emotionally lonely than females. . . . The trends for the males in the sample to have lower self-esteem and score higher on the UCLA loneliness scale than females were not statistically significant.

Not surprisingly, face-to-face friendship group was also related to the wellbeing measures. Specifically, those with more face-to-face friends had higher self-esteem than those in the low face-to-face friendship group. . . . The high friendship group was also less socially lonely, . . . and less generally lonely on the UCLA scale than the low face-to-face friendship group. . . .

There were gender-by-friendship group interactions for both online and face-to-face friendship groups. . . . [Females] with more online friends were higher on self-esteem and lower on loneliness than females with fewer online friends, but . . . the opposite was true for males. Higher numbers of online regular friendships seemed to militate against self-esteem and be related to greater loneliness for males. . . .

For face-to-face friendships, the effects on wellbeing were in the same direction for males and females, but they were stronger for males. [Those] with more face-to-face friendships were higher on self-esteem and less lonely, with males showing greater extremes of loneliness and low self-esteem than females, and wellbeing as more strongly associated with face-to-face friendships for males than for females.

Predicting Wellbeing from Number of Friends (On- and Offline), Social Network Importance (On- and Offline) and Time Spent on the Internet

Regressions were conducted (separately for males and females) to assess whether the set of variables including number of online and face-to-face friends, perceived importance of online and face-to-face networks and time spent on the Internet predicted wellbeing (self-esteem and 3 measures of loneliness). None of the potential predictor variables were correlated at greater than .6. . . . Correlations . . . showed a pattern for girls of significant positive correlations between wellbeing and face-to-face friendship indicators, and weak or nonsignificant correlations between wellbeing and online friendship indicators. There were no significant correlations between time spent on the Internet and wellbeing for girls. For boys, the correlations between wellbeing and face-to-face friendship indicators were significant and positive and between wellbeing and both time spent on the Internet and online friendship indicators were significant and negative. . . .

The regressions show a similar pattern of findings to the MANOVA, in the sense that the results for males suggest a greater implication of Internet use in loneliness and lower self-esteem. While the importance associated with face-to-face friendships and, to some extent, the number of face-to-face friends were the strongest predictors of loneliness and self-esteem, online relationship activity was also consistently associated with wellbeing for males, but in a negative direction. In other words, young men who rated their online friendship networks as very important were more likely to have lower self-esteem and to be lonely. None of the measures of the spent online (for communication, entertainment or information-related activities) were significant predictors of wellbeing.

Discussion

The present study supported previous research suggesting that young males would spend more time on the Internet on an average day than young females (Kraut & Mukopadhyay, 1999; Odell et al., 2000). Both sexes indicated that they spent large amounts of time with this medium, three hours per day for girls and four for boys. While these times may have been overestimated due to the form of measurement used (assessing minutes per average day across several categories of activity), they do suggest some cause for concern. The gender gap had closed for the Internet activities of personal communication and information-seeking, but was still very much in evidence for Internet entertainment, an activity on which boys spent about two hours per day—twice as long as the girls. In addition, boys had more Internet friends and fewer face-to-face friends than girls, although the total friendship numbers were equal. Boys who ascribed high importance to their Internet friends tended to estimate their face-to-face networks as less important, while girls rated the importance of their Internet and face-to-face friendships similarly. The picture that emerges is of young people spending long hours at the computer, with boys in particular limiting their time for face-to-face interactions and, to some extent, discounting these. Time available for offline activities is thus reduced, particularly for boys. How do these findings relate to wellbeing?

Young people reported that the number of face-to-face friendships were clearly related to wellbeing, with more friends associated with higher self-esteem and lower social and general loneliness. These effects were stronger for boys, indicating that offline friends were particularly important as markers of wellbeing for them. In addition, while online friendships were associated with better wellbeing for girls, the opposite was true for boys. Higher numbers of regular online friendships amongst boys were related to lower self-esteem and greater loneliness. In the regressions, offline friendship number and perceived importance positively predicted wellbeing for both sexes, while online friendship number and importance negatively predicted wellbeing for boys only. These effects of friendship patterns swamped any relationships between wellbeing and time spent online.

Thus, the answer to the question of whether online social interactions can substitute for (or enhance) offline face-to-face friendships for young people during adolescence and early adulthood appears to be a definite 'no' for boys. There is a great deal of evidence that peer relations play an important role in promoting adolescent and youth social–emotional development, act as a buffer against loneliness and enhance self-esteem (e.g., Demir & Tarhan, 2001; Parkhurst & Asher, 1992). This study suggests a need for young men to experience a significant proportion of these peer relationships in the real-world domain. Those young men who strongly emphasise the importance of their online relationships may be cutting off options for psychosocial development through the give and take of face-to-face friendships. This may be a result of lack of social confidence and poor social skills leading to avoidance of real-world friendships with all their difficulties. Or it may be that the nature of Internet relationships (e.g., possibilities for anonymity and role-playing, reduced need to 'work at' friendships) can undermine skills needed in face-to-face relationships. Or, more simply, online friendships may reduce time available for offline friendships which appear to have a greater potential to relate positively to wellbeing. Kraut and colleagues (1998) speculated that negative effects of Internet use could result from both the displacement of social activities and of strong ties. According to this view, the time an individual spends online might interrupt or replace time they had previously spent engaged in real-life social activities. Furthermore, by using the Internet, an individual may be substituting their better real-life relationships or 'strong ties', which are thought to lead to better psychological outcomes, for artificial online relationships or 'weak ties'.

Girls, on the other hand, seem to have developed mechanisms by which their online activity does not interfere with offline friendships, and may even enhance it. For girls, more friendships either on- or offline related to positive indicators of wellbeing. This may relate in part to the fact that girls spend less time on the Internet altogether. In addition, when they do access the Internet, around one-third of this time is devoted to personal communication activities, some of which may involve relating to friends who are substantially of the face-to-face type. Boys, on the other hand, spend only about one-quarter of their time in such activities, preferring to engage in Internet entertainment, games and so on, which have a greater potential to be socially isolating.

It has been suggested that the lack of clarity in the literature to date regarding the association between wellbeing and Internet use may relate to issues surrounding the measurement of wellbeing (Moody, 2001). We used 4 measures and, in particular, were able to test out Moody's (2001) idea that time spent on the Internet communicating with friends would be related to higher emotional, but not higher social, loneliness. This was not the case. In fact, all wellbeing measures were negatively related to Internet focus (time spent on the Internet, Internet friendships, and their perceived importance) for boys. For girls, the relationships between Internet activity and measures of loneliness were weakly negative or nonexistent. Thus boys appear to be disadvantaged both socially and emotionally by their reliance on Internet friendships, while social and emotional advantage is associated with online and offline friendships for girls, and offline friendships for both sexes. . . .

References

Armstrong, L., Phillips, J.G., & Saling, L.L. (2000). Potential determinants of heavier Internet usage. *International Journal of Human-Computer Studies, 53,* 537–550.

Australian Bureau of Statistics (2001). *Use of the Internet by householders, Australia: Catalogue No. 8147.0,* Canberra: Author.

Demir, A., & Tarhan, N. (2001). Loneliness and social dissatisfaction in Turkish adolescents. *Journal of Psychology, 135,* 113–124.

Gross, E.F., Juvonen, J., & Gable, S.L. (2002). Internet use and wellbeing in adolescence. *Journal of Social Issues, 58,* 75–91.

Kraut, R., Kiesler, S., Boneva, B., Cummings, J., Helgeson, V., & Crawford, A. (2002). Internet paradox revisited. *Journal of Social Issues, 58,* 49–74.

Kraut, R., & Mukopadhyay, T. (1999). Information and communication: Alternative uses of the Internet in households. *Information Systems Research, 10,* 287–304.

Kraut, R., Patterson, M., Lundmark, V., Kiesler, S., Mukopadhyay, T., & Scherlis, W. (1998). Internet paradox: A social technology that reduces social involvement and psychological well-being? *American Psychologist, 53,* 1017–1031.

Moody, E.J. (2001). Internet use and its relationship to loneliness. *CyberPsychology & Behaviour, 4,* 393–401.

Odell, P., Korgen, K., Schumacher, P., & Delucchi, M. (2000). Internet use among female and male college students. *CyberPsychology & Behaviour 3,* 855–862.

Parkhurst, J.T., & Asher, S.R. (1992). Peer rejection in middle school: Subgroup differences in behaviour, loneliness, and interpersonal concerns. *Developmental Psychology, 28,* 231–241.

Parks, M.R., & Floyd, K. (1996). Making friends in cyberspace. *Journal of Communication, 46.* Retrieved March 20, 2002, from http://www.ascusc.org/jcmc/vol1/issue4/parks.html

Pew Internet & American Life Project. (2001). *Teenage life online: The rise of the instant-message generation and the Internet's impact on friendships and family relationships.* Retrieved August 20, 2002, from http://www.pewinternet.org/reports/pdfs/PIP_Teens_Report.pdf

Shaw, L.H., & Gant, L.M. (2002). In defense of the Internet: The relationship between Internet communication and depression, loneliness, self-esteem, and perceived social support. *CyberPsychology & Behavior, 5,* 157–171.

Weiss, R.S. (1973). *Loneliness: The experience of emotional and social isolation.* Boston, MA: The MIT Press.

Elisheva F. Gross, Jaana Juvonen, and Shelly L. Gable

Internet Use and Well-Being in Adolescence

$\mathbf{A}$s Internet use among teenagers has grown exponentially in the last 10 years, so has concern over its effect on their psychological well-being. Of over 1,000 U.S. parents surveyed in 1999, almost two thirds expressed concern that "going on-line too often may lead children to become isolated from other people," whereas 40% endorsed the belief that "children who spend too much time on the Internet develop antisocial behavior" (Turow, 1999).

Such apprehensions are not simply the fears of overprotective parents; they received initial empirical support from the first major study of the Internet's psychological impact. A longitudinal investigation of first-time Internet users known as the HomeNet study (Kraut et al., 1998) reported that using the Internet for as little as 3 [hrs] weekly led to increased levels of depression and reductions in social support over the course of 2 years. Results showed teenagers to be the population most vulnerable to these negative effects. Kraut and colleagues speculated that adolescents' heavy usage of the Internet for on-line communication led them to forsake critical bonds with local friends and family for weak relations with strangers.

In considering the application of Kraut and colleagues' findings to adolescents, two concerns in particular should be noted. First, because the HomeNet sample did not include a non-Internet-using control group, we cannot determine how much of the downward trend in participants' well-being was due to their Internet use or to the unfortunate but steady decline in perceived social support and overall contentment *typically* reported by youth as they proceed through adolescence. Second, the Kraut et al. study (like most studies of youth Internet use, did not gather detailed accounts of on-line social activity (i.e., with whom and about what Internet users were communicating). Given the importance of supportive peer relationships to healthy adolescent development, we argue that an understanding of the relation between youth Internet use and psychological well-being requires a consideration of *with whom* adolescents communicate on-line.

Well-Being and Close Relationships

The need to form and maintain strong interpersonal bonds has been described as a fundamental need and one that is critical to healthy development (Sullivan, 1953). Research on young adults has found that feeling close and

From *Journal of Social Issues*, vol. 58, no. 1, 2002, pp. 75–90. Copyright © 2002 by Blackwell Publishing, Ltd. Reprinted by permission. Note: The complete text of this article contains many references to specific studies described. The interested individual should refer to the original publication for these extensive citations. These references have been omitted here in the interest of brevity.

connected to others on a daily basis is associated with higher daily well-being, and in particular, feeling understood and appreciated and sharing pleasant interactions are especially strong predictors of well-being (Reis, Sheldon, Gable, Roscoe, & Ryan, 2000). As outlined by Reis and Shaver (1988), intimacy is developed and sustained through social exchanges with responsive others (e.g., pleasant interactions and feeling understood). Intimacy emerges as an expectation for peer relationships in late childhood or early adolescence (Sullivan, 1953), and the expectations and meanings of friendships remain constant throughout adolescence and adulthood. Thus close and meaningful interactions with peers are likely to be at least as important to adolescent well-being as they are to adult well-being. Indeed, research affirms that close peer relationships contribute positively to adolescent self-esteem and well-being, whereas peer relationship problems such as peer rejection and a lack of close friends are among the strongest predictors of depression and negative self-views. From the perspective of intimacy theory (Reis & Shaver, 1988), Internet use could undermine *or* foster well-being, depending on whether it supplants (as suggested by Kraut et al., 1998) or expands opportunities for meaningful, daily contact with close peers.

Adolescent Internet Use

Two advances in the use of the Internet are important to our understanding of the nature of on-line relationships and social exchanges. First, new technologies have been developed to further facilitate synchronous on-line interaction with known others. One such feature, instant messages (IMs), allows users to be informed when friends are on-line and to chat with them through text windows that appear on the screens of the two parties involved. Because of its dyadic, real-time, and private format, the IM is structurally and functionally comparable to other important and pervasive forms of social interaction in adolescence: "hanging out" face to face and talking on the phone. Indeed, a recent study by the Pew Internet and American Life Project (2001) indicates that for a fifth of American teenage Internet users, instant messaging (IMing) has become the primary means of contacting friends. Second, with more youth (particularly from middle- and upper-income households) accessing the Internet from home than ever before, teens are increasingly likely to find their close friends on-line. Thus, youth need not necessarily forsake their school-based relationships when they log on; the Internet can now be both a space in which to interact with distant associates and strangers and a supplemental medium for communication with one's established, off-line peer network.

The Present Study

We present findings from a study on adolescents' daily Internet use and psychological adjustment, with a specific focus on IMing. Participants in this research completed three daily reports of their overall well-being, socially specific adjustment (loneliness and social anxiety in school), and after-school activity, including Internet use. Dispositional measures of these variables were also collected in participants' classrooms prior to the daily reporting. Given the tendency for psychological well-being (Reis et al., 2000) and loneliness to fluctuate within and across days as a function of social contact, we expected that daily indicators of well-being would be especially important to consider.

Analyses will be presented in two parts: descriptive and correlational. First, distinct forms of Internet use will be explored in the context of both overall time on-line and time in non-Internet activities. The second set of results will be devoted to the investigation of associations among on-line activity and well-being. It is proposed that with the increasing ease and speed of on-line communication with friends, adolescents' psychological well-being is not associated with how much time they spend either on the Internet or in specific on-line domains. Rather, we predict that socially specific aspects of psychological adjustment—loneliness and social anxiety with school peers— are related to the closeness of relationships with on-line communication partners. In order to enable the collection of detailed communication variables, we focus on the characteristics of discrete, dyadic IM exchanges. Specifically, we test the prediction that adolescents who report lower levels of loneliness and social anxiety, relative to their peers, would be more likely to IM with people to whom they felt close. In addition, we expected the daily indicators of loneliness and social anxiety to improve predictions of partner closeness beyond the contributions of trait indicators. Given the centrality of motives for and content of self-relevant disclosure to the process of intimacy (Reis & Shaver, 1988), we also explored the associations among well-being and IM motives and topics. Finally, in light of previously reported gender differences in early adolescents' verbal intimacy with friends and Internet use, we took gender into account in our analyses.

Method

Demographic data (age, gender, ethnicity), background information on Internet use (e.g., on-line tenure, parental rules regarding Internet use, shared phone access, and speed of Internet connectivity), and dispositional measures of psychological adjustment (depression, social anxiety, and loneliness) were collected from participants in school. For the same night as the data were collected (8–14 hr later) and for two consecutive nights thereafter, participants provided daily reports on three general sets of variables: specific on-line activities, general after-school activity, and psychological adjustment.

Participants

To allow us to examine an adolescent peer context in which Internet use is widespread, we sampled from a relatively homogenous mid- to high-socioeconomic-status community. . . . The participants [49 males; 81 females] ranged in age from 11 to 13 years. . . . Of the 120 participants who reported their ethnicity, 59.2% identified themselves as European American, 17.5% as Asian American, 10% as being of mixed heritage, 5.8% as Latino/a, 1.7% as African American, and 5.8% as other.

Procedure

. . . All participants first completed a confidential self-report questionnaire in class. Participants were then directed to complete the daily report just before going to sleep each night. . . .

A total of 17 participants did not complete any nightly logs, resulting in 113 participants reporting a total of 275 days, an average of 2.12 of 3 possible days per person. Girls were more compliant, on average completing more logs than boys. . . . There was no significant difference in either psychological measures or levels of typical Internet use between participants who submitted at least one versus no daily reports.

One-Time Measures

Typical after-school activity. To enable comparisons of our data with other studies of Internet use, participants were asked to estimate how much time they spend "on a typical day" using the Internet at home. In addition, in order to situate Internet use in the context of daily after-school activity, five other types of after-school activity were assessed: homework, organized activity, . . . hanging out with friends, talking on the phone, and watching television. . . .

Loneliness. Nine items from the 30-item UCLA Loneliness Scale, Version 3 were used to assess global feelings of isolation. . . .

Social anxiety. Global social anxiety was measured using the generalized social anxiety subscale of the Social Anxiety Scale for Adolescents (SAD-G). . . . This instrument assesses adolescents' subjective experience of generalized social avoidance, inhibition, and distress. . . .

Friendship. A quantitative measure of friendship (number of close friends at school) was included to provide construct validity for the measures of school-based loneliness and social anxiety, as well as to serve as a proxy for the size of social circle assessment used in the HomeNet study (Kraut et al., 1998).

Depressed mood. The 10-item short form of the Child Depression Inventory was administered with eight filler items. . . .

Daily Measures

Our primary aim in using a dual-survey approach at this preliminary stage of investigation was to verify participants' in-school global self-reports of peer-related adjustment and after-school behavior with daily reports of their behaviors across three weekdays. Therefore, daily scores across the three days were combined as a mean, despite the potential loss of key information regarding within-person variability.

Daily after-school activity. Participants were asked to estimate how much time they spent that day on the six after-school activities mentioned. . . . In addition, eight categories of on-line activity were listed: e-mail, games, multiuser dimensions (MUDs), message boards, list-servs/newsgroups, chat rooms, IMs, and Web or America Online (AOL) sites. Next to each activity, participants rated engagement. . . .

Characteristics of on-line communication. In order to balance our interest in the details of interaction with our concern for participant attrition and fatigue, the log required participants to provide more extensive information for only their single lengthiest IM interaction that day, as follows: relational identity of IM partner (stranger, acquaintance, friend, best friend, girlfriend/boyfriend, or family member); origin of contact with partner (on-line, off-line in school or off-line outside of school); duration of relationship (six possible categories, from *this is the first time we've met* to *over 2 years*); gender of partner; relative age of partner; their own motives for IMing; and topics discussed. Participants were asked to indicate how much they discussed each of 13 communication topics ranging from less intimate (e.g., politics, schoolwork/college, sports) to more intimate topics (e.g., gossip, boyfriend/girlfriend stuff, friends). . . .

Loneliness. A daily index of loneliness was developed from the UCLA Loneliness Scale. . . .

Social anxiety. [The] SAD-G scale was adapted for use as a daily measure, [of social anxiety]. . . .

Subjective well-being. The Student's Life Satisfaction Scale was adapted for use [as] a daily assessment of student's global life satisfaction (cf., depression) beyond such specific domains as peer relations at school. . . .

Results

Internet Usage in the Context of Adolescents' After-School Time

Using the traditional response format of how often participants use the Internet, the in-school survey revealed that 90% of participants use the Internet "occasionally" or "regularly" at home. Similarly, 84% of respondents reported that they go on-line on a "typical day." Consistent with these figures, 70% of participants . . . reported at least one Internet session during the 3 days of our study. On a given single day, however, between 40% and 57% of participants . . . reported that they did *not* go on-line. Thus, global questions seemed to bias usage estimates to be somewhat higher (14–21%) than those reported in daily logs. In order to portray an average daily assessment, all activities and psychological measures were averaged across days for all participants.

On average, the Internet consumed less of participants' daily after-school time than any of the other five activities measured. Participants reported over 1 hr in organized activities . . . and watching television . . . , and more than 2 hr doing homework. . . . Average daily time on-line . . . most closely approximated time spent on the phone . . . and with friends. . . .

. . . [On] average, participants devoted the majority of their daily time on-line to three domains: IMing . . . , visiting Web sites and "surfing the Web" . . . , and e-mail. . . . No significant gender differences in levels of overall or specific types of Internet usage were revealed by t-tests, after excluding the 5 boys . . . who comprised the long tail . . . of high daily game activity (i.e., 75 min or more of on-line game play per day). . . .

Characteristics of IMs

Participants reported exchanging IMs with an average of 2.68 . . . different people per day. Additional data were collected about participants' longest IM interaction each day. The median interaction duration was 30 min, and 54% of participants who reported IMing . . . indicated that they communicated with the person "every day" or "almost every day." An additional 14% reported weekly contact with the IM partner. In contrast, only 7% of instant messengers stated that the reported interaction was the first IM they had ever exchanged with that particular person.

IM motives and topics.   Participants' motives for and topics of IM communication convey the social and personal nature of participants' interactions. The topics most commonly reported by both boys and girls were friends (58%), gossip (51%), and "boyfriend/girlfriend stuff" (50%). The most widely reported motive for IMing was "to hang out with a friend," endorsed by 92% of instant messengers . . . , and nearly three fourths of instant messengers reported IMing because they were bored. . . .

IM partners.   Consistent with our expectations, participants' relationships with IM partners ($n = 86$) were described, on average, as relatively long-standing friendships with peers first met in school. Most IM partners (86%) were reported to be "about the same age" (i.e., less than 2 years older or younger) as the participant, whereas the remaining 14% were described as 2 or more years older. Just over half (54%) of reported IM interactions occurred in same-sex dyads. Of the partners, 88% were first-met off-line, predominantly at school (67%). Only 12% of partners were first encountered on-line. Sixty-five percent of participants reported knowing their IM partner for more than a year, and 35% had known their partner for more than 2 years. No participants reported knowing their partner for less than a week.

To be able to describe the closeness of participants' relationships with IM partners, partner type was ordered on the dimension of closeness. First, we excluded three low-frequency categories (boyfriend/girlfriend, family member, other) because the closeness of these relationships varies considerably among young adolescents. . . . Second, we represented the remaining categories as a 4-point closeness scale (1 = *stranger,* 2 = *acquaintance,* 3 = *friend,* and 4 = *best friend*). Third, we averaged closeness of the communication partner across days. Reported closeness of the relationship with primary IM partners was fairly consistent across the three days . . . and reflected participants' tendency to communicate with friends. . . . Examination of cross-tabulations of IM partner closeness and origin of the relationship (i.e., off-line vs. on-line) showed that the vast majority of friends and all best friends were initially met *off-line*. The few strangers with whom participants communicated were largely met on-line (five out of six). Closeness differed neither by gender nor by tenure on-line.

Internet Usage and Psychological Adjustment

Overall usage levels. Consistent with our predictions, time on-line . . . was not correlated with psychological adjustment. In addition, analysis of variance comparisons among groups of Internet users of varying levels of tenure (e.g., 0–6 months vs. 2 years or more using the Internet) yielded no significant differences on any psychological measures.

Predicting closeness of relationship with IM partner from daily adjustment. Pearson correlations between IM partner closeness and all psychological measures . . . yielded significant associations with daily levels of loneliness, $r(38) = -.43, p = .01$, and social anxiety, . . . suggesting that participants who felt relatively socially anxious and/or lonely in school *on a daily basis* were more likely to communicate in IMs with people with whom they did not have a close affiliation.

Hierarchical multiple regressions were performed to test the multivariate model: the contribution of average daily social anxiety to the average closeness of IM partners. . . .

[Results indicated] daily measure of social anxiety significantly predicted closeness of IM partner, $\beta = .45$, $p < .02$, adding 13% to the total variance explained by the model, $\Delta R^2 = .13, p < .02$. . . .

As predicted, daily loneliness predicted an additional 8% of the total variance. . . . In predicting the closeness of IM partners, then, daily loneliness and daily anxiety are important. Teens who, on average, reported feeling more daily loneliness and/or social anxiety in school were more likely to communicate with a stranger than with a friend or close friend after school. To provide discriminant evidence for our claim that IM partner characteristics were associated with socially specific rather than overall well-being, correlations were computed between closeness and both dispositional (CDI) and daily (SLSS) global well-being. Associations were nonsignificant, indicating that general feelings of life contentment or dissatisfaction could not predict the closeness of participants' IM partners.

Exploratory analyses: IM motives and topics. Consistent with the pattern of our main findings, exploratory analyses revealed that time spent discussing certain social topics was associated with interpersonal adjustment. Specifically, participants who reported feeling lonely in school both in general and on a daily basis were less likely to talk about friends when IMing. . . . Similarly, participants with higher dispositional social anxiety were less likely than their more comfortable peers to discuss romantic topics. . . .

Examination of participants' motives for IMing also supports the hypothesis that on-line communication serves distinct functions for adolescents experiencing peer-related distress. Although the most commonly reported motive for IMing was to "hang out with a friend," the motive "to avoid being alone" was unique in demonstrating significant associations with psychological adjustment. Daily average social anxiety was significantly and positively correlated with solitude avoidance. . . . In addition, youth reporting fewer close friends in school were significantly more likely to report IMing to avoid being alone. . . .

Discussion

The aim of the present study was twofold: first, to examine more closely what adolescents were doing on-line, and second, to examine whether distinctions among on-line activities and communication partners allow us to better understand the relation between Internet use and well-being.

In spite of the growing role of on-line communication in the lives of young people, even regular Internet users in our sample continued to spend most of their after-school time on traditional activities, many of which involved peer interaction. . . . Moreover, on-line communication appears to be similar in several ways to traditional means of youth social interaction: it occurred largely in private settings (i.e., e-mail and IMs) with friends who were also part of participants' daily, off-line (e.g., school) lives. In addition, on-line communication was reported to be mainly devoted to ordinary yet intimate topics (e.g., friends, gossip) and motivated by a desire for companionship.

Given that participants reported spending much of their on-line time engaged in interactions with close others, the null association between time spent on-line and psychological well-being is not surprising. According to intimacy theory (Reis & Shaver, 1988), such interactions should be *positively* related to well-being. Likewise, on-line usage by specific domain (e.g., downloading music, chatting) were not associated with well-being. Indeed, the very meaning of time spent in individual on-line domains may be complicated by the prevalence of on-line multi-tasking among participants. . . .

As expected, *whom adolescents communicated with on-line* was found to predict peer-related psychological well-being. Although most social interaction through IMs occurred between friends known from off-line, the closeness of participants' relationships with IM partners was predicted by daily social functioning. Specifically, participants who reported feeling lonely or socially anxious in school on a daily basis were more likely to communicate through IMs with people they did not know well (i.e., strangers vs. friends).

These findings suggest that when they feel connected and comfortable with school-based peers, early adolescents use the Internet to seek out additional opportunities to interact with them. In the case of chronic or even temporary feelings of social discomfort or detachment, however, adolescents may use the Internet to avoid being alone, and, in doing so, turn to people disconnected from their daily life.

But do Internet-based relations provide anxious and lonely youth with the intimacy and companionship that are missing in their off-line lives? Alternatively, because these youth are more likely to communicate with strangers, are they more vulnerable to on-line predators? . . . In our sample, the closeness of participants' relationships with their IM partners was significantly associated with the relationship's origin, meaning that there were few cases of close friendships developed on-line. Given the growing evidence that close relationships can and do originate on the Internet, especially for individuals experiencing difficulty in their off-line social life (McKenna & Bargh, 2000), we suspect that their absence in the present sample may be at least in part the result of our sample's limited size and frequency of lonely individuals. . . .

In contrast to previously reported gender differences in both levels and types of on-line communication (Kraut et al., 1998), boys and girls in the present study reported equivalent levels and characteristics of interpersonal communication not only on the Internet, but also on the telephone. . . .

Finally, although in the present sample parental rules regarding Internet usage were not found to be influential, further research is needed on the family context of use, particularly in light of the differing depictions of parental on-line monitoring offered by youth and their parents (Pew Internet and American Life Project, 2001). . . .

Conclusions

The findings presented here suggest that McKenna and Bargh's (2000) claim that "there is no simple main effect of the Internet on the average person" (p. 59) applies to the case of early adolescents. Our results are not inconsistent with their and others' evidence that the Internet may serve distinct functions for socially anxious and lonely individuals. At the same time, we find that normatively adjusted adolescents use the Internet as yet another tool in their communications repertoire. This finding conveys a very different picture from that provided by early studies and media reports on adolescent Internet use. We have argued that advances in communications technology and the continuing growth in youth Internet access may help to explain the discrepancy across studies (e.g., early and more recent investigations) and samples (e.g., of adults vs. teenagers). This said, continuing research is needed to further examine the functions and potential long-term effects of the many distinct and rapidly evolving uses of the Internet. In conducting such research, researchers are urged to take into account the social and developmental context of adolescents' daily lives.

References

Kraut, R., Patterson, M., Lundmark, V., Kiesler S., Mukopadhyay, T., & Scherlis, W. (1998). Internet paradox: A social technology that reduces social involvement and psychological well-being? *American Psychologist, 53,* 1017–1031.

McKenna, K. Y. A., & Bargh, J. A. (2000). Plan 9 from cyberspace: The implications of the Internet for personality and social psychology. *Personality and Social Psychology Review, 4,* 57–75.

Pew Internet and American Life Project (2001). *Teenage life online: The rise of the instant message generation and the Internet's impact on friendships and family relationships* [On-line, retrieved July 19, 2001]. Available: http://www.pewinternet. org/reports/pdfs/PIP_Teens_Report.pdf.

Reis, H. T., & Shaver, P. (1988). Intimacy as an interpersonal process. In S. Duck (Ed.), *Handbook of personal relationships* (pp. 367–389). Chichester, UK: Wiley.

Reis, H. T., & Sheldon, K. M., Gable, S. L., Roscoe, J., & Ryan, R. M. (2000). Daily well-being: The role of autonomy, competence, and relatedness. *Personality and Social Psychology Bulletin, 26,* 419–435.

Sullivan, H. S. (1953). *The interpersonal theory of psychiatry.* New York: Norton.

Turow, J. (1999, May 4). The Internet and the family: The view from the family, the view from the press [On-line, retrieved July 19, 2001]. The Annenberg Public Policy Center of the University of Pennsylvania. Available: http://www. appcpenn.org/internet/family/rep27.pdf.

POSTSCRIPT

Do Cyber-Friendships Hinder Healthy Adolescent Development?

Lauren Donchi and Susan Moore assessed the relationship between psychological well-being and Internet use among adolescents, focusing on time spent on-line as well as the differences between face-to-face and cyber-friendships. Their results indicated that females with more on-line friends had more self-esteem and less loneliness than females with few on-line friends. The opposite, however, was true for males. Specifically, the more cyber-friends, the lower the self-esteem and the greater the loneliness for males.

On the other hand, Elisheva Gross, Jaana Juvonen and Shelly Gable found that time spent on-line was not associated with psychological well-being. Furthermore, they found that psychological well-being was not a function of having cyber-friends. For well-adjusted adolescents, the Internet was used to seek out additional opportunities to interact with close friends. Gender differences with respect to cyber-friendships and psychological well-being were not found. Interestingly, Gross, Juvonen, and Gable did report that socially anxious adolescents were more likely to communicate with strangers.

These two selections contribute to our understanding of cyber-friendships and address our concerns in several ways. Cyber-friendships can be unhealthy for boys, especially if the boys are socially anxious. The results reported by Donchi and Moore support previous research findings such as those by Moody (2001) who found that high levels of Internet use were associated with high levels of emotional loneliness as measured by a sense of emptiness brought on by the absence of intimate relationships. Moody argued that emptiness was a result of too much time on-line, removed from face-to-face peer interaction. Mazalin and Moore (2004), also supporting the negative effects of on-line communications, found that participating in chat rooms was associated with less mature identity status and higher levels of social anxiety for males. They argue that because the peer group plays an important role in adolescent development (i.e., social learning theory), the diminished proximity of the peer group limits social learning and hence has a negative effect on development. According to Erikson's theory, healthy adolescent development leads to a strong sense of self and a strong identity. If development is impaired, an adolescent is at risk for a weak sense of self and a less mature identity. The gender differences found with respect to cyber-friendships could imply that males are more vulnerable with respect to the formation of a healthy identify and sense of self. Males may need more face-to-face friendships than females in order to establish a strong sense of self. It is recommended that this be examined in future studies.

The positive outcomes reported by Gross, Juvonen, and Gable, whereby well-adjusted adolescents use on-line communications to further strengthen face-to-face friendship, can be linked to the "rich get richer model" proposed in previous studies (Kraut et al, 1998; 2002). Kraut and colleagues argue that individuals who are highly sociable and have strong support systems get more social benefit from on-line communication. In other words, they found that, for extraverts, using the Internet was associated with increases in community involvement, better self-esteem, and decreases in negative affect such as loneliness and depression. Those who are already comfortable in social situations can take away the many benefits of Internet communication (e.g., strengthening off-line relationships).

Kraut et al. further argue that introverts, who are anxious and/or lonely, are more likely to communicate on-line rather than face-to-face to avoid physical proximity. For these individuals, and perhaps for boys more than girls, cyber-friendships can do more harm than good, especially if they are friendships with strangers. McKenna and Bargh (1999) found that socially anxious and lonely individuals were more likely to form very close intimate friendships on the Internet. For these individuals, the Internet replaced face-to-face interactions. However, as the on-line relationship strengthened, McKenna and Bargh found the more likely it was these socially anxious individuals would integrate their on-line friendships into their off-line lives. If the on-line "friends" are predators, this could be dangerous for the vulnerable anxious adolescent. Apart from the risk of forming relationships with dangerous strangers, there could also be concern that socially anxious adolescents are forming electronic friendships with the machine, instead of forming healthy peer friendships. This could interfere with learning effective social skills.

References/Further Readings

Kraut, R., Patterson, M., Lundmark, V., Kiesler, S., Mukhopadhyay, T., & Scherlis, W. (1998). Internet paradox: A social technology that reduces social involvement and psychological well-being. *American Psychologist,* 53, 1017–1031.

Kraut, R., Kiesler, S., Boneva, B., Cummings, J., Helgeson, V., & Crawford, A. (2002). Internet paradox revisited. *Journal of Scoial issues,* 58, 49–74.

Mazalin, D., & Moore, S. (2004). Internet use, identity development and social anxiety among young adults. *Behaviour Change,* 21, 90–102.

McKenna, K.Y.A., & Bargh, J.A. (1999). Causes and consequences of social interaction on the Internet. A conceptual framework. *Media Psychology,* 1, 259–270.

Moody, E.J. (2001). Internet use and its relationship to loneliness. *Cyber Psychology and Behavior,* 4, 393–401.

Statistics Canada (2004). Household Internet Use Survey. http://www. statcan.ca/daily/english/040708/d040708a.htm.

Parks, M., & Roberts, L. (1998). Making MOOsic: The development of personal relationships on-line and a comparison to their off-line counterparts. *Journal of Social and Personal Relationships,* 15, 517–537.

Pew Internet and American Life Project (2004). How Americans use instant messaging. http://www.pewinternet.org/pdfs/PIP_Instantmessage_Report.pdf.

Pew Internet and American Life Project (2005a). Internet Tracking Survey. http://www.pewinternet.org/pdfs/PIP-Broadband_questionnaire.pdf.

Pew Internet and American Life Project (2005b). The Internet at school. http://www.pewinternet.org/PPF/r/163/report_display.asp.

On the Internet . . .

Office of Juvenile Justice and Delinquency Prevention

Office of Juvenile Justice and Delinquency Prevention is part of the U.S. Department of Justice, which develops and implements effective programs for juveniles. This Web site provides information on legislation and programs that are available to youth such as the Gang Reduction Program and Internet Crimes Against Children Task Force Program.

http://www.ojjdp.ncjrs.org

Youth Criminal Justice Act

The Department of Justice updates this Web site with information on the Youth Criminal Justice Act. This Web site not only outlines the Youth Criminal Justice Act, it also has information on sentencing, judicial measures, and the court system.

http://laws.justice.gc.ca/cgi-bin/notice.pl?redirect=/en/Y-1.5/index.html

National Center for Injury Prevention and Control

The National Center for Injury Prevention and Control works to reduce morbidity, disability, mortality, and costs associated with injuries. This Web site offers a wide variety of information on child maltreatment, intimate partner violence, sexual violence, suicide, and youth violence.

http://www.cdc.gov/ncipc/dvp/dvp.htm

Keep Schools Safe

This Web site provides information to students, parents, and teachers on dealing with school violence, fighting, bullying, and aggression in youth.

http://www.keepschoolssafe.org/

The Children Left Behind Project

The Children Left Behind Project is a joint initiative of the Indiana Youth Services Association and the Center for Evaluation and Education Policy, sharing data on the use and effect of school suspension and expulsion.

http://www.ceep.indiana.edu/ChildrenLeftBehind/

National Institute on Drug Abuse

This Web site is dedicated to club drugs, which are widely used by young adults in club settings. It has statistics and trends on current club drug problems.

http://www.clubdrugs.org/

DanceSafe

DanceSafe promotes health and safety within the rave and nightclub community. It has articles and research literature regarding drugs in clubs.

http://www.dancesafe.org/

PART 4

Antisocial Behaviors

*T*here are many areas where adolescent behavior can cause problems for the developing teen. This area of study is sometimes called abnormal adolescent psychology or the sociology of juvenile delinquency. By studying these behaviors, we can attempt to prevent problems before they occur and intervene when problems do occur. What is defined as a "problem" or an antisocial behavior can change depending on the social, political, and economic climate of the time. The following part deals with four issues of adolescent problems that are currently hot topics in antisocial adolescent behavior.

- Should Adolescents Who Commit Serious Offenses Be Tried and Convicted as Adults?

- Is School-Related Violence Increasing?

- Are Girls Bigger Bullies Than Boys?

- Is the Use of "Club Drugs" a Problem Among Adolescents?

ISSUE 15

Should Adolescents Who Commit Serious Offenses Be Tried and Convicted as Adults?

YES: Daniel P. Mears, from "Getting Tough with Juvenile Offenders: Explaining Support for Sanctioning Youths as Adults," *Criminal Justice and Behavior* (April 2001)

NO: Laurence Steinberg and Elizabeth S. Scott, from "Less Guilty by Reason of Adolescence: Developmental Immaturity, Diminished Responsibility, and the Juvenile Death Penalty," *American Psychologist* (December 2003)

ISSUE SUMMARY

YES: Daniel Mears, an associate professor for the College of Criminology and Criminal Justice at Florida State University, reports that for serious offenses, there is widespread support for sanctioning youths as adults. He points to a conservative group, fearful of crime, worrying about social order and public safety.

NO: Laurence Steinberg, Distinguished University Professor at Temple University, and Elizabeth Scott, law professor at the University of Virginia, argue that adolescents often lack the capabilities to make mature judgments, control impulses, and resist coercion from peers and therefore should not be held to the same standards of criminal conduct as adults.

Not much more than a century ago, little distinction was made between how children and adults were tried and convicted. This changed, however, when child development researchers recognized the time between childhood and adulthood as a distinct period of development. As such, child advocacy groups argued that children and adolescents should be removed from adult courts and prisons. This led to the first juvenile court in the United States in 1899 and the Juvenile Delinquent's Act of 1908 in Canada. These changes to the justice system were based on arguments of providing care and custody to vulnerable children with a focus on rehabilitation and reintegration.

For over 50 years, both systems ran smoothly. It was not until the 1960s when the recognition and protection of children's legal rights were questioned. Child welfare groups argued that juveniles within the system were not being rehabilitated and were being given long and cruel sentences. By the 1970s, following several class-action lawsuits alleging cruel and unusual punishment, governments reexamined the way youth were tried, convicted, and rehabilitated, resulting in the U.S. 1974 Juvenile Justice and Delinquency Prevention Act (JJDPA) and Canada's 1984 Young Offenders Act (YOA). Both acts, focusing on children's rights, rehabilitation, and reintegration, mandated that juveniles be protected and cared for and not be placed in adult jails. The JJDPA is still in effect in the United States, while the YOA was replaced in 2003 with the Youth Criminal Justice Act (YCJA). The change in Canada was made to address the escalating incarceration rates that had been higher than other Western countries. Custody in Canada is now reserved for violent offenders and serious repeat offenders.

Although the JJDPA and YCJA addressed the rehabilitation of youth, problems continue to exist. As youth violence and crime rates rose through the 1980s and 1990s, there was public demand for a "get tougher" approach to juvenile crime. Public perception was that the JJDPA and YCJA protected youth too much, resulting in higher crime rates and compromised social order. In the United States, this "get tougher" approach resulted in government action and in the majority of states having laws making it easier to try young juveniles in adult criminal court. For example, the youngest in American history was Michigan's Nathaniel Abraham. In 1999, he was 11 when he was charged and prosecuted as an adult for murder (Tuell, 2002). Interestingly, youth crime rates have dropped since the mid-1990s.

If adolescents can be tried and convicted as adults, can they also be executed like adults? In the United States, the answer is yes. Every nation in the world prohibits the execution of juvenile offenders, except for the United States, where only 13 U.S. jurisdictions prohibit the execution of juveniles (Tuell, 2002). Between 1973 and 2003, 2.6 percent (22 of 859) of the total executions in the United States were juvenile offenders. How are these decisions made? Who essentially decides which juveniles to transfer to adult court and on what factors do they consider in the decision? In the United States and in Canada, judicial waiver (i.e., one method of transfer to adult court) is initiated by the prosecutor, decided by the judge, and usually based on age, criminal history, seriousness of offense, likelihood to rehabilitate, and threat to the public. Is this the right way to deal with young offenders? Should adolescents who commit serious offenses be tried and convicted as adults? Should the decision be based on public opinion, threat to society, seriousness of the crime, or age and maturity of the defendant? How do we balance the individuals' rights against those of society?

These questions will be addressed in the selections that follow. Steinberg and Scott argue that juveniles cannot be held blameworthy for their crimes in the same way as adults because of cognitive and psychosocial deficits resulting in immature decision making, vulnerability to external pressure, and unformed character. Daniel Mears, on the other hand, argues that there is support for sanctioning juveniles as adults. He points to a conservative group, fearful of crime, worrying about social order and public safety.

YES

Daniel P. Mears

Getting Tough with Juvenile Offenders: Explaining Support for Sanctioning Youths as Adults

In recent years, getting tough with juvenile offenders has become a prominent focus of reforms and political campaigns (Roberts & Stalans, 1998). Central to these efforts has been the increased expansion of laws enabling youths to be transferred from juvenile to criminal court, especially for the commission of violent and drug offenses (Torbet & Szymanski, 1998). This trend clearly runs counter to the *parens patriae* (state as parent) foundation of the juvenile court, in which rehabilitation and the "best interests" of the child were viewed as being of paramount importance (Feld, 1999). It also runs counter to public opinion in America, which generally holds that rehabilitation, particularly for juveniles, should be a central feature of sanctioning (Roberts & Stalans, 1998, p. 52). Indeed, survey research consistently reveals considerable support among Americans for investing in nonpunitive, rehabilitative sanctioning, especially where youths are concerned (Stalans & Henry, 1994). Given recent expansions in juvenile transfer laws, the question thus emerges as to the link between support for rehabilitative sanctioning and transfer of youths to adult court. The more general question is, Who supports sanctioning youths as adults and why?

Although substantial research has been conducted on public opinion and punishment, much of it remains primarily descriptive, prompting calls for more nuanced and theoretical analyses. The situation is particularly acute in the area of public attitudes about juvenile justice (Stalans & Henry, 1994), especially given the transfonnation of the juvenile court in recent years to an increasingly criminal-like institution (Feld, 1999). Taking these observations as a point of departure, this article has the following three goals: (a) to focus attention on theorizing and explaining views toward sanctioning youths in adult courts, (b) to examine specific factors that to date have not been sufficiently addressed in the context of juvenile justice sanctioning, and (c) to investigate specific mechanisms, including marital status and political orientation, through which a rehabilitative philosophy of punishment may affect support for sanctioning youths as adults. The latter focus stems from what appears to be an emerging tension between conservative "tough love" approaches (e.g.,

From *Criminal Justice and Behavior*, vol. 28, no. 2, April 2001, pp. 206–226. Copyright © 2001 by Sage Publications. Reprinted by permission. Note: The complete text of this article contains many references to specific studies described. The interested individual should refer to the original publication for these extensive citations. These references have been omitted here in the interest of brevity.

George W. Bush's recent calls for "compassionate conservatism"; see Lardner & Walsh, 1999) and more liberal/traditional rehabilitative emphases. . . .

Support for Sanctioning Youths in the Adult Justice System

Despite the considerable research focused on public attitudes toward juvenile justice, much of this research has focused primarily on use of the death penalty for youths, rehabilitative sanctioning, funding for treatment and vocational training, and fear of victimization (Schwartz et al., 1993). One notable exception is Schwartz et al.'s national study of demographic factors associated with support for trying juveniles in adult court and sentencing them to adult prisons. They found that the profile of those most likely to support sanctioning youths as adults for selling illicit drugs or committing property or violent crimes consisted primarily of males, persons approaching middle age, African American parents, and those who are fearful of being the victim of violent crime. However, they did not assess the role of philosophy of punishment or political or religious orientation or of factors such as income or marital status, each of which previous research suggests may be related to punitiveness (Jelen, 1998). Moreover, contextual factors such as public disorder, urbanization, and crime rates, which research on the death penalty and fear of crime has highlighted as being of potential importance (Taylor, Scheppele, & Stinchcombe, 1979), remain largely unexamined in studies of support for sanctioning youths as adults.

Perhaps of more immediate importance than assessing whether such factors indeed are related to support for more punitive sanctioning of youths is the need to understand better why and how. In the context of juvenile justice, a focus on rehabilitative attitudes toward sanctioning is particularly warranted, given the foundation of the juvenile court on the idea of rehabilitation and the best interests of the child. One avenue by which to explore this relationship is to examine links between rehabilitative orientations and whether an individual is married. The latter distinction is important because marriage can be viewed as reflecting a commitment to mainstream conventional values, particularly those bearing on the notion of the sacredness of childhood. As Plissner (1983) has noted, "married people are more likely . . . to have, or to expect, children and, if so, to take a benign view of authority and a dim view of social disorder" (p. 53).

In theorizing possible linkages, two competing possibilities present themselves. On one hand, those who are married may adhere more strongly to conventional societal values (Plissner, 1983), which may contribute to their viewing youthful offenders as young adults. In turn, this view may temper the influence of a rehabilitative philosophy of punishment and enhance a nonrehabilitative, more punitive orientation. On the other hand, those who are married may be more likely to view youthful offenders as less culpable for their behavior, which may enhance the influence of a rehabilitative philosophy of punishment while diminishing that of a punitive orientation. Finally, insofar as an interaction exists between sanctioning philosophy and marital status, the question emerges as to whether it can be explained by reference to political ideology. The latter clearly is linked to sentencing policy formation generally (Roberts & Stalans, 1998) as well as to marital status not broadly but for specific political issues, thus raising the possibility that sanctioning philosophy and marital status may be linked to political orientation.

Method

Data

The data for this study came from the National Opinion Survey of Crime and Justice (NOSCJ). . . . Three dependent variables were examined: Juveniles should be tried as adults if charged with (a) selling illegal drugs, (b) committing a property crime, or (c) committing a violent crime. Each of these variables was coded 1 (*agree* or *strongly agree*) or 0 (*neutral, disagree,* or *strongly disagree*) to focus on the issue of who actively supports adult sanctioning of youths. . . .

Three sets of independent variables were used in the analyses: sociodemographic, attitudinal, and contextual factors. Sociodemographic factors included age as well as age squared (to examine curvilinearity in the effect of age), . . . race, . . . annual household income, . . . education, . . . marital status, . . . and number of people in household. . . .

Attitudinal factors included political ideology, which was coded dichotomously to emphasize conservative ideological orientations (1 = conservative, 0 = moderate or liberal), as well as views on parents having legal responsibility for their children's actions, . . . religious denomination (1 = conservative Protestant, 0 = other), and rehabilitative philosophy of sanctioning juveniles (1 = rehabilitation, 0 = other). For religion, respondents were given denominational categories from which to choose; those who listed a specific denomination were coded as conservative Protestant if they described themselves as being Christian, evangelical, embracing the "full gospel," or as belonging to any of the following: Apostolic, Assembly of God, Baptist, Church of Christ, Church of the Nazarene, Faith United, Jehovah's Witness, Mormon, Pentecostal, Reformed Church, or Unity. For punishment philosophy, . . . "other" included three options from which respondents could choose as representing the main purpose of punishing juveniles: deterrence, incapacitation, and retribution. The contrast thus was between rehabilitative and nonrehabilitative approaches to sanctioning.

Finally, contextual factors included a public disorder index . . . composed of views about eight items (trash and litter, neighborhood dogs running loose, graffiti, vacant houses and unkempt lots, unsupervised youths, noise, people drunk or high in public places, and abandoned cars and car parts); urbanization . . . and state-level juvenile (ages 10 to 17) property and violent crime rates (number of arrests per 100,000 persons ages 10 to 17). . . .

Design and Analyses

Given the considerable attention state legislatures have given to violent and drug offenses, the analyses center on three types of offenses (selling illegal drugs, property crime, and violent crime) rather than a composite measure of attitudes toward sanctioning youths as adults. Also, because the focus of this article is on examining support for or against sanctioning youths as adults, the dependent variables have been coded dichotomously. . . .

Results

. . . [There] is slight evidence of a curvilinear relationship between age and support for more punitive (i.e., adult-like) sanctioning of youths who engaged in property crime, with support declining until middle age and increasing thereafter. . . . [For] property offending, . . . males were more likely than females to support more punitive sanctioning when juveniles committed this type of offense. Those who had higher incomes were somewhat more likely to support more punitive sanctioning of juveniles when the offense involved selling drugs, whereas those who were married were more likely to support harsher sanctioning when the crime involved a violent offense. By contrast, both higher levels of education and adherence to a rehabilitative philosophy of punishment consistently were associated with a reduced likelihood of supporting the sanctioning of youths as adults, regardless of offense. . . . [Many] of the other identified factors . . . were either unassociated with or inconsistently associated with support for more punitive sanctioning, including race, . . . the number of people in a household (significant only for violent crime), adherence to a conservative political ideology or to the belief that parents should be held legally responsible for their children's actions, affiliation with a conservative Protestant denomination, perception of public disorder, and living in an urbanized area (significant only for selling illegal drugs) or in a state with higher juvenile property and violent crime rates. . . .

[The] effect of sanctioning philosophy on support for sanctioning youths as adults varied depending on whether an individual was married. . . . [Those] most supportive of sanctioning youths as adults were married and adhered to a nonrehabilitative philosophy of punishment, whereas those least supportive were married and adhered to a rehabilitative philosophy of punishment.

In attempting to account for the interaction between philosophy of punishment and marital status, it was theorized that an individual's political ideology might play a role and perhaps even eliminate any observed interactive relationship. To test this hypothesis, a three-way interaction term was created using rehabilitative philosophy (R), being married (M), and conservative ideology (C) as constituent terms. . . .

The only model for which a three-way interaction effect surfaced was support for adult-like sanctioning of youths who sold illegal drugs. . . .

In the two-way interaction model, . . . the effect of being married increased the predicted probability that a nonrehabilitative philosophy would result in support for adult-like sanctioning of youthful drug dealers. . . . Conversely, among those adhering to a rehabilitative philosophy of punishment, being married only marginally affected the probability of supporting more punitive sanctioning. In the three-way interaction model for selling illegal drugs, the initial difference identified in the two-way interactive model was not eliminated but rather was differentially present among different groups . . . That is, being married increased the probability of supporting more punitive sanctioning among those adhering (a) to a conservative political orientation and a rehabilitative philosophy of punishment . . . or (b) to a nonconservative political orientation and a non-rehabilitative philosophy of punishment. . . .

Discussion

Findings from this research parallel that of other research (Schwartz et al., 1993). . . . When the offense was property crime, slight evidence of a curvilinear relationship between age and support for sanctioning youths as adults emerged, with the greatest support among the youngest and oldest age groups. For this same offense, males were more likely than females to support more punitive sanctioning of youths. By contrast, an effect of income emerged only for youths tried for selling illegal drugs, with wealthier individuals more likely to support punitive sanctioning. Nonetheless, some general patterns consistently emerged across the three types of offenses examined in this study (selling illegal drugs, committing property crime, or committing violent crimes): Support for sanctioning youths as adults was greater among the married, and it was markedly lower among the better educated and adherents to a rehabilitative philosophy of punishment. In addition, few if any direct effects were evident for race, number of people in household, conservative political ideology, belief that parents should be legally responsible for their children's actions, conservative Protestantism, perception of public disorder, or living in an urbanized area or in a state with higher juvenile property and violent crime rates.

The fact that there is relatively widespread support for adult-like sanctioning of youths tried for selling illegal drugs or committing property or violent crimes and that, for the most part, this support cuts across many sociodemographic groups, contexts, and political ideologies, is striking. It does not belie the fact that widespread support also exists for rehabilitation, especially for youths. However, it does suggest the prevalence of a tough love approach to juvenile sanctioning that perhaps always has underlain the juvenile court but that today clearly is more pronounced (Feld, 1999; Roberts & Stalans, 1998; Schwartz et al., 1993) and is, it appears, independent of juvenile crime rates (Taylor et al., 1979). That certain factors, including marital status and philosophy of punishment, exert an influence that seemingly is independent of political ideology suggests also that views about punishment to some extent transcend political boundaries. . . .

In examining potential interactive effects, several notable patterns arose. First, an interaction between philosophy of punishment and marital status was evident across offenses. Specifically, among those with a nonrehabilitative orientation, the married were considerably more likely than the nonmarried to support sanctioning youths as adults; by contrast, marital status exerted little differential influence among those with a rehabilitative orientation. Second, a three-way interaction between philosophy of punishment, marital status, and political ideology surfaced but only for the crime of selling illegal drugs. Specifically, among those holding political orientations and philosophies of punishment that were inconsistent (e.g., a conservative political orientation coupled with a rehabilitative philosophy), being married significantly increased punitiveness.

The initial two-way interaction suggests that being married enhances a nonrehabilitative orientation, thus generating more support for tougher sanctioning of youths. This accords with the idea that those who are married have a greater stake in conventional mainstream societal values (Plissner, 1983) and therefore may be more likely to be threatened by affronts to society. The image thus is one of a group (i.e., those who are married and who adhere to punitive philosophies of punishment) that is especially fearful of crime and its potential consequences and, as a result, is more likely to view juveniles as young adults who warrant adult-like sanctioning. . . .

Given that crime and social disorder have been prominent concerns among conservatives, the question is whether the observed interaction can be explained by reference to political ideology. The three-way interactive models provided tentative support for this possibility, but only for the offense of selling illegal drugs: Being married significantly increased the probability of supporting more punitive sanctioning of youthful drug dealers, but only among those adhering to inconsistent political and punishment orientations. One potential explanation for this finding . . . is that holding a consistent set of beliefs in essence may "trump" any effect of being married. By contrast, holding an inconsistent set of beliefs may lead those who are married to tend toward a more punitive punishment philosophy and, in turn, to support more punitive sanctioning of youths. . . .

The interactive effects of sanctioning philosophy, marital status, and political ideology suggest the intriguing possibility that calls for tough love approaches to sanctioning—most recently and prominently the compassionate conservatism promoted by George W. Bush (Lardner & Walsh, 1999)—have a basis not only in conservative politics but in broader social and philosophical trends in society. The fact that a three-way interaction emerged only for selling illegal drugs lends potential support to this view, especially given the long-standing concern in the United States about the role of drugs in undermining social order. More generally, the interactive effects suggest that our knowledge to date about how exactly different groups view sanctioning and its effect merits renewed attention. . . .

Conclusion

Recent increases in more punitive, adult-like laws for juvenile sanctioning raise questions about the extent to which and why there is public support for such laws. Thus, this article has focused broadly on exploring previously identified factors, including those that have been less systematically examined, and, more specifically, on explicating the interactive role of sanctioning philosophy, marital status, and political orientation in support for sanctioning youths as adults. These issues are important because juvenile sanctioning has become a pressing social issue nationally (Torbet & Szymanski, 1998). However, they also provide a unique opportunity to understand better the basis on which the juvenile court has been transformed from an informal, rehabilitative institution founded on the notion of *parens patriae* to a formal, punitive-based institution that increasingly resembles the criminal justice system (Feld, 1999).

Clearly, public support for sanctioning youths as adults is widespread and cuts across many sociodemographic groups and social settings. . . .

Beyond these observations, there are critical issues that require closer scrutiny if we are to understand better who supports sanctioning youths as adults and, to the extent that they do, why. Such understanding is important not only for its own sake but to provide policy makers with insight into the kinds of policies that reflect public sentiment. Foremost among these issues is the understanding that public opinion is neither monolithic nor simple. As Roberts (1992) has written, "Public perceptions of offenders . . . are complex and far from unidimensional" (p. 138). As but one example, the support for trying juveniles in adult court for commission of select offenses should not be taken as support for adult sentencing. Indeed, Schwartz et al. (1993) found that although the "public prefers having juveniles accused of serious crimes (felonies) tried in adult criminal courts . . . [they do] not favor giving juveniles the same sentences as adults or sentencing them to adult prisons" (p. 24). Moreover and as noted earlier, research consistently shows that the public supports rehabilitative programming, especially of youths (Roberts, 1992).

Echoing calls from others for closer attention to support for tougher sanctioning of juveniles (Roberts & Stalans, 1998; Stalans & Henry, 1994), findings from this article suggest the need for considerably more attention to studying the relationship between philosophy of punishment and other factors. . . . For example, previous research has emphasized the role of fear of crime and of having children (Schwartz et al., 1993), but there are many other situational and social contextual factors that remain to be examined closely, including the role of victimization of family or friends, views toward the potentially mitigating influence of a youth's history of abuse, media coverage of crime, age composition of a given area, unemployment rates, religious heterogeneity, and so forth (Stalans & Henry, 1994). . . .

In short, there is much empirical and theoretical work to be done to further our understanding of public support for sanctioning youths as adults. Given the profound changes to the juvenile court in recent years (Feld, 1999), there is a compelling need for such work. Indeed, if the juvenile justice system is to develop on a more rational basis or at least is to reflect accurately public opinion, the complexity behind their views will require more realistic and nuanced accounts. On the 100th anniversary of the first juvenile court in the United States, it is none too soon to begin developing a sounder foundation for juvenile justice policy.

References

Feld, B.C. (1999). *Bad kids: Race and the transformation of the juvenile court.* New York: Oxford University Press.

Jelen, T.G. (1998). Research in religion and mass political behavior in the United States: Looking both ways after two decades of scholarship. *American Politics Quarterly, 26,* 110–134.

Lardner, G., Jr., & Walsh, E. (1999, October 24). George W. Bush: The Texas record; Compassion collides with the bottom line. *The Washington Post,* p. A1.

Plissner, M. (1983). The marriage gap. *Public Opinion, 6,* 53.

Plutzer, E., & McBurnett, M. (1991). Family life and American politics: The "marriage gap" reconsidered. *Public Opinion Quarterly, 55,* 113–127.

Roberts, J.V. (1992). Public opinion, crime, and criminal justice. In M. H. Tonry (Ed.), *Crime and justice: A review of research* (Vol. 16, pp. 99–180). Chicago: University of Chicago Press.

Roberts, J.V., & Stalans, L.J. (1998). Crime, criminal justice, and public opinion. In M. H. Tonry (Ed.), *The handbook of crime and punishment* (pp. 31–57). New York: Oxford University Press.

Schwartz, I.M., Guo, S., & Kerbs, J.J. (1993). The impact of demographic variables on public opinion regarding juvenile justice: Implications for public policy. *Crime & Delinquency, 39,* 5–28.

Stalans, L. J., & Henry, G. T. (1994). Societal views of justice for adolescents accused of murder: Inconsistency between community sentiment and automatic legislative transfers. *Law and Human Behavior, 18,* 675–696.

Taylor, D.G., Scheppele, K.L., & Stinchcombe, A.L. (1979). Salience of crime and support for harsher criminal sanctions. *Social Problems, 26,* 411–424.

Torbet, P.M., & Szymanski, L. (1998). *State legislative responses to violent juvenile crime: 1996–1997 update.* Washington, DC: Department of Justice, Office of Juvenile Justice and Delinquency Prevention.

Laurence Steinberg and
Elizabeth S. Scott

 **NO**

Less Guilty by Reason of Adolescence: Developmental Immaturity, Diminished Responsibility, and the Juvenile Death Penalty

Since 1990, only a handful of countries in the world . . . have executed individuals whose crimes were committed when they were juveniles. Twenty-one states in the United States allow the execution of individuals under the age of 18, and in most of these states, adolescent offenders as young as 16 can be sentenced to death (Streib, 2002). The United States Supreme Court has held that the death penalty is unconstitutional for youths who are under 16 at the time of their offense (*Thompson v. Oklahoma,* 1998) but has declined to categorically prohibit capital punishment for 16- and 17-year-olds. . . .

The juvenile death penalty is a critically important issue in juvenile crime policy, but it is not our sole focus in this article. We are interested in the broader question of whether juveniles should be punished to the same extent as adults who have committed comparable crimes. Capital punishment is the extreme case, but in practical effect, it is not the most important one in an era in which youth crime policy has become increasingly punitive. The question of whether juveniles should be punished like adults is important to discussions about sentencing guidelines, the transfer of juvenile offenders into the adult criminal justice system, and the incarceration of juveniles in adult facilities (Fagan & Zimring, 2000). High-profile murder cases, like those involving Lee Malvo [the 17-year-old Washington-area serial sniper,] or Lionel Tate, the Florida 14-year-old who was sentenced to life in prison for killing a playmate during a wrestling match, generate public attention to these matters, but questions about the appropriate punishment of juvenile offenders arise in many less visible cases, including those involving nonviolent crimes such as drug selling.

In this article, we draw on research and theory about adolescent development to examine questions about the criminal culpability of juveniles. Recent shifts in juvenile justice policy and practice toward the harsher treatment of youthful offenders are grounded in concerns about public protection and the belief that there is no good reason to exercise leniency with young offenders. This view rejects the conventional wisdom behind traditional juvenile justice policy and challenges those who support reduced punishment for juveniles to

From *American Psychologist*, vol. 58, no. 12, December 2003, pp. 1009–1018. Copyright © 2003 by American Psychological Association. Reprinted by permission. Note: The complete text of this article contains many references to specific studies described. The interested individual should refer to the original publication for these extensive citations. These references have been omitted here in the interest of brevity.

justify a separate, more lenient justice regime for young offenders. We accept this challenge, and we argue that emerging knowledge about cognitive, psychosocial, and neurobiological development in adolescence supports the conclusion that juveniles should not be held to the same standards of criminal responsibility as adults. . . .

Excuse and Mitigation in the Criminal Law

The starting point for our argument is the core principle of penal proportionality . . . (Bonnie, Coughlin, & Jeffries, 1997). Proportionality holds that fair criminal punishment is measured not only by the amount of harm caused or threatened by the actor but also by his or her blameworthiness. Thus, the question we address is whether, and in what ways, the immaturity of adolescent offenders is relevant to their blameworthiness and, in turn, to appropriate punishment for their criminal acts. Answering this question requires a careful examination of the developmental capacities and processes that are relevant to adolescent criminal choices, as well as the conditions and circumstances that reduce culpability in the criminal law (Scott & Steinberg, 2003).

As a preliminary matter, it is important to distinguish between excuse and mitigation, two constructs that are distinct within the law but that are often blurred in laypersons' discussions of crime and punishment. In legal parlance, *excuse* refers to the complete exculpation of a criminal defendant; he or she bears no responsibility for the crime and should receive no punishment. Not surprisingly, defenses that excuse actors altogether from criminal liability are very narrowly drawn. For example, crimes committed under extreme duress may be excused—one who acts with a gun to one's head, for instance—whereas crimes committed under less stressful conditions would not (Robinson, 1997). Unlike excuse, which calls for a binary judgment—guilty or not guilty—*mitigation* places the culpability of a guilty actor somewhere on a continuum of criminal culpability and, by extension, a continuum of punishment. Thus, mitigation is a consideration when a harmful act is sufficiently blameworthy to meet the minimum threshold of criminal responsibility, but the actor's capacities are sufficiently compromised, or the circumstances of the crime sufficiently coercive, to warrant *less* punishment than the typical offender would receive. For example, mental illness that distorts an individual's decision making, but that is not severe enough to support an insanity defense, can reduce the grade of an offense or result in a less punitive disposition (Bonnie et al., 1997).

The public debate about the criminal punishment of juveniles is often heated and ill-informed, in part because the focus is typically on excuse when it should be on mitigation. It is often assumed, in other words, that the only alternative to adult punishment of juveniles is no punishment at all—or a slap on the hand. Instead, we argue that the developmental immaturity of adolescence mitigates culpability and justifies more lenient punishment, but that it is not, generally, a basis for excuse. . . . That is, a juvenile offender, owing to his or her developmental immaturity, should be viewed as *less* culpable than a comparable adult offender, but not as an actor who is without any responsibility for the crime. . . .

Criminal law doctrine takes account of excuse and mitigation in many ways in calculating the seriousness of offenses and the amount of punishment that is appropriate. For example, [defense factors] such as duress, insanity, and self-defense recognize that actors can cause the harm of the offense but be less culpable than the typical offender—or, in extreme cases, not culpable at all (Robinson, 1997). . . .

[Factors] that reduce criminal culpability can be grouped roughly into three categories. The first category includes endogenous impairments . . . in the actor's decision-making capacity [i.e., mental illness, MR, extreme distress] that affect his or her choice to engage in criminal activity (Kadish, 1987). . . .

Under the second category, culpability is reduced when the external circumstances faced by the actor are so compelling that an ordinary (or "reasonable") person might have succumbed to the pressure in the same way as did the defendant (Morse, 1994). . . .

The third category of mitigation includes evidence that the criminal act was out of character for the actor. . . . For example, a reduced sentence might result if the crime was a first offense; if the actor expressed genuine remorse . . . or, more generally, if the criminal act was aberrant in light of the defendant's established character traits and respect for the law's values (United States Sentencing Commission, 1998).

Developmental Immaturity and Mitigation

Each of the categories of mitigation described in the previous section is important to an assessment of the culpability of adolescents who become involved in crime, and each sheds light on differences between normative adolescents and adults. First, and most obviously, adolescents' levels of cognitive and psychosocial development are likely to shape their choices, including their criminal choices, in ways that distinguish them from adults and that may undermine competent decision making. Second, because adolescents' decision-making capacities are immature and their autonomy constrained, they are more vulnerable than are adults to the influence of coercive circumstances that mitigate culpability for all persons, such as provocation, duress, or threat. Finally, because adolescents are still in the process of forming their personal identity, their criminal behavior is less likely than that of an adult to reflect bad character. Thus, for each of the sources of mitigation in criminal law, typical adolescents are less culpable than are adults because adolescent criminal conduct is driven by transitory influences that are constitutive of this developmental stage.

Deficiencies in Decision-Making Capacity

It is well established that reasoning capabilities increase through childhood into adolescence and that preadolescents and younger teens differ substantially from adults in their cognitive abilities (Keating, 1990). . . . Although few psychologists would challenge the assertion that most adults have better reasoning skills than preadolescent children, it is often asserted that, by mid-adolescence, teens' capacities for understanding and reasoning in making decisions roughly approximate those of adults (Furby & Beyth-Marom, 1992). . . . However, . . . there is good reason to question whether age differences in decision making disappear by mid-adolescence. . . . Laboratory studies that are the basis of the assertion that adolescents' reasoning ability is equivalent to that of adults are only modestly useful in understanding how youths compare with adults. . . . In typical laboratory studies of decision making, individual adolescents are presented with hypothetical dilemmas under conditions of low emotional arousal and then asked to make and explain their decisions. In the real world, and especially in situations in which crimes are committed, however, adolescents' decisions are not hypothetical, they are generally made under conditions of emotional arousal (whether negative or positive), and they usually are made in groups. In our view, it is an open and unstudied question whether, under real-world conditions, the decision making of mid- adolescents is truly comparable with that of adults.

More important, even when teenagers' cognitive capacities come close to those of adults, adolescent judgment and their actual decisions may differ from that of adults as a result of psychosocial immaturity. Among the psychosocial factors that are most relevant to understanding differences in judgment and decision making are (a) susceptibility to peer influence, (b) attitudes toward and perception of risk, (c) future orientation, and (d) the capacity for self-management. Whereas cognitive capacities shape the *process* of decision making, psychosocial immaturity can affect decision-making *outcomes*. . . .

There is considerable evidence that the four dimensions of psychosocial maturity described in the previous paragraph continue to develop during the adolescent years. First, substantial research supports . . . that . . . teenagers are more responsive to peer influence than are adults. Studies in which adolescents are presented with hypothetical dilemmas in which they are asked to choose between an antisocial course of action suggested by their peers and a prosocial one of their own choosing indicate that susceptibility to peer influence increases between childhood and early adolescence as adolescents begin to individuate from parental control, peaks around age 14, and declines slowly during the high school years (Steinberg & Silverberg, 1986). Peer influence affects adolescent judgment both directly and indirectly. . . . [Adolescents] make choices in response to direct peer pressure. . . . More indirectly, adolescents' desire for peer approval . . . affect their choices, even without direct coercion. . . .

Second, it is well established that over an extended period between childhood and young adulthood, individuals become more future-oriented. Studies in which individuals are asked to envision themselves or their circumstances in the future find that adults project out their visions over a significantly longer time frame than do adolescents (Nurmi, 1991). . . . There are at least two plausible explanations for this age difference in future orientation. First, owing to cognitive limitations in their ability to think in hypothetical terms, adolescents simply may be less able than adults to think about events that have not yet occurred. . . . Second, the weaker future orientation of adolescents may reflect their more limited life experience. For adolescents, a consequence 5 years in the future may seem very remote in relation to how long they have been alive; teens may simply attach more weight to short-term consequences because they seem more salient to their lives (Gardner, 1993).

Third, adolescents differ from adults in their assessment of and attitude toward risk. In general, adolescents use a risk–reward calculus that places relatively less weight on risk, in relation to reward, than that used by adults. When asked to advise peers on making a potentially risky decision, . . . adults spontaneously mentioned more potential risks than did adolescents (Halpern-Felsher & Cauffman, 2001). . . .

A number of explanations for this age difference have been offered. First, youths' relatively weaker risk aversion may be related to their more limited time perspective, because taking risks is less costly for those with a smaller stake in the future (Gardner & Herman, 1990). Second, . . . considerable evidence indicates that people generally make riskier decisions in groups than they do alone (Vinokur, 1971); there is evidence both that adolescents spend more time in groups than do adults and, as noted earlier, that adolescents are relatively more susceptible to the influence of others.

Fourth, . . . the widely held stereotype that adolescents are more impulsive than adults finds some support in research on developmental changes in impulsivity and self-reliance over the course of adolescence. As assessed on standardized self-report personality measures, impulsivity increases between middle adolescence and early adulthood and declines thereafter, and gains in self-management skills take place during early, middle, and late adolescence (Steinberg & Cauffman, 1996). . . . [Adolescents] have more rapid and more extreme mood swings . . . than adults, which may lead them to act more impulsively. Taken together, these findings indicate that adolescents may have more difficulty regulating their moods, impulses, and behaviors than do adults.

Most of the developmental research on cognitive and psychosocial functioning in adolescence measures behaviors, self-perceptions, or attitudes, but mounting evidence suggests that at least some of the differences between adults and adolescents have neuropsychological and neurobiological underpinnings. . . . [Studies] of brain development during adolescence, and of differences in patterns of brain activation between adolescents and adults, indicate that the most important developments during adolescence occur in regions that are implicated in processes of long-term planning, the regulation of emotion, impulse control, and the evaluation of risk and reward. For example, changes in the limbic system around puberty may stimulate adolescents to seek higher levels of novelty and to take more risks and may contribute to increased emotionality and vulnerability to stress (Dahl, 2001). At the same time, patterns of development in the prefrontal cortex, which is active during the performance of complicated tasks involving long-term planning and judgment and decision making, suggest that these higher order cognitive capacities may be immature well into late adolescence (Geidd et al., 1999).

At this point, the connection between neurobiological and psychological evidence of age differences in decision-making capacity is indirect and suggestive. However, the results of studies using paper-and-pencil measures of future orientation, impulsivity, and susceptibility to peer pressure point in the same direction as the neurobiological evidence, namely, that brain systems implicated in planning, judgment, impulse control, and decision making continue to mature into late adolescence. Thus, there is good reason to believe that adolescents, as compared with adults, are more susceptible to influence, less future oriented, less risk averse, and less able to manage their impulses and behavior, and that these differences likely have a neurobiological basis. The important conclusion for our purposes is that . . . like offenders who are mentally retarded and mentally ill, adolescents are less culpable than typical adults because of diminished decision-making capacity. . . .

Moreover, like offenders who are mentally retarded, there is good reason to believe that the deficiencies of adolescent judgment are [biological in origin.] . . . [During] adolescence, immature judgment is likely no more subject to the volitional control of the youth than is the poor judgment of adults who are mentally retarded.

Heightened Vulnerability to Coercive Circumstances

. . . As we noted earlier, criminal culpability can be reduced on the basis of circumstances that impose extraordinary pressures on the actor. The criminal law does not require exceptional fortitude or bravery of citizens and, in general, recognizes mitigation where an ordinary (or in legal parlance, "reasonable") person might have responded in the same way as the defendant under similar circumstances. In evaluating the behavior of an adolescent in responding to extenuating circumstances, however, the correct basis for evaluation is not comparison of the actor's behavior with that of an "ordinary" adult but rather with that of an "ordinary" adolescent (Scott & Steinberg, 2003).

Because of their developmental immaturity, normative (i.e., "ordinary") adolescents may respond adversely to external pressures that adults are able to resist. If adolescents are more susceptible to *hypothetical* peer pressure than are adults . . . , it stands to reason that age differences in susceptibility to *real* peer pressure will be even more considerable. Thus, it seems reasonable to hypothesize that a youth would succumb more readily to peer influence than would an adult in the same situation. Similarly, if adolescents are more impulsive than adults, it may take less of a threat to provoke an aggressive response from a juvenile. And, because adolescents are less likely than adults to think through the future consequences of their actions, the same level of duress may have a more disruptive impact on juveniles' decision making than on that of adults. . . .

Recent evidence on age differences in the processing of emotionally arousing information supports the hypothesis that adolescents may tend to respond to threats more viscerally and emotionally than adults (Baird, Gruber, & Fein, 1999), but far more research on this topic is needed.

Unformed Character as Mitigation

In addition to the mitigating effects of adolescents' diminished decision-making capacity and greater vulnerability to external pressures, youthful culpability is also mitigated by the relatively unformed nature of their characters. As we have noted, the criminal law implicitly assumes that harmful conduct reflects the actor's bad character and treats evidence that this assumption is inaccurate as mitigating of culpability. For most adolescents, the assumption *is* inaccurate, and thus their crimes are less culpable than those of typical criminals.

The emergence of personal identity is an important developmental task of adolescence and one in which the aspects of psychosocial development discussed earlier play a key role. As documented in many empirical tests of Erikson's (1968) theory of the adolescent *identity crisis*, the process of identity formation includes considerable exploration and experimentation over the course of adolescence. . . . Often this experimentation involves risky, illegal, or dangerous activities like alcohol use, drug use, unsafe sex, and antisocial behavior. For most teens, these behaviors are fleeting; they cease with maturity as individual identity becomes settled. Only a relatively small proportion of adolescents who experiment in risky or illegal activities develop entrenched patterns of problem behavior that persist into adulthood (Farrington, 1986). Thus, making predictions about the development of relatively more permanent and enduring traits on the basis of patterns of risky behavior observed in adolescence is an uncertain business. At least until late adolescence, individuals' values, attitudes, beliefs, and plans are likely to be tentative and exploratory expressions rather than enduring representations of personhood. Thus, research on identity development in adolescence supports the view that much youth crime stems from normative experimentation with risky behavior and not from deep-seated moral deficiency reflective of "bad" character. . . .

In view of what we know about identity development, it seems likely that the criminal conduct of most young wrongdoers is quite different from that of typical adult criminals. Most adults who engage in criminal conduct act on subjectively defined preferences and values, and their choices can fairly be charged to deficient moral character. This cannot be said of typical juvenile actors, whose behaviors are more likely to be shaped by developmental forces that are constitutive of adolescence. To be sure, some adolescents may be in the early stages of developing a criminal identity and reprehensible moral character traits, but most are not. Indeed, studies of criminal careers indicate that the vast majority of adolescents who engage in criminal or delinquent behavior desist from crime as they mature into adulthood (Farrington, 1986). Thus the criminal choices of typical young offenders differ from those of adults not only because the choice, *qua* choice, is deficient as the product of immature judgment, but also because the adolescent's criminal act does not express the actor's bad character.

The notion that individuals are less blameworthy when their crimes are out of character is significant in assessing the culpability of typical young offenders. In one sense, young wrongdoers are not like adults whose acts are less culpable on this ground. A claim that an adult's criminal act was out of character requires a demonstration that his or her established character is good. The criminal choice of the typical adolescent cannot be evaluated in this manner because the adolescent's personal identity is in flux and his or her character has not yet stabilized. However, like the adult offender whose crime is mitigated because it is out of character, adolescent offenders lack an important component of culpability—the connection between a bad act and a bad character. . . .

Developmental Immaturity, Diminished Culpability, and the Juvenile Crime Policy

The adolescent who commits a crime typically is not so deficient in his or her decision-making capacity that the adolescent cannot understand the immediate harmful consequences of his or her choice or its wrongfulness, as might be true of a mentally disordered person or a child. Yet, in ways that we have described, the developmental factors that drive adolescent decision making may predictably contribute to choices reflective of immature judgment and unformed character. Thus, youthful criminal choices may share much in common with those of adults whose criminal behavior is treated as less blameworthy than that of the typical offender, because their criminal behavior is out of character, their decision-making capacities are impaired by emotional disturbance, mental illness, or retardation, or their criminal choices were influenced by unusually coercive circumstances.

If, in fact, adolescent offenders are generally less culpable than their adult counterparts, how should the legal system recognize their diminished responsibility? An important policy choice is whether immaturity should be considered on an individualized basis, as is typical of most mitigating conditions, or as the basis for treating young law violators as a separate category of offenders (Scott & Steinberg, 2003).

We believe that the uniqueness of immaturity as a mitigating condition argues for the adoption of, or renewed commitment to, a categorical approach, under which most youths are dealt with in a separate justice system, in which rehabilitation is a central aim, and none are eligible for the ultimate punishment of death. Other mitigators—emotional disturbance and coercive external circumstances, for example—affect criminal choices with endless variety and have idiosyncratic effects on behavior; thus, individualized consideration of mitigation is appropriate where these phenomena are involved. . . .

Ongoing research on the links between brain maturation and psychological development in adolescence has begun to shed light on why adolescents are not as planful, thoughtful, or self-controlled as adults, and, more importantly, it clarifies that these "deficiencies" may be physiological as well as psychological in nature. Nevertheless, we are a long way from comprehensive scientific understanding in this area, and research findings are unlikely to ever be sufficiently precise to draw a chronological age boundary between those who have adult decision-making capacity and those who do not. Some of the relevant abilities (e.g., logical reasoning) may reach adultlike levels in middle adolescence, whereas others (e.g., the ability to resist peer influence or think through the future consequences of one's actions) may not become fully mature until young adulthood.

Many perspectives can inform debates about youth crime policy and the juvenile death penalty, but surely one should be the science of developmental psychology. Psychologists have much to contribute to discussions about the underpinnings, biological bases, and developmental course of the capacities and competencies relevant to criminal culpability and to the appropriateness of capital punishment for juveniles. Especially needed are studies that link developmental changes in decision making to changes in brain structure and function, and studies that examine age differences in decision making under more ecologically valid conditions.

In our view, however, there is sufficient indirect and suggestive evidence of age differences in capacities that are relevant to criminal blameworthiness to support the position that youths who commit crimes should be punished more leniently than their adult counterparts. Although, as we have noted, the definitive developmental research has not yet been conducted, until we have better and more conclusive data, it would be prudent to err on the side of caution, especially when life and death decisions are concerned. The Supreme Court has repeatedly emphasized that the death penalty is acceptable punishment only for the most blameworthy killers (*Gregg v. Georgia*, 1976; *Lockett v. Ohio*, 1978). All other developed countries have adopted a policy that assumes that adolescents, because of developmental immaturity, simply do not satisfy this criterion. The United States should join the majority of countries around the world in prohibiting the execution of individuals for crimes committed under the age of 18.

References

Baird, A., Gruber, S., & Fein, D. (1999). Functional magnetic resonance imaging of facial affect recognition in children and adolescents. *Journal of the American Academy of Child and Adolescent Psychiatry, 38,* 195–199.

Bonnie, R., Coughlin, A., & Jeffries, J. (Eds.). (1997). *Criminal law.* New York: Foundation Press.

Dahl, R. (2001). Affect regulation, brain development, and behavioral/emotional health in adolescence. *CNS Spectrums, 6,* 1–12.

Erikson, E. (1968). *Identity: Youth and crisis.* New York: Norton.

Fagan, J., & Zimring, F. (2000). *The changing borders of juvenile justice: Transfer of adolescents to the criminal court.* Chicago: University of Chicago Press.

Farrington, D. (1986). Age and crime. In M. Tonry & N. Morris (Eds.), *Crime and justice: An annual review of research* (pp. 189–217). Chicago: University of Chicago Press.

Furby, L., & Beyth-Marom, R. (1992). Risk taking in adolescence: A decision-making perspective. *Developmental Review, 12,* 1–44.

Gardner, W. (1993). A life-span rational choice theory of risk taking. In N. Bell & R. Bell (Eds.), *Adolescent risk taking* (pp. 66–83). Newbury Park, CA: Sage.

Gardner, W., & Herman, J. (1990). Adolescents' AIDS risk taking: A rational choice perspective. In W. Gardner, S. Millstein, & B. Wilcox (Eds.), *Adolescents in the AIDS epidemic* (pp. 17–34). San Francisco: Jossey-Bass.

Gregg v. Georgia, 428 U.S. 153 (1976).

Giedd, J., Blumenthal, J., Jeffries, N., Castllanos, F., Liu, H., & Zijdenbos, A., et al. (1999). Brain development during childhood and adolescence: A longitudinal MRI study. *Nature Neuroscience, 2,* 861–863.

Halpern-Felsher, B., & Cauffman, E. (2001). Costs and benefits of a decision: Decision-making competence in adolescents and adults. *Journal of Applied Developmental Psychology, 22,* 257–273.

Kadish, S. (1987). Excusing crime. *California Law Review, 75,* 257–296.

Keating, D. (1990). Adolescent thinking. In S. S. Feldman & G. R. Elliot (Eds.), *At the threshold: The developing adolescent* (pp. 54–89). Cambridge, MA: Harvard University Press.

Lockett v. Ohio, 438 U.S. 586 (1978).

Morse, S. (1994). Culpability and control. *Pennsylvania Law Review, 142,* 1587–1660.

Nurmi, J. (1991). How do adolescents see their future? A review of the development of future orientation and planning. *Developmental Review, 11,* 1–59.

Robinson, P. (1997). *Criminal law.* New York: Aspen.

Scott, E., & Steinberg, L. (2003). Blaming youth. *Texas Law Review, 81,* 799–840.

Steinberg, L., & Cauffman, E. (1996). Maturity of judgment in adolescence: Psychosocial factors in adolescent decision-making. *Law and Human Behavior, 20,* 249–272.

Steinberg, L., & Silverberg, S. (1986). The vicissitudes of autonomy in early adolescence. *Child Development, 57,* 841–851.

Streib, V. (2002). *The juvenile death penalty today: Death sentences and executions for juvenile crimes, January 1, 1973–November 15, 2002* [Unpublished report]. Retrieved from http://www.law.onu.edu/faculty/streib/juvdeath.pdf

Thompson v. Oklahoma, 487 U.S. 815 (1998).

United States Sentencing Commission, (1998). *United States sentencing guidelines manual: Section 5K2.20.* Washington, DC: Author.

Vinokur, A. (1971). Review and theoretical analysis of the effects of group processes upon individual and group decisions involving risk. *Psychological Bulletin, 76,* 231–250.

POSTSCRIPT

Should Adolescents Who Commit Serious Offenses Be Tried and Convicted as Adults?

Steinberg and Scott address the issue of culpability or blameworthiness. They explain the factors that reduce culpability among adolescents, which they argue should reduce the grade of an offense and subsequently the punishment. The adolescent cognitive and psychosocial characteristics described include immature decision making because of still-developing cognitive capacities, greater vulnerability to external pressures such as peer coercion, and a still-developing identity resulting in tentative values, attitudes, and beliefs. Because of these factors, Steinberg and Scott recommend a separate justice system for adolescents with a focus on rehabilitation, more lenient punishments, and laws prohibiting their execution.

Mears does not necessarily argue against Steinberg and Scott but instead addresses the public opinion of sanctioning youth as adults. Public opinion is strong when it comes to implementing laws and policies and as such, it is necessary to know who supports the "tough love" approach and why. He reports that a conservative group comprised of married individuals with a philosophy of punishment is more likely to support transfer of youth to adult court, especially for serious offenses. This conservative group with conventional mainstream values is especially fearful of crime and its potential consequences, such as the threat to public safety and social disorder. The argument here is one of collective rights.

Many brain researchers support Steinbergís argument stating that structurally, the brain is still growing and maturing during adolescence. Jay Giedd of the National Institute of Mental Health (NIMH) considers 25 the age at which the brain has reached maturity, especially in the areas of the frontal lobe, the region responsible for planning, reasoning, and impulse control. Because the adolescent brain is not fully developed, adolescents are more prone to erratic behaviour driven by emotions and are not as morally culpable as adults. Fried & Reppucci (2001) also support this view, arguing that throughout adolescence, judgment is impaired because "the development of several psychosocial factors that are presumed to influence decision making lags behind the development of the cognitive capacities that are required to make mature decisions" (p. 45).

U.S. law views decision making differently than what is stated above. Essentially, past the age of 14 years, adolescents are competent decision makers under the informed-consent model as long as they are of average or above-average intelligence and can make a knowing, voluntary, intelligent decision (Ambuel & Rappaport, 1992). Steinberg and Scott, however, argue that the informed-consent model is inadequate because it overemphasizes the cognitive components at the expense of the non-cognitive components (e.g., social factors such as peer influence) that may influence mature judgment and sound decision making. Adolescents at 14 may or may not have the cognitive capacity necessary to make good choices, and therefore deciding on an exact age for informed consent or transfer to adult court is impossible. Steinberg and Scott recommend that adolescents who are being considered for transfer to adult court undergo psychological testing to determine their level of maturity.

Jon Sparks, a lawyer in California and past chief of police in Arizona, supports the findings by Mears. He argues that juveniles should be tried as adults if they commit serious crimes such as rape, robbery, or murder, regardless of their age, because children should know at a very young age that "if they do the crime, they will do the time." He further states that many young offenders think the juvenile justice system is a joke, knowing they will not receive harsh punishments. He agrees with them, stating that justice is served only when a juvenile is handled as an adult http://www.newdawnpublishing.com/article_2.htm.

Support for sanctioning youth as adults was also documented by Moon, Wright, Cullen, and Pealer (2000). They found that the majority of respondents in their study favored juvenile capital punishment, often for young offenders. More respondents, however, preferred alternative sentencing options such as life in prison without parole or life in prison with work requirements. Although somewhat dated, a public opinion pole in 1996 also showed that Americans in general supported the transfer of juveniles who have committed serious crimes to adult court (Triplett, 1996).

The arguments are well laid out with respect to trying and convicting youth in adult court when they commit serious crimes. Do lenient penalties protect the public? Are harsh adult penalties fair for an adolescent who lacks the cognitive capacities to reason and make decisions effectively? Should policies reflect public sentiment? Are individual rights more important than collective rights, or how can we balance the two?

References/Further Readings

Ambuel, B., & Rappaport, J. (1992). Developmental trends in adolescents' psychological and legal competence to consent to abortion. *Law and Human Behavior, 16,* 129–154.

Beckman, M. (2004). Crime, culpability, and the adolescent brain. *Science, 305,* 596–599.

Butts, J., & Mitchell, O. (2000). Brick by brick: Dismantling the border between juvenile and adult justice. *Criminal Justice, 2,* 167–213.

Fried, C. S., & Reppucci, N. D. (2001). Criminal decision making: The development of adolescent judgment, criminal responsibility, and culpability. *Law and Human Behavior, 25,* 45–61.

Giedd, J. N. (2004). Structural magnetic resonance imaging of the adolescent brain. *Annals of the New York Academy of Science,* 1021, 77–85.

Grisso, T., Steinberg, L., Woolard, J., Cauffman, E., Scott, E., Graham, S., Lexcen, F., Reppucci, N. D., & Schwartz, R. (2003). Juveniles' competence to stand trial: A comparison of adolescents' and adults' capacities as trial defendants. *Law and Human Behavior,* 27, 333–363.

Kennedy, D. (1997). Let's hold juveniles responsible for their crimes. National Policy Analysis: A Publication of the National Center for Public Policy Research, 166. http://www.nationalecenter.org.

Moon, M. M., Wright, J. P., Cullen, F. T., & Pealer, J. A. (2000). Putting kids to death: Specifying public support for juvenile capital punishment. *Justice Quarterly,* 17, 663–684.

Office of Juvenile Justice and Delinquency Prevention. (1999). Juvenile justice: A century of change. Washington DC: Office of juvenile Justice.

Sabbagh, L. (2006). The teen brain hard at work: No, really. *Scientific American Mind,* 17, 21–25.

Shook, J. J. (2005). Contesting childhood in the US justice system: The transfer of juveniles to adult criminal court. *Childhood,* 12, 461–478.

Statistics Canada (1997 through 2000). Youth Court Statistics. Ottawa: Canadian Centre for Justice Statistics.

Streib, V. L. (2003). The juvenile death penalty today: Death sentences and executions for juvenile crimes, January 1, 1973–June 30, 2003. http://www.law.onu.edu/faculty/streib.

Triplett, R. (1996). The growing threat: Gangs and juvenile offenders. In T. J. Flanagan & D. R. Longmire (Eds.). *Americans view crime and justice: A national public opinion survey* (pp. 137–150). Thousand Oaks, CA: Sage.

Tuell, J. A. (2002). Juvenile offenders and the death penalty. Child Welfare League of America. National Center for Program Standards and Development. Washington, DC.

ISSUE 16

Is School-Related
Violence Increasing?

YES: Kathryne M. Speaker and George J. Petersen, from "School Violence and Adolescent Suicide: Strategies for Effective Intervention," *Educational Review* (vol. 52, no. 1, 2000)

NO: Dewey G. Cornell, from "Myths about Youth Violence and School Safety," *Virginia Youth Violence Project*

ISSUE SUMMARY

YES: Kathryne Speaker, assistant professor of education at The College of New Jersey, and George Petersen, associate professor of education at California Polytechnic State University, argue that the number of incidents of violence and the severity of these acts have dramatically increased.

NO: Dewey Cornell, professor in the Curry School of Education at the University of Virginia and director of the Virginia Youth Violence Project, provides evidence that violence in schools is not increasing.

School violence is a serious problem that has received a great deal of attention in recent years. The publicized incidents of school violence—in particular the school shootings in the late 1990s—resulted in national concern about the safety of North American schools. One of the most covered stories occurred in 1999 when two adolescent boys went on a shooting rampage in Columbine High School in Littleton, Colorado. Shortly after Columbine, a copycat incident occurred in a high school in Taber, Alberta. Media coverage of these school shootings generated widespread belief that our schools were not safe and that school violence was in fact an epidemic. This public reaction resulted in governments in both Canada and the United States taking action. For example, the U.S. Senate and the House of Representatives held hearings on youth and school violence, while Canadian Ministers of Education began exploring ways to ensure school safety. In both countries, a "zero-tolerance policy" was implemented in all schools, stating that anyone carrying a weapon or exhibiting violent behavior would be suspended or expelled immediately. As part of this movement, security measures were increased, and departments of education distributed guidebooks to schools giving advice on identifying potentially violent students.

The Center for Disease Control defines violence as "The threatened or actual physical force or power initiated by an individual that results in or has a high likelihood of resulting in physical or psychological injury or death (Youth Violence and Suicide Prevention Team, 1999). Physical violence (a subtype of the more general term) is defined as "an act carried out with the intention, or perceived intention, of physically injuring another person. This could include pushing, shoving, slapping, kicking, hitting, threatening with a weapon or using a weapon (Lockwood, 1997). School violence, encompassing both the previous definitions, is any violence occurring on school property, on school buses, and at school events. Further, school violence can be categorized as either serious violent crime (e.g., murder, rape, robbery) or less serious crime (e.g., threat, theft, vandalism) (Youth Violence and Suicide Prevention Team, 1999).

In 1997, 10 percent of all public schools reported at least one serious crime to police. Another 47 percent reported a less serious crime (DeVoe et al., 2002). Police-reported violence occurs more frequently in junior high/ middle schools and in high schools as opposed to elementary schools. Specifically, in 2002, the rate of serious violent crime for elementary school students was 0.1 per 1,000. For students in junior high/middle school and high school, rates were 0.9 per 1,000 and 1.0 per 1,000 respectively. Rates for less serious crimes were 3 per 1,000 for elementary schools, 15 per 1,000 for junior high/middle schools, and 17 per 1,000 for high schools (DeVoe et al., 2002). Urban schools as opposed to suburban, rural, or small-town schools reported more school violence.

Student testimonies of school violence are quite different than those reported to the police, indicating that many incidents of violence go unreported. For example, according to high school students, the rate of serious violent crime was 7 per 1,000 for boys and 2 per 1,000 for girls. For boys, this rate is seven times higher than the rate reported to police by school administrators. For less serious offenses such as theft, students reported 47 per 1,000 for boys and 45 per 1,000 for girls. It appears that students experience far more crime than what is reported to police. Shafii and Shafii (2003) report that in a typical Midwest, midsize city, 30–50 cases of school violence are reported daily, with guns involved in 50 percent of the cases. Interpreting this statistic with respect to the police and student testimony rates reported above could mean that over 200 cases of school violence are occurring every day in a typical Midwest school.

These are alarming statistics; however, we ask if the rates are worse than they were 10 years ago. Is school violence an epidemic or as rampant as the media portrays it to be? Is the learning environment becoming more dangerous than in the past? Essentially, is school-related violence increasing? Kathryne Speaker and George Petersen argue that school violence is becoming commonplace and cross all economic, social, and ethnic lives. Dewey Cornell, on the other hand, argues that violence in schools is not increasing, and our schools are in fact very safe.

**Kathryne M. Speaker and
George J. Petersen**

School Violence and Adolescent Suicide: Strategies for Effective Intervention

Introduction

The public school system in the United States has always represented itself as being the hallmark of vital socialization, equality in education, hope for the future and sense of community. This picture has changed drastically in the past 20 years. Chaos seems to be replacing community. Juvenile violence and suicide are becoming increasingly commonplace and occurrences of both phenomena cross all economic, social and ethnic lines. While the increasing tide of juvenile violence in the streets is alarming, it is particularly problematic because of its insidious encroachment into the public school system. Violence disrupts normal school operation, students do not learn and teachers cannot teach. It degrades the quality of life and the education of children, and it forces some schools to allocate many of their already limited resources to security and prevention measures.

The causes of violence in our culture are extremely complicated. Literature in the area has pointed to the complex interaction between poverty, racism, drugs and alcohol, the loss of employment, inadequate hand gun regulation, lack of personal opportunity and responsibility, disinvestment in schools and family violence as all playing a crucial role in America's culture of violence (Prothrow-Stith, 1994). In a recent survey of school administrators, over 50% of the respondents felt that lack of parental involvement was the single most important contributor to school violence (Stephens, 1994). Societal changes, the breakdown of family relationships and violent role models in the media have also been cited as contributing factors . . . (Met Life, 1994).

The American family structure has shifted away from the idealized two-parent family with dad working and mom at home with the children. According to the US Department of Health and Human Services 75% of all mothers of school-age children are in the labor force. . . . One in four children live in families with only one parent, . . . and 22% of all children . . . live in families below the poverty line, the highest number and rate since 1965.

From *Educational Review*, vol. 52, no. 1, 2000, pp. 65–73. Copyright © 2000 by Taylor & Francis, Ltd. Reprinted by permission. Note: The complete text of this article contains many references to specific studies described. The interested individual should refer to the original publication for these extensive citations. These references have been omitted here in the interest of brevity.

As a result of the deteriorating social environment and growing fiscal crisis, many children face substantial hurdles on their journey toward adulthood. Dryfoos (1994) refers to these barriers as the 'new morbidities'—unprotected sex, drugs, violence, and depression . . . in contrast to the 'old morbidities'—chronic diseases, nutritional deficiencies, acne and infestation of head lice. Needless to say, these 'new morbidities' also create significant problems for schools.

> Today's schools feel pressured to feed children; provide psychological sup-
> port services; offer health screening; establish referral networks related to
> substance abuse, child welfare, and sexual abuse; cooperate with the local
> police and probation officers; add curricula for prevention of substance
> abuse, teen pregnancy, suicide, and violence; and actively promote social
> skills, good nutrition, safety, and general health. (Dryfoos, 1994, p. 5)

. . . Research has [also] demonstrated that many of the same negative societal changes are . . . the components identified as significant contributors to adolescent suicide (McGuire & Ely, 1984). . . . The increase in the number of firearms in this country is [also] important in both violence and suicide. . . . In 1994 almost 3350 of the suicides aged 15–24 . . . were by firearms (NCHS, 1997). We also know, just as violence in the school has increased dramatically, that suicide among adolescents has increased 300% in the past 30 years. . . .

For many reasons American schools have not focused adequate attention on either youth violence or suicide. The search for solutions to these problems has generated a collection of approaches that parallel those used by law enforcement personnel to combat violence and crime in United States society. Yet budgetary, scheduling and resource constraints on American education force schools to deal with violence and suicide in a piecemeal fashion, and recent research has shown that this fragmented approach is meeting with little success. In a recent study, 1200 educators were queried about suicide prevention plans at their school site. Only 20% indicated that their school had such a plan.

The majority of violence prevention programs target the areas of parental involvement, gang activity, drugs and conflict resolution skills and are being piloted in middle schools/junior high and senior high schools with little attention paid to the problem at the elementary level (Stephens, 1994). Other programs, including police partnerships/liaisons, use of advanced technologies (metal detectors, cameras, etc.), removal of lockers (or not installing them), etc., have also been tried, but the results of these efforts have been less than successful in overcoming the enigmatic problem of school violence. Suicide prevention programs are also often implemented after the fact and deal with post-traumatic reaction rather than prevention. . . . No concentrated effort has been made to determine what programs might effectively prevent violent behavior before it starts (Johnson & Johnson, 1995). . . .

Many professionals in the field do recognize, however, that schools must lead in the development and assessment of programs that address the specific needs of adolescents in order to help them with the knowledge, skills and values to make more positive choices in dealing with life and death issues (Kalafat & Ellis, 1994). Rarely is information about the effectiveness of these programs reported in professional journals because of the difficulty in demonstrating that they do prevent adolescent suicide. While empirically based information is beginning to be accumulated, the acquisition of data is difficult because of the small numbers and the lack of documentation of both attempts and completions. . . .

A review of the literature on the subject of teenage suicide would suggest that many of the components in a school-based suicide prevention and intervention program parallel the components detailed in an empirically derived model focused on the remediation of school violence in elementary schools. The concepts of proactive, early and inclusive intervention and education are mandated in this violence reduction model. Research in the area of adolescent suicide has indicated that these components are equally essential in a comprehensive and systematic school-based suicide prevention program (Henry, 1996).

Violence—Suicide Reduction Model

The model presented in this article is based on the conclusions of a national study conducted by the authors of the present paper. The study surveyed teachers, site administrators and district administrators in 15 school districts in 12 states. The student populations in the participating districts ranged from fewer than 1000 students to districts with student populations of well over 50,000. A primary focus of the study was to identify education professionals' perceptions of the causes, frequencies and changes in demographics, types and costs associated with violence in P-12 (i.e. primary) settings. In order to identify the underlying elements of the perceived causes for school violence data were subjected to a factor analytic investigation. . . . [Results indicated] five factors seen as contributing most significantly to school violence: (1) a decline in the family structure [(>30% of the variance)]; (2) a lack of school resources or skills to deal with violence; (3) the breakdown in moral/ethical education of youth; (4) family violence combined with drug-related factors; and (5) violence in the media. These data confirm previous research which implicated the role of declining societal modeling, media violence and declining family structure as root causes in the escalation of school violence (Met Life, 1994; Prothrow-Stith, 1994). The data further suggest that a lack of skills and resources for professional educators combined with the lack of a moral/ethical education are crucial elements contributing to the serious problems of school violence and adolescent suicide. Studies of adolescent suicide ideation indicate that a lack of effective coping strategies may also be a significant contributor. [It is therefore recommended that intervention programs focus on these factors.] The need for such intervention at the elementary level is essential to both violence and suicide prevention for at least two reasons. First, studies have demonstrated that prevention models focused on at-risk populations have been shown to be effective when implemented at the preschool/elementary level (Baker, 1992), and [second,] data from the authors' study point to the fact that the greatest rise in the frequency of violent acts is at the preschool/elementary level. Suicide rates among those aged 10–14 years are increasing at the highest rate during adolescence, indicating that intervention must begin before age 10. Developmentally, it also follows that major coping strategy changes occur early and waiting until high-school age may be too late to make major changes (Wolfle & Siehl, 1992). . . .

Family Inclusion

While schools struggle to implement reactive measures of violence prevention, the data suggest that to successfully address the problem a proactive, comprehensive reorganization of the existing school structure must be undertaken. A key element in this reorganization is the recognition that schools will need to incorporate not only an academic focus for the student but include the family within the educational structure (Dryfoos, 1994). The restructuring of schools should include a new definition of the school as 'town' or 'community center', which supports, includes and engages the entire family in the scope of the educational setting. As the basic structure of the family disintegrates, violence among family members increases and this domestic violence spills into the classroom. This disintegration of family structure is also distinguished as a chronic stressor, one of the categories often related to depression and suicidal ideation (Adams *et al.*, 1996). . . . A new picture of the school must emerge to provide the variety of services that are needed by families and students in order to alleviate incidents of school violence and potential student suicide.

Evolution of Teacher/Administrator Roles

This component would require schools at the preschool/elementary level to staff their buildings with personnel trained not only in traditional pedagogical methodologies but also in a comprehensive values education. The role of school counselor should be integral to the entire process of prevention and intervention in the joint program of violence and suicide prevention. All school personnel should be involved in implementing an ethical and social skills curriculum and developing an integrated and inclusive school environment involving the daily modeling of these skills by school personnel for students.

Student Success

The third component of the model involves creating a 'success identity' . . . (Glasser, 1992). The critical factor in meeting the basic needs of individuals is the creation of individual responsibility that significantly impacts upon personality development. If parents are able to demonstrate and convey a sense of responsibility for themselves as well as in their children, children will develop an integrated concept of self-worth. This ultimately leads to what Glasser refers to as a 'success identity.' . . . Learning effective ways to satisfy basic needs actively and to effectively cope with life's ups and downs contributes to building positive self-esteem and sense of identity. Adolescent violence and suicide can be viewed as a reaction to unmet physical and emotional needs. The establishment and encouragement of self-esteem in students is an absolute requirement of any successful model since self-esteem is, in itself, a deterrent to participation in violent acts.

Conflict Mediation

This component of the elementary model does not suggest that there is one specific program of mediation that should be implemented in every classroom. Rather, this component emphasizes that the teaching of some form of empirically field-tested conflict mediation, negotiation procedures and constructive resolution skills should be included in the curriculum of every classroom. As Johnson and Johnson (1995) have repeatedly suggested, the norms, values and culture of a school should promote negotiation and mediation procedures by including classroom lessons on improving communication skills, ways to control anger, appropriate assertiveness, problem-solving skills, perspective-taking, creative thinking and other related interpersonal and small-group skills. . . .

Media Intervention

There have been numerous conclusive studies that indicate a causal relationship between television violence and actual violence. Regardless of whether the relationship has a direct correlation, educators should address the power of the media when discussing the subject of school violence. Teachers must be equipped to deal with the influences children are exposed to outside the classroom and to be aware that non-attention to media issues is translated by children as acceptance of the violence that they see, hear and live with on a daily basis. There are certain inclusive strategies that every teacher should implement in the classroom. These key elements include creating a safe classroom atmosphere; planning a curriculum which presents alternative reading material that meets each child's developmental needs and allows for the resolution of personal and ethical questions; communicating with children in the classroom while creating the opportunity to make informed choices; and reaching out to parents to involve them in discussions and decisions concerning family choices for viewing, listening and reading. The influence of the media in the lives of children is pervasive. As Healy (1990) states, schools will have to assume a more positive and educational role in guiding children who are 'visually vulnerable' in analysis and evaluation of media content (p. 320). Visual literacy must now be taught in addition to print literacy. Teaching children to evaluate critically the violence they see on a screen teaches them to interact with their viewing choices and evaluate the impact of those choices on their own lives.

Conclusion

The search for effective solutions to the problems of violence and suicide will require vigilance on the part of practitioners and more intensive and integrated research on the part of university and educational researchers. The suggestions and ideas presented in this article are not conclusive, yet they compare the documented similarities of violence and suicide. The intention of this article is to focus the reader's attention on the significance and rapid increase in school violence and suicide among our nation's school population. Using a holistic and inclusive model, suggestions for the reduction and remediation of these two phenomena have been presented.

References

Adams, D., Overholser J., Spirito, A. (1996) Suicide attempts and stressful life events, *The Prevention Researcher*, 3(3), pp. 5–8.

Baker, S. (1992) *School Counseling for the Twenty-first Century* (New York, Merrill).

Dryfoos, J. (1994) *Full Service Schools: a revolution in health services for children, youth and families* (San Francisco, CA, Jossey-Bass).

Glasser, S. (1992) Violence in schools, *Congressional Quarterly*, pp. 787–802.

Review of the literature and implications for school counselors, *School Counselor*, 37, pp. 328–335.

Healy, J. (1990) *Endangered Minds* (New York, Simon & Schuster).

Henry, C. (1996) A human ecological approach to adolescent suicide, *Prevention Researcher*, 3(3), pp. 5–8.

Johnson, D. & Johnson, T. (1995a) Why violence prevention programs don't work and what does, *Educational Leadership*, 52(5), pp. 63–68.

Kalafat, J. & Elias, M. (1994) An evaluation of a school-based suicide awareness intervention, *Suicide and Life-Threatening Behavior*, 24(3), pp. 224–233.

McGuire, D. & Ely, M. (1984) Child suicide, *Child Welfare*, 1, pp. 17–26.

Met Life (1994) *The Metropolitan Life Survey of the American Teacher 1994. Violence in America's public schools: the family perspective* (Metropolitan Life Insurance Company).

National Center for Health Statistics (1997) Advance report of final mortality statistics, 1994, *NCHS Monthly Vital Statistics Report*, 45(3, suppl.), pp. 63–80.

Prothrow-Stith, D. (1994) Building violence prevention into the curriculum : a physician-administrator applies a public health model to schools, *School Administrator*, 4(51), pp. 8–12.

Stephens, R.D. (1994) Gangs guns and school violence, *USA Today*, 122(2584) , pp. 29–32.

Wolfle, J. & Siehl, P. (1992) The role of school and family in the prevention of adolescent suicide. Paper presented at the Annual Association of Teacher Educators, Orlando, Florida.

Dewey G. Cornell  **NO**

Myths about Youth Violence and School Safety

T he highly publicized school shootings of the 1990's generated nationwide concern about the safety of our schools. The news media focused national attention on little-known places such as Pearl, Mississippi; Paducah, Kentucky; and Jonesboro, Arkansas where young boys opened fire on their classmates. In 1999, Columbine High School became the best-known high school in America when two boys went on a shooting rampage that killed twelve students and a teacher before they killed themselves. Live television coverage of the Columbine tragedy began while students were still hiding in the school and police were attempting to find the shooters. In the following weeks the American public was exposed to numerous images of bloody victims and interviews with traumatized, grief-stricken survivors.

There was a dramatic national response to the school shootings. Both the U.S. Senate and the House of Representatives held hearings on youth violence, the White House held a conference on school violence, and both the FBI and Secret Service conducted studies of school shootings. The U.S. Department of Education distributed "warning signs" guidebooks to schools giving advice on identifying potentially violent students (Dwyer, Osher, & Warger, 1998) and the U.S. Surgeon General (2001) released a major report on youth violence. Less obvious, but even more important, local school authorities across the country adopted new security measures, implemented tougher zero tolerance policies, and greatly expanded their use of school resource officers and school security officers.

Although the school shootings stimulated new attention to the problem of school safety and brought about many positive changes in relationships between schools and law enforcement agencies, *public perceptions are easily skewed by media attention to a handful of extreme cases*. The school shootings frightened the public and generated a widespread belief that there was an epidemic of violence in our schools. As the facts presented here demonstrate, this epidemic was a myth. School violence did not increase in the 1990's, it declined.

Consequently, it is important to guard against fear-based perceptions of school violence. Policy decisions about school safety must be based on objective information. School administrators and policy-makers must maintain a rational and factual perspective on school safety. Here are five myths about youth violence and school safety that threaten to distort school safety policy and practices:

Myth 1. Juvenile Violence Is Increasing

Facts According to FBI national arrest statistics, the arrest rate of juveniles for violent crime (murder, robbery, rape, and aggravated assault) peaked in 1994 and has declined each year since then. This rate is lower now than in any year since at least 1980. The most dramatic decline in juvenile violence is seen for homicides, the category with the most complete and reliable data. . . . [There] were more than three times as many juveniles arrested for murder in 1993 [n = 3284] than in 2002 [n = 973].

Myth 2. Juveniles Are More Violent Than Adults

Facts Juveniles account for just 12% of all violent crimes cleared by arrest. The peak years for violent crime occur in young adults [between the ages 17 and 23].

Myth 3. School Violence Is Increasing

Facts The rate of violent crimes in U.S. public schools has declined since 1994 (DeVoe et al., 2002). The serious violent crime rate (total number of murders, aggravated assaults, robberies, and rapes per 100,000 students) in 2001 was less than half what it was in 1994.

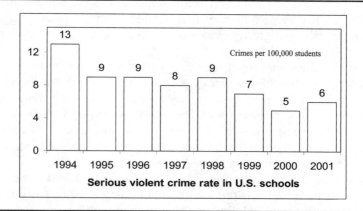

Myth 4. School Homicides Are Increasing

Facts Media attention to several school shootings resulted in a series of copycat crimes during the late 1990's, briefly interrupting an otherwise downward trend (National School Safety Center, 2003).

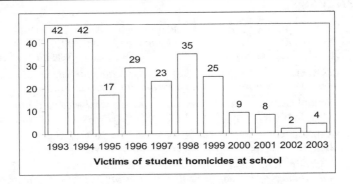

Victims of student homicides at school

Myth 5. There Is a Realistic Possibility of a Student-Perpetrated Homicide at Your School

News media attention to school shootings in the 1990's made them seem like frequent events, but actually homicides committed by students at school are rare events when you consider that there are more than 53 million students attending 119,000 public and private schools in the United States (U.S. Department of Education, 2002). According to the National School Safety Center (2003), there were 93 incidents in which a student murdered someone at school during the ten years from the 1992–93 school year to the 2001–02 school year. Considering that 93 incidents occurred in ten years, you can expect 9.3 incidents per year in the nation's 119,000 schools. This means that the annual probability of any one school experiencing a student-perpetrated homicide is 9.3 ÷ 119,000, which is .0000781 or about 1 in 12,804. In other words, an educator can expect a student to commit a murder at his or her school once very 12,804 years.

How Dangerous Are Our Schools?

Schools are not dangerous places. The perception that schools are dangerous is a misperception generated by a series of extreme, high profile cases that are not representative of most schools. In fact, very few serious violent crimes take place at school. From the standpoint of violent crime, students are safer at school than at home. Moreover, schools have become even safer during the past decade, such that the serious violent crime rate at school is less than half what it was in 1994. Although there are relatively few serious violent crimes at school, there are many less serious crimes and there are numerous discipline problems—primarily disorderly conduct and fights that do not result in injuries—that demand attention. Bullying, teasing, and harassment are common problems that deserve attention in every school, too.

Schools are relatively safe, but they are not crime-free and we have an obligation to keep them as safe as possible. To keep schools safe, it is important to recognize what kinds of crimes are likely or unlikely to occur, and to base decisions on facts rather than fears.

References

DeVoe, J.F., Ruddy, S.A., Miller, A.K., Planty, M., Snyder, T.D., Duhart, D.T., & Rand, M.R. (2002). *Indicators of school crime and safety: 2002* (NCES 2003-009/NCJ196753). U.S. Departments of Education and Justice. Washington, DC.

Dwyer, K., Osher, D., & Warger, C. (1998). *Early warning, timely response: A guide to safe schools.* Washington, DC: U.S. Department of Education.

National School Safety Center (2003). *School associated violent deaths.* Westlake Village, CA. Retrieved January 29, 2003 from http://www.nssc1.org.

U.S. Surgeon General (2001). *Youth violence: A report of the Surgeon General.* Rockville, MD: U.S. Dept. of Health and Human Services.

Vossekuil, B., Fein, R.A., Reddy, M., Borum, R., & Modzeleski, W. (2002). *The final report and findings of the Safe School Initiative: Implications for the prevention of school attacks in the United States.* U.S. Secret Service and U.S. Department of Education. Washington, D.C.

POSTSCRIPT

Is School-Related
Violence Increasing?

Speaker and Petersen present evidence that youth violence and in particular school violence is increasing. They address five factors contributing to school violence: breakdown in family structure, lack of resources to deal with violence, breakdown of moral and ethical education, violent role models in the family, and violence in the media. They also state that gang activity and drugs are contributing to the increasing rates and that measures taken to increase security in schools have not been successful. Finally, they argue that violence disrupts normal school operations, negatively affecting the teaching and learning environment and degrading the quality of life and education of our students.

In his brief but relevant paper, Dewey Cornell addresses five common myths of youth violence and school safety. He reports that the arrest rate of juveniles for violent crimes has decreased in recent years. He also reports that the rate of violence in our schools has declined, and school homicides, despite what the media say, have decreased significantly since 1999. Finally, Dr. Cornell states that although our schools are not dangerous places, less serious acts of violence such as bullying and teasing deserve more attention.

In support of Cornell's argument, the Center for Disease Control (CDC) examined school violence between 1991 and 2003 and reported that in general, most violence-related behaviors had decreased. More specifically, the prevalence of weapon carrying on school property had decreased significantly, from 11.8 percent in 1993 to 6.1 percent in 2003. Physical fighting on school property also declined significantly from 16.2 percent in 1993 to 12.8 percent in 2003. Interestingly, they also reported that student fear of violence increased significantly with more students reporting "not going to school" because of safety concerns in 2003 versus 1993 (5.4 percent and 4.4 percent, respectively).

In support of Speaker and Petersen's argument linking gang activity to increasing rates of school violence, Chandler, Chapman, Rand, and Taylor (1998) found that the presence of gangs more than doubled the likelihood of violent victimization at school. In addition, they found a positive correlation between the presence of gangs at school and the presence of guns and drugs on school property. Adding to this, Shafii and Shafii (2003) argue that although school violence in general (i.e., number of reported cases) has stabilized in recent years, violence against females (students and teachers) and violence involving gang activity has actually increased. Gangs affect more cities and jurisdictions than ever before (Flannery, Hussey, Biebelhausen, & Wester, 2003), and given that gang members are often adolescents between the ages of 14 and 24, it may not be surprising that we are experiencing increases in gang-related violence in our schools. If there are more gangs in our schools, perhaps it is also not surprising that the CDC found that students were more concerned about school safety, despite the reported decrease in school violence.

Student fear as reported by the CDC may also be a by-product of the intense media coverage of school violence, in particular the school shootings. Cornell (2005) for example, states that research supports the argument that the media largely exaggerate the risk of violent crime in schools. The number of murders by students at school has declined since 1999, and serious crimes involving gangs, weapons, or drugs constitute less than 10 percent of the problems (Skiba, 2004). Less serious forms of violence, on the other hand, are more pervasive. This would include theft, vandalism, bullying, and fighting. With their fragile egos and self-esteem, adolescents are perhaps afraid to go to school because they do not want to be victims of bullying and fighting. This issue certainly deserves attention in the literature.

In summary, the question of whether or not school-related violence is increasing is more complex than a simple yes/no debate. On the one hand, school violence as reported by school officials and law enforcement agencies appears to be decreasing, yet according to students, violence is commonplace and is taking place without being reported to police (DeVoe et al., 2002). The fact that students are concerned for their safety coupled with the increase in gang-related violence in North American schools adds to the complexity of this issue.

References/Further Readings

Center for Disease Control and Prevention (2004). Violence-related behaviors among high school students—United States, 1991–2003. *Morbidity and Morality Weekly Report, 53,* 651–655.

Chandler, K.A., Chapman, C.D., Rand, M.R., & Taylor, B.M. (1998). Students' reports of school crime: 1989 and 1995. Washington, DC: U.S. Department of Education, Office of Educational Research and Improvement, National Center for Education Statistics, and U.S. Department of Justice, Office of Justice Programs, Bureau of Justice Statistics.

Cornell, D. G. (2005). School violence: Fears versus facts. In K. Heilbrun, N. Goldstein, & R. Redding (eds). *Juvenile delinquency: Prevention, assessment, and intervention* (pp. 45–66). New York: Oxford University Press.

DeVoe, J.F., Ruddy, S.A., Miller, A.K., Planty, M., Snyder, T.D., Duhart, D. T., et al. (2002). Indicators of school crime and safety: 2002 (National Crime Victimization Study 2003–009/NCJ196753). Washington, DC: Departments of Education and Justice.

Flannery, D.J., Hussey, D.L., Biebelhausen, L., & Wester, K.L. (2003). Crime, delinquency, and youth gangs. In G. Adams & M. Berzonsky (eds.).

Blackwell handbook of adolescence (pp.503–522). Malden, MA: Blackwell Publishing.

Herda-Rapp, A. (2003). The social construction of local school violence threats by the news media and professional organizations. *Sociological Inquiry, 73*, 545–574.

Howell, J.C., & Lynch, J.P. (2000). Youth gangs in schools. Juvenile Justice Bulletin. Washington, DC: U.S. Department of Justice, Office of Justice Programs, Office of Juvenile Justice and Delinquency Prevention.

Morrell, R. (2002). A calm after the storm? Beyond schooling as violence. *Educational Review, 54*, 37–46.

National School Safety Center (2003). School associated violent deaths. Westlake Village, CA. http://www.nssc1.org.

Shafii, M., & Shafii, S. L. (2003). School violence, depression, and suicide. *Journal of Applied Psychoanalytic Studies, 5*, 155–169.

Skiba, R. (2004). Zero tolerance: The assumptions and the facts. *Education Policy Briefs, 2*, 1–8. Indiana Youth Services Association and the Center for Evaluation & Education Policy. http://www.ceep.indiana.edu/ChildrenLeftBehind.

Vossekuil, B., Fein, R.A., Reddy, M., Borum, R., & Modzeleski, W. (2002). The final report and findings of the Safe School Initiative: Implications for the prevention of school attacks in the United States. U.S. Secret Service and U.S. Department of education. Washington, D.C.

Youth Violence and Suicide Prevention Team: Preventing Violence and Suicide. (1999). Centers for Disease Control and Prevention, National Center for Injury Prevention and Control. Atlanta, GA.

ISSUE 17

Are Girls Bigger Bullies Than Boys?

YES: Melanie J. Zimmer-Gembeck, Tasha C. Geiger, and Nicki R. Crick, from "Relational and Physical Aggression, Prosocial Behavior, and Peer Relations: Gender Moderation and Bidirectional Association," *Journal of Early Adolescence* (November 2005)

NO: Christina Salmivalli and Ari Kaukiainen, "'Female Aggression' Revisited: Variable- and Person-Centered Approaches to Studying Gender Differences in Different Types of Aggression," *Aggressive Behavior* (vol. 30, 2004)

ISSUE SUMMARY

YES: Melanie Zimmer-Gembeck, an assistant professor of psychology at Griffith University in Australia, and her colleagues report gender differences in levels of relational aggression, which is a type of bullying. In early adolescence, girls are more relationally aggressive than boys. The authors argue that girls may use relational aggression to gain and keep friends.

NO: Christina Salmivalli, professor of applied psychology, and psychologist Ari Kaukiainen, both from University of Turku, argue that boys use all types of aggression more than girls in early adolescence. This included direct aggression, verbal aggression, and indirect or relational aggression.

In recent years, bullying has become increasingly more serious among today's youth. Conflict and misunderstanding are part of normal development. As cognitive capacities become more sophisticated, adolescents learn to argue. This is part of gaining independence and learning to think for themselves. Bullying, however, introduces risk to normal development.

Bullying is a relationship problem, defined as a subset of aggression occurring when one or more individuals verbally, physically, and/or psychologically harass another person (Olweus, 1997). Olweus also states that there are three core characteristics of bullying: It is aggressive behavior, it occurs over time, and it involves a power imbalance. With respect to the aggressive behavior, bullying also involves physical aggression (e.g., hitting, punching, pushing), verbal aggression (e.g., name-calling, insulting, yelling obscenities), and the more psychological form of aggression often referred to as indirect, relational, or social aggression. Indirect, relational, or social aggression can each be defined differently, yet each has similar characteristics with respect to the type of manipulation involved.

Indirect aggression is defined as a "type of behavior in which the perpetrator attempts to inflict pain in such a manner that he or she makes it seem as though there is no intention to hurt at all" (Bjoörkqvist, Österman & Kaukiainen, 1992, p. 118). Essentially, it's a "behind-the back" aggression. A related term is "stabbing in the back." Relational aggression is defined as behaviors that hurt others by damaging relationships or feelings (Crick & Grotpeter, 1995). This type of mainly covert aggression is about the endpoint, where the goal is to disrupt friendships. Social aggression is also focused on the endpoint and is defined as the "manipulation of group acceptance through alienation, ostracism, or character defamation" (Cairns, Cairns, Neckerman, Ferguson, & Gariépy, 1989, p. 323). Social aggression involves damaging another's self-esteem and/or social status. Indirect, relational, and social aggression have the following characteristics in common: gossiping, spreading rumors, ignoring, deliberately leaving someone out of a group, turning others against others, embarrassing others in public, performing practical jokes, and sending abusive phone calls (Archer & Coyne, 2005).

There is evidence that physical and verbal aggressions decline in early adolescence, at the same time as the more covert types escalate. Research has indicated that between the ages of 8 and 18, physical aggression declines in both males and females, whereas indirect aggression increases significantly between 8 and 11 years of age and then starts to decline. There is the argument that with the development of social intelligence, direct physical and verbal aggressions are replaced with indirect, relational, or social aggression (Björkqvist et al, 1992). The decline in physical and verbal aggressions after age 11 can also be linked to adolescent moral and cognitive development. Essentially, with advanced cognitions and moral reasoning, adolescents make better choices (e.g., aggression is unacceptable), have enhanced perspective-taking skills, and they have more mature conflict resolution (i.e., talking it through versus using aggression). Development is gradual and individual; therefore, the decline in physical aggression and the initial increase followed by a decrease in relational aggression will be different for each individual and dependent on a number of factors.

During this transition, are girls as aggressive as boys? Do they bully as much as boys? Past research has reported males to be bigger bullies and more aggressive than females. However, findings indicate that while girls engage in fewer acts of physical aggression, they engage in equal if not higher levels of indirect, relational, or social aggression (Moretti, Catchpole, & Odgers, 2005). Does this make them as aggressive as boys? During adolescence, do boys continually engage in more aggressive acts than girls? These questions will be addressed in the selections. Melanie Zimmer-Gembeck and her colleagues report gender differences in levels of aggression during early adolescence, while Christina Salmivalli and Ari Kaukiainen argue that boys use all types of aggression more than girls in early adolescence.

Melanie J. Zimmer-Gembeck,
Tasha C. Geiger, and Nicki R. Crick

Relational and Physical Aggression, Prosocial Behavior, and Peer Relations Gender Moderation and Bidirectional Associations

Relationships among children, and children's reputation and status in the peer group, are important for social and emotional development. Being held in positive regard by peers has been associated with future social competence and relatively fewer behavioral problems. Furthermore, in numerous studies, peer rejection has been consistently associated with later individual maladjustment, such as learning difficulties, poor academic achievement, loneliness and depressive symptoms in childhood, and mental health problems and criminality in adolescence and adulthood.

Because children's status with their peers is one of the most robust indicators of maladjustment, both cross-sectional and prospective studies have been conducted to investigate why some children and adolescents are more preferred by peers than other children. In particular, researchers have focused on whether children's own behaviors predict acceptance and rejection by peers. Convincing evidence has emerged showing that children's physically aggressive behaviors are predictive of rejection by the peer group. . . .

Few longitudinal studies of behavior and peer relationships have followed children as they [age.] . . . This is an important question to address as the progression from childhood into early adolescence is a time marked by significant change in the nature and form of peer groups and friendships. . . .

Peer Status, Children's Behaviors, and Gender

A . . . key objective . . . was to investigate gender differences in associations between peer status and children's behaviors (gender moderation). Physical and relational aggression and prosocial behavior were the behaviors examined. . . . [In] addition to physical aggression, relational aggression and prosocial behavior were measured . . . to expand the study of children's behavior, peer status, and gender.

From *Journal of Early Adolescence*, vol. 25, no. 4, November 2005, pp. 421–452. Copyright © 2005 by Sage Publications. Reprinted by permission. Note: The complete text of this article contains many references to specific studies described. The interested individual should refer to the original publication for these extensive citations. These references have been omitted here in the interest of brevity.

Relational aggression.   Relational aggression involves "behaviors that harm others through damage (or threat of damage) to relationships or feelings of acceptance, friendship, or group inclusion." For example, relational aggression includes the use of social exclusion to harm others. . . . [Relational] aggression and related behaviors have been found to increase around early adolescence (about age 11 through 12). As desires for intimacy and exclusivity in relationships increase from late childhood to early adolescence, some young people may increasingly use relationally aggressive strategies rather than physical aggression to harm others or influence their relationships. In past studies of early adolescents, relational aggression has been more common than physical aggression, and relational aggression has been associated with poorer peer relationships. . . .

Prosocial behavior.   There have been recent appeals to expand the study of peer interactions by placing more emphasis on positive behaviors during the transition into adolescence. A link has been established between prosocial behavior and peer acceptance, with prosocial children being more accepted by their peers. . . .

Social preference and social impact.   Social preference and social impact were the measures of peer status in the current study. . . . Social preference has been referred to as a measure of likability and peer acceptance, whereas social impact has been referred to as a measure of prominence and visibility in the peer group. . . . [Likability], dominance, and prominence in the peer group [become] increasingly salient in adolescence after a transition to middle school. . . .

Gender moderation hypotheses.   . . . [We] expected that gender would moderate associations between peer status and children's behaviors. First, the association between physical aggression and social preference was expected to be greater among males than females. . . .

Second, associations between relational aggression and social preference and between relational aggression and social impact were expected to be stronger for girls than for boys. With regards to peer preference, we expected that engagement in relational aggression in Grade 3 will be associated with lower peer preference in early adolescence because these behaviors can violate the emphasis on trust that is becoming more salient and characteristic of peer relationships during this transitional period. Yet previous research findings have shown that relational aggression is associated with lower peer preference for girl (but not for boys), after physical aggression was taken into account. Earlier relational aggression was also expected to be associated with greater social impact in early adolescence as . . . one motivation for relational aggression may be to increase dominance and prominence in the peer group. A recent study found associations between relational aggression and social impact among girls (Lease, Kennedy, & Axelrod, 2002). Using a combination of reports of who is popular and who is liked, girls who were popular but not as well liked were more relationally aggressive. It appears that relationally aggressive girls can have more social impact in the peer group but be less preferred when compared to girls who are less relationally aggressive. However, overall, we did anticipate that relational as well as physical aggression would have independent effects on later social preference and impact for both genders. . . .

Finally, we expected . . . earlier prosocial behavior would predict later peer status, and earlier social preference and impact would be associated with prosocial behavior by early adolescence. We expected these associations to be stronger among females as compared to males. . . .

Three-Year Stability of Peer Status and Children's Behaviors

In addition to examining the associations between peer status and children's behaviors and the moderation of these associations by gender, a final aim of the current study was to examine the stability of social preference, social impact, and children's behaviors across a 3-year interval spanning entry into adolescence and a middle school environment. A particular interest was in the 3-year stability of relationally aggressive behavior. . . .

Method

Participants

Children participated in sociometric assessments in their classrooms in Grades 3 (T1) and 6 (T2). . . . The longitudinal sample for this study consisted of [458] children who completed assessments at T1 and T2. . . .

Procedure

Peer nominations were collected in Grades 3 and 6. . . . Children were supplied with alphabetized rosters of their classmates and nomination forms. Each child on a roster was assigned an identification number. Students used identification numbers to nominate three classmates (male or female) for each item. . . .

Measures

Social preference and impact.   Students nominated the three classmates they liked most and the three classmates they liked least. Peer acceptance scores for each child were calculated by summing liked most nominations. Peer rejection scores for each child were calculated by summing liked least nominations. . . . Social preference and social impact scores were computed as acceptance score minus rejection score and acceptance score plus rejection score, respectively. . . . Hence, social preference is the extent to which children are liked versus disliked by peers (assessed as peer acceptance minus peer rejection), whereas social impact reflects a child's visibility in the peer group (assessed as peer acceptance plus peer rejection). . . .

Children's aggression and prosocial behavior.   . . . The physical aggression scale contained three items: "classmates who hit, kick, or punch others at school," "kids who push and shove others around," and "kids who tell others that they will beat them up unless kids do what they say," The relational aggression scale contained five items, including "kids who try to make another kid not like a certain person by spreading rumors about them or talking behind their backs"; "kids, who when they are mad at a person, get even by keeping that person from being in their group of friends"; "people who, when they are mad at a person, ignore the person or stop talking to them"; "kids who let their friends know that they will stop liking them unless the friends do what they want them to do"; and "people who try to exclude or keep certain people from being in their group when doing things together (like having lunch in the cafeteria or going to the movies)." The prosocial behavior scale contained three items, including "people who say or do nice things for other classmates,' "kids who help others join a group or make friends,' and "people who try to cheer up other classmates who are upset or sad about something.'. . .

Results

Gender Differences . . .

. . . In Grades 3 and 6, girls were more preferred by peers than boys, and boys had slightly more social impact than girls in Grade 6. Females were more prosocial than males, whereas males were more physically aggressive than females. No significant gender difference was obtained in relational aggression in third grade, but by sixth grade, females were significantly more relationally aggressive than boys. . . .

Social Preference

. . . *[Children's] behavior and social preference, and gender moderation.* In Grade 3, . . . [aggressive behavior (including relational aggression)] was negatively associated, and prosocial behavior was positively associated with social preference for boys and girls. In Grade 6, children's behaviors and social preference were intercorrelated with only one exception for boys and three exceptions for girls. In Grade 6, relational aggression was not associated with prosocial behavior in either gender, and relational and physical aggression scores were not significantly associated with social preference among females. . . .

In Grade 3, the positive association between relational and physical aggression was stronger for boys than girls, and the positive association between prosocial behavior and preference was weaker among boys than girls. In Grade 6, . . . the negative associations between relational aggression and social preference and between physical aggression and social preference were stronger among boys than girls.

. . . *[Children's] behavior, social preference, and gender moderation [across time.]* . . . [In] Grade 3, relational aggression was negatively associated with later social preference, and this association was only significant among girls. . . . [Social] preference in Grade 3 predicted children's behaviors within Grade 6.

Children who were more preferred in Grade 3 were less often nominated as relationally . . . and physically aggressive and more often nominated as prosocial in Grade 6. . . . [There were no] significant gender differences [across time]. . . .

Social Impact

. . . *[Children's] behavior and social impact, and gender moderation.* In Grade 3, all children's behaviors and social impact scores were significantly intercorrelated for boys and girls with the exception of prosocial behavior and social impact for boys and physical aggression and social impact for girls. In Grade 6, with the exception of physical aggression and social impact among boys, children's behaviors and social impact were significantly intercorrelated. . . . [Aggressive (including relational aggression)] and prosocial behaviors were positively associated with social impact. . . .

In Grade 3, the positive association between relational aggression and social impact, and the positive association between physical aggression and social impact were stronger among boys than girls. The positive association between prosocial behavior and impact was weaker among boys than girls in both Grade 3 and Grade 6.

. . . *[Children's behaviors, social preference, and gender moderation [across time].* . . . Physical aggression in Grade 3 predicted social impact only among boys, whereas relational aggression in Grade 3 predicted later social impact only among girls. Prosocial behavior in Grade 3 was positively associated with social impact in Grade 6 for boys and girls.

Conversely, children with higher social impact scores in Grade 3 were more often nominated as aggressive in Grade 6, but the [social] impact in Grade 3 and relational aggression in Grade 6 was not significant for girls. Additionally, the influence of social impact on later physical aggression was significant and stronger among boys than girls.

Discussion

Researchers have identified some of the correlates of peer status, and this work has revealed the significant role of peer reputation in the social development of children. However, few empirical investigations have had the opportunity to examine the independent effects of boys' and girls' physical aggression, relational aggression, and prosocial behavior on social preference and impact from childhood to early adolescence. Evidence exists concerning the negative influence of physical aggression on peer status, but the present investigation illustrated the additional importance of relational aggression and prosocial behavior as well as the gender of the child when explaining children's concurrent and future status with peers. Not only do children's aggressive and prosocial behaviors predict future peer relations, but the balance of being liked and disliked by classmates is important for shaping future aggressive and prosocial behaviors when interacting with peers.

. . . Associations Between Children's Behavior and Peer Relations [Across Time]

. . . *Social preference.* Peer social preference, where high scores indicate being highly liked and rarely disliked by others . . . seemed to have a [great] influence on children's later physical aggression, relational aggression, and prosocial behaviors . . . among both boys and girls. Preference scores in Grade 3 predicted all later behaviors among boys and all behaviors with the exception of relational aggression among girls. These results concur with [the idea] that positive peer experiences are important for learning appropriate social skills such as negotiating conflict and helping others as well as indicating that the lack of these opportunities may be detrimental to interactions with schoolmates. . . .

Social impact. . . . [Analyses] of peer social impact, where high scores indicate a higher level of like and dislike by peers . . . supported a gender normative hypothesis with behaviors more commonly associated with boys (physical aggression) linked to later social impact for boys and behaviors more commonly associated with girls (relational aggression) linked more strongly to later social impact for girls. Gender normative aggressive behaviors appear to be having an [effect] on status with other children at the transition from childhood to early adolescence. . . .

[Social] impact in Grade 3 also predicts children's aggressive behaviors in Grade 6. Earlier social impact is associated with increasing physical aggression for all children and relational aggression among boys only. Yet the association between earlier social impact and later physical aggression is stronger among boys compared to girls. Peers are increasingly noticing children with relatively more negative or positive behaviors, and this recognition seems to play a role in maintaining and escalating children's, especially boys', aggressive behaviors.

Aggression, peer status and gender. Although previous research has consistently found negative associations between physical aggression and rejection and acceptance by peers, when both physical and relational aggression are considered, the current findings show that it is girls' relational aggression, and not physical aggression, that predicts both social preference and impact 3 years later. In contrast, . . . associations between social impact and physical aggression were stronger among boys as compared to girls. Additionally, the associations between earlier social preference and impact and later relational aggression were significant among boys, but not girls. Together, findings suggest that aggression may partly escalate among boys between Grades 3 and 6 as a reaction to their peer experiences rather than vice versa. Girls may use relational aggression for reasons other than as a response to their peer status, such as gender socialization or arising from their greater focus on dyadic friendship interactions. In other words, girls' relational aggression emerges and, in turn, affects their peer status; boys' aggression may be more of an outcome of their peer status and associated peer experiences. However, this interpretation of the findings is speculative. . . .

. . . Associations and Gender . . .

. . . [Relational] aggression and physical aggression co-occurred among boys and girls, but this was more likely among boys than girls. Thus, boys who have the highest physical aggression scores are often the same boys who have the highest relational aggression scores. However, the correlation between relational and physical aggression was not as strong for girls, indicating that these two forms of aggression do not as strongly covary among girls. These findings indicate that it continues to be important for researchers interested in aggression and gender to include separate assessments of relational and physical aggression. . . .

Among males, aggression (physical and relational) was consistently associated with social preference and impact in both Grade 3 and Grade 6. Among females, the impact of physically and relationally aggressive behaviors on their peer status changed with age. Aggressive behaviors were increasingly reflected in girls' peer social impact scores (like and dislike scores combined) rather than only in lower peer social preference scores (like scores net of dislike scores). These findings are supportive of other evidence that aggression can be associated with social dominance and liking by some peers, and dislike by other peers, especially in early adolescence. For example, Crick and Grotpeter (1995) found that relationally aggressive children (in Grades 3 to 6) are more likely than nonrelationally aggressive children to be classified as controversial (highly liked and disliked by others). Others (Henington, Hughes, Cavell, & Thompson, 1998; Salmivalli, Kaukiainen, & Lagerspetz, 2000) have reported that relational aggression is associated with higher status with some peers, especially in adolescence. Relational aggression may be increasingly used as a strategy to gain and keep friends at this time of heightened peer interactions. . . .

Stability of Children's Behaviors and Peer Relations

[An] objective of this investigation was to examine the 3-year stability of all constructs with particular focus on relational aggression and girls. It was clear that children's early social behavior, including relational aggression, and reputations established with classmates tend to accompany children into early adolescence even after they change schools and classrooms. . . . In the current study, social preference scores were somewhat more stable than impact scores, but there was moderate 3-year stability in physical aggression, relational aggression, and prosocial behavior. . . .

Gender Differences and Relational Aggression

There have recently been questions regarding whether relational aggression is more prevalent among females or males (for reviews on this topic see Geiger et al., 2004; Underwood, Galen, & Paquette, 2001). The current study findings regarding relational aggression by gender and age are important to consider in conjunction with these questions. We found that gender differences in levels of relational aggression differed depending on children's age. There was no gender difference in relational aggression among third grade children (about age 9); however, by sixth grade (about age 12), girls were more relationally aggressive than their male peers. Findings are consistent with that of Bjoerkqvist and colleagues (Bjoerkqvist, Lagerspetz, & Kaukiainen, 1992) who reported that gender differences in indirect aggression did not occur until about age 10. However, because girls have been found to be more relationally aggressive than boys as early as preschool (see Geiger et al., 2004), firm conclusions await further research. . . . [Gender] differences in relational aggression may depend on the measurement techniques used at different ages (e.g., peer nominations, observations). Gender differences in relational aggression are sometimes found when using observational or teacher report measures but not as often found when using peer nominations. The current studies relied on one reporting source: classmates. This may have resulted in slightly inflated associations. . . .

Summary and Conclusion

. . . It is important to consider gender, relational aggression, and prosocial behavior in addition to the more commonly studied behavior of physical aggression when investigating stability and change in peer status during childhood and adolescence. Furthermore, differential results across the two gender-moderation models presented here indicate the importance of examining both social preference and social impact as distinct constructs. Doing so allowed a more complete understanding of the age-related and gendered interface between children's positive and negative behaviors when interacting with peers and schoolmates' perceptions of others as liked or disliked members of the group.

References

Bjoerkqvist, K., Lagerspetz, K.M., & Kaukiainen, A. (1992). Do girls manipulate and boys fight? Developmental trends in regard to direct and indirect aggression. *Aggressive Behavior, 18,* 117–127.

Crick, N.R., & Crotpeter, J.K. (1995). Relational aggression, gender, and social-psychological adjustment. *Child Development, 66,* 710–722.

Geiger, T.C., Zimmer-Gembeck, M.J., & Crick, N. R. (2004). The science of relational aggression: Can we guide intervention? In M. M. Moretti, C. Odgers, & M. Jackson (Eds.), *Girls and aggression: Contributing factors and intervention strategies, Perspectives in law and psychology series* (pp. 27–40). New York: Kluwer.

Henington, C., Hughes, J.N., Cavell, T.A., & Thompson, B. (1998). The role of relational aggression in identifying aggressive girls and boys. *Journal of School Psycology, 36,* 457–477.

Lease, A.M., Kennedy, C.A., & Axelrod, J.L. (2002). Children's social constructions of popularity. *Social Development, 11,* 87–109.

Salmivalli, C., Kaukiainen, A., & Lagerspetz, K. (2000). Aggression and sociometric status among peers: Do gender and type of aggression matter? *Scandinavian Journal of Psychology, 41,* 17–24.

Underwood, M. K., Galen, B. R.,& Paquette, J. A. (2001). Top ten challenges for understanding gender and aggression in children: Why can't we all just get along? *Social Development, 10,* 248–266.

Christina Salmivalli and
Ari Kaukiainen

 **NO**

"Female Aggression" Revisited: Variable- and Person-Centered Approaches to Studying Gender Differences in Different Types of Aggression

Introduction

During recent decades, increasing attention has been drawn to subtle forms of aggression, in which the perpetrator harms the target person by damaging or manipulating his/her relationships or status in the peer group rather than by making any overt (physical or verbal) attacks. Such forms of aggression have been referred to as indirect, relational, or social aggression. Each of these concepts emphasizes slightly different aspects of, or strategies by which, the harm is delivered. . . . In the present paper, we refer to the above forms of aggression as *indirect*.

When studies on indirect forms of aggression started to emerge, it was a common argument that while boys are more directly (i.e., physically and/or verbally) aggressive than girls, girls in turn use more indirect forms of aggression than boys. Since then, this statement has been taken more or less as a universal truth, even if the evidence seems to be far from conclusive.

What seems quite clear now is that females use more indirect than direct, at least physical, aggression, and in proportional terms, i.e., when expressed as proportions of the total aggression scores, girls may even use more indirect aggression than boys. For instance, Österman et al. [1998] found that 55 per cent of all aggression used by 8-year-old girls was indirect, while the corresponding proportion for boys was 26 per cent (among the 11- and 15-year-old adolescents, the proportions were 41 per cent and 52 per cent for girls vs. 23 per cent and 20 per cent for boys, respectively).

It might, however, be premature to say that 'the claim that human males are more aggressive than females appears to be false,' or that indirect aggression would be an exclusively 'female' type of aggression.

Already among the early studies, there were some that found few or no gender differences in indirect aggression, while some even found that boys used more indirect aggression than girls. These findings were, however, generally

From *Aggressive Behavior*, vol. 30, no. 2, March 26, 2004. Copyright © 2004 by Wiley Agency. Reprinted by permission. Note: The complete text of this article contains many references to specific studies described. The interested individual should refer to the original publication for these extensive citations. These references have been omitted here in the interest of brevity.

ignored in the ongoing academic debate, which was dominated by the view of females being more indirectly aggressive than males. There are, again, some recent studies showing very mixed patterns of findings regarding the use of indirect aggression. Underwood [2002], studying different subtypes of gender exclusivity and social aggression in children (10 to 14 years old), found no gender difference in verbal social aggression towards a provoking playmate in a laboratory setting, while girls showed more nonverbal, i.e., facial and gestural social aggression, than boys. On the other hand, there was a trend for boys to report using more relational aggression toward others than girls. Preliminary results from a meta-analysis by Scheithauer and Petermann [2002] showed no gender difference in the use of indirect, or what they call 'unprototypical' aggression across 70 studies. However, the effect sizes found varied according to age: adolescent girls, for instance, showed more this type of aggression than boys.

The aim of the present report is to participate in the ongoing discussion about gender differences in aggression by presenting results based on questionnaire data from three age groups in middle childhood and adolescence. In addition to comparing the mean scores of boys and girls on different types of aggression, we took a person-oriented approach and formed clusters with different 'aggression profiles' [using a technique called cluster analysis.]. In the latter approach, individuals' value profiles rather than their scores on single variables are taken into consideration, and the person (with his/her unique combination of values on the relevant variables) is the central unit of analysis.

We were looking for two kinds of manifestations of 'female aggression.' If indirect aggression is typical of females, this would become apparent, first, in girls scoring higher than boys on indirect (while not on physical and verbal) aggression. Another manifestation of female indirect aggression would be the identification of a group of highly aggressive girls employing indirect, rather than direct aggressive strategies.

Method

The participants were 526 children (274 girls, 252 boys) from 22 school classes in two towns in Finland. They were from three grade levels, aged 10, 12, and 14 years. Aggression was measured by . . . a peer- and self-report procedure in which children evaluated all their same-sex classmates, as well as themselves, in terms of their use of direct physical (e.g. hits, kicks), direct verbal (e.g. yells, insults), and indirect aggression (e.g. says bad things behind the other's back, tries to get the others to dislike the person), on a five-point scale ranging from 0 = 'never' to 4 = 'very often'.

Results

[Analyses] (with both self- and peer-reports of physical, verbal, and indirect aggression as dependent variables) were conducted across all age groups and in each age group separately [and] were significant at the p = .000 level in all cases. Across age groups, *boys used all three types of aggression more than girls*, with only one exception: in self-reported indirect aggression, the difference between boys and girls was not significant. Looking at the three age groups separately, boys were again, in most cases, significantly more aggressive than girls. In indirect aggression, however, a significant gender difference was found only among the 10-year-old children, and only in peer reports.

[A] cluster analysis was performed with the . . . peer-reported scores on the three aggression scales [used] for forming the clusters. Five ["clusters"] with different aggression profiles were identified. According to . . . analyses, . . . the members of these clusters differed significantly from each other in self-, as well as peer-reported physical, verbal, and indirect aggression. . . .

Girls and boys were not evenly distributed in the clusters. . . . There were more boys than would have been expected by chance in [the extremely aggressive group] and [the high direct aggressive group], which were characterized by extremely high scores on all kinds of aggression [(the extremely aggressive group) and] high score on direct aggression [, respectively]. Girls on the other hand, were overrepresented in [. . . the low aggressive group and the high indirect aggressive group.] The former cluster was a group of nonaggressive children. The latter consisted of children with very high scores on indirect, above-average scores on verbal, and average scores on physical aggression. *All 36 children in this cluster were girls.* This suggests that even if girls are not—when comparing the average scores of all girls and all boys—more indirectly aggressive than boys are, there is a group of girls who are very aggressive, and predominantly indirectly so.

Discussion

While there seems to be clear evidence of boys being more physically (and perhaps verbally) aggressive than girls, a debate is going on regarding the gender difference—or lack of it—in indirect/social/relational aggression [Crick and Grotpeter, 1995; Lagerspetz and Björkqvist, 1994; Underwood et al., 2001]. In the present study, boys and girls in middle childhood and adolescence were compared with respect to 1) their average scores on direct, verbal, and indirect aggression, and 2) their 'aggression profiles', i.e., their combinations of values on the three aggression scales. Comparing the mean scores of boys and girls on the different types of aggression used (direct physical, direct verbal, and indirect), all the differences found showed boys being more aggressive than girls. The differences were largest in physical aggression, somewhat smaller in verbal aggression, and smallest, or in many cases non-existent in indirect aggression.

The person-oriented approach, however, revealed two cluster groups in which girls were overrepresented: the nonaggressive group, and the indirectly aggressive group. This suggests that, first, girls are nonaggressive as compared with boys, and second, highly aggressive girls rarely use all types of aggression to any great extent. There is a group of highly aggressive girls whose use of aggression was *predominantly indirect.* When boys were aggressive, on the other hand, they either tended to prefer direct (physical and verbal) strategies or to use quite high levels of *all kinds of aggression.* The latter is in line with Scheithauer and Petermann's [2002] finding that boys showed a combination of direct and indirect aggression more often than girls.

Should indirect aggression be called 'female aggression' at all? In the light of our data [as well as several other studies, see Galen and Underwood, 1997; Tomada and Schneider, 1997; Österman et al., 1998] we argue that it should not, at least in the sense of girls being, on average, more indirectly aggressive than males. But, perhaps in the sense that for a group of highly aggressive girls, it is the predominant way of being aggressive, we can talk about 'female aggression'.

From the methodological point of view, we suggest that studies of psychosocial adjustment and direct and indirect aggression might benefit from a person-oriented approach. Although direct and indirect aggression are highly intercorrelated, their common variance is often neglected when studying associations between indirect aggression and adjustment. For instance, direct aggression is rarely controlled for, when predicting concurrent or longitudinal adjustment from indirect aggression. It would be enlightening to see whether students in our [high indirect aggressive group] . . . suffer from adjustment difficulties, or whether they are in fact relatively well-adjusted. Unfortunately, our data do not allow such observations.

References

Crick N, Grotpeter J. 1995. Relational aggression, gender, and social-psychological adjustment. Child Dev 66:710–722.

Galen B, Underwood M. 1997. A developmental investigation of social aggression among children. Dev Psychol 33:589–600.

Lagerspetz K, Björkqvist K. 1994. Indirect aggression in girls and boys. In: Huessmann R, editor. Aggressive Behavior. Current perspectives. New York: Plenum Press.

Österman K, Björkqvist K, Lagerspetz K, Kaukiainen A, Landau S, Fraczek A, Caprara G. 1998. Crosscultural evidence of female indirect aggression. Aggr Behav 24:1–8.

Scheithauer H, Petermann F. 2002. Indirect/social/ relational aggression in children and adolescents: A meta-analysis of gender- and age-specific differences. Paper presented in the XV world meeting of International Society for Research on Aggression, 28–31 July 2002, Montreal, Canada.

Tomada G, Schneider B. 1997. Relational aggression, gender, and peer acceptance: Invariance across culture, stability over time, and concordance among informants. Dev Psychol 33:601–609.

Underwood M. 2002. Developmental differences in friendship exclusivity and social aggression from middle childhood trough early adolescence. Paper presented in the XV world meeting of International Society for Research on Aggression, 28–31 July 2002, Montreal, Canada.

Underwood M, Galen B, Paquette J. 2001. Top ten challenges for understanding gender and aggression in children: Why can't we all just get along? Soc Dev 10:248–266.

POSTSCRIPT

Are Girls Bigger Bullies Than Boys?

Melanie Zimmer-Gembeck and colleagues examined the association between aggression and peer acceptance. In doing so, they found gender differences with respect to physical aggression, relational aggression, and prosocial behavior. More specifically, they argue that although young adolescent boys (i.e., grade 6) are more physically aggressive, girls of the same age are more relationally aggressive. Given that both physical aggression and relational aggression are forms of bullying, these results indicate that girls bully as much as boys, just in a different way. Instead of hurting their victims physically, they hurt them psychologically.

Christina Salmivalli and Ari Kaukiainen examined gender differences in direct (both physical and verbal) and indirect aggression during early adolescence. According to their results, boys use all three types of aggression more than girls. Differences were largest in physical aggression, smaller in verbal aggression, and smallest in indirect aggression. Cluster analyses revealed that, overall, girls are nonaggressive compared to boys and that highly aggressive girls rarely use all three types of aggression to any great extent, compared to highly aggressive boys.

In support of Zimmer-Gembeck, Geiger, and Cricks' argument, Viljoen et al. (2005), in their sample of male and female adolescent offenders, found that a higher proportion of females compared to males were involved in some form of bullying; however, the nature of bullying differed across genders. Significantly more males than females used both physical and verbal bullying, whereas significantly more females used only verbal and more indirect forms of bullying. To summarize, females bullied more but tended to use only verbal and indirect aggression. Björkqvist et al. 1992) suggest that the cognitive and verbal superiority of girls might explain why indirect aggression is more common among them. Moretti, Catchpole and Odgers (2005), in reviewing the literature, also support the findings of Zimmer-Gembeck, Geiger, and Crick. They report that social and relational forms of aggression are as common or more common in girls compared with boys, and such behavior may be used to secure high social status. They also report that the initial gains in social dominance are short-lived and that many are likely to be rejected if the aggression continues.

In support of the argument that boys bully more than girls, Peets and Kikas (2006), in a very similar study to Salmivalli and Kaukiainen, found that "boys, compared with girls, tended to manage their anger and conflict by using all the aggressive strategies more frequently, which indicates that aggression, regardless of the forms it takes, belongs to the behavioral repertoire of boys rather than girls" (p. 75). In a review of research studies using peer nominations (a typical method for relational aggression), Archer and Coyne (2005) also found that girls were not always more relationally aggressive than boys; however, girls used relational aggression more than physical aggression, and boys used more physical versus relational aggression. These differences were small during preaadolescence, larger between 8 and 11, and peaking thereafter. Scheithauer and Petermann (2002) also found that adolescent boys compared to adolescent girls used more direct as well as indirect aggression. Finally, Tiet, Wasserman, Loeber, McReynolds, & Miller (2001) found that there were no significant differences between girls and boys' relational aggression; however, boys were significantly more physically aggressive than girls, perhaps indicating that overall, boys are bigger bullies.

The above arguments provide evidence that both boys and girls engage in multiple forms of hurtful behavior. The debate is whether or not the amount of bullying is equal regardless of whether it is direct or indirect. Boys are more physically aggressive than girls; however, the findings are mixed as to whether girls engage in more relational aggression than boys. More specifically, it may be that when we think about social or verbal aggression, we access the most typical "social aggressor." Based on Salmivalli and Kaukiainen, this would involve girls (recall the highly indirectly aggressive cluster of all girls and no boys); thus, we may overestimate all girls' social aggression. Those who are highly socially aggressive are usually girls, but this does not mean that all girls are highly socially aggressive. This is called the "availability heuristic bias."

Adolescent aggression—and more specifically, bullying—is a serious problem for today's youth. Students who are bullied are more likely to have both physical and emotional problems lasting into adulthood. Adolescents who bully are also at risk for long-term problems such as being rejected by their peer group, academic failure, and criminal behavior. Given these negative effects both for the bully and the victim, this issue deserves continued attention in the research.

References/Further Readings

Archer, J. (2004). Sex differences in aggression in real-world settings: A meta-analytic review. *Review of General Psychology*, 4, 291–322.

Archer, J., & Coyne, S. M. (2005). An integrated review of indirect, relational, and social aggression. *Personality and Social Psychology Review*, 9, 212–230.

Bjoörkqvist, K., Österman, K., & Kaukiainen, A. (1992). The development of direct and indirect aggressive strategies in males and females. In K. Bjoörkqvist & P. Niemelä (Eds.), *Of Mice and Women. Aspects of Female Aggression* (pp. 51–64). San Diego, CA: Academic Press.

Cairns, R. B., Cairns, B., Neckerman, H., Ferguson, L., & Gariépy, J. (1989). Growth and aggression: 1. Children to early adolescence. *Developmental Psychology*, 25, 320–330.

Crick, N. R., & Grotpeter, J. (1995). Relational aggression, gender, and social-psychological adjustment. *Child Development*, 66, 710–722.

Moretti, M. M., Catchpole, R. E. H., & Odgers, C. (2005). The dark side of girlhood: Recent trends, risk factors and trajectories to aggression and violence. *The Canadian Child and adolescent Psychiatry Review*, 14, 21–25.

Olweus, D. (1997). Bully/victim problems in school: Facts and intervention. *European Journal of Psychology of Education*, 12, 495–510.

Peets, K., & Kikas, E. (2006). Aggressive strategies and victimization during adolescence: Grade and gender differences, and cross-informant agreement. *Aggressive Behaviour*, 32, 48–79.

Scheithauer, H., & Petermann, F. (2002). Indirect/social/relational aggression in children and adolescents: A meta-analysis of gender- and age-specific differences. Paper presented in the XV world meeting of International Society for research on Aggression, July 2002, Montreal, Canada.

Tiet, Q. Q., Wasserman, G. A., Loeber, R., McReynolds, L. S., & Miller, L. S. (2001). Developmental and sex differences in types of conduct problems. *Journal of Child and Family Studies*, 10, 181–197.

Viljoen, J. L., O'Neill, M. L., & Sidhu, A. (2005). Bullying behaviors in female and male adolescent offenders: Prevalence, types, and association with psychological adjustment. *Aggressive Behavior*, 31, 521–535.

ISSUE 18

Is the Use of "Club Drugs" a Problem Among Adolescents?

YES: Eric Sigel, from "Club Drugs: Nothing to Rave About," *Contemporary Pediatrics* (October 2002)

NO: Jacob Sullum, from "Sex, Drugs and Techno Music," *Reason* (January 2002)

ISSUE SUMMARY

YES: Eric Sigel, assistant professor of pediatrics and adolescent medicine, argues that club drugs such as Ecstasy, GHB, Rohypnol, and Special K are dangerous. Their use, especially at rave parties, allows participants to overlook social barriers and helps individuals to relate better to others. Sigel cautions that some drugs that are taken at rave parties, especially GHB, have led to date rape.

NO: Jacob Sullum, a senior editor at *Reason* magazine, contends that the effects of drugs such as Ecstasy, particularly with regard to sexual behavior, are exaggerated. He refers to the history of marijuana and how it too was deemed a drug that would make people engage in behaviors in which they would not typically engage. Sullum maintains that the public's reaction to club drugs is unjustified.

$\mathbf{S}$ince the early 1990s, club drugs have attracted significant attention in North America. Although use of most club drugs has declined in recent years (methamphetamine continues to increase), prevalence rates among today's adolescents are still alarming. In 2002, 2.2 percent of 12- to 17-year-olds, and 5.8 percent of 18- to 25-year-olds reported using Ecstasy (MDMA) in the past year. Approximately 1.3 percent and 1.8 percent of 12- to 17- and 18- to 25-year-olds, respectively, reported using LSD in the same time frame, and 0.9 percent and 1.7 percent of the same age groups reported using methamphetamine in the past year (Maxwell, 2004). Not surprisingly, the number of people admitted to emergency rooms due to adverse reactions to Ecstasy, methamphetamine, and other club drugs is also alarming. In the year 2002, more than 4,000 people were admitted to emergency rooms because of Ecstasy, and more than 17,500 emergency room visits were because of methamphetamine use

(Maxwell, 2004). Methamphetamine, in particular, is a major concern. The World Health Organization (WHO) recently stated that methamphetamine is the most widely used illicit club drug after marijuana.

The taking of club drugs such as methamphetamine, Ecstasy, LSD, GHB, Ketamine, and Rohypnol are not limited to rave parties. A *Time* magazine article indicates that these drugs are showing up at hip-hop parties, on Bourbon Street in New Orleans, and in many other places. However, their use at rave parties is not unusual. Many people agree that making rave parties illegal will not stop the use of these drugs, but it would remove one venue where their use occurs. Also, drug use is deeply embedded in the culture of rave parties. This raises the question, Is making rave parties illegal an effective strategy for reducing the use of club drugs? Further, would people who attend rave parties but who do not use drugs be unfairly penalized if such parties were outlawed?

Attempts to make rave parties and similar activities illegal are being made on the national level as well as on the local level in both Canada and the United States. For example, a bipartisan bill was introduced into the U.S. Senate "to prohibit an individual from knowingly opening, maintaining, managing, controlling, renting, leasing, making available for use, or profiting from any place for the purpose of manufacturing, distributing, or using any controlled substance, and for other purposes." This act is referred to as the Reducing Americans' Vulnerability to Ecstasy Act of 2002, or the RAVE Act. Canada has taken similar action with the Controlled Drugs and Substance Act.

One reason for implementing these acts, and in particular the RAVE Act, is that raves have become a way to exploit North American youth. These parties are said to be manipulating young people as a means of making money. There is concern that drug use at these parties leads to adverse physical reactions as well as reckless behavior. For example, one consequence of Ecstasy use is dehydration. To capitalize on this effect, some club owners charge excessive amounts of money for water. Others have "chilling rooms" one can go into—for a price. Those who object to rave parties point to these examples as proof that club owners are engaging in exploitation.

Another problem with raves and similar club parties is that they become venues for buying and selling illegal drugs. One of the problems associated with buying illegal drugs is that they are not always what they are purported to be. One cannot be sure of the authenticity of the drug being purchased. If an adolescent buys a "bogus" drug or a modified drug, there can be serious side effects above and beyond the harmful effects of the pure drug. In addition, the buyer has no legal recourse. This is one reason why groups such as DanceSafe attend raves. This group tests pills for purity. Essentially, someone who purchases an Ecstasy pill can have it tested to determine whether or not it is indeed Ecstasy. DanceSafe attempts to reduce the harmful effects associated with misidentified drugs. What message does this send to adolescents? Is it one of protection coupled with permission? In other words, does it give the impression that it is ok to use the real thing because the real thing is safe as long as it is tested? Can club drugs be used safely? Are club drugs dangerous regardless of whether they are pure or not? In summary, should we be concerned about club drugs?

YES

Eric Sigel

Club Drugs: Nothing to Rave About

Ecstasy and other so-called club drugs have caught on with many teens and young adults as a way to enhance the fun of rave parties. Here's what you need to know to counsel your patients about the dangers—including date rape—of this risky kind of recreation.

Club drugs, considered novel in the early 1990s have become mainstream. (1) In particular, we have witnessed a striking rise in the use of Ecstasy since the mid-1990s. The use of club drugs has its roots in the club and rave scene, which originated in the late 1980s and has, like the drugs associated with it, moved from the margins toward the mainstream of teenage culture. It is essential for any health-care practitioner who cares for youth to understand the epidemiology, biology, and psychological impact of club drugs on teenagers and young adults.

Raves: Cradle of Club Drugs

Recognizing the nature of raves is important to understanding the evolution of club drugs into popular culture. (2) Raves are all-night dance parties that began underground, hidden from the law and mainstream culture. Originally, they represented an alternative to mainstream socialization, an outlet for teens and young adults who did not identify with the popular peer groups. Because of the desire to stay separate from the mainstream and the law, rave organizers would send out notices at the last minute letting concertgoers know where the upcoming event was to be held—usually an abandoned warehouse or remote area of the countryside.

Rave music was initially noncommercial and computer generated, reflecting the so-called techno age. It has been described as repetitive, remorseless, loud, and fast, surging past the listener in mind-numbing waves. Over the last 10 to 15 years, rave music has evolved into a new genre, appealing to a wide range of teenagers and adults. Some of the different types of music within this genre are referred to as techno, house, and trance.

Raves also have become increasingly popular. It is easy to log on to the World Wide Web and find out where a rave is being held on any given night. (3,4) Concert promoters sponsor raves (legally) at prominent venues in most major cities.

From *Contemporary Pediatrics*, vol. 19, no. 10, October 1, 2002, pp. 47–58. Copyright © 2002 by Advanstar Medical Economics. Reprinted by permission.

The link between raves and drugs derives in part from the nature of raves. Raves typically last all night. Drug use helps participants stay up all night and then come down when dawn arrives. The drugs also enable participants to dismiss classic social barriers and connect to peers, regardless of sex, ethnic background, or social class.

In general, adolescent substance use in the United States reached a peak in the mid-1990s; the use of some substances has leveled off since then and the use of others has declined slightly. (5) Ecstasy is the one drug whose use has increased dramatically over the last five years, though the rate of increase slowed somewhat for the first time in 2001. (6) Nearly 12% of high school seniors have tried Ecstasy at least once.

When interpreting statistics concerning club drug use, physicians must apply the numbers to clinical situations to get an accurate picture. We tend not to attach great significance to drugs that "only 1% to 2%" of a population are using, as is the case with some club drugs. Consider, however, that if 2% of high school students are using Gamma-hydroxybutyrate (GHB), for example, and you are working in a clinic that sees 50 adolescents a week, you will likely see one GHB user weekly, which is significant.

Ecstasy: Euphoria at a Price

MDMA (3-4-methylenedioxymethamphetamine), or "Ecstasy," is an amphetamine that has hallucinogenic properties similar to mescaline. (7,8) Street names include, in addition to Ecstasy, Adam, Bean, E, M, Roll, X, XTC, and Lovers Speed. In the 1970s, psychiatrists used Ecstasy to decrease patients' inhibitions, allowing them to talk freely and openly. In 1985, once the physical dangers of the drug were recognized, the US Drug Enforcement Agency reclassified MDMA as a schedule I drug, and it became a banned substance. Media attention has focused increasingly on Ecstasy in recent years, both because of the rapid rise in its use and much-publicized deaths connected with the drug.

Ecstasy is readily available; more than 50% of high school students say they can obtain it easily. Forty-one percent of tenth graders and 61% of 12th graders say that Ecstasy is "fairly easy" or "very easy" to get. (5) It comes in the form of tablets, often with names such as Playboy bunnies or Nike swoosh CK. Each "brand" of tablet is thought to have a slightly different effect. The drug can be made in home labs but is most often imported from Europe.

Studies have shown different tablets to contain anywhere from 0 mg to 140 mg of MDMA. The average dose is 100 mg. A point to stress when talking to patients about Ecstasy is that the user has no way to know what is actually in the tablet; it may be cut with any one of a number of undesirable drugs, such as ephedrine, dextromethorphan, or amphetamine.

Effects   Onset of action occurs 20 minutes after ingestion of the drug and can last up to six hours. Ecstasy increases sensory input. Users report that they feel extremely happy, peaceful, and euphoric with enhanced sensation from touch and other sensory systems. Social inhibitions disappear, sexual sensation increases, and people feel close, or connected, to others.

MDMA is metabolized by the liver and excreted by the kidney. It produces its effects by indirect sympathetic activation, releasing norepinephrine, dopamine, and serotonin from terminals in the central and autonomic nervous systems. It can inhibit monoamine oxidase. Alcohol potentiates toxicity.

Ecstasy produces multiple physiologic effects. (9) Short-term cardiac effects include tachycardia, vasoconstriction, unpredictable blood pressure changes, arrhythmias, hypertension, and paradoxical hypotension (with depletion of catecholamines). (10) Users may develop myocardial ischemia or infarction, as well as coronary artery spasm. Longer term cardiac effects include irreversible cardiomyopathy, noncardiogenic pulmonary edema, and pulmonary hypertension.

Other medical consequences of Ecstasy use include increased muscle tension, involuntary teeth clenching, malignant hyperthermia, blurred vision, syncope, chills, sweating, dehydration, and seizures. Users may develop hepatitis, which is thought to result from hepatic cell damage related to metabolism of MDMA by the liver. The effects are usually similar to viral hepatitis, with elevated liver enzymes that return to normal after weeks or months. One study found Ecstasy to be the second leading cause of liver damage in people under 25 years of age. (11) In rare cases, the damage can lead to liver failure.

Neurologic effects of MDMA result primarily from its action on the serotonin system. Ecstasy releases serotonin, reducing levels of serotonin (5-hydroxytryptamine [5-HT]) and its metabolite 5HIAA as well as 5-HT transporter. This effect has been demonstrated in several species, including primates. (12) Increasing doses of MDMA lead to degeneration of serotenergic axon terminals throughout the entire brain.

Brain changes in the axonal terminals are detectable seven years after recreational Ecstasy use. Positron emission tomography scans . . . have shown decreased brain 5-HT transporter binding that correlates with the extent of prior use. (13) In addition, Ecstasy produces a demonstrated up-regulation of postsynaptic 5-[HT.sub.2] receptors, which may put users at risk for microvascular changes in the brain and subsequent cerebrovascular accidents. (14)

Persons who have used Ecstasy recreationally show impaired cognitive function affecting performance in complex tasks requiring attention, memory, and learning, and tasks that reflect general intelligence. (15) Performance deteriorates with heavier use of the drug.

Short-term psychological difficulties associated with Ecstasy use include confusion, depression, sleep problems, drug craving, severe anxiety, and paranoia while and sometimes weeks after taking MDMA. Other psychological effects include increased somatization, obsessionality, and hostility. (16)

Deaths from Ecstasy have been attributed to a wide range of medical complications, including rhabdomyolysis, hyperpyrexia, intravascular coagulopathy, hepatic necrosis, cardiac arrhythmias, cerebrovascular accidents, and suicide.

Treatment   Acute MDMA intoxication can be treated initially by administering activated charcoal within the first hour after ingestion to decrease absorption of the drug. General treatment is supportive. In cases of severe intoxication, monitor serum electrolytes, renal and liver function tests, creatine phosphoki-nase, complete blood count, and coagulation studies. Anxiety and agitation should be treated with a benzodiazepine. Seizures and hypertension should be treated appropriately. (17) No indication exists at present to evaluate brain function or learning ability specifically, although such an assessment should be considered if unusual or specific deficits are observed.

Because Ecstasy has so much appeal, counseling is important, especially in the early teen years. Healthcare professionals need to be aware of several myths about MDMA use that they may encounter among their patients. Many users of MDMA believe that using the drug "the right way" prevents sequelae. The "right way" includes drinking appropriate fluids, avoiding getting over-heated, and having enough energy in one's system. As with any drug, users believe they cannot get addicted to MDMA, which is false.

In some countries, such as Canada, raves have health stations and tools to help attendees determine the purity of their Ecstasy. If the content of a pill is determined to be less than 90% MDMA, users usually will not take it. If "ravers" develop acute medical symptoms, the medical team can intervene and send patients to emergency rooms if necessary. Ethical questions have been raised as to whether providing health stations condones the use of Ecstasy and other drugs.

GHB: Date Rape Drug of Choice

Gamma-hydroxybutyrate is a sedative and amnestic that is often used at the end of a rave to help people come down from their Ecstasy high. Street names include Liquid Ecstasy, Soap, Easy Lay, and Georgia Home Boy.

GHB has been used clinically outside the US to treat narcolepsy and opi-ate and ethanol withdrawal. It has also been used as an anesthetic (for single-agent intravenous anesthesia for emergency procedures and anesthesia for cat-aract surgery and labor, for example), although other, more effective agents have largely supplanted it.

Since about 1990, GHB has been abused in the US for its euphoric, seda-tive, and anabolic (bodybuilding) effects. (18) It was widely available over the counter in health food stores from the 1980s until 1992 and was purchased mostly by body builders to aid fat reduction and muscle building. Ingredients in GHB, gamma-butyrolactone (GBL) and 1,4-butanediol, can be converted by the body into GHB. These ingredients are still found in a number of dietary supplements available in health food stores and gymnasiums to induce sleep, build muscles, and enhance sexual performance despite warnings about GBL-related products issued by the Food and Drug Administration in 1997 and 1999. (19) GHB is now more often used as a club drug than a dietary supple-ment and, because of its amnestic properties, is one of the most commonly used "date rape" drugs. Around 1.6% of high school seniors report having used GHB in the last year. (5)

GHB can be produced in clear liquid, white powder, tablet, and capsule forms and is tasteless if mixed in drinks. (20) Like many other club drugs, it can be made in home laboratories.

Because of GHB's toxicity, overdoses have increased dramatically—from 55 in 1994 to 2,973 in 1999. (21) In 1999, GHB accounted for 32% of illicit-drug-related calls to poison centers in Boston. (21)

Effects   Onset of action occurs 10 to 20 minutes after the drug is taken. Effects can last up to four hours, depending on the dosage. Alcohol potentiates the effects. At lower doses, GHB can relieve anxiety and produce relaxation. As the dose increases, however, the sedative effects may result in sleep and eventual coma or death.

GHB is a naturally occurring metabolite of the inhibitory neurotransmitter gamma-aminobutyric acid and also functions as a neurotransmitter on its own. It binds to receptors in the hippocampus, cortex, midbrain, basal ganglia, and substantia nigra. GHB mediates sleep cycles, temperature regulation, cerebral glucose metabolism and blood flow, memory, and emotional control. (22) In low doses, it inhibits dopamine release, but at high doses it stimulates dopamine release.

The neurologic effects are primary, leading to central nervous system depression with sedation, confusion, amnesia, and coma. It can decrease the seizure threshold and intracranial pressure and cause nystagmus, dizziness, and ataxia.

Other effects include decreased heart rate and blood pressure (at low doses), nausea, and respiratory depression and apnea, which can lead to hypoxia and respiratory failure.

Treatment is generally supportive. If the patient is unconscious, aspiration precautions should be taken. Pulse oximetry should be initiated, and the patient should be observed for respiratory depression and bradycardia. Bradycardia can be treated with epinephrine or, if the rhythm disturbance is getting worse, with atropine. (23) Patients typically return to consciousness two to six hours after ingestion.

Ketamine: Not for Dogs Only

Ketamine is an injectable anesthetic that has been approved for both human and animal use in medical settings since 1970. (24) About 90% of the ketamine sold legally today is intended for veterinary use. Street names include Special K, K, Vitamin K, Cat Valium.

Ketamine became popular as a drug of abuse in the 1980s, when it was realized that a large dose causes a dream-like state and hallucinations similar to those associated with phencyclidine (PCP). Around 1.3% of eighth graders and 2.5% of 12th graders report using ketamine in the past year. (5)

Ketamine is produced in liquid form or as a white powder that is often snorted or smoked with marijuana or tobacco. Recently, intramuscular injection of the drug has been reported.

Effects   Ketamine has receptors in the hippocampus and cerebral cortex. It is a noncompetitive N-methyl-D-aspartate (NMDA) receptor antagonist that prevents excretion of excitatory neurotransmitters. It produces a dissociative state characterized by profound analgesia and amnesia without loss of consciousness. (25) Drug abusers seek the delusional effects of ketamine.

Neurologic effects include sedation, anxiety, agitation, slurred speech, dilated pupils, and psychotic symptoms such as delusions and hallucinations. Low-dose intoxication impairs attention, learning ability, and memory. Systemic effects resulting from an increase in catecholamines include increased heart rate and blood pressure, palpitations, chest pain, and tachypnea. A high dose can lead to respiratory depression.

Treatment is supportive. For acute anxiety reactions, a benzodiazepine may be indicated.

Rohypnol: Forget About It!

Rohypnol (flunitrazepam) is a benzodiazepine that is not approved for prescribing in the US. It is approved in Europe and is used in more than 60 countries as a treatment for insomnia, a sedative, and a presurgical anesthetic. It is produced in tablet form and smuggled into the US from Latin America and Europe. Street names include Roofies, Rophies, Roche, and Forget-me Pill.

Relatively few adolescents admit to using Rohypnol—around 1.7% of high school seniors say they have used it during their lifetime. Fewer than 1% of eighth and 12th graders say they have used Rohypnol in the last year. (5)

Effects   Rohypnol causes profound "anterograde amnesia." (26) Users may not remember events they experienced while under the influence of the drug but do not necessarily lose consciousness. Rohypnol's amnestic effect—along with the fact that it is tasteless and odorless and dissolves easily in carbonated beverages—makes it attractive as a date rape drug. Concurrent use of alcohol aggravates the sedative and toxic effects of Rohypnol. Even without alcohol, a dose of Rohypnol as small as 1 mg can cause impairment for eight to 12 hours. It has been used to enhance highs produced by heroin and to ease the negative effects of cocaine.

Rohypnol is a central nervous system depressant. Users become drowsy and may lose consciousness. Other side effects include decreased blood pressure, respiratory depression, visual disturbances, dizziness, confusion, nausea, vomiting, and urinary retention.

Treatment for Rohypnol intoxication is supportive and, except in an acute overdose with respiratory depression or hypotension, medical intervention is unnecessary. (27) Exploring with the patient's peers what may have occurred under the influence is important, because it may reveal other medical concerns that need to be evaluated, such as sexual assault.

Methamphetamine: The Downside of Uppers

Methamphetamine is an addictive stimulant drug that causes the body to release norepinephrine, dopamine, and serotonin in the central and autonomic nervous system. (28) It is a crystal-like powdered substance—usually white or slightly yellow, depending on purity—that sometimes comes in large rock-like chunks. When the powder flakes off the rock, the shards look like glass, which is a nickname for the drug. Other street names include Chalk, Crank, Croak, Crypto, Crystal, Fire, Meth, Speed, and White Cross. (29) Methamphetamine can be taken orally, injected, snorted, or smoked.

Methamphetamine can be made easily using a combination of over-the-counter products including cold preparations containing pseudophedrine. The drug has received much media attention because police raids of methamphetamine labs have increased substantially, consuming significant resources of local drug agencies.

About 2.2% of eighth graders and 6% of high school seniors report using methamphetamine within the last year; 10% of high school seniors report having used the drug over their lifetimes. (5)

Methamphetamine overdoses treated in emergency rooms increased 30% nationwide between 1999 and 2000. (30)

Effects   Immediately after smoking or intravenously injecting methamphetamine, the user experiences an intense sensation, called a "rush" or "flash," caused by the catecholamine release. The sensation lasts only a few minutes and is described as extremely pleasurable. Oral or intranasal use produces euphoria—a high, but not a rush. Other short-term effects include irritability and aggression, anxiety, nervousness, convulsions, and insomnia.

Generally, methamphetamine has similar sympathomimetic side effects to those caused by Ecstasy. Short-term effects include tachycardia, hypertension, hyperthermia, mydriasis, and diaphoresis. Cardiac arrhythmia can lead to stroke or myocardial infarctions. (28) Necrotizing vasculitis involving medium and small arteries in most organs can lead to widespread ischemia and intracranial hemorrhage. Alcohol can potentiate toxicity.

Methamphetamine is neurotoxic. Abusers may have significant reductions in dopamine transporters. Research shows that users risk long-term damage to their brain cells similar to that caused by a stroke or Alzheimer's disease. (31) Irreversible cardiomyopathy also has been noted. Psychological symptoms of prolonged use include paranoia, hallucinations, repetitive behavior patterns, and delusions of parasites or insects under the skin. Users often obsessively scratch their skin to get rid of the imagined insects.

As noted, methamphetamine is addictive, and users can develop a tolerance quickly, needing higher doses to get high and going on longer binges to achieve the desired effect. Some users avoid sleep for three to 15 days while on a binge.

Treatment   Emergent treatment targets the symptoms of overdose—hyperthermia, tachycardia, and hypertension. (32) Hyperthermia above 40[degrees] C requires cooling measures, such as cooling blankets. Seizures can be controlled with a benzodiazepine. Unless hypertension is life-threatening and requires aggressive treatment, monitoring vital signs until they stabilize is appropriate. Activated charcoal, administered within one hour of ingestion, can help decrease absorption of methamphetamine.

Symptomatic patients require monitoring of electrolytes, renal and hepatic function, creatine phosphokinase, and the electrocardiogram. A specific urine test—a semiquantitative homogeneous enzyme-multiplied immunoassay test (EMIT)—can detect the class of amphetamine that was used.

Methamphetamine addiction is generally treated with cognitive-behavioral therapy. Support groups can also help addicts.

LSD: Still a Bad Trip

Lysergic acid diethylamide (LSD) is a hallucinogen. It alters cognitive and perceptual states, leading to auditory and visual hallucinations. Street names include Acid, Boomers, and Yellow Sunshines.

LSD is manufactured from lysergic acid, which is found in ergot, a fungus that grows on rye and other grains. (33) It is sold in tablet, capsule, and liquid forms as well as on pieces of blotter paper impregnated with the drug. It is typically taken by mouth. Around 3.4% of eighth graders and 10.9% of 12th graders have used LSD in their lifetime; 6.6% of 12th graders have used the drug in the past year. (5)

Effects LSD is a potent 5-[HT.sub.1] (serotonin) agonist. Its effects are unpredictable and depend on the amount taken, the surroundings in which the drug is used, and the user's personality, mood, and expectations. Typically the user feels the effects of the drug 30 to 90 minutes after taking it. Initial physical effects include dilated pupils, hyperthermia, tachycardia, hypertension, diaphoresis, lightheadedness, and tremors. In the next phase of intoxication, the visual, auditory, and sensory alterations develop; they can last several hours. The user's sense of time and self changes. Sensations may seem to "cross over," giving the user the feeling of hearing colors and seeing sounds. These changes can be frightening and cause panic.

The late phase of intoxication produces euphoria, mood swings, and depression. Tension and anxiety may develop, leading to panic attacks. Sensations and feelings change much more dramatically than the physical signs. The user may feel several different emotions at once or swing rapidly from one emotion to another.

A high dose of LSD can lead to hyperventilation, and severe toxicity can cause apnea, seizures, coma, and respiratory arrest. Other life-threatening sequelae include neuroleptic malignant syndrome, characterized by hyperthermia, muscle rigidity, rhabdomyolysis, and stupor, which may progress to coma and death.

Two long-term disorders are associated with LSD use: persistent psychosis and posthallucinogen perception disorder, a condition marked by visual disturbances, such as trails of light. LSD users may experience acute psychotic reactions and paranoia, which can develop in persons without a history of schizophrenia.

Flashbacks occur in 15% to 77% of LSD users, often weeks or years after taking LSD. (43) They are generally related to the chronicity of LSD use, but can happen to anyone who has used LSD.

Although users do not become physically addicted to LSD, they often need to increase the dose to achieve similar effects. This results in increased risk of medical side effects.

Treatment General treatment IS supportive. Activated charcoal administered within one hour of ingestion can help decrease absorption, but is not typically recommended for recreational LSD use. A benzodiazepine can benefit those who are significantly agitated. For those undergoing a so-called bad trip, talking them down in a quiet, dimly lit room can be helpful. For acute psychosis, haloperidol can be effective. Hospital admission may be warranted for prolonged psychosis. (35)

Screening and Counseling

In-depth assessment of drug use is beyond the scope of this article. Primary care health providers should recognize that any adolescent who demonstrates "at-risk behavior" is more likely than other youth to use club drugs. Early onset of any drug use, younger age of sexual debut, and academic difficulties are just a few of the risk factors. High-functioning teenagers are not immune to risk, however, as they may experiment out of boredom or curiosity.

Adolescents and young adults should be asked about the availability of MDMA and other club drugs, what their philosophy is on using these drugs—especially Ecstasy because of its popularity—and whether they have experimented. Counseling college-bound youth about what they may be exposed to on campus and their responsibilities regarding drug use is an additional avenue to pursue.

Counseling about side effects and risks associated with acute toxicity is essential. Use of any amphetamine puts the user at risk of death the next time he or she uses it because of the idiosyncratic cardiovascular effects of these drugs. Some practitioners believe use of club drugs is reason to bring parents into the discussion, breaking confidentiality if a patient is in imminent danger. . . .

Evaluating youth for depression or other mental health disorders is vital and can help determine the appropriate course of intervention. If the patient seems addicted, referral to a drug treatment program is indicated. If the patient has been experimenting and appears to have a comorbid psychiatric condition such as depression, treating the condition with counseling and medication is appropriate.

Although most drugs are metabolized within a few days, performing random Monday urine screening can be used to monitor drug use as an adjunct to treatment. Some club drugs—including MDMA, methamphetamine, and Rohypnol (as a benzodiazepine)—can be detected on comprehensive drug screens. Specific screens must be ordered for other drugs, such as LSD and ketamine. The physician needs to know what is available from the lab he or she uses and customize drug testing accordingly.

So that adolescents can make responsible, informed decisions, they need to be made aware that club drugs have potentially high morbidity and mortality. In counseling adolescents and young adults, it is essential to remind them always to be on the lookout for themselves and each other, especially at parties or in bars where they do not know everyone. Because it is easy to dope drinks in these situations, youth need to know exactly where a drink came from and who made it.

The availability and properties of date rape drugs may make the idea of sexually victimizing peers more enticing, so a serious conversation with males about the morality and legal aspects of date rape is worth pursuing. Young women need to be aware of how date rape may be perpetrated and how they can team up with peers to prevent it. Encouraging young women to buddy-up at parties and in bars and check in with each other consistently during the evening is one way to prevent such consequences as sexual assault.

Physicians should familiarize themselves with drug treatment resources in the community. Schools often offer mini-courses on drug use. Most cities have drug treatment facilities that can help assess the extent of an adolescent's drug use and determine whether significant intervention, such as residential treatment or day treatment, is indicated. Adolescent specialists can help the primary care practitioner work through complicated situations.

References

1. National Institute on Drug Abuse: Club drugs. Community Drug Alert Bulletin, December 1999. http://www.nida.nih.gov/ClubAlert/ClubDrugAlert.html

2. Weir E: Raves: A review of the culture, the drugs, and the prevention of harm. CMAJ 2000; 162(13):1843

3. http://www.come.to/DenverRaves

4. http://www.ravehousetech.about.com/mbody.htm

5. The Monitoring the Future Study: Trends in the use of various drugs. 2001 data from in-school surveys of 6th, 10th, and 12th grade students. Ann Arbor, Mich., University of Michigan News and Information Services, December 2001. www.monitoringthefuture.org

6. Johnson LD, O'Malley PM, Bachman JG: Rise in ecstasy use among American teens begins to slow. Ann Arbor, Mich., University of Michigan News and Information Services, December 19, 2001. www.monitoringthefuture.org

7. Schwartz R, Miller N: MDMA (Ecstasy) and the rave: A review. Pediatrics 1997; 100:705

8. National Institute on Drug Abuse: Ecstasy. 2001. http://www.nida.nih.gov/Infofax/Clubdrugs.html

9. Kalant H: The pharmacology and toxicology of "Ecstasy" (MDMA) and related drugs. CMAJ 2001; 165(7):917

10. Lester SJ, Baggott M, Welm S, et al: Cardiovascular effects of 3,4-methylene-dioxymethamphetamine: A double-blind, placebo-controlled trial. Ann Intern Med 2000; 133:969

11. Andreu V: Ecstasy: A common cause of severe acute hepatotoxicity. J Hepatol 1998; 29:94

12. Ricaurte GA, Yuan J, McCann UD: 3,4 Methylenedioxymethamphetamine ("Ecstasy")-induced serotonin neurotoxicity: Studies in animals. Neuropsychobiology 2000; 42:5

13. McCann UD, Szabo S, Scheffel U, et al: Positron emission tomographic evidence of toxic effect of MDMA ("Ecstasy") on brain serotonin neurons in human beings. Lancet 1998; 352:1433

14. Reneman L, Habraken J: MDMA (Ecstasy) and its association with cerebrovascular accidents: Preliminary findings. Am J Neuroradiol 2000; 21:1001

15. Gouzoulis-May F: Impaired cognitive performance in drug-free use of recreational Ecstasy. J Neurol Neuorosurg Psychiatry 2000; 68:719

16. Parrot AC, Sisk E, Turner JJD: Psychobiologic problems in heavy "Ecstasy" (MDMA) polydrug users. Drug and Alcohol Dependence 2000; 60:105

17. Hallucinogenic amphetamines. Poisindex, Micromedex Inc, vol 113

18. O'Connell T, Kaye L, Plosay J: Gamma-hydroxybutyrate (GHB): A newer drug of abuse. Am Fam Physician 2000; 62:2478

19. US Department of Health and Human Services, Food and Drug Administration: FDA warns about GBL-related products. January 21, 1999. www.cfsan.fda.gov

20. National Institute on Drug Abuse: GHB. 2001. http://www.nida.nih.gov/Infofax/Clubdrugs.html

21. Substance Abuse and Mental Health Services Administration (SAMHSA): The DAWN Report, December 2000. www.samhsa.org

22. U J, Stokes SA, Woeckener A: A tale of novel intoxication: A review of the effects of gamma-hydroxybutyric acid with recommendations for management. Ann Emerg Med 1998; 31(6):739

23. GHB. Poisindex, Micromedex Inc, vol 113

24. National Institute on Drug Abuse: Ketamine. 2001. http://www.nida.nih.gov/Infofax/Clubdrugs.html

25. Kohrs R, Duriex M: Ketamine: Teaching an old drug new tricks. Anesth Analg 1998; 87:1186

26. National Institute on Drug Abuse: Rohypnol. 2001. http://www.nida.nih.gov/Infofax/Clubdrugs.html

27. Rohypnol. Poisindex, Micromedex Inc, vol 113

28. Ghuran A, Nolan J: Recreational drug misuse: Issues for the cardiologist. Heart 2000; 83:627

29. National Institute on Drug Abuse: Methamphetamine. 2001. http://www.nida.nih.gov/Infofax/Clubdrugs.html

30. Drug Abuse Warning Network (DAWN Report): Year-end 2000 emergency department data, www.whitehousedrugpolicy.gov/news/yearend2000

31. National Institute on Drug Abuse: Methamphetamine: Abuse and addiction. Research Report series, 1998. http://www.nida.nih.gov/ResearchReports/methamph/Methamph.html

32. Amphetamines and related drugs. Poisindex, Micromedex Inc, vol 113

33. National Institute on Drug Abuse: LSD. 2001. http://www.nida.nih.gov/infofax/lsd.html

34. Haddad LM, Shannon MW, Winchester JF: Clinical Management of Poisoning and Drug Overdose, ed 3. Philadelphia, WB Saunders, 1998

35. LSD. Poisindex, Micromedex Inc, vol 113

Jacob Sullum  **NO**

Sex, Drugs, and Techno Music

[In 2001], the Chicago City Council decided "to crack down on wild rave parties that lure youngsters into environments loaded with dangerous club drugs, underage drinking and sometimes predatory sexual behavior," as the *Chicago Tribune* put it. The newspaper described raves as "one-night-only parties . . . often held in warehouses or secret locations where people pay to dance, do drugs, play loud music, and engage in random sex acts." Taking a dim view of such goings-on, the city council passed an ordinance threatening to jail building owners or managers who allowed raves to be held on their property. Mayor Richard Daley took the occasion to "lash out at the people who produce the huge rogue dance parties where Ecstasy and other designer drugs are widely used." In Daley's view, rave promoters were deliberately seducing the innocent. "They are after all of our children," he warned. "Parents should be outraged by this."

The reaction against raves reflects familiar anxieties about what the kids are up to, especially when it comes to sex. As the chemical symbol of raves, MDMA—a.k.a. Ecstasy—has come to represent sexual abandon and, partly through association with other "club drugs," sexual assault. These are not the only fears raised by MDMA. The drug, whose full name is methylenedioxymethamphetamine, has also been accused of causing brain damage and of leading people astray with ersatz feelings of empathy and euphoria (concerns discussed later in this article). But the sexual angle is interesting because it has little to do with the drug's actual properties, a situation for which there is considerable precedent in the history of reputed aphrodisiacs.

A relative of both amphetamine and mescaline, MDMA is often described as a stimulant with psychedelic qualities. But its effects are primarily emotional, without the perceptual changes caused by LSD. Although MDMA was first synthesized by the German drug company Merck in 1912, it did not gain a following until the 1970s, when the psychonautical chemist Alexander Shulgin, a Dow researcher turned independent consultant, tried some at the suggestion of a graduate student he was helping a friend supervise. "It was not a psychedelic in the visual or interpretive sense," he later wrote, "but the lightness and warmth of the psychedelic was present and quite remarkable." MDMA created a "window," he decided. "It enabled me to see out, and to see my own insides, without distortions or reservations."

From *Reason*, vol. 33, no. 8, January 2002, pp. 26–34. Copyright © 2002 by Reason Foundation. Reprinted by permission.

After observing some striking examples of people who claimed to have overcome serious personal problems (including a severe stutter and oppressive guilt) with the help of MDMA, Shulgin introduced the drug to a psychologist he knew who had already used psychedelics as an aid to therapy. "Adam," the pseudonym that Shulgin gave him (also a nickname for the drug), was on the verge of retiring, but was so impressed by MDMA's effects that he decided to continue working. He shared his techniques with other psychologists and psychiatrists, and under his influence thousands of people reportedly used the drug to enhance communication and self-insight. "It seemed to dissolve fear for a few hours," says a psychiatrist who tried MDMA in the early '80s. "I thought it would have been very useful for working with people with trauma disorders." Shulgin concedes that there was "a hint of snake-oil" in MDMA's reputed versatility, but he himself considered it "an incredible tool." He quotes one psychiatrist as saying, "MDMA is penicillin for the soul, and you don't give up penicillin, once you've seen what it can do."

Shulgin did not see MDMA exclusively as a psychotherapeutic tool. He also referred to it as "my low-calorie martini," a way of loosening up and relating more easily to others at social gatherings. This aspect of the drug came to the fore in the '80s, when MDMA became popular among nightclubbers in Texas, where it was marketed as a party drug under the name *Ecstasy*. The open recreational use of Ecstasy at clubs in Dallas and Austin brought down the wrath of the Drug Enforcement Administration [DEA], which decided to put MDMA in the same legal category as heroin. Researchers who emphasized the drug's psychotherapeutic potential opposed the ban. "We had no idea psychiatrists were using it," a DEA pharmacologist told *Newsweek* in 1985. Nor did they care: Despite an administrative law judge's recommendation that doctors be allowed to prescribe the drug, the ban on MDMA took effect the following year.

Thus MDMA followed the same pattern as LSD, moving from discreet psychotherapeutic use to the sort of conspicuous consumption that was bound to provoke a government reaction. Like LSD, it became illegal because too many people started to enjoy it. Although the DEA probably would have sought to ban any newly popular intoxicant, the name change certainly didn't help. In *Ecstasy: The MDMA Story*, Bruce Eisner quotes a distributor who claimed to have originated the name *Ecstasy*. He said he picked it "because it would sell better than calling it 'Empathy.' 'Empathy' would be more appropriate, but how many people know what it means?" In its traditional sense, *ecstasy* has a spiritual connotation, but in common usage it simply means intense pleasure—often the kind associated with sex. As David Smith, director of the Haight-Ashbury Free Clinic, observed, the name "suggested that it made sex better." Some marketers have been more explicit: A 1999 article in the *Journal of Toxicology* (headlined "SEX on the Streets of Cincinnati") reported an analysis of "unknown tablets imprinted with 'SEX'" that turned out to contain MDMA.

Hyperbolic comments by some users have reinforced Ecstasy's sexual connotations. "One enthusiast described the feeling as a six-hour orgasm!" exclaimed the author of a 2000 op-ed piece in Malaysia's *New Straits Times*, picking up a phrase quoted in *Time* a couple of months before. A column in *The Toronto Sun*, meanwhile, stated matter-of-factly that MDMA "can even make you feel like a six-hour orgasm." If simply taking MDMA makes you feel that way, readers might reasonably conclude, MDMA-enhanced sex must be indescribably good.

Another reason MDMA came to be associated with sex is its reputation as a "hug drug" that breaks down emotional barriers and brings out feelings of affection. The warmth and candor of people who've taken MDMA may be interpreted as flirtatiousness. More generally, MDMA is said to remove fear, which is one reason psychotherapists have found it so useful. The same effect could also be described as a loss of inhibitions, often a precursor to sexual liaisons. Finally, users report enhanced pleasure from physical sensations, especially the sense of touch. They often trade hugs, caresses, and back rubs.

Yet the consensus among users seems to be that MDMA's effects are more sensual than sexual. According to a therapist quoted by Jerome Beck and Marsha Rosenbaum in their book *Pursuit of Ecstasy*, "MDMA and sex do not go very well together. For most people, MDMA turns off the ability to function as a lover, to put it indelicately. It's called the love drug because it opens up the capacity to feel loving and affectionate and trusting." At the same time, however, it makes the "focusing of the body and the psychic energy necessary to achieve orgasm . . . very difficult. And most men find it impossible. . . . So it is a love drug but not a sex drug for most people."

Although this distinction is widely reported by users, press coverage has tended to perpetuate the connection between MDMA and sex. In 1985 *Newsweek* said the drug "is considered an aphrodisiac," while *Maclean's* played up one user's claim of "very good sexual possibilities." *Life* also cited "the drug's reputation for good sex," even while noting that it "blocks male ejaculation." More recently, a 2000 story about MDMA in *Time* began by describing "a classic Southeast Asian den of iniquity" where prostitutes used Ecstasy so they could be "friendly and outgoing." It warned that "because users feel empathetic, ecstasy can lower sexual inhibitions. Men generally cannot get erections when high on e, but they are often ferociously randy when its effects begin to fade." The story cited a correlation between MDMA use and "unprotected sex." A cautionary article in *Cosmopolitan* began with the account of "a 28-year-old lawyer from Los Angeles" who brought home a man with whom she felt "deeply connected" under the influence of MDMA. "We would have had sex, but he couldn't get an erection," she reported. "The next day, I was horrified that I had let a guy I couldn't even stand into my bed!"

Rape Drugs

MDMA has been linked not just to regrettable sexual encounters but to rapes in which drugs are used as weapons. The connection is usually made indirectly, by way of other drugs whose effects are quite different but which are also popular at raves and dance clubs. In particular, the depressants GHB and Rohypnol have acquired reputations as "date rape drugs," used to incapacitate victims to whom they are given surreptitiously. Needless to say, this is not the main use for these substances, which people generally take on purpose because they like their effects. It's not clear exactly how often rapists use GHB or Rohypnol, but such cases are surely much rarer than the hysterical reaction from the press and Congress (which passed a Date Rape Drug Prohibition Act [in 2001]) would lead one to believe. The public has nonetheless come to view these intoxicants primarily as instruments of assault, an impression that has affected the image of other "club drugs," especially MDMA.

Grouping MDMA with GHB and Rohypnol, a 2000 Knight Ridder story warned that the dangers of "club drugs" include "vulnerability to sexual assault." Similarly, the *Chicago Tribune* cited Ecstasy as the most popular "club drug" before referring to "women who suspect they were raped after they used or were slipped a club drug." In a *Columbus Dispatch* op-ed piece, pediatrician Peter D. Rogers further obscured the distinction between MDMA and the so-called rape drugs by saying that "Ecstasy . . . comes in three forms," including "GHB, also called liquid Ecstasy," and "Herbal Ecstasy, also known as ma huang or ephedra" (a legal stimulant), as well as "MDMA, or chemical Ecstasy." He asserted, without citing a source, that "so-called Ecstasy"—it's not clear which one he meant—"has been implicated nationally in the sexual assaults of approximately 5,000 teen-age and young adult women." Rogers described a 16-year-old patient who "took Ecstasy and was raped twice. She told me that she remembers the rapes but, high on the drug, was powerless to stop them. She couldn't even scream, let alone fight back." If Rogers, identified as a member of the American Academy of Pediatrics' Committee on Substance Abuse, had trouble keeping the "club drugs" straight, it's not surprising that the general public saw little difference between giving a date MDMA and slipping her a mickey.

As the alleged connections between MDMA and sex illustrate, the concept of an aphrodisiac is complex and ambiguous. A drug could be considered an aphrodisiac because it reduces resistance, because it increases interest, because it improves ability, or because it enhances enjoyment. A particular drug could be effective for one or two of these purposes but useless (or worse) for the others. Shakespeare observed that alcohol "provokes the desire, but it takes away the performance." Something similar seems to be true of MDMA, except that the desire is more emotional than sexual, a sense of closeness that may find expression in sex that is apt to be aborted because of difficulty in getting an erection or reaching orgasm. Also like alcohol, MDMA is blamed for causing people to act against their considered judgment. The concern is not just that people might have casual sex but that they might regret it afterward.

Surely this concern is not entirely misplaced. As the old saw has it, "Candy is dandy, but liquor is quicker." When drinking precedes sex, there may be a fine line between seducing someone and taking advantage, between lowering inhibitions and impairing judgment. But the possibility of crossing that line does not mean that alcohol is nothing but a trick employed by cads. Nor does the possibility of using alcohol to render someone incapable of resistance condemn it as a tool of rapists.

The closest thing we have to a genuine aphrodisiac—increasing interest, ability, and enjoyment—is Viagra, the avowed purpose of which is to enable people to have more and better sex. Instead of being deplored as an aid to hedonism, it is widely praised for increasing the net sum of human happiness. Instead of being sold on the sly in dark nightclubs, it's pitched on television by a former Senate majority leader. The difference seems to be that Viagra is viewed as a legitimate medicine, approved by the government and prescribed by doctors.

But as Joann Ellison Rodgers, author of *Drugs and Sexual Behavior*, observes, "there is great unease with the idea of encouraging sexual prowess. . . . At the very least, drugs in the service of sex do seem to subvert or at least trivialize important aspects of sexual experiences, such as love, romance, commitment, trust and health." If we've managed to accept Viagra and (to a lesser extent) alcohol as aphrodisiacs, it may be only because we've projected their darker possibilities onto other substances, of which the "club drugs" are just the latest examples.

Signal of Misunderstanding

The current worries about raves in some ways resemble the fears once symbolized by the opium den. The country's first anti-opium laws, passed by Western states in the late 19th century, were motivated largely by hostility toward the low-cost Chinese laborers who competed for work with native whites. Supporters of such legislation, together with a sensationalist press, popularized the image of the sinister Chinaman who lured white women into his opium den, turning them into concubines, prostitutes, or sex slaves. Although users generally find that opiates dampen their sex drive, "it was commonly reported that opium smoking aroused sexual desire," writes historian David Courtwright, "and that some shameless smokers persuaded 'innocent girls to smoke in order to excite their passions and effect their ruin.'" San Francisco authorities lamented that the police "have found white women and Chinamen side by side under the effects of this drug—a humiliating sight to anyone who has anything left of manhood." In 1910 Hamilton Wright, a U.S. diplomat who was a key player in the passage of federal anti-drug legislation, told Congress that "one of the most unfortunate phases of the habit of smoking opium in this country" was "the large number of women who [had] become involved and were living as common-law wives or cohabiting with Chinese in the Chinatowns of our various cities."

Fears of miscegenation also played a role in popular outrage about cocaine, which was said to make blacks uppity and prone to violence against whites, especially sexual assault. In 1910 Christopher Koch, a member of the Pennsylvania Pharmacy Board who pushed for a federal ban on cocaine, informed Congress that "the colored people seem to have a weakness for it. . . . They would just as leave rape a woman as anything else, and a great many of the southern rape cases have been traced to cocaine." Describing cocaine's effect on "hitherto inoffensive, law abiding negroes" in the *Medical Record*, Edward Huntington Williams warned that "sexual desires are increased and perverted."

Marijuana, another drug that was believed to cause violence, was also linked to sex crimes and, like opium, seduction. Under marijuana's influence, according to a widely cited 1932 report in *The Journal of Criminal Law and Criminology,* "sexual desires are stimulated and may lead to unnatural acts, such as indecent exposure and rape." The authors quoted an informant who "reported several instances of which he claimed to have positive knowledge, where boys had induced girls to use the weed for the purpose of seducing them." The federal Bureau of Narcotics, which collected anecdotes about marijuana's baneful effects to support a national ban on the drug, cited "colored students at the Univ. of Minn. partying with female students (white) smoking [marijuana] and getting their sympathy with stories of racial persecution. Result pregnancy." The bureau also described a case in which "two Negroes took a girl fourteen years old and kept her for two days in a hut under the influence of marijuana. Upon recovery she was found to be suffering from syphilis."

Drug-related horror stories nowadays are rarely so explicitly racist. A notable and surprising exception appears in the 2000 film *Traffic,* which is critical of the war on drugs but nevertheless represents the utter degradation of an upper-middle-class white teenager who gets hooked on crack by showing her having sex with a black man. Whether related to race or not, parental anxieties about sexual activity among teenagers have not gone away, and drugs are a convenient scapegoat when kids seem to be growing up too fast.

The link between drugs and sex was reinforced by the free-love ethos of the '60s counterculture that embraced marijuana and LSD. In the public mind, pot smoking, acid dropping, and promiscuous sex were all part of the same lifestyle; a chaste hippie chick was a contradiction in terms. When Timothy Leary extolled LSD's sex-enhancing qualities in a 1966 interview with *Playboy,* he fueled the fears of parents who worried that their daughters would be seduced into a decadent world of sex, drugs, and rock 'n' roll. The Charles Manson case added a sinister twist to this scenario, raising the possibility of losing one's daughter to an evil cult leader who uses LSD to brainwash his followers, in much the same way as Chinese men were once imagined to enthrall formerly respectable white girls with opium.

The alarm about the sexual repercussions of "club drugs," then, has to be understood in the context of warnings about other alleged aphrodisiacs, often identified with particular groups perceived as inferior, threatening, or both. The fear of uncontrolled sexual impulses, of the chaos that would result if we let our basic instincts run wild, is projected onto these groups and, by extension, their intoxicants. In the case of "club drugs," adolescents are both victims and perpetrators. Parents fear for their children, but they also fear them. When Mayor Daley warned that "they are after all of our children," he may have been imagining predators in the mold of Fu Manchu or Charles Manson. But the reality is that raves—which grew out of the British "acid house" movement, itself reminiscent of the psychedelic dance scene that emerged in San Francisco during the late '60s—are overwhelmingly a youth phenomenon.

The experience of moving all night to a throbbing beat amid flickering light has been likened to tribal dancing around a fire. But for most people over 30, the appeal of dancing for hours on end to the fast, repetitive rhythm of techno music is hard to fathom. "The sensationalist reaction that greets every mention of the word *Ecstasy* in this country is part of a wider, almost unconscious fear of young people," writes Jonathan Keane in the British *New Statesman*, and the observation applies equally to the United States. For "middle-aged and middle-class opinion leaders . . . E is a symbol of a youth culture they don't understand."

This is not to say that no one ever felt horny after taking MDMA. Individual reactions to drugs are highly variable, and one could probably find anecdotes suggesting aphrodisiac properties for almost any psychoactive substance. And it is no doubt true that some MDMA users, like the woman quoted in *Cosmo*, have paired up with sexual partners they found less attractive the morning after. But once MDMA is stripped of its symbolism, these issues are no different from those raised by alcohol. In fact, since MDMA users tend to be more lucid than drinkers, the chances that they will do something regrettable are probably lower.

I Love You Guys

Another alcohol-related hazard, one that seems to be more characteristic of MDMA than the risk of casual sex or rape, is the possibility of inappropriate emotional intimacy. The maudlin drunk who proclaims his affection for everyone and reveals secrets he might later wish he had kept is a widely recognized character, either comical or pathetic depending upon one's point of view. Given MDMA's reputation as a "love drug," it's natural to wonder whether it fosters the same sort of embarrassing behavior.

Tom Cowan, a systems analyst in his 30s, has used MDMA a few times, and he doesn't think it revealed any deep emotional truths. (All names of drug users in this story are pseudonyms.) "For me," he says, "it was almost too much of a fake. . . . It was too artificial for me. . . . I felt warm. I felt loved. All of those sensations came upon me. . . . I had all these feelings, but I knew that deep down I didn't feel that, so at the same time there was that inner struggle as far as just letting loose and just being. . . . That was difficult because of the fakeness about it for me." More typically, MDMA users perceive the warm feelings as real, both at the time and in retrospect. Some emphasize an enhanced connection to friends, while others report a feeling of benevolence toward people in general.

"I was very alert but very relaxed at the same time," says Alison Witt, a software engineer in her 20s. "I didn't love everybody. . . . It's a very social drug, and you do feel connected to other people, but I think it's more because it creates a sense of relaxation and pleasure with people you're familiar with." Walter Stevenson, a neuroscientist in his late 20s, gives a similar account: "I felt really happy to have my friends around me. I just enjoyed sitting there and spending time with them, not necessarily talking about anything, but not to the degree that I felt particularly attracted or warm to people I didn't know. I was very friendly and open to meeting people, but there wasn't anything inappropriate about the feeling."

Adam Newman, an Internet specialist in his 20s, believes his MDMA use has helped improve his social life. "It kind of catapulted me past a bunch of shyness and other mental and emotional blocks," he says. Even when he wasn't using MDMA, "I felt a lot better than I had in social interactions before." Bruce Rogers, a horticulturist in his 40s, says one thing he likes about MDMA is that "you can find something good in somebody that you dislike." He thinks "it would make the world a better place if everybody did it just once."

That's the kind of assertion, reminiscent of claims about LSD's earthshaking potential, that tends to elicit skeptical smiles. But the important point is that many MDMA users believe the drug has lasting psychological benefits, even when it's taken in a recreational context—the sort of thing you don't often hear about alcohol.

Not surprisingly, people who use MDMA in clubs and at raves emphasize its sensual and stimulant properties, the way it enhances music and dancing. But they also talk about a sense of connectedness, especially at raves. Jasmine Menendez, a public relations director in her early 20s who has used MDMA both at raves and with small groups of friends, says it provides "a great body high. I lose all sense of inhibition and my full potential is released. . . . It allows me to get closer to people and to myself."

Too Much Fun

Euphoria is a commonly reported effect of MDMA, which raises the usual concerns about the lure of artificial pleasure. "It was an incredible feeling of being tremendously happy where I was and being content in a basic way," Stevenson recalls of the first time he felt MDMA's effects. He used it several more times after that, but it never became a regular habit.

Menendez, on the other hand, found MDMA "easy to become addicted to" because "you see the full potential in yourself and others; you feel like you won the lottery." She began chasing that feeling one weekend after another, often taking several pills in one night. "Doing e as much as I did affected my relationship with my mother," she says. "I would come home cracked out from a night of partying and sleep the whole day. She couldn't invite anyone over because I was always sleeping. She said that my party habits were out of control. We fought constantly. I would also go to work high from the party, if I had to work weekends. The comedown was horrible because I wanted to sleep and instead I had to be running around doing errands."

Menendez decided to cut back on her MDMA consumption, and recently she has been using it only on special occasions. "I think I've outgrown it finally," she says. "I used e to do some serious soul-searching and to come out of my shell, learning all I could about who I really am. I'm grateful that I had the experiences that I did and wouldn't change it for the world. But now, being 23, I'm ready to embrace mental clarity fully. Ecstasy is definitely a constructive tool and if used correctly can benefit the user. It changed my life for the better, and because of what I learned about myself, I'm ready to start a new life without it."

Sustained heavy use of MDMA is rare, partly because it's impractical. MDMA works mainly by stimulating the release of the neurotransmitter serotonin. Taking it depletes the brain's supply, which may not return to normal levels for a week or more. Some users report a hangover period of melancholy and woolly-headedness that can last a few days. As frequency of use increases, MDMA's euphoric and empathetic effects diminish and its unpleasant side effects, including jitteriness and hangovers, intensify. Like LSD, it has a self-limiting quality, which is reflected in patterns of use. In a 2000 survey, 8.2 percent of high school seniors reported trying MDMA in the previous year. Less than half of them (3.6 percent) had used it in the previous month, and virtually none reported "daily" use (defined as use on 20 or more occasions in the previous 30 days). To parents, of course, any use of MDMA is alarming, and the share of seniors who said they'd ever tried the drug nearly doubled between 1996 and 2000, when it reached 11 percent.

Parental fears have been stoked by reports of sudden fatalities among MDMA users. Given the millions of doses consumed each year, such cases are remarkably rare: The Drug Abuse Warning Network counted nine MDMA-related deaths in 1998. The most common cause of death is dehydration and overheating. MDMA impairs body temperature regulation and accelerates fluid loss, which can be especially dangerous for people dancing vigorously in crowded, poorly ventilated spaces for hours at a time. The solution to this problem, well-known to experienced ravers, is pretty straightforward: avoid clubs and parties where conditions are stifling, take frequent rests, abstain from alcohol (which compounds dehydration), and drink plenty of water. MDMA also interacts dangerously with some prescription drugs (including monoamine oxidase inhibitors, a class of antidepressants), and it raises heart rate and blood pressure, of special concern for people with cardiovascular conditions.

Another hazard is a product of the black market created by prohibition: Tablets or capsules sold as Ecstasy may in fact contain other, possibly more dangerous drugs. In tests by private U.S. laboratories, more than one-third of "Ecstasy" pills turned out to be bogus. (The samples were not necessarily representative, and the results may be on the high side, since the drugs were submitted voluntarily for testing, perhaps by buyers who had reason to be suspicious.) Most of the MDMA substitutes, which included caffeine, ephedrine, and aspirin, were relatively harmless, but one of them, the cough suppressant dextromethorphan (DXM), has disturbing psychoactive effects in high doses, impedes the metabolism of MDMA, and blocks perspiration, raising the risk of overheating. Another drug that has been passed off as MDMA is parametethoxyamphetamine (PMA), which is potentially lethal in doses over 50 milligrams, especially when combined with other drugs. In 2000 the DEA reported 10 deaths tied to PMA. Wary Ecstasy users can buy test kits or have pills analyzed by organizations such as DanceSafe, which sets up booths at raves and nightclubs.

Nervous Breakdown

Generally speaking, a careful user can avoid the short-term dangers of MDMA. Of more concern is the possibility of long-term brain damage. In animal studies, high or repeated doses of MDMA cause degeneration of serotonin nerve receptors, and some of the changes appear to be permanent. The relevance of these studies to human use of MDMA is unclear because we don't know whether the same changes occur in people or, if they do, at what doses and with what practical consequences. Studies of human users, which often have serious methodological shortcomings, so far have been inconclusive.

Still, the possibility of lasting damage to memory should not be lightly dismissed. There's enough reason for concern that MDMA should no longer be treated as casually as "a low-calorie martini." If the fears of neurotoxicity prove to be well-founded and a safe dose cannot be estimated with any confidence, a prudent person would need a good reason—probably better than a fun night out—to take the risk. On the other hand, the animal research suggests that it may be possible to avoid neural damage by preventing hyperthermia or by taking certain drugs (for example, Prozac) in conjunction with MDMA. In that case, such precautions would be a requirement of responsible use.

However the debate about MDMA's long-term effects turns out, we should be wary of claims that it (or any drug) makes people "engage in random sex acts." Like the idea that certain intoxicants make people lazy, crazy, or violent, it vastly oversimplifies a complex interaction between the drug, the user, and the context. As MDMA's versatility demonstrates, the same drug can be different things to different people. Michael Buchanan, a retired professor in his early 70s, has used MDMA several times with one or two other people. "It's just wonderful," he says, "to bring closeness, intimacy—not erotic intimacy at all, but a kind of spiritual intimacy, a loving relationship, an openness to dialogue that nothing else can quite match." When I mention MDMA use at raves, he says, "I don't understand how the kids can use it that way."

POSTSCRIPT

Is the Use of "Club Drugs" a Problem Among Adolescents?

There is little argument that mind-altering drugs can cause physical and emotional havoc for the user. On drugs, people might become less inhibited and engage in behaviors they would not typically exhibit. However, if one attends a rave party, is one more likely to use drugs? Are individuals who go to raves the types of people who would use drugs regardless? If going to raves increases the likelihood of drug use, is that a valid argument for making raves illegal?

Sigel contends that club drugs are readily available at rave parties. Furthermore, the clandestine nature of rave parties offers some degree of obscurity from law enforcement officials. Earmarking raves as places where drugs may be used might increase the probability that drug use will occur. One might think that it is appropriate, perhaps expected, to engage in drug use at a rave party.

Sullum argues that history shows that bringing attention to certain drugs results in their increased use. Young people would not know to alter their consciousness with certain drugs unless they were alerted to their effects. However, if young people participate in an activity that is potentially harmful to them, one could argue that it is the government's responsibility to step in. At what point is too much information counterproductive? How should we balance the right to know about certain drugs with the publicity generated by informing the public about these drugs?

There are many interesting questions associated with the issue of whether or not we should be concerned about club drugs. For example, when is a drug a club drug? Can people just get together to enjoy music and to socialize without being looked upon suspiciously? If a club brings in a musical group that plays techno music, does the club become a front for a rave? If patrons at a club use illegal drugs, is that the responsibility of the club owner or manager? These questions deserve further investigation from researchers.

References/Further Readings

Arria, A. M., Yacoubian, G. S., Jr., Fost, E., & Wish, E. D. (2002). The pediatric forum: Ecstasy use among club rave attendees. *Archives of Pediatrics and Adolescent Medicine, 156,* 295–296.

Cloud, J. (2000). The lure of Ecstasy. *Time,* June 5, 2000.

Jensen, P. (2000). Ecstasy and its agony. *The Baltimore Sun,* January 28, 2000.

Leinwand, D. (2002). As raves go uptown, cities take aim at drugs, noise. *USA Today,* November 12, 2002.

Maxwell, J. C. (2003). Response to club drug use. *Current Opinion in Psychiatry,* 16, 279–289.

Maxwell, J. C. (2004). Patterns of club drug use in the U. S., 2004. The Gulf Coast Addiction Technology Transfer Center (GCATTC). University of Texas, Austin Texas.

Some Facts About Club Drugs. The National Institute on Drug Abuse (NIDA); The National Institute of Health (NIH); U.S. Department of Health and Human Services. http://www.nida.nih.gov/ClubAlert/Clubdrugalert. html

Yacoubian, G. S., Arria, A. M., Fost, E., & Wish, E. D. (2002). Estimating the prevalence of Ecstasy use among juvenile offenders. *Journal of Psychoactive Drugs,* 34, 209–213.

Contributors to This Volume

AUTHORS

MAUREEN DRYSDALE is an assistant professor of psychology and acting director of the Sexuality, Marriage, and Family Studies program at St. Jerome's University at the University of Waterloo in Waterloo, Ontario, Canada. She is also an associate with the Waterloo Centre for the Advancement of Co-operative Education. Dr. Drysdale teaches courses in adolescence, educational psychology, child abnormal psychology, and problem behaviors in the classroom. Her research interests include the many factors that impact academic achievement and, more specifically, problem behaviors in the classroom (e.g., autism, ADHD, conduct problems, depression, and eating disorders). She also researches adolescent transitions, such as high school–to–postsecondary and postsecondary-to-work transitions. She has presented her research findings at numerous professional conferences (SRA, CPA, AERA, WACE) and published in journals such as *The Journal for Students Placed at Risk* and the *Journal of Cooperative Education.* Dr. Drysdale received her PhD in educational psychology from the University of Calgary, specializing in human development and learning.

B.J. RYE is an associate professor of psychology and human sexuality as well as the director (currently on leave) of the Sexuality, Marriage, and Family Studies program at St. Jerome's University at the University of Waterloo in Waterloo, Ontario, Canada. Dr. Rye teaches such courses as Introduction to Human Sexuality, The Psychology of Gender, and The Psychology of Sexual Orientation. Her research focuses on attitudes toward sexual minority groups (e.g., attitudes toward gay and lesbian parenting, persons with HIV/AIDS, transgender individuals, and intersex people). She has also evaluated the efficacy of sexual health education programs and interventions, as

STAFF

Larry Loeppke	Managing Editor
Jill Peter	Senior Developmental Editor
Susan Brusch	Senior Developmental Editor
Beth Kundert	Production Manager
Jane Mohr	Project Manager
Tara McDermott	Design Coordinator
Nancy Meissner	Editorial Assistant
Julie Keck	Senior Marketing Manager
Mary Klein	Marketing Communications Specialist
Alice Link	Marketing Coordinator
Tracie Kammerude	Senior Marketing Assistant
Lori Church	Pemissions Coordinator

well as investigated sexual health behavior practices from social psychological perspectives. Her writings have appeared in such journals as *AIDS & Behavior, The Journal of Sex Research*, and *Health Psychology*. Dr. Rye sits on the editorial board of *The Canadian Journal of Human Sexuality*. She received her PhD in social psychology from the University of Western Ontario, with a specialization in human sexuality.

AUTHORS

NANCY E. ADLER is the network chair of the John D. and Catherine T. MacArthur Research Network on Socioeconomic Status and Health. She is a professor of medical psychology, the director of both the health psychology program and the Center for Health and Community, and is the vice-chair of the department of psychiatry at the University of California, San Francisco. Her research interests include the impact of socioeconomic status on health and health behaviours.

PAUL R. AMATO is a professor and the department head of sociology at Pennsylvania State University. His research interests include marital quality, causes and consequences of divorce, parent-child relationships over the life course, psychological distress, and well-being.

SANDRA H. BERRY is the senior director of RAND's Survey Research Group and co-director of the RAND Health Center for the Study of HIV, STDs, and Sexual Behavior. She specializes in instrument designs, experimental designs, and data collection in unusual settings.

SUSAN M. BLAKE is an associate research professor in the department of prevention and community health of the School of Public Health and Health Services in the George Washington University. Her research focuses primarily on child, adolescent, and women's health.

LISA BRAUN is a student and the student senator for Queers & Allies: LesBiGayTrans Services of Kansas at the University of Kansas.

SANDRA A. BROWN is an associate clinical professor of psychiatry at the University of California–San Diego and an adjunct faculty at San Diego State University. Her research focuses on neuropsychological correlates of learning disabilities in children and adolescents.

E. SANDRA BYERS is a professor and chair in the department of psychology at the University of New Brunswick. Her research interests include sexual satisfaction, sex education, sexual communication, and sexual and dating violence. She teaches human sexuality, sex therapy, and psychotherapy.

JACQUELINE N. COHEN is a Ph.D. student in clinical psychology at the University of New Brunswick. Her research interests are mental health and relationships of women and minority group members. Her primary research area is the sexual well-being of lesbian and bisexual women.

TERESA STANTON COLLETT is a law professor at the University of St. Thomas School of Law in Minnesota. She is the author of *Cases and Materials on the Rules of the Legal Profession* (West Publishers, 2003) and

Teacher's Manual for Cases and Materials on the Rules of the Legal Profession (West Publishers, 1997).

REBECCA L. COLLINS is a behavioral scientist at RAND Corporation. Her research interests include child policy in adolescents, HIV, STDs, and sexual behavior.

DEWEY G. CORNELL is the Curry Memorial Professor of Education in the Curry School of Education at the University of Virginia, and the director of the Virginia Youth Violence Project, whose mission is to identify effective methods and policies for youth violence prevention, especially in school settings. Dr. Cornell is also a forensic clinical psychologist and a faculty associate of the Institute of Law, Psychiatry, and Public Policy. He is the author of "Designing Safer Schools for Virginia: A Guide to Keeping Students Safe from Violence."

MARY CRAWFORD is a psychology professor at the University of Connecticut. Her research interests include gender and communication, feminist research methods, and gender and cognition. She is the author of *Women and Gender: A Feminist Psychology,* 4th ed. (McGraw-Hill, 2003) and *Practicing Perfection: Memory and Piano Performance* (Lawrence Erlbaum Associates, 2002).

NICKI R. CRICK is a professor and the director of Institute of Child Development at the University of Minnesota. Her research interests are relational and overt aggression, peer victimization, social information processing, and gender.

RAYMOND de KEMP is a researcher at the Institute of Family and Child Care Studies at the Nijmegen University and at the Behavioural Science of the Radbound University Nijmegen in the Netherlands. His research focuses mainly on adolescent smoking.

LISA M. DIAMOND is an assistant professor of psychology and gender studies at University of Utah, Salt Lake City. Her research interest is primarily on the emotional dynamics of attachment relationships between romantic partners and family members. She is also interested in researching same-sex sexuality in women.

LAUREN DONCHI has a bachelor's degree with honors from Swinburne University in Melbourne, Australia. She is a registered psychologist with a strong background in schools and education and is currently employed by the Department of Education & Training to provide psychology services within a network of schools in outer eastern Melbourne.

ANDRE J.A. ELFERINK is a member of the Dutch Medicines Evaluation Board of the Netherlands.

MARC N. ELLIOTT is a statistician of the RAND Statistics Group in Santa Monica.

RUTGER C.M.E. ENGELS is a professor of the department of special education and a member of the Behavioural Science Institute at the Radbound University Nijmegen, in the Netherlands. He teaches educational and family psychology. He was the co-organizer of the international conference on "Hot Topics in Peer Relations" at Radbound University Nijmegen. His research is focused on the role of self-regulatory processes in romantic encounters.

R. CHRIS FRALEY is an assistant professor at the department of psychology at the University of Illinois at Urbana–Champaign. His research focuses on attachment, personality, and emotion between infant-parent and adult romantic relationships.

WYNDOL FURMAN is a child clinical psychology professor at the University of Denver. His research interests include childhood and adolescent relationships. He is the director of the Relationship Center in the psychology department of the University of Denver, where they study children's and adolescent's relationships with different people. He is the co-editor of *The Development of Romantic Relationships in Adolescence* (Cambridge University Press, 1999).

SHELLY L. GABLE is an assistant professor of psychology at the University of California, Los Angeles. She conducts research on motivation, close relationships, daily well-being, and appetitive social processes.

TASHA C. GEIGER is an instructor in the department of pediatrics at the University of Rochester School of Medicine and Dentistry. Her research interests include autism spectrum disorders.

CHRISTINE C. GISPEN-DE WIED is a medical researcher at the KNAW Research Information Centre in Netherlands. She is also the clinical coordinator at the pharmacotherapeutical group of the Dutch Medicines Evaluation Board of the Netherlands.

CAROL GOODENOW is the director of coordinated school health at the Massachusetts department of education's nutrition, health, and safety department.

CATHERINE M. GRELLO is a clinical psychology graduate student at the University of Tennessee. She is interested in researching adolescent sexual behaviour.

ELISHEVA F. GROSS is doctoral student at the University of California, Los Angeles. She developed and directed new media projects in nonprofit community organizations dedicated to developing communication, technical, and creative skills among youth from diverse backgrounds. Her current research focuses on adolescent social cognitive development as a function of social and cultural context.

DUANE A. HARGREAVES is a researcher at the School of Psychology of Flinders University in Australia. His focus is on media and its effects on body image.

MELINDA S. HARPER is an assistant professor of psychology at the University of Tennessee.

JOYCE HUNTER is the co-director of the Community Collaboration Core at the HIV Center for Clinical and Behavioral Studies at the New York State Psychiatric Institute and Columbia University. She is the principal investigator of the Working It Out Project, a community-based research project for HIV prevention program for gay, lesbian, and bisexual adolescents.

SARAH B. HUNTER is an associate behavioral scientist at RAND Corporation. She researches on substance abuse prevention.

SHARON JAYSON is a reporter of *USA Today*. She mainly writes and examines sexuality, especially regarding adolescents and family relationships.

JAANA JUVONEN is a behavioral scientist at RAND and an adjunct associate professor in the psychology department at the University of California, Los Angeles. Her area of expertise is in early adolescent peer relationships and psychosocial adjustment. She has co-edited two books: *Social Motivation: Understanding Children's School Adjustment* (Cambridge University Press, 1996) and *Peer Harassment in School: The Plight of the Vulnerable and Victimized* (2001).

DAVID E. KANOUSE is a senior behavioral scientist of the RAND Corporation. He specializes in HIV, STDs, and sexual behavior. He is the co-director of the Prevention and Treatment Services Core of the Center for HIV Identification, Prevention, and Treatment Services.

ARI KAUKIAINEN is a psychologist at the department of psychology at the University of Turku, Finland. His research interests include learning difficulties, aggression, bullying, and social skills, and how they are connected to each other.

DALE KUNKEL is a professor of communication at the University of Arizona. He studies children and media issues, television effects, and assessments of media industry.

YVON D. LAPIERRE is a professor emeritus at the department of psychiatry at the University of Ottawa and founded the Institute of Mental Health Research. His research focuses on anxiety disorders, mood disorders, schizophrenia, youth psychiatry, and forensic psychiatry. His articles are often published in the *Journal of Psychiatry & Neuroscience*.

REBECCA LEDSKY is part of the Evaluation and Research Methods Practice Area Lead at the Health Systems Research, Inc. She provides technical assistance to conduct policy assessments and analysis, program assessment, evaluation design, and data collection. Her projects predominantly focus on evaluation of health care program development and delivery that address HIV and STDs.

FRITS J. LEKKERKERKER is the chairman of the Dutch Medicines Evaluation Board of the Netherlands. He oversees the registration of different medicines and studies the patients' effects on the medicines.

DAVID LOHRMANN is the project director for the Academy for Educational Development in Washington, D.C. He is also the graduate coordinator and associate professor at the Indiana University School of Health, Physical Education, and Recreation, department of applied health science. He is also the president of the American School Health Association. He focuses on researching on secondary school health education.

MAUREEN LYON is a licensed clinical psychologist and assistant research professor in pediatrics at George Washington University Medical Center, in the Division of Adolescent and Young Adult Medicine at Children's National Medical Center, located in Washington, D.C.

MICHAEL J. MARKS is a graduate student in the department of psychology at the University of Illinois at Urbana–Champaign. His research focuses on the sexual double standard.

SHANNAN MARTIN is a sex and abstinence educator and researcher of The Heritage Foundation.

DONALD R. McCREARY is a psychology adjunct professor at the Brock University, York University, and University of Regina. His research interests include gender differences, men's health concerns, and gender roles in body image. He is the editor of *Applied Social Psychology* (Prentice Hall, 1997).

ALEXANDER McKAY is the research coordinator for the Sex Information and Education Council of Canada, associate editor of *The Canadian Journal of Human Sexuality,* and an instructor at Ryerson University. His work focuses on adolescent sexual and reproductive health and the development of high-quality sexual health education programming for youth.

DANIEL P. MEARS is an associate professor for the College of Criminology and Criminal Justice at Florida State University and a senior research associate for Justice Policy Center at the Urban Institute. His research interests include crime and delinquency, juvenile and criminal justice, mental health, drug offending, and sentencing.

ANGELA MIU is a senior programmer analyst at the RAND Corporation.

SUSAN MOORE is a social psychologist and a research professor in the department of psychology at Swinburne University in Melbourne, Australia. Her research interests include adolescent sexuality and risk-taking, attitude research, and beliefs about romance and love.

AIDA ORGOCKA is a gender and development expert. She is the development officer for the Christian Children's Fund, Albania. Her research focuses on mother and child health, child development and education, and child protection.

MARY A. OTT is an assistant professor of clinical pediatrics and adolescent medicine at the Indiana University School of Medicine.

GEERTJAN OVERBEEK is a professor at the Behavioural Science Institute, Radbound University Nijmegen. His research interests are parent-peer linkages and romantic relationships.

EMILY J. OZER is an assistant professor at the School of Public Health, University of California, Berkeley. Her research interests include school and community-based interventions, promotion of mental and physical health among adolescents, violence prevention, and trauma and post-traumatic stress disorder.

MELISSA G. PARDUE is a heritage scholar at the White House in Washington, D.C. She was a social welfare policy analyst at The Heritage Foundation.

DANIELLE POPP is a graduate student in the University of Connecticut's social psychology graduate program. Her research interests include social perception, interpersonal expectancies in social interaction, and research methods for studying behavior in social interaction.

MARGOT PRIOR is a professor of psychology at the University of Melbourne. She was a founder of the Victorian Parenting Center and the Learning Difficulties Centre at the Royal Children's Hospital. Her research interests include autism, learning difficulties, communication disorders, and social inequalities in children's health and well-being. She is the co-author of *Pathways from Infancy to Adolescence–Australian Temperament Project 1983-2000* (Australian Institute of Family Studies, 2000) and is the editor of *Learning and Behaviour Problems in Asperger Syndrome* (Guildford Press, 2003).

HILARY E.S. RANDALL researches on sexual health education at the University of New Brunswick.

ALISON CAMPBELL RATE is the executive director of Open Doors Counselling and Educational Services. She is a specialist in counseling services for crisis pregnancy and pregnancy loss and in promoting sexuality education in primary and secondary schools.

ROBERT E. RECTOR is a policy analyst focusing on welfare and family poverty. He is the senior research fellow of The Heritage Foundation. He is the author of *America's Failed $5.4 Trillion War on Poverty* (Heritage Foundation, 1995), a comprehensive examination of the U.S. welfare programs.

JENNIFER ROGERS is the program manager for the adolescent health committee of the American College of Preventive Medicine.

MARGARET ROSARIO is an associate professor of psychology at the City College of New York. Her research interests include multidimensional interfaces of personal and social identity and the exposure of community violence on health-related outcomes.

JERRY R. RUIS is a member of the Dutch Medicines Evaluation Board of the Netherlands.

EDA RUSCHENA is a psychologist at the Catholic Education Office in Melbourne, Australia.

CHRISTINA SALMIVALLI is a professor and the deputy director of applied psychology at University of Turku, Finland. Her research interests include peer relations in childhood, bullying and victimization, and social cognition and social adjustment.

ANN SANSON is the associate professor of psychology at the University of Melbourne. Her research interests include developmental psychology, child temperament, parenting, and problems in early childhood. She is the co-author of *Pathways from Infancy to Adolescence–Australian Temperament Project 1983-2000* (Australian Institute of Family Studies, 2000) and *Introducing the Longitudinal Study of Australian Children* (Australian Institute of Family Studies, 2002).

JOHN SANTELLI is the department chair and professor of clinical population and family health, and the professor of clinical pediatrics at the Mailman School of Public Health in Columbia University. His research focuses on HIV/STD risk behaviors, prevention of HIV/STD/unintended pregnancy among adolescents and women, and adolescent health.

DORIS K. SASSE is a researcher in psychology for Brock University and for Synovate of Canada, Ltd. She has frequently published articles regarding adolescent psychology in various journals.

RICHARD SAWYER is a researcher at the Academy of Educational Development in Washington, D.C.

REBECCA SCHLEIFER is a researcher with the HIV/AIDS and Human Rights Program of Human Rights Watch. She is interested in lesbian, gay, and transgender rights.

RON H.J. SCHOLTE is a professor at the department of development psychology at the University of Nijmegen in the Netherlands. He is also the treasurer at the Institute of Family and Child Care Studies in the University of Nijmegen and a researcher of the Behavioural Science Institute of the Radbound University Nijmegen. His research is focused on abnormal child psychology and peer interaction among adolescents.

ERIC W. SCHRIMSHAW is a graduate student at the City College of New York. He is also the project director at the Center for Psychosocial Study of Health & Illness, at Columbia University's Mailman School of Public Health. His research interest is on the relations between social and individual resources in psychological adjustment to stress and HIV/AIDS on women.

ELIZABETH S. SCOTT is a law professor at the University of Virginia. She is the co-director of the Center for Children, Families and the Law at the University of Virginia. Her research is interdisciplinary, applying behavioral economics, social science research, and developmental theory to legal policy issues involving children and families.

LAURA SHAFFER is a graduate student at the University of Denver. She is interested in researching late-adolescent sexual relationships.

ERIC SIGEL is an assistant professor of pediatrics, an adolescent medicine specialist, and the program director of the Eating Disorders Treatment Program at The Children's Hospital in Denver, Colorado.

DIANA SMART is a research fellow at the Australian Institute of Family Studies and the project manager for the Australian Temperament Project. Her research interests include adolescent and youth development, transitions to young adulthood, developmental pathways and transition points, and fostering social competence and social responsibility.

KATHRYNE M. SPEAKER is an assistant professor for the department of special education, language, and literacy at The College of New Jersey.

LAURENCE STEINBERG is the Distinguished University Professor and Laura H. Carnell Professor of Psychology at Temple University. His research focuses on adolescent development. He is the author or the editor of many books, including *Adolescence* (McGraw-Hill, 2005), *Handbook of Adolescent Psychology* (Wiley, 2004), and *The Ten Basic Principles of Good Parenting* (Simon & Schuster, 2004).

JITSCHAK G. STOROSUM is a member of the Dutch Medicines Evaluation Board in the Netherlands and the psychiatric department of the Academic Medical Center in Amsterdam, the Netherlands.

JACOB SULLUM is a syndicated newspaper columnist and a senior editor at *Reason* magazine. He is the author of *For Your Own Good: The Anti-Smoking Crusade and the Tyranny of Public Health* (Free Press, 1998) and *Saying Yes: In Defense of Drug Use* (Tarcher, 2003).

DANIEL SUMMERS is a specialist in adolescent medicine at the Mount Sinai Adolescent Health Center of Mount Sinai School of Medicine in New York.

MARIKA TIGGEMAN is a psychology professor at the Flinders University, Australia. Her major research interest is in the field of body image, including development of body image in children, effect of dieting on psychological well-being and cognitive performance, and the stereotyping of fat.

JEANNE TSCHANN is a professor of psychology at the University of California, San Francisco. Her research focuses on personal relationships and their influence on health-related functioning of adolescents of Latino populations.

CORNELIUS F.M. van LIESHOUT is a researcher at the Behavioural Science Institute of the Radbound University Nijmegen. He is the editor of *Developing Talent Across the Lifespan* (Psychology Press, 2000). His research is mainly in child and adolescent studies.

BARBARA J. van ZWIETEN is one of the two Dutch regulators in the Committee for Proprietary Medicinal Products and a member of the Dutch Medicines Evaluation Board of the Netherlands.

ANGELA D. WEAVER is an instructor at the University of New Brunswick and St. Thomas University in Fredericton, New Brunswick. She is currently studying in the doctoral program in clinical psychology at the University of New Brunswick.

DEBORAH P. WELSH is an associate professor of psychology at the University of Tennessee. Her research interests include clinical psychology, adolescent romantic and family relationships, and the development of sexuality.

RICHARD WINDSOR is a professor in the department of prevention and community health and is the director of the department's doctoral program in health behavior at the School of Public Health and Health Services in the George Washington University. He focuses on prevention research and evaluation in the areas of smoking and pregnancy, cancer control, and adolescent health.

TAMAR WOHLFARTH is a clinical assessor of the Dutch Medicines Evaluation Board in the Netherlands.

MELANIE J. ZIMMER-GEMBECK is an assistant professor of psychology at Griffith University, Australia. Her research areas include the interface of relationships with peers, the development of self-system, adolescent sexual behavior and the development of sexuality, and intervention programs for children and adolescents.

Index